FARM-FRESH *and* FAST

FARM-FRESH *and* FAST

EASY RECIPES AND TIPS FOR MAKING THE MOST
OF FRESH, SEASONAL FOODS

FAIRSHARE
CSA COALITION

This book is a labor of love and, as such, is dedicated to the farmers in our community who labor over and love our food and land, and the eaters who love our farmers and the scrumptious food they produce.

Brought to you by FairShare CSA Coalition

303 S. Paterson St., Suite 1B
Madison, WI 53703
608-226-0300
www.csacoalition.org

FairShare CSA Coalition (formerly MACSAC) supports and connects CSA growers and eaters.

Individual copies and discounted wholesale orders are available through FairShare. Contact us at the address above or visit our website at www.csacoalition.org for more information.

Ten recipes were previously published by and generously donated to us by *Edible Madison*, a quarterly publication dedicated to celebrating the local food and agriculture of southern Wisconsin. These recipes are credited to *Edible Madison*, along with the individual contributor, below their respective titles.

Printed in the United States of America

ISBN 978-0-615-72782-0

CONTENTS

FARM-FRESH FARE

MENUS, TIPS, AND OTHER RESOURCES

DIRECTORY

Here's a visual introduction to the vegetables and fruits (plus a few extras) you'll find inside. Items are grouped according to plant anatomy to highlight similarities among ingredients. Check out pages 3 and 4 for details on how to put this book to work in your kitchen!

3 // KERNELS, LEGUMES, AND PODS *pages 61–82*

bean

corn

okra

pea

1 // ROOT VEGETABLES *pages 7–48*

beet	parsnip	salsify
burdock	potato	sweet potato
carrot	radish	turnip
celeriac	rutabaga	
Jerusalem artichoke		
jicama		
kohlrabi		
parsley root		

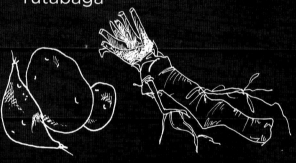

4 // FRUITS EATEN AS VEGETABLES

pages 83–122

bell pepper

cucumber

eggplant

summer squash

tomatillo

tomato

winter squash

2 // STALKS AND SHOOTS

pages 49–60

asparagus

celery

fennel

fiddlehead fern

5 // SWEET FRUITS *pages 123–56*

apple	grape	pear	rhubarb
apricot	ground cherry	plum	
berry	melon	pluot	
cherry	peach/nectarine	quince	

6 // LEAFY GREENS *pages 157–92*

amaranth	lettuce
arugula	mâche
broccoli rabe	miner's lettuce
cabbage	
chard	mizuna
chicory	nettle
Chinese broccoli	purslane
choy	sorrel
greens	spinach
kale	watercress
lamb's quarters	

7 // CROWNS, BUDS, AND FLOWERS

pages 193–206

artichoke
broccoflower
broccoli
broccolini
brussels sprout
cauliflower
Romanesco

9 // EXTRAS

pages 225–42

eggs
flowers
honey
maple syrup
meat and poultry
mushrooms
preserves

8 // AROMATIC ACCENTS

pages 207–24

chile pepper	leek
garlic	onion
ginger	ramp
herbs	shallot

ACKNOWLEDGMENTS

Many hands, mouths, fields, and kitchen tables contributed to the realization of this quirky *Farm-Fresh and Fast* project. Many, many minds wrapped around the seedling of an idea and then nourished it to fruition: to preserve the core concepts of *From Asparagus to Zucchini*—simple, delicious recipes presented in an easy-to-use format—while creating a resource to encourage flexible, creative cooking. We'd like to give special thanks to some of these folks for their leadership, dedication, and passion.

This book could never have come together without the sustained effort of the core committee: FairShare Executive Director Kiera Mulvey assembled a team of food lovers and facilitated many brainstorming sessions to keep the project moving throughout its development. Project manager Danielle Pacha coordinated the *whole enchilada* (so to speak!), overseeing recipe submission and testing, editing recipes and text, and shaping our collective contributions into a cohesive whole; without her tireless attention to detail, pure dedication, and endless patience, we'd still be in book concept land! Food writer and stylist Beth Fortune wrote the main text and helped significantly with recipe development, style, and thoughtful content development; Beth's professional food life and passion for good, clean food is literally written all over this book. Pat Mulvey, one half of the dynamic duo of "CSA Chefs" that is *Local Thyme*, lent her talents, vision, and chef's eye to book concept development and master recipe realization. Erika Janik, known for her writer's wit and foodie style, played a key role and served as Jack-of-all-cookbook-projects, from writing to editing to titling.

We thank our excellent design team for their impeccable style and for bringing our words to life: Sarah LaTarte, FairShare's Graphic Guru, again wowed the town (and beyond!) with her fresh, clean, creative reinvention of our style and her quirky, timeless ideas; Heather Silecchia of Little H Designs, a.k.a "doodler in residence," contributed her fabulous whimsy and spot-on drawings throughout the book; and Mallory Shotwell provided breathtaking photographs for the front cover.

We are indebted to the following epicures for supplying the "meat" of the book: contributing chefs Terese Allen, Lee Davenport, Laura Gilliam (the other half of *Local Thyme*), and Sam Kanson-Benanav provided a taste of their flavorful, fabulous foods; Jamie DeCaria and a community of home cooks added their culinary creations to our recipe collection; expert mixologists Grant Hurless (*Forequarter* and *Merchant*), Hastings Cameron and Mark Bystrom (*Underground Food Collective*), and John Kinder (*Death's Door Spirits*) concocted delectable cocktails featuring farm-fresh foods; Jim Klousia and Jamie Lamonde of *Edible Madison* generously contributed recipes and mouthwatering photographs; Jen Christman-Kelly made helpful recommendations for master recipe presentation; and REAP Food Group donated a number of recipes from past *Food for Thought* contests.

Finally, this book benefited greatly from the support and assistance of the following friends: Natasha Sattin provided the sweat and organization to launch this book from infancy to a board-approved and vetted real project; Rachel Armstrong and a dedicated group of cookbook enthusiasts helped refine the book's core concepts during discussions and focus groups in the early stages of development; an army of discriminating testers were instrumental in recipe selection and fine tuning, especially Lindsay Christians, Nichole Fromm, Nicole Miller, Sue Steinmann, and Edith Thayer, whose detailed evaluations were much appreciated; FairShare CSA Coalition staff Julie Garrett, Erika Jones, Beth Nitz, and Lauren Wells tested and tasted recipes and patiently tolerated the project's impact on their office space; Edith Hines read the manuscript in its final stages and made many excellent suggestions for improvement; and Susan Park served as our trusty indexer and final set of eyes on the proofs.

Our heartfelt thanks go to all of these contributors, and to many more; it sure takes a village to make a community cookbook!

INTRODUCTION

We envision a future where Community Supported Agriculture is the backbone of a strong local food system; where all families have access to locally produced, organic food and have strong connections to their farms, food, and community.

We are FairShare CSA Coalition (formerly MACSAC), a coalition of food enthusiasts passionate about Community Supported Agriculture (CSA). Since 1992, we have worked hard to build and sustain a vital, strong CSA community in Madison, Wisconsin, and beyond, through education, outreach, and resource sharing. We hope that you will find this book, a follow-up to our popular *From Asparagus to Zucchini*, an invaluable guide to cooking successfully with fresh ingredients from your CSA box, farmers' market, co-op, or any local food sources.

Joining a CSA is a financial commitment to a farm in return for a weekly box containing seasonal produce, and perhaps eggs, honey, herbs, flowers, meat, and even cheese, depending on the farm. Complementing CSA memberships are farmers' markets, where shoppers can find fresh, local produce, meat, dairy products, flowers, and an ever-changing selection of goods from local artisans. Opening a CSA box or returning from the farmers' market with overflowing bags can evoke one of two reactions: excitement at the thought of a week of delicious home-cooked meals, or trepidation about now having to cook all that food!

This book is meant to help both seasoned and new CSA members make the most of their fresh local bounty. For experienced cooks, we'll keep the pick-up day excitement going all week long with great recipes and creative serving suggestions. We're also here to help those who aren't sure where to start with managing their first CSA deliveries. In *Farm-Fresh and Fast* you'll find at-a-glance storage and preparation information, pictures and thorough descriptions of seventy-eight vegetables and fruits (and a selection of fresh-food "extras"), and easy-to-follow, quick recipes. All cooks will benefit from the tips and tricks scattered throughout the book, as well as our guide to pantry basics, menu suggestions, and glossary of cooking terms.

LOCALLY GROWN PRODUCTS ARE DIFFERENT FROM STANDARDIZED COMMERCIAL CROPS. WE THINK THEY'RE BETTER.

Fruits and vegetables straight from the farm are fresher, more delicious, and even more intriguing than large-scale commercial crops. Food from industrial farms often travels thousands of miles, so farmers are limited to growing varieties that will survive the long journey rather than those that taste best. By contrast, local farmers in close proximity to their customer bases can tailor their crops to local growing conditions and select varieties for flavor and interest rather than durability. Locally grown fruits and vegetables also last longer after purchase, because they haven't already spent days or weeks in storage, shipping, or on supermarket shelves. And since the trip from farm to table is short and quick, local produce stays in the field longer, until it is fully mature. For the CSA member and farmers' market shopper, then, buying locally results in an abundance of fruits and vegetables that are available at the peak of freshness, when flavor and texture are optimal and maximum storage life remains.

Eating locally involves an element of surprise that can be both fascinating and frustrating for the cook. Garlic scapes look beautiful curling out of the box, but how do you transform them into a meal? How do you make the gratin you were planning when turnips arrived in your box instead of potatoes? When is it okay to swap things out, and when will it ruin the whole dish? We hope to inspire confidence in both beginning and experienced cooks (and everyone in between) by providing all the information you need to prepare your CSA bounty quickly and confidently, with or without recipes, and by presenting it in a way that is well organized, accessible, and easy to understand.

ABOUT THIS BOOK

SECTIONS

In this book produce is grouped into sections according to plant anatomy—specifically, the part of the plant that is used in cooking—with individual vegetables and fruits listed alphabetically within each section. Of course, many vegetables play different roles in different contexts; for example, both carrots and celery serve as flavorings when added to soups, but their primary association is not with "Aromatics" like onions and garlic, so they are assigned instead to the common-sense categories of "Root Vegetables" (carrots) and "Stalks and Shoots" (celery). This practical approach to categorization is meant to highlight similarities among ingredients, so it's easy to see how one vegetable may be substituted for another. It also facilitates finding unusual ingredients, or those that have several common names. How might this organization work for you?

♦ Imagine that you would like to make a salad with shaved fennel, goat cheese, and walnuts, but fennel is not yet in season. By skimming the "Stalks and Shoots" section, you'll see that celery is similar to fennel: both are crunchy and have fresh, herbaceous flavors. You decide to make your salad with celery and find that the flavor combination is just as good as, maybe better than, your original recipe.

♦ Perhaps you have received something in your CSA box that looks like a gnarled, white carrot gone mad. Your newsletter says it's white salsify—so should you look for it under *W*, then, or *S*? Or perhaps you bought it at the farmers' market, where (you think) the name had something to do with oysters but you can't remember the specifics. You just want to know if you can add it to your soup. It's easy to find the answer in *Farm-Fresh and Fast*. Since it looks like a root, you try "Root Vegetables," and there it is, salsify, with its alternative name, oyster plant, and a description of its ideal uses. And yes, you can add it to soup, but you probably won't want to serve it raw on a veggie platter.

Of course, you can also find featured ingredients listed alphabetically in the handy directory at the front of the book, or in the index, which lists recipes as well.

AT-A-GLANCE GUIDES

We want to make it easy to find answers. That's why we've supplied a guide at the end of every section outlining basic storage and cooking methods for most entries in the book. This way, you don't have to read an entire section to find out whether carrot leaves are edible (they are), whether to refrigerate sweet potatoes (don't), or if you can freeze tomatoes (you can). These guides are not meant to be the last word in food storage and preparation. Rather, they are generalized indications of preferred methods.

RECIPES

Community recipes. As in *From Asparagus to Zucchini*, we bring you more excellent recipes from our community of CSA members, farmers, chefs, and food lovers. All involve active preparation time of sixty minutes or less, and most will be ready to serve in under an hour. Additionally, we've suggested ways to adapt the recipes to your own palate or pantry, noted potential ingredient substitutions, and included tips for success from the contributors. Each vegetable and fruit is featured in three or more community recipes when possible. For produce that isn't specifically called for in the recipes in our collection, such as mâche and miner's lettuce, we've recommend recipes in which it will work as a substitute.

Master recipes. We're also including something a little different in this book. We're calling them master recipes, but you can think of them as templates. For example, our pesto master recipe in the "Aromatic Accents" section has a basic pesto formula. It also has measurements to make pesto four different ways, and a list of ideas for different herb, nut, and cheese combinations. Finally, it has suggestions for what to do with all that pesto. The techniques and guides in the master recipes are meant to help turn followers of recipes into confident, versatile cooks. Please, remember us when you're famous, and be sure to write down your best creations for the next book.

MENUS, TIPS, AND OTHER RESOURCES

At the back of the book you'll find the following supplementary information:

Theme menus and cocktails. We've compiled some of our favorite recipes into menus for all seasons and occasions, taking the guesswork out of cooking for groups large and small. Of course, delicious meals aren't the only way to enjoy fresh produce, and we've solicited a selection of handcrafted cocktails for your sipping pleasure. (Look for the cocktail symbol to find fruits and vegetables that shine in these creative concoctions.)

Food handling tips and terminology. In dedicated food safety and storage sections we've outlined common-sense methods for keeping your food healthy and fresh. We've also developed a glossary of cooking terms to explain techniques like *chiffonade*, to clarify the difference between *blanch* and *boil*, and to illustrate the best practices for sautéing, braising, deep-frying, and other techniques.

Pantry basics. A cook cannot create with fruits and veggies alone, so we've put together a shopping list of pantry staples to help ensure that you have what you need to whip up satisfying meals at a moment's notice.

Books we love and use. Finally, for those who wish to learn more about culinary techniques, food preservation, and food industry issues, we've compiled a list of our favorite resources.

This book has been a labor of love for us. We hope that you find it useful, and that it helps you enjoy two of the best things in life: fresh, locally grown food, and time with your family and friends. Now go on, cook something. Cheers.

FARM-FRESH FARE

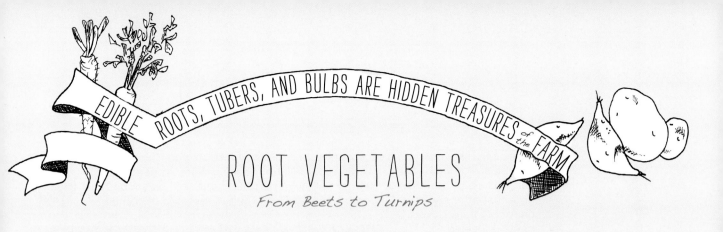

ROOT VEGETABLES

From Beets to Turnips

Edible roots, tubers, and bulbs are the hidden treasures of the farm. Colorful and shapely, these nutrient-packed vegetables grow unseen beneath the ground. In the field, they are the energy reservoirs of plants, storing natural sugars and starches produced during photosynthesis. Some, like potatoes, store energy in the form of starch, becoming dry and pleasantly fluffy when cooked. Others, like beets, store energy as sugar and are deliciously sweet, staying moist and firm after cooking. Once harvested, versatile root vegetables can be sliced and eaten raw, roasted to caramelized perfection, or pureed into silky soups. A little information—and a few simple techniques—is all that's needed to unlock the potential of these indispensable vegetables.

Selection. Look for root vegetables that are firm and heavy for their size. If greens are intact, choose those that appear fresh. If the greens have been removed, check the stem end to make sure the vegetable has not sprung new shoots; vegetables that are putting energy into new growth have already used up their stores of tasty sugars or starches.

Storage. Wipe off any excess dirt, but do not wash root vegetables until ready to use, as the residual moisture will hasten decay. Many root vegetable greens are edible, including turnip, kohlrabi, beet, and even carrot greens (see "Leafy Greens" on page 157). Remove the greens from the roots and store them separately; otherwise the leaves will continue to draw moisture and nutrients from the root. For beets, leave about one inch of stem attached during storage to preserve nutrients and flavor, and keep the long taproot intact.

With the exception of potatoes and sweet potatoes, store root vegetables loosely wrapped in the vegetable drawer of the refrigerator. Store potatoes and sweet potatoes in a dark, cool environment, between about 45° and 60°.

Preparation. Many root vegetables can be delicious raw, depending not only on the type of vegetable but also on its age and size. Slice very dense vegetables thin, or grate them into salads. Soak slices or sticks in ice water for added crispness. Older, bigger roots may become too woody and strongly flavored to eat raw. When in doubt, try a slice. If it's too strong, reserve it for cooking and add it to soup broths, mashed potatoes, or purees. Some root vegetables will darken when they are exposed to air. To slow this reaction, try:

◆ **Acidulated water.** Dip cut pieces of Jerusalem artichoke, burdock root, and salsify in water with lemon juice or vinegar added (about a teaspoon of acid to two cups of water). Note that these vegetables will uniformly darken when they are cooked, regardless of pretreatment.

◆ **Cold water.** Keep raw cut potatoes and celeriac submerged in water to slow browning. Keep soaking times short to prevent them from absorbing too much water.

◆ **Amended cooking water.** To prevent boiled potatoes from darkening in the center, add cream of tartar or lemon juice to the cooking water halfway through the cooking time.

> *The beet is the most intense of vegetables. The radish, admittedly, is the more feverish, but the fire of the radish is a cold fire, the fire of discontent not passion. Tomatoes are lusty enough, yet there runs through tomatoes an undercurrent of frivolity. Beets are deadly serious.*
> —TOM ROBBINS,
> *Jitterbug Perfume*

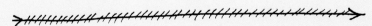

Root vegetables can be cooked in almost any way. See the usage guide at the end of this chapter for recommendations.

BEET

Beets can be classic red, yellow, white, or red-and-white-striped Chioggia. Red beet pigment is water soluble, so it will tint cooking water, other foods, cutting boards, and hands. Neither yellow nor striped beets will bleed, but note that after cooking, Chioggia beets will lose their stripes and become uniformly pale. Cook beets unpeeled to retain nutrients that lie just under the skin; the skins will rub off easily after they have cooled.

Naturally bleach away vegetable stains from cutting boards by placing the board stain-side out in a sunny window for a day. Clean hands stained by beets, salsify, or burdock with vinegar or lemon juice and salt.

BURDOCK

Also called gobo, burdock is cultivated primarily in Japan, and to a lesser extent in Europe and the United States. It also grows wild in much of North America. It is a very long, slender root with brown skin and grayish flesh, with a sweet, earthy flavor and a crisp-tender texture. It works best as a supporting player in most dishes, as the flavor is very subtle. Burdock is used for a popular pickle that accompanies sushi and rice dishes. Choose firm roots, preferably no more than one inch in diameter. If the skin is thin, it need not be peeled. Precook burdock if your dish calls for larger pieces; otherwise it may be stringy. To precook, add the chopped burdock to cold water with a pinch of baking soda; bring to a boil, then drain. Finish cooking as desired.

CARROT

White, yellow, purple, red, or orange, carrots from the farm can be a revelation in flavor as well as color. Only large carrots need to be peeled before using; most can be simply scrubbed clean. Acids will intensify the color of red or purple carrots; consider slicing these and serving them as a salad with a simple lemon- or vinegar-based dressing. Store carrots away from apples, pears, and potatoes, as these foods emit ethylene gas, which makes carrots bitter (for more details about storing fruits with high ethylene emission, see "Food Storage" on page 258).

CELERIAC

Celeriac, or celery root, is a knobby brown vegetable with a flavor profile similar to its stalky cousin's, but a little stronger and deeper. It can substitute for celery in vegetable medleys or stand on its own in purees, gratins, or soups. Remove the thick, bumpy outer layer with a paring knife to ensure that it is thoroughly clean. Once peeled, celeriac can be eaten either raw or cooked. For raw preparation, marinate slices or shreds in vinaigrette for a few hours before serving to tenderize and mellow the flavor. Alternatively, toss slices with salt and lemon juice and let them stand for an hour; then rinse, drain, and dry before dressing.

JERUSALEM ARTICHOKE

Tubers of the sunflower plant, Jerusalem artichokes are also known as sunchokes. They resemble small ginger roots, with lumpy, brown skin and white flesh that is nutty, sweet, and crunchy. They can be peeled or merely scrubbed clean, and can be served raw or cooked.

JICAMA

Jicama is a large, round root with thin brown skin and white, crunchy flesh. Its flavor is mild, slightly sweet, and watery. When cooked, it is similar in taste and texture to water chestnuts. Raw jicama is a great choice for crudités, salads, and salsas, as it does not soften, discolor, or lose its crunch. Jicama should be peeled, with the fibrous layer of flesh under the skin removed along with the brown peel.

KOHLRABI

A member of the vast mustard family (Brassicaceae), kohlrabi is a juicy, crunchy vegetable with mild sweetness and very little of the heat that characterizes its relatives. When raw or lightly blanched, it's a crunchy addition to vegetable platters and salads. When cooked, it's a versatile ingredient best served in dishes that don't overpower its delicate sweetness. Trim tough stalks and peel kohlrabi before using (baby kohlrabies need not be peeled).

PARSLEY ROOT

Also called Dutch, Holland, or Hamburg parsley, parsley root resembles a white carrot or a small parsnip. Aromatic and complex, it adds depth of flavor to purees, soups, braises, and stews. It can be cooked by itself, although it is probably best used in combination with other flavors. It can be peeled or merely scrubbed clean. Use parsley root in place of, or in addition to celeriac in "Cheesy Celeriac and Potato Mash" (page 28), or add it to "Grilled Shrimp, Fennel, and White Bean Salad" (page 58).

Note that parsnips are very similar in appearance to parsley root. Parsley root usually has long, feathery fronds still attached, while parsnips have their leaves removed (if your parsnips have leaves, remove them carefully—they cause skin irritation for many people). A taste will quickly resolve the issue, since parsley root is quite pungent, while parsnips are sweet.

PARSNIP

Related to carrots, celeriac, and parsley root, parsnips have a complex, herbaceous flavor. They are similar in appearance to large white carrots and are edible raw, but unlike carrots, they are quite dense and are thus best cooked. Parsnips from the farm can simply be scrubbed clean if they are thin skinned, but grocery-store parsnips are sometimes coated in wax and should be peeled.

POTATO

Baking. Also categorized as mealy or starchy, baking potatoes such as russet, Kennebec, and Idaho are high in starch, with low moisture. These potatoes are left in the ground for several weeks after they are harvested to toughen the skin and allow the flavor to develop. When cooked, they have a fine, dry, fluffy texture that makes them excellent for baking and frying. These potatoes make for a smooth, creamy-textured mashed potato with the addition of fats and liquids. They are best stored in a cool (45°–60°), dark environment. They may sprout or decay at warmer temperatures, and when refrigerated their starches convert to sugars, which unpleasantly alters the flavor of the potato and causes it to darken when cooked. Cold-stored potatoes can be reconditioned, however, by bringing them to room temperature for several weeks before use, as potato chip makers do to assure a quality chip.

While some enjoy the flavor of raw potatoes, the starch they contain is hard to digest until it is transformed by cooking, so they can cause stomach upset. If you find raw potatoes to be irresistible, stick to a slice or two to avoid digestive difficulties, and always make sure that they are thoroughly washed. Green potatoes contain a toxic alkaloid called solanine, and they should not be consumed either raw or cooked.

POTATO (CONTINUED)

Waxy.   In general, round white, round red, Yukon Gold, fingerling, purple, blue, and rose potatoes are considered waxy, although there are exceptions. (When in doubt, ask your farmer about the specific varieties he or she grows.) Waxy, when describing potatoes, means less starch and more sugar and moisture than starchy potatoes. After cooking, they hold their shape and stay moist. They are good for boiling, frying, braising, or roasting. To help boiled potatoes keep their shape, start them in cold water. Store these potatoes under the same conditions as baking potatoes.

New.   Any variety of potato can be a new potato if it's tender and young. New potatoes are harvested from green vines, usually in the spring or summer. They are considered waxy, regardless of variety, because their sugars haven't converted to starch, and their skin is still thin. They are often small enough to cook whole and are good steamed, boiled, or roasted. They should be stored in a cool, dry place, as with baking and waxy potatoes, but unlike those, they are best used within a few days.

RADISH

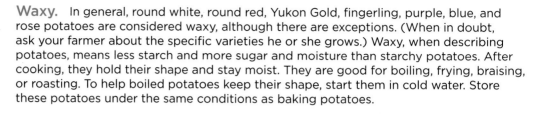

Table.   The radishes most familiar to Americans are table radishes (also called spring or summer radishes). These are the small, round, red varieties, as well as the oblong French Breakfast and multicolored Easter Egg radishes. These members of the mustard family (Brassicaceae) tend to be hotter than Asian radishes, although the only way to know the bite of a particular radish is to sample it. Choose radishes that feel firm when gently squeezed to avoid pithy interiors. While usually served raw, table radishes are also delicious cooked.

Asian.   Large, white daikons are probably the most familiar radishes in this category, but these staples of Asian cuisine come in all sizes, shapes, and colors. Chefs love the Beauty Heart or watermelon radish for its sweet flavor and beautiful appearance—a pale green exterior and vibrant fuchsia-pink center that fades to white at the edges. Asian radishes are generally milder than the smaller red table varieties. Delicious both raw and cooked, they make a fine substitute for crackers in crudités and a crunchy addition to stir-fries. In Chinese cuisine, cooked radish often accompanies seafood, as it both adds sweetness and removes undesirable fishy tastes. If cutting a large Asian radish for use in both cooked and raw preparations, use the half nearest the stem for serving raw, since it is the sweetest.

Black.   Black, or Spanish, radishes are rare, but they are quite different from Asian and table radishes and thus deserve their own category. They are firm and dry, with white flesh and a strong taste similar to horseradish. Before serving raw, they should be cut and soaked in cold water for several hours, or even days, to mellow; even then, the flavor will still be strong. Black radish adds a pleasing bite to creamy spreads and rich meats or fish. Cooked, it resembles a firm turnip, and can be peeled or merely scrubbed clean. Black radishes will last for months in the refrigerator if wrapped in newspaper or perforated plastic and kept dry.

RUTABAGA

Rutabaga, a species of Brassica, also goes by the names swede or yellow, winter, Swedish, Russian, or Canadian turnip. Rutabaga's checkered past has left it with a slightly tarnished reputation. During World War I, it was often the only food available in continental Europe, particularly in Germany, where the 1916–17 famine caused by the British blockade was dubbed the Rutabaga Winter. Although in some circles it remains unpopular, golden rutabaga is a versatile vegetable with a smooth texture and a pleasant, sweet taste (with a bite when raw). It is quite dense, but cooking it in a microwave for a minute will make it easier to cut. It is easier to peel after it has been cut into chunks. Slice it thin to eat it raw, or cook it in nearly any way. Use it as you would turnips.

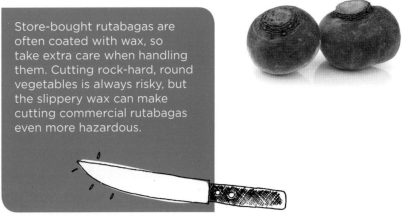

Store-bought rutabagas are often coated with wax, so take extra care when handling them. Cutting rock-hard, round vegetables is always risky, but the slippery wax can make cutting commercial rutabagas even more hazardous.

SALSIFY

White and black salsify are two different plants with culinary similarities. White salsify is pale, forked, and scraggly with fuzzy rootlets (its genus name is Tragopogon, meaning "goat's beard"). Black salsify looks similar to burdock root: dark brown, smooth, and carrotlike. Both have a flavor similar to artichoke hearts and Jerusalem artichokes. When cooked, salsify is sometimes compared to oysters, and both varieties are sometimes called oyster plant. Salsify should be scrubbed and then peeled; it is best served cooked. Cook salsify gently until it is just tender, as it quickly passes from perfect to mushy.

SWEET POTATO

Sweet potatoes can be either white or orange, but they are never "yams." (True yams grow only in the tropics and rarely appear in the United States outside specialty markets.) White sweet potatoes are dry and crumbly after cooking. The orange variety is sweeter, more pumpkinlike, and moist. Sweet potatoes are best stored between 55° and 60°. Refrigerating sweet potatoes may cause their cores to remain hard even after cooking. Sweet potatoes are good cooked every way.

TURNIP

Turnips, like their Brassica relatives rutabagas, deserve an image makeover. When fresh, turnips are crisp and juicy, with a slightly sweet flavor and a mild bite. They do dehydrate and turn bitter rather quickly, however, so they are best when used within a few days. Turnips can be enjoyed raw, but taste them for bitterness before serving. They are also excellent cooked, especially in savory stews and braises or with roasts. Unfortunately, poor-quality turnips do not improve with cooking. It's best to use strong-tasting, woody specimens in broths, or to add them (cooked and pureed) in small amounts to mashed potatoes or soup.

ROOT VEGETABLES
Storage and Usage Guide

VEGETABLE	STORAGE AND PRESERVATION				USAGE SUGGESTIONS						
	IDEAL CONDITIONS	PICKLE	FREEZE	DEHYDRATE	EDIBLE GREENS*	RAW	STEAM	GRILL	BAKE	ROAST	SAUTÉ
BEET	1-inch stem and taproot intact, wrapped, refrigerated	•	•	•	•	•	•	•	•	•	
BURDOCK	wrapped in damp paper towel, then plastic, refrigerated	•	•	•		•					•
CARROT	refrigerated	•	•	•	•	•	•	•		•	•
CELERIAC	refrigerated	•	•	•	•	•		•		•	
JERUSALEM ARTICHOKE	refrigerated	•									
JICAMA	refrigerated	•				•	•	•			•
KOHLRABI	refrigerated	•	•	•	•	•	•	•		•	•
PARSLEY ROOT	wrapped in dry paper towel, then plastic, refrigerated	•	•	•	•			•		•	•
PARSNIP	refrigerated	•	•	•		•		•		•	•
POTATO											
baking	cool and dry		•	•				•	•	•	
waxy	cool and dry		•	•			•			•	•
new	cool and dry		•	•			•			•	•
RADISH											
table	refrigerated	•			•	•					
Asian	refrigerated	•		•	•	•	•	•		•	•
black	wrapped in dry paper towel, then plastic, refrigerated	•				•				•	•
RUTABAGA	wrapped in damp paper towel, then plastic, refrigerated	•	•	•	•	•	•	•		•	•
SALSIFY	refrigerated				•		•				
SWEET POTATO	cool and dry	•	•	•			•	•	•	•	
TURNIP	refrigerated	•	•	•	•	•	•	•		•	•

*For more information, see "Leafy Greens" on page 157.

MASTER RECIPE: FOUR-WAY PUREED SOUP

Always delicious served hot, often tasty served cold, pureed vegetable soups are fine comfort food all year long. Virtually any vegetable or vegetable combination can star in a pureed soup, but the creamy flesh of hearty root vegetables—and winter squash too—makes an especially good puree that helps to thicken the soup and give it a sumptuous, smooth texture. The technique for pureed soups is easy to master, and since they freeze and reheat well, they are a handy means for preserving fresh vegetables for future use.

THE BASICS

Fat: oil or butter

Aromatics: chopped onions, garlic, celery, carrots, fennel

Main vegetable(s): nearly any (single or a combination), chopped

Uncooked grain(s): rice, barley, wheat berries (optional)

Liquid: broth, water, juice, wine (or a combination)

Flavorings: herbs, spices, dairy, accent vegetables, wine or liqueur

Seasoning: salt and pepper

Garnishes: flavored oil, sour cream, cheese, nuts, croutons, finely diced raw vegetables, cooked seafood or meats

PROCESS

Heat the **fat** in a large stockpot and sauté the **aromatics** until softened. Add the chopped **main vegetable(s)** and **uncooked grain(s)** (if desired). Cover with the cooking **liquid** and bring to a boil, skimming off any foam that rises to the surface. Reduce to a simmer and cook until the vegetables are soft and the grains are cooked. If you prefer a hearty texture, reserve some of the cooked vegetables and puree the rest with an immersion blender, a food processor, or a food mill, or CAREFULLY in a blender (use caution when pureeing hot liquids—they can splash up explosively!). Return the puree and reserved vegetables to the pot and heat through. Remove from the heat and stir in any **flavorings**, such as dairy, herbs, or wilted greens. **Season** to taste. **Garnish** with flavored oil, a swirl of cream, raw vegetables cut small, nuts, croutons, or any other creamy, crunchy, or flavorful accent.

VARIATIONS

CREAMY RADISH GREENS SOUP

By Sara Schroeder

SERVES 4

2 tablespoons butter or olive oil

1 medium onion, chopped

1 bunch radish greens, chopped

2 medium potatoes, sliced

4 cups vegetable broth

Salt and ground black pepper to taste

ADD AS GARNISH:

⅓ cup Greek-style yogurt

4 radishes, thinly sliced

POTATO AND KALE SOUP

By Elizabeth Abbene

SERVES 4–6

2 tablespoons olive oil

2 onions, chopped

4 cloves garlic, chopped

6 potatoes, cut into bite-size pieces

Water to cover the vegetables

COOK 10 MINUTES, THEN ADD:

3 cups chopped kale

Sea salt to taste

ADD AS GARNISH:

1 carrot or golden beet, shredded

CREAMY CELERY AND POTATO SOUP

By Patricia Mulvey and Laura Gilliam

SERVES 6–8

2 tablespoons olive oil

1 onion, chopped

1 bunch celery, chopped

2 baking potatoes, peeled and cubed

6 cups chicken or vegetable broth

½ cup white wine

1 tablespoon dried thyme

Salt to taste

KABOCHA SQUASH SOUP WITH APPLE BRANDY

By Patricia Mulvey and Laura Gilliam

SERVES 4–6

2 tablespoons unsalted butter

1 onion, chopped

2 pounds kabocha squash, peeled, seeded, and cubed

2 apples, peeled, cored, and chopped

⅓ cup rice

3 cups chicken broth

1½ cups apple cider

¼ cup Calvados apple brandy

Salt to taste

ADD AS GARNISH:

1 tablespoon chopped fresh sage

FOUR-WAY PUREED SOUP (CONTINUED)

IDEA STARTERS

Leek, medley of fall root vegetables, thyme; garnishes: whipping cream, frizzled leek

Shallot, broccoli, potato, bay leaf, nutmeg; garnish: grated Cheddar

Onion, cauliflower, rice, ginger, curry powder (cooked in coconut milk); garnish: reserved cauliflower florets

Onion, kohlrabi, parsley root, carrot; garnishes: sour cream, grated carrots and kohlrabi

Fennel, beet, ginger; garnishes: kefir (a fermented milk product), fennel fronds

Cipolline onion, carrot, rice (cooked in carrot juice); garnishes: dill, crispy onions

Garlic, sweet potato, chipotle in adobo sauce, cumin; garnishes: sour cream, toasted pumpkin seeds

Roasted garlic, salsify, bay leaf; garnishes: crème fraîche, chopped savory, grated lemon peel

SERVING SUGGESTIONS

◆ For an elegant appetizer, puree until very smooth and serve in shot glasses.

◆ For a rustic, hearty soup, keep half of the vegetables cooked but unpureed; serve with crusty bread.

◆ Chilled soups will thicken; thin with water, broth, or milk.

◆ Gently reheat leftover pureed soups without thinning and use them as sauces.

ANIA'S BORSCHT (BEET)

BY HEIDI ACCOLA OF ROOTS & SHOOTS FARM

Every family from Russia to Romania has its own recipe for borscht, a hearty and classic eastern European soup that highlights the rich, sweet flavor of beets. Borscht is delicious served hot or cold. The beets will turn the whole dish a vibrant reddish-pink.

SERVES 12-16 // VEGAN // SIDE DISH

INGREDIENTS

2 tablespoons olive oil

1–2 onions, chopped

1–2 leeks, chopped

2 cups shredded cabbage

1 (28-ounce) can tomatoes (crushed or diced)

3–4 beets, chopped

2–3 carrots, chopped

Several celery stalks, sliced

12 cups broth and water (6 cups of each)

3 bay leaves

½ tablespoon dried marjoram

Salt and ground black pepper to taste

1 teaspoon sugar (optional)

1 sweet apple (Pink Lady, Golden Delicious, etc.), peeled, cored, and shredded

1 bunch leafy greens
(beet greens, parsley, Swiss chard), chopped

1 (15-ounce) can white beans

1 tablespoon lemon juice

Sour cream (optional)

PROCESS

Heat the olive oil in a large stockpot over low heat and sauté the onions and leeks for 1–2 minutes. Add the cabbage and sauté some more (at least 10 minutes). Add the tomatoes, beets, carrots, and celery. Stir everything and sauté a few minutes more. Add the broth and water (enough so that everything in the pot is covered and there is still room for the greens), bay leaves, marjoram, salt, pepper, and sugar (if desired). Cook until everything is tender, 30–40 minutes. Add the apple, greens, beans, and lemon juice. Cook for a few minutes more. You may use an immersion blender to puree the soup, but it's not necessary. Serve with a dollop of sour cream (if desired).

BABY BEETS WITH BEET GREENS

BY DOROTHY PARKS, COURTESY OF REAP

Dorothy begs her farmer to harvest beets early so she'll have tender treats for this tasty dish. We love the resourceful use of both parts of the beet—a great way to minimize waste.

SERVES 2 // FISH/SEAFOOD // SIDE DISH

INGREDIENTS

1 pound baby beets with greens attached

2 tablespoons olive oil

1 medium Walla Walla sweet onion, roughly chopped

4 cloves garlic, smashed

Salt and ground black pepper to taste

2 tablespoons oyster sauce

4–5 tablespoons balsamic vinegar

PROCESS

Cut the stems off the beets and slice the bigger beets in half. Cut the leaves off the stems and discard the stems. In a large nonstick skillet, heat the olive oil, beets, and onion and sauté over high heat until the onion begins to soften, about 5 minutes. Add the beet greens. Reduce the heat to medium and add the garlic, salt, and pepper. Cook, stirring constantly, for 2–3 minutes. Add the oyster sauce and balsamic vinegar and mix well. Cover and cook for another 5 minutes. Drain slightly, but do not press. Serve hot.

> Nourishing the link between land and table, REAP Food Group is a longtime partner and friend of FairShare (thanks for the recipes!). Check out their website, www.reapfoodgroup.org, for more on their groundbreaking work in farm-to-school, farm-to-restaurant, and food system development in Wisconsin.

BEAUTIFUL BEET SALAD WITH HONEY-LIME VINAIGRETTE

BY BETHANY NELSON

This salad is particularly lovely with candy-cane-striped Chioggia beets (try slicing them thin to show their rings) or mixed golden and red beets. Taste a slice of your beets to make sure they are juicy enough for this salad. If they seem tough, steam them whole until just tender, let cool, and then proceed.

SERVES 4-6 // VEGETARIAN // SIDE DISH

INGREDIENTS

SALAD:

1 bunch salad greens (about 6 cups)

3–4 small raw beets, peeled and shredded or thinly sliced (about 2 cups)

½ small red onion, thinly sliced

¾ cup crumbled feta

½ cup sunflower seeds

HONEY-LIME VINAIGRETTE:

Juice from 1 lime (plus grated peel; optional)

1 tablespoon balsamic vinegar (or to taste)

1 tablespoon honey

¼ cup olive oil

Salt and ground black pepper to taste

PROCESS

SALAD: Place the salad greens in a serving bowl. Add the beets and onion and sprinkle the feta over the vegetables. Top with sunflower seeds.

HONEY-LIME VINAIGRETTE: Whisk all ingredients together, adjusting amounts to suit your taste. Pour over the salad and toss. Let the salad sit in the refrigerator for 15 minutes prior to serving to blend the flavors.

BEET SALSA

BY TERI FORD

Looking for a way to use beets (and admittedly not a beet lover), Teri tried adding one to her favorite salsa. To her surprise, the beet added such vibrant color that now salsa just doesn't seem the same without it. Choose young, juicy beets for this recipe. Serve with lime wedges and your favorite tortilla chips, or as a topping for grilled fish.

YIELDS ABOUT 10 CUPS // VEGAN // CONDIMENT

INGREDIENTS

2 tomatoes, cored

2 green chiles, seeded for less heat if desired

1 orange or red bell pepper, seeded

1 cucumber, peeled if desired

2 cloves garlic

½ medium sweet onion

1 beet, peeled

1 bunch green onions

¼ cup chopped fresh cilantro

Pinch each paprika, garlic salt, celery seed, and cayenne, or more to taste

Salt and ground black pepper to taste

PROCESS

Coarsely chop all the vegetables and place them into the bowl of a food processor. Add the herbs and seasonings. Pulse until blended but still chunky. Adjust the seasonings. If necessary, work in batches and transfer the blended salsa to a large bowl for final seasoning.

BEET, ORANGE, AND BLUE CHEESE SALAD

BY NANCY STILLWELL, COURTESY OF REAP

With the assertive flavors of citrus and blue cheese, this outstanding salad will turn an otherwise "everyday" meal into an occasion.

SERVES 4 // VEGETARIAN // SIDE DISH

INGREDIENTS

DRESSING:

¼ cup olive oil

¼ cup cider vinegar

¾ teaspoon salt

¼ teaspoon ground black pepper

½ teaspoon Dijon mustard

1 tablespoon minced fresh thyme

2 tablespoons minced fresh basil

2 teaspoons chopped fresh oregano

SALAD:

2 pounds fresh beets (about 8), roots and stems retained

1 small red onion, thinly sliced

Mixed salad greens

2 oranges, peeled and sliced

⅓ cup crumbled blue cheese

PROCESS

Whisk together all the dressing ingredients until emulsified. Set aside.

Preheat an oven to 425°. Wrap each beet in aluminum foil and roast in the oven for 45 minutes. Cool slightly. Trim off the roots and stems and rub off the skin. Cut the beets into ½-inch slices, then cut the slices into quarters. Toss the warm beets with 3 tablespoons of the dressing. Let stand for about 30 minutes.

Just before serving, divide the mixed greens among four salad plates. Arrange the beets, red onion, and orange slices on top of the greens. Drizzle with the remaining dressing and sprinkle with blue cheese.

BEETS AND LENTILS WITH GOAT CHEESE

BY RICH AND JESS BERNSTEIN

The deep, earthy flavors of lentils and beets are complemented with the bright, fresh flavor of goat cheese in this hearty salad. Serve it warm or cool, and add a sprinkling of fresh herbs for flavor and color.

SERVES 6-8 // VEGETARIAN // MAIN DISH

INGREDIENTS

6 medium beets (about 1½ pounds)

2 cups lentils, rinsed

Greens from 6 medium beets, chopped (optional)

¼ cup sunflower or olive oil

1½ teaspoons Dijon mustard

1½ tablespoons red wine vinegar

2 cloves garlic, minced

¼ teaspoon salt

Freshly ground black pepper to taste

1 small onion, quartered lengthwise and thinly sliced

8 ounces fresh goat cheese

PROCESS

Place the beets and lentils in a large stockpot with water to cover and bring to a boil. Cook for 30–60 minutes, until the lentils are tender and a knife slips easily into the centers of the beets. Larger beets may take longer. Add the beet greens to the pot 5–10 minutes before the beets are finished cooking (if desired). Remove the beets from the pot with a slotted spoon and set aside to cool. Drain the lentils if necessary and set aside in a large bowl.

Meanwhile, place the oil, mustard, vinegar, garlic, salt, and pepper in a jar and shake to emulsify.

When the beets are cool enough to handle, peel them and cut into 1-inch chunks. Add them to the bowl with the lentils, along with the onion. Toss with the oil and vinegar mixture and adjust the seasonings as desired. Serve warm, cold, or at room temperature, topping each serving with a dollop of goat cheese.

Try pickling the onion slices while you wait for the lentils and beets to cook: Combine 1 cup cider vinegar and ¼ cup sugar in a saucepan. Heat over medium heat, stirring until the sugar is dissolved. Pour the mixture over the sliced onion in a nonreactive bowl and let stand, stirring occasionally, for at least 20 minutes, or until the beets are done. Drain and use as directed in the recipe.

WHEAT BERRY AND BEET SALAD
WITH MAPLE-BALSAMIC VINAIGRETTE

BY SAM KANSON-BENANAV OF THE UNDERGROUND FOOD COLLECTIVE

Sam and his fellow Underground chefs cook as a collective, drawing on their combined training and world travels to produce food that's better than any one of them could make alone. In this classic salad, Sam highlights the natural sweetness of beets with a maple-balsamic glaze and balances them with nutty wheat berries and pungent greens.

SERVES 6-8 // VEGAN // SIDE DISH

INGREDIENTS

SALAD:

4 medium beets

Maple syrup

Balsamic vinegar

Salt

1¼ cups wheat berries

MAPLE-BALSAMIC VINAIGRETTE:

1 tablespoon Dijon mustard

¼ cup maple syrup

¼ cup balsamic vinegar

½ cup grape seed oil

Salt and ground black pepper to taste

1 bunch baby greens (try kale, beet greens, frisée, arugula, or spinach)

PROCESS

Preheat an oven to 400°. Place the whole beets in an oven-safe baking dish filled with ¼ inch of water. Drizzle the beets with maple syrup and balsamic vinegar and season heavily with salt. Cover with aluminum foil and roast until the beets are tender, 30–45 minutes.

Meanwhile, cook the wheat berries like pasta: bring 4 cups of salted water to a boil, add the wheat berries, and cook uncovered over low heat until soft, 45–55 minutes. Drain and set aside to cool.

For the vinaigrette, start with the Dijon, whisk in the maple syrup and balsamic vinegar, and then slowly add the grape seed oil, whisking until the vinaigrette is thick and emulsified. Season with salt and pepper.

When the beets are done cooking, allow them to cool, then remove the skins by rubbing with a paper or cotton towel or peeling with a vegetable peeler. Chop into bite-size cubes. Mix together the wheat berries, beet cubes, and vinaigrette. Serve on a bed of greens.

BURDOCK SOUP WITH HON TSAI TAI AND GREEN GARLIC
BY EDITH THAYER

Undaunted by the inclusion of homely burdock root in her CSA box, Edith developed this recipe to highlight its assets. She notes that long, slow simmering is the best way to cook burdock, as it maximizes flavor and tenderness. Any member of the choy family can be used in this soup, but hon tsai tai is particularly attractive.

SERVES 6-8 // FISH/SEAFOOD // SIDE DISH

INGREDIENTS

1 (8-ounce) package soba noodles

1 tablespoon sesame oil

1 small knob fresh ginger, peeled and sliced

A few green onions, thinly sliced

3 stalks green garlic, sliced; or 1–2 cloves garlic, minced

½ cup soy sauce or tamari

2–3 tablespoons sugar

6 cups chicken or vegetable broth

2–3 large burdock roots, cut into ¼-inch slices (1½–2 cups)

¼ pound mushrooms (whatever variety you like), sliced

1 bunch hon tsai tai or bok choy, roughly chopped (about 4 cups)

¼–½ pound shrimp, peeled and chopped

2 eggs, beaten (optional)

PROCESS

In a large stockpot of simmering water, cook the soba noodles until al dente and drain in a colander. Let cool, then roughly chop. Return the pot to low heat, heat the sesame oil, and sauté the ginger, green onions, and green garlic for 2–3 minutes; do not allow to brown. Add the soy sauce, sugar, and broth and heat through. Add the burdock and cook until tender, about 10 minutes. Add the mushrooms and hon tsai tai and simmer for 5–10 minutes. Next add the chopped soba noodles and shrimp and cook until warmed through (the shrimp will cook in the hot broth).

When everything is hot, remove from the heat and pour in the beaten eggs (if desired); they help to thicken the soup slightly and increase the protein a bit. (Note: If using the eggs, be sure to add them only if you are serving the soup immediately; leftovers will not keep well in the refrigerator after the egg has been added.)

GLAZED JAPANESE SHREDDED BURDOCK AND CARROT

BY PATRICIA MULVEY AND LAURA GILLIAM OF LOCAL THYME

This quick and tasty sauté scales up or down quite easily, so you can effortlessly adapt it to the amount of burdock you have on hand, or the number of mouths you need to feed.

SERVES 4 // VEGETARIAN // SIDE DISH

Patricia Mulvey and Laura Gilliam are Madison-area chefs who share the mission of "Ending Veggie Guilt One Box at a Time." Visit their website at localthyme.com for details about their CSA menu-planning service.

INGREDIENTS

2 teaspoons toasted sesame oil

½ pound burdock, peeled and shredded

½ pound carrots, peeled and shredded

1½ tablespoons mirin

1 tablespoon honey

1½ teaspoons sake

1 tablespoon soy sauce

2 teaspoons black sesame seeds

PROCESS

Heat the sesame oil in a large skillet over medium heat. Add the burdock and carrot and sauté until softened, about 5 minutes. Stir in the mirin, honey, sake, and soy sauce. Increase the heat and boil until the vegetables are well glazed with sauce, a few minutes longer. Sprinkle with black sesame seeds and serve.

MOMOFUKU'S BRAISED CHICKEN WITH BURDOCK AND MISO

BY PATRICIA MULVEY AND LAURA GILLIAM OF LOCAL THYME

When Pat saw Momofuku chef/founder David Chang's "Clay-Pot Miso Chicken" recipe in Gourmet *magazine (October 2007), she knew she had to make the dish pronto. A Japanese take on a traditional Mexican stew, Chang's original dish requires over two hours of cooking time. Pat and Laura adapted the recipe to fit their busy schedules, creating a quicker version that's equally rich and satisfying.*

SERVES 4 // POULTRY // MAIN DISH

INGREDIENTS

9 cups water, divided

½ cup dried wood ear mushrooms*

½ cup dried shiitake mushrooms

1 medium burdock root

½ teaspoon rice vinegar

3 tablespoons canola oil, divided

8 chicken thighs, bone in and skin on

1 onion, chopped

1 tablespoon minced ginger

1 tablespoon minced garlic

½ cup mirin

½ cup white miso

½ cup soy sauce

2 cups reduced-sodium chicken broth

Cooked rice (optional)

*Available in Asian markets or in the specialty aisle of many grocery stores.

PROCESS

Preheat an oven to 300°. Bring 6 cups of the water to a boil and then remove from the heat. Submerge the dried wood ear and shiitake mushrooms in the hot water and soak for about 15 minutes to soften. Drain the mushrooms, rinse, discard any tough pieces, squeeze out the excess water, and chop. While the mushrooms soak, peel and dice the burdock and soak it in 1 cup of water with a little rice vinegar added.

Meanwhile, heat a heavy stockpot or Dutch oven over medium-high heat. Add 2 tablespoons of the oil and heat until shimmering. Without crowding the pot, brown the chicken in batches. Once browned, remove the chicken from the pot and, if needed, add the remaining oil. Sauté the onion until softened and beginning to brown (about 5 minutes), then add the ginger and garlic and sauté for 30 seconds more. Add the mirin, scraping up any browned bits, and boil for about 1 minute. Stir in the miso and soy sauce. Drain the burdock and add it to the pot, along with the reconstituted mushrooms, the browned chicken, the broth, and the remaining 2 cups of water. Bring to a boil, skimming off any foam that rises to the surface. Cover, and place the pot in the oven to braise for 45–60 minutes, until the internal temperature of the chicken reaches 165°. Serve over rice (if desired).

CARROT BREAKFAST PANCAKES

BY EDITH THAYER

Carrots lend sweetness and moisture to these pancakes, and they are thoroughly blended with the batter, so picky kids won't even know they're included. The pancakes also freeze well and can be popped in a toaster to thaw.

SERVES 6-8 // VEGETARIAN // MAIN DISH

INGREDIENTS

1¾ cups milk

2 eggs

¼ cup butter, melted

4 medium carrots, roughly chopped

1¼ cups all-purpose flour

1¼ cups whole-wheat pastry flour

2 tablespoons flaxseed meal (optional)

2 tablespoons baking powder

1 teaspoon salt

¼ cup sugar

½ teaspoon ground nutmeg

½ teaspoon ground cinnamon

Maple syrup (optional)

PROCESS

Put the milk, eggs, and butter in a blender or food processor and blend. Add the carrots and blend well, until the carrots are completely integrated with no visible pieces. Pour the mixture into a bowl and add the flours, flaxseed meal (if desired), baking powder, salt, sugar, and spices and mix until thoroughly combined. If you think the batter is too thin, add a little more flour.

Spray a large skillet or griddle with cooking spray (or oil lightly) and heat. Pour the batter onto the hot surface using a ¼-cup measure. Cook the pancakes until bubbles appear on the top, and then turn over and cook until the other side is golden brown. Serve with maple syrup (if desired).

CARROT SLAW

BY DAX PHILLIPS

This quick and easy slaw is an excellent way to showcase multicolored carrots. Our testers loved it on fish tacos; it's also great with grilled chicken and fish.

SERVES 4 // VEGAN // SIDE DISH

INGREDIENTS

5 carrots (any size), peeled

2 stalks celery

½ cup diced yellow onion

½ cup roughly chopped fresh cilantro

1½ tablespoons olive oil

1½ tablespoons cider vinegar

Salt and freshly ground black pepper to taste

PROCESS

Shred the carrots and celery with a food processor or box grater. Toss with the remaining ingredients. Taste and adjust the seasonings as desired.

> Try this slaw recipe with beets, kohlrabi, or radishes instead of carrots. It's also delicious with mint or parsley in addition to, or in place of, cilantro.

GINGERED CARROTS

BY PATRICIA MULVEY AND LAURA GILLIAM OF LOCAL THYME

The spicy-sweet combination of ginger and carrots makes this super-simple dish taste sophisticated and complex. It's perfect when served as an accompaniment to rich meats, like duck or lamb, or as part of an Asian-themed meal.

SERVES 4 // VEGETARIAN // SIDE DISH

INGREDIENTS

1 pound carrots, peeled and sliced

1 tablespoon butter

1 tablespoon minced fresh ginger

Salt and ground black pepper to taste

PROCESS

Fill a medium pot with water and bring to a boil over medium-high heat. Add the carrots, reduce the heat to medium, and cook until the carrots float and are tender (8–10 minutes). Drain the carrots in a colander. Melt the butter in the pot used for the carrots. Return the carrots to the pot and add the ginger, tossing to coat the carrots evenly with ginger and melted butter. Season with salt and pepper and serve hot.

HOT AND SOUR SOUP (CARROT)

BY JEN FILBERT

Jen adapted this traditional recipe to suit Harmony Valley Farm's winter harvest by replacing water chestnuts with winter radish, and the result was beautiful as well as delicious. If Beauty Heart radish is not available, any mild radish can be substituted, including daikon.

SERVES 4 // VEGAN // SIDE DISH

INGREDIENTS

4 cups vegetable broth

1 tablespoon sherry

1 onion, chopped

1 large carrot, grated

1 large Beauty Heart radish, peeled and grated

4 ounces firm tofu, cut into ½-inch cubes

1½ tablespoons soy sauce or tamari

2 tablespoons red wine vinegar

¼ cup water

2 tablespoons cornstarch

1 teaspoon sesame oil

½ teaspoon ground black pepper (or more to taste)

¼ cup or less finely chopped green onion or chives (optional)

PROCESS

Combine the broth, sherry, onion, carrot, and radish in a large stockpot. Cover and cook over medium-high heat until the mixture comes to a boil. Reduce the heat to medium-low and simmer, covered, for 5 minutes. Add the tofu, soy sauce, and vinegar. Increase the heat to medium-high and return to a boil. Uncover and cook for 3 minutes.

Combine the water and cornstarch; stir well and add to the pot. Cook and stir for 2 minutes more, until the soup thickens slightly. Remove from the heat and add the sesame oil, pepper, and green onions or chives (if desired).

YOĞURTLU HAVUÇ SALATASI (CARROT SALAD WITH YOGURT)
BY BARBARA WRIGHT/FAIRSHARE CSA COALITION

This Turkish salad is commonly paired with raki, an anise-flavored aperitif. We recommend serving it in the Turkish way: as part of a sumptuous meze table for festive celebrations.

SERVES 4 // VEGETARIAN // SIDE DISH

INGREDIENTS

2 tablespoons olive oil

3 medium carrots, grated

½ teaspoon salt

½–1 cup yogurt

1 tablespoon mayonnaise (optional)

1–2 cloves garlic, grated (optional)

1 tablespoon finely chopped fresh dill (optional)

PROCESS

Heat the oil in a medium skillet over medium heat and add the carrots and salt. Sauté until the carrots change color, about 5 minutes. Transfer the carrots to a bowl, add the yogurt and the mayonnaise, garlic, and dill (if desired), and mix well. To serve, place the carrot mixture onto a serving platter alongside various meat and vegetable dishes.

CELERIAC AND KOHLRABI RÖSTI
BY JAMIE BAKER OF PRIMROSE VALLEY FARM

Rösti is a classic Swiss fried potato dish that is a little like a cross between latkes and hash browns. This version uses celeriac and kohlrabi in place of the standard potatoes.

SERVES 2-4 // VEGETARIAN // SIDE OR MAIN DISH

INGREDIENTS

1 small celeriac (about 12 ounces), peeled and coarsely shredded

½ kohlrabi (about 4 ounces), peeled and coarsely shredded

¼–½ cup chickpea or all-purpose flour (chickpea flour adds a nutty flavor)

¼ cup chopped parsley (stems and leaves)

2 eggs, beaten

2 tablespoons cold water

1 teaspoon sea salt

1 teaspoon freshly ground black pepper

Olive oil for frying

PROCESS

Place the shredded celeriac and kohlrabi, ¼ cup of the flour, and the parsley, egg, water, salt, and pepper in a large bowl or a food processor with the chopping blade attached. Stir or process until well combined. If necessary, add more flour—the batter should be stiff enough to hold together when scooped with a spoon.

Heat about 1 tablespoon of oil in a skillet over medium-high heat (the oil should cover the bottom of the skillet). Drop heaping tablespoons of the celeriac-kohlrabi mixture into the hot oil, flatten with the back of a spoon or spatula, and cook for 2–3 minutes on each side, until browned and cooked through. Set aside in a warm oven until all the batter is cooked (you may need to cook them in multiple batches).

CELERIAC RISOTTO WITH PESTO

BY EDITH THAYER

Risotto is rich and satisfying, especially on a cold day. The creamy rice dish is also versatile; any manner of vegetables, cheese, and/or meat can be added for a delicious side dish or main course. The celeriac in this version makes for a rich and warming meal.

SERVES 4 // VEGETARIAN // MAIN DISH

You can make a pesto with celeriac leaves if your celeriac happens to come with its greens still intact; simply blend the leaves with ¼ cup of olive oil. See the pesto master recipe on page 213 for additional ideas.

INGREDIENTS

4 cups chicken or vegetable broth

3 tablespoons butter

1 good-size celeriac, peeled and sliced (about 2 cups)

1½ cups sliced leeks

1½ cups Arborio rice

½ cup white wine

1 cup shredded Parmesan, divided

Salt and ground black pepper to taste

Premade pesto to taste (Edith uses about ½ cup)

PROCESS

Heat the broth in a saucepan and keep it warm on the stove while you prepare the vegetables. Melt the butter in a separate saucepan and stir in the celeriac and leeks. Cover and cook, stirring often, until the vegetables are tender but not brown, about 5 minutes. Mix in the rice and stir for 1 minute. Add the wine and let boil, continuing to stir until it is absorbed into the rice. Add about ½ cup of the hot broth and stir until it is absorbed into the rice. Continue adding broth in this way until all the broth is absorbed and the risotto is creamy yet still al dente (this process should take about 25 minutes). Remove the risotto from the heat and mix in ¾ cup of the cheese. Season with salt and pepper, then stir in the pesto. Serve with the remaining cheese sprinkled on top.

CELERIAC SOUP WITH CILANTRO

BY EDITH THAYER

A simple soup with a complex flavor, this recipe combines earthy celeriac and fresh-tasting cilantro with intriguing results. It's an excellent first course, bringing the palate alive with heat and nuance.

SERVES 4 // VEGETARIAN // SIDE DISH

INGREDIENTS

1 medium onion, finely chopped (about ½ cup)

1 jalapeño, chopped (with or without seeds)

2–3 cloves garlic, finely chopped

1 tablespoon olive oil

1 teaspoon ground cumin

Salt and freshly ground black pepper to taste

1½ pounds celeriac, peeled and cut into cubes*

4 cups chicken or vegetable broth

¼ cup chopped fresh cilantro, or more to taste

⅓ cup milk

*If you don't have enough celeriac, substitute some potatoes.

PROCESS

In a large stockpot, sauté the onion, jalapeño, and garlic in the olive oil for 2–3 minutes over medium-high heat. Stir in the cumin and season with salt and pepper. Add the celeriac and the broth. Bring to a boil, then reduce the heat, cover the pot, and let simmer for 10–15 minutes, or until the celeriac is cooked but not mushy. Remove from the heat and use an immersion blender or food processor to puree the soup until it has the consistency you want. Stir in the chopped cilantro and milk and adjust the seasonings.

CHEESY CELERIAC AND POTATO MASH
BY APRIL PRUSIA/FAIRSHARE CSA COALITION

Flavorful and satisfying, this riff on mashed potatoes works as well for an elegant dinner party as it does for a casual family dinner. Celeriac adds a bright and herbaceous note. Try turnips, rutabaga, or even radishes instead for sweet variations.

SERVES 6 // VEGETARIAN // SIDE DISH

INGREDIENTS

1½ pounds celeriac

1½ pounds potatoes

1 cup sour cream, milk, or yogurt

2 tablespoons butter

Salt, ground black pepper, and dried thyme to taste

Cheese of choice for grating

PROCESS

Peel the celeriac and potatoes and cut into 1- to 2-inch cubes. Drop only the celeriac into a stockpot with enough water to cover both the celeriac and the potatoes. Cover the pot, heat over medium-high heat, and boil for 5 minutes. Add the potatoes and boil until everything is very tender, about 15 minutes. Drain off the water and add the sour cream and butter. Mash the mixture and add the salt, pepper, and thyme. Top with grated cheese.

CREAM OF ASPARAGUS AND JERUSALEM ARTICHOKE SOUP WITH DILL
BY PATRICIA MULVEY AND LAURA GILLIAM OF LOCAL THYME

The addition of Jerusalem artichokes adds a delicate taste and rich texture to this extravagant soup. If you prefer a lighter soup, substitute nonfat evaporated milk or nondairy half-and-half for the cream.

SERVES 6 // VEGETARIAN // SIDE DISH

INGREDIENTS

1 tablespoon unsalted butter or olive oil

½ bunch green onions, chopped (about ½ cup)

1 pound asparagus, cut into 1-inch lengths

1 pound Jerusalem artichokes, peeled and chopped

6 cups chicken or vegetable broth, plus more to adjust the consistency if necessary

½ cup whipping cream

1 teaspoon lemon juice

Salt and ground black pepper to taste

½ bunch dill, finely chopped (about ¼ cup)

PROCESS

Melt the butter (or heat the oil) in a stockpot and add the green onions, asparagus, and Jerusalem artichokes. Pour the broth over the vegetables, bring to a boil, and reduce the heat to a simmer. Simmer until the vegetables are quite soft, 6–8 minutes. Allow the soup to cool a little before pureeing in small batches in a blender or food processor.

Return the soup to the pot and return briefly to a boil. Remove from the heat, stir in the cream and lemon juice, and season with salt and pepper. If you want a thinner consistency, add a little more broth, water, or cream. Serve warm garnished with chopped dill, or let cool and chill—this soup is just as delicious served cold.

JERUSALEM ARTICHOKE PENNE WITH SPINACH PESTO

BY PATRICIA MULVEY AND LAURA GILLIAM OF LOCAL THYME

Sweet, overwintered Jerusalem artichokes are the highlight of this pasta dish, which works equally well served hot or cold. If you have a gas grill with a side burner, this dish can be cooked outdoors.

SERVES 6–8 // VEGETARIAN // MAIN DISH

INGREDIENTS

1 tablespoon plus 1 teaspoon salt

½ pound Jerusalem artichokes

1 pound penne

½ pound spinach, large stems removed

¼ cup walnuts, toasted

1 stalk green garlic, chopped

½ cup extra-virgin olive oil

1 tablespoon grated lemon peel

½ bunch green onions, thinly sliced

1 ounce Parmesan, shaved

½ cup chopped pitted Kalamata olives

Salt and ground black pepper to taste

PROCESS

Bring a large pot of water to a boil over medium-high heat and add 1 tablespoon of the salt. Using a sharp paring knife, remove any blemishes or crevices on the Jerusalem artichokes; slice them in half lengthwise, then into ¼-inch half-moons. Place the Jerusalem artichokes in a steamer insert, set them over the boiling water, and cover. Steam the Jerusalem artichokes for 5–10 minutes, or until they are crisp-tender and easily pierced with a fork.

Cook the pasta according to the package directions (if you have a pot with a stacking steamer insert, you can cook it in the water that's steaming the vegetables; otherwise, boil some water for the pasta in a separate pot).

While the Jerusalem artichokes steam and the penne boils, make the spinach pesto: place the spinach into the bowl of a food processor along with the nuts, green garlic, and the remaining teaspoon of salt, and process until smooth. Scrape down the sides of the bowl if necessary. With the motor running, drizzle the olive oil into the spinach mixture and blend until smooth, about 1 minute, then stir in the grated lemon peel.

Drain the pasta and toss with the Jerusalem artichokes, spinach pesto, green onions, cheese, and olives. Season with salt and pepper and serve hot, or refrigerate and serve chilled.

JERUSALEM ARTICHOKE SALAD

BY ELIZABETH ABBENE

In this simple salad, sunflower seeds emphasize the flavor of Jerusalem artichokes, which are, after all, sunflower tubers. This recipe is a good way to introduce Jerusalem artichokes to the uninitiated, and a good starting point for variations. Think about serving it on a bed of butterhead lettuce, or adding kale, olives, or cherry tomatoes in any combination.

SERVES 6 // VEGAN // SIDE DISH

INGREDIENTS

DRESSING:

2 tablespoons cider vinegar

2 tablespoons olive oil

4 tablespoons minced garlic

SALAD:

2 pounds Jerusalem artichokes, chopped into bite-size pieces

4 cups salted water or vegetable broth

¾ cup sunflower seeds, toasted

Sea salt to taste

PROCESS

Combine the dressing ingredients and shake or whisk until combined. In a medium stockpot, cover the Jerusalem artichokes with the salted water or broth, bring to a boil over medium-high heat, and cook until tender, 10–15 minutes. Drain well and toss with the dressing. Let cool. Stir in the sunflower seeds. Add more salt if necessary.

SAUTÉED JERUSALEM ARTICHOKES

BY JAMIE DECARIA OF SAVORRA.COM

Jamie and her husband tried Jerusalem artichokes at a restaurant and didn't really care for them, but when they showed up in her CSA box she was determined to give them a second chance. She's happy she did, as hers were perfectly tender and absolutely delicious. If you can't find Jerusalem artichokes or are not interested in trying them, you can prepare this dish with red potatoes.

Jamie DeCaria is on a quest to eat more real food, and she generously shares what she's learned in the kitchen at her website, savorra.com. Visit Jamie's site to find more simple recipes for turning fresh ingredients into tasty meals.

SERVES 4 // VEGAN // SIDE DISH

INGREDIENTS

3 tablespoons olive oil

½ tablespoon finely chopped garlic

1 small onion, cut into ¼-inch slices (about ½ cup)

6–8 Jerusalem artichokes, cut into ⅛- to ¼-inch slices (or substitute red potatoes)

1 teaspoon kosher salt, or to taste

¼ teaspoon freshly ground black pepper

1½ tablespoons freshly squeezed lemon juice (omit if using potatoes)

PROCESS

Heat the oil in a small skillet over medium-low heat. Add the garlic and sauté for 1 minute, until fragrant. Add the onion and Jerusalem artichokes; sprinkle with salt, pepper, and lemon juice, and cook, covered, stirring occasionally, until the Jerusalem artichokes are tender (about 20 minutes).

CHILE-RUBBED JICAMA

BY PATRICIA MULVEY AND LAURA GILLIAM OF LOCAL THYME

With just a few additional ingredients, crunchy jicama makes a tasty, quick, and refreshing snack.

SERVES 2-4 // VEGAN // APPETIZER

INGREDIENTS

1 pound jicama, peeled and cut into 1-inch matchsticks

½ teaspoon (or more) ancho chile powder

¼ lime

Salt to taste

PROCESS

Using your hands, rub the jicama sticks with a dusting of ancho chile powder, adding more if you like some heat. Squeeze lime juice over the jicama, sprinkle with salt, and toss to distribute evenly.

JICAMA SLAW

BY PATRICIA MULVEY AND LAURA GILLIAM OF LOCAL THYME

In this peppy side dish, a tangy, lightly spicy lime dressing complements the sweet crunch of jicama, carrot, cabbage, and peppers. It's great on its own or served atop fish tacos or alongside barbecue. If you shred the vegetables using a food processor's shredding disk (for the jicama and carrots) and slicing disk (for the cabbage), the prep time will fly by.

SERVES 6 // VEGETARIAN // SIDE DISH

INGREDIENTS

3 tablespoons lime juice

½ teaspoon hot pepper sauce

½ teaspoon chili powder

6 tablespoons rice vinegar

1 teaspoon honey

6 tablespoons olive or sunflower oil

Salt and ground black pepper to taste

3 cups peeled, shredded jicama

1 cup peeled, shredded carrot

1 cup peeled, shredded red cabbage

1 cup julienned yellow bell pepper

4 green onions, chopped

1 tablespoon minced fresh cilantro

PROCESS

Combine the lime juice, hot pepper sauce, chili powder, vinegar, honey, and oil in a bowl and whisk to form an emulsified dressing. Season with salt and pepper. Toss the dressing with the remaining ingredients (jicama through cilantro) in a large bowl, adjust the seasonings, and serve immediately.

JICAMA AND WATERMELON SALAD

BY PATRICIA MULVEY AND LAURA GILLIAM OF LOCAL THYME

The cooling ingredients in this bright and refreshing summer salad pair perfectly with spicy entrées.

SERVES 4 // VEGETARIAN // SIDE DISH

INGREDIENTS

1 medium jicama, peeled and julienned

2 cups diced watermelon

2 cups peeled, seeded, and chopped cucumber

3 tablespoons roughly torn mint

½ cup orange juice

¼ cup lime juice

2 tablespoons honey

Salt and ground black pepper to taste

PROCESS

Combine the jicama, watermelon, cucumber, and mint in a salad bowl. In a small bowl, whisk together the orange juice, lime juice, and honey, and then toss with the jicama mixture. Season with salt and pepper and serve immediately.

MEDITERRANEAN POTATO SALAD WITH KOHLRABI

BY DEE SYVERUD

The peppery crunch of kohlrabi is a welcome addition to this lively potato salad. Dee says it's great with anything grilled, and she particularly loves it with wild Alaskan salmon. It's also delicious prepared with other tender, crunchy root vegetables, like turnips, celeriac, or radish, if kohlrabi is not yet in season.

SERVES 8-10 // VEGETARIAN // SIDE DISH

INGREDIENTS

SALAD:

Salt for cooking water

4 pounds tiny red potatoes, cut into 1-inch pieces

2 pounds kohlrabi, peeled and cut into long strips

½ cup halved, pitted Kalamata olives

2 bunches green onions (white and light green parts only), diced

1 bunch fresh mint leaves, minced

2–3 sprigs flat-leaf parsley, minced

DRESSING:

1½ tablespoons coarse-grain mustard

1 tablespoon yellow mustard

2 large cloves garlic, minced

1 teaspoon honey

1 tablespoon white wine vinegar

1 tablespoon cider vinegar

3–4 tablespoons grape seed oil

Freshly ground black pepper to taste

Coarsely ground sea salt to taste

PROCESS

Bring a pot of salted water to a boil. Add the potatoes and cook until a knife pierces them easily, about 10 minutes. Remove the potatoes from the water, place on a baking sheet, and let cool. (Placing them in the refrigerator during cooling will help them hold their shape and dry out a bit so they absorb the dressing more readily.)

Combine the remaining salad ingredients in a large bowl and set aside. Whisk the dressing ingredients in a small bowl until emulsified. When the potatoes are cool, add them to the vegetable mixture, drizzle with the dressing, and toss gently so as not to damage the potatoes. Serve at room temperature.

PETITE ASIAN-INSPIRED KOHLRABI SALAD
BY SARA GOMACH

Savory sesame oil and crushed red pepper accent juicy, sweet kohlrabi in this deliciously simple salad. Our tester loved this recipe exactly as written, but we're betting this salad would also be delicious with fresh, tender turnips, carrots, or Asian radish instead of kohlrabi. Try this salad as a side dish for delicate fish or seared scallops.

SERVES 2 // VEGAN // SIDE DISH

INGREDIENTS

1 kohlrabi, peeled

Juice from ½ lemon

1 tablespoon sesame oil

1 teaspoon white wine vinegar

½ teaspoon crushed red pepper

2 tablespoons chopped fresh cilantro

Salt and ground black pepper to taste

1 tablespoon slivered almonds, toasted or raw

PROCESS

Cut the kohlrabi in half lengthwise and slice into half-moons. In a small bowl, combine the kohlrabi, lemon juice, sesame oil, white wine vinegar, crushed red pepper, cilantro, salt, and pepper. Toss to fully coat the kohlrabi. To serve, arrange 5–7 slices on each plate and top with slivered almonds.

SAUTÉED SHREDDED KOHLRABI WITH CHEESE
BY JULI MCGUIRE OF TWO ONION FARM

Mild and crisp when raw, kohlrabi cooks up sweet and tender. This recipe is a nice option for a vegetable that can be intimidating with its thick skin. Serve alongside roasted meats or baked salmon.

SERVES 2-4 // VEGETARIAN // SIDE DISH

INGREDIENTS

1 tablespoon unsalted butter

2 kohlrabi (about ¾ pound), peeled and shredded

2–3 tablespoons grated Pecorino Romano

Salt and ground black pepper to taste

PROCESS

Melt the butter in a skillet over medium-high heat. Add the kohlrabi and cook, stirring frequently, until the juice evaporates and the kohlrabi is tender and beginning to brown, 10–12 minutes. Add the cheese, salt, and pepper, stir, and continue cooking until the cheese melts. Serve warm.

CURRIED PARSNIP SOUP

BY PATRICIA MULVEY AND LAURA GILLIAM OF LOCAL THYME

Pat based this heavenly soup on a recipe shared by one of her clients. The sweet parsnips pair well with the classic curry-coconut milk combination; sherry adds a welcome bright note to round out the flavor.

SERVES 6 // VEGETARIAN // SIDE DISH

INGREDIENTS

2 tablespoons butter

1 large onion, chopped

2 tablespoons minced fresh ginger

2 stalks celery, chopped

5 medium parsnips, peeled and chopped

1 large russet potato, peeled and diced

4 cups vegetable broth

1 tablespoon curry powder

3 tablespoons sherry

1 (14-ounce) can coconut milk

Salt and ground black pepper to taste

PROCESS

Melt the butter in a stockpot over medium-high heat. Sauté the onion, ginger, and celery until the onion is translucent, 5–6 minutes. Mix in the next 6 ingredients (parsnips through coconut milk), bring to a boil, reduce the heat, and simmer until the vegetables are all tender, about 20 minutes. Puree the soup with an immersion blender or in a food processor. Season with salt and pepper. If you prefer a slightly thinner soup, thin it with water or vegetable broth.

HONEY BALSAMIC GLAZED PARSNIPS

BY PATRICIA MULVEY AND LAURA GILLIAM OF LOCAL THYME

Honey enhances the natural sweetness of the parsnips in this flavorful side dish.

SERVES 4 // VEGETARIAN // SIDE DISH

INGREDIENTS

1½ pounds parsnips, peeled, halved lengthwise, and cut into 1-inch lengths

2 tablespoons olive oil

Salt and ground black pepper to taste

1 tablespoon butter

1 tablespoon honey

1 teaspoon balsamic vinegar

PROCESS

Preheat an oven to 400°. Toss the parsnips with the oil, salt, and pepper. Spread in a single layer on a baking sheet. Roast for 35–40 minutes, stirring twice, until tender and uniformly browned.

Meanwhile, stir together the butter, honey, and vinegar in a small saucepan over medium heat. When the parsnips are cooked, remove them from the oven and toss them in the honey mixture. Serve immediately.

FARM-FRESH AND FAST // ROOT VEGETABLES // 34

PARSNIP OR CELERIAC OVEN FRIES
BY ALISSA MOORE OF WELLSPRING CSA

Healthier than traditional French fries and just as delicious, these easy "fries" can be made to suit any palate or occasion by substituting different seasonings.

SERVES 4 // VEGAN // SIDE DISH

INGREDIENTS

1 pound parsnips and/or celeriac

3 tablespoons olive oil

Salt and ground black pepper to taste

1–2 teaspoons other seasonings (minced garlic, chili powder, dried herbs, etc.) (optional)

PROCESS

Preheat an oven to 375°. Trim the ends of the parsnips or peel the celeriac and cut into uniform wedges. Place in a bowl and drizzle with the olive oil, tossing to coat each piece. Sprinkle with salt and pepper and mix in the other seasonings (if desired). Spread the vegetables in a single layer on a baking sheet. Bake for 45–60 minutes, turning over each piece after 20–30 minutes. When finished, the edges of the oven fries will be starting to brown.

AUTUMN HARVEST SOUP (POTATO)
BY EDITH THAYER

Sweet carrots and apples enlivened with bright curry powder make for a rich, warming autumn soup. This soup is a popular dinner party or potluck dish and can be served with sour cream or Greek-style yogurt, chopped parsley or cilantro, lime wedges, and even toasted sliced almonds for garnish.

SERVES 4 // VEGAN // SIDE DISH

INGREDIENTS

1 large onion, diced (about 1 cup)

1 stalk celery, diced

1 red bell pepper, diced (about ½ cup)

2 tablespoons vegetable oil or butter

1 tablespoon curry powder

2 carrots, peeled and diced (about 3 cups)

2 apples, diced (about 3 cups)

1 large Yukon Gold potato, diced

1 bay leaf

4 cups chicken or vegetable broth

¼ cup currants or raisins

½ teaspoon dried thyme

½–1 cup half-and-half or coconut milk

Salt and ground black pepper to taste

Sour cream and chopped fresh parsley (optional)

PROCESS

In a large stockpot, sauté the onion, celery, and red pepper in the oil or butter until the onion is softened and translucent, about 5 minutes (do not brown). Stir in the curry powder, then add the carrots, apples, potatoes, and bay leaf. Sauté for 2–3 minutes. Add the broth, currants, and thyme. Bring the soup to a boil, cover, and cook until the vegetables are tender, about 25 minutes. Remove the bay leaf. Use an immersion blender to puree the soup to the desired consistency (leave a few chunks for a more "rustic" soup). Add half-and-half or coconut milk if the soup is too thick. Season with salt and pepper. Serve garnished with a dollop of sour cream and a sprinkling of parsley (if desired).

JOSEPHINE'S POTATO DUMPLINGS
BY JOSEPHINE HESS, COURTESY OF REAP

Josephine has been making these time-tested dumplings for decades. Simple and mild, they can be paired with almost any accompaniment. Josephine loves them served with pork and sauerkraut, or simply dressed with butter, salt, and pepper.

SERVES 4 // VEGETARIAN // SIDE DISH

If you have any leftovers, cut the dumplings into ¼-inch slices. Dip the slices in beaten egg and fry in butter until golden brown. Sprinkle with salt and pepper.

INGREDIENTS

1 cup boiled, mashed potatoes (about 3 medium potatoes)

1 egg

1 teaspoon salt

2 cups all-purpose flour

PROCESS

Bring a large pot of water to a boil. In a medium bowl, combine the mashed potatoes, egg, and salt and mix well. Add the flour 1 cup at a time and knead until the mixture resembles bread dough. Shape into 8 (2- to 3-inch) balls. Cook the dumplings in the boiling water for 15–20 minutes. They will float when ready, but make sure they boil for at least 15 minutes.

MILI JULI SABZI (MIXED VEGETABLE CURRY) (POTATO)
BY HUMA SIDDIQUI, COURTESY OF REAP

In the temperate climate of Pakistan, Huma enjoyed mili juli sabzi *all year long. Its lively mix of spices accommodates lots of vegetable combinations, making it easily adaptable to regions where the produce changes with the seasons.*

SERVES 3-4 // VEGAN // MAIN DISH

INGREDIENTS

3 tablespoons vegetable oil

1 teaspoon cumin seeds

1 medium onion, diced

1 medium eggplant, diced

2 medium potatoes, diced

1 medium zucchini, diced

4 medium tomatoes, diced

1 green bell pepper, seeded and diced

½ teaspoon turmeric

1½ teaspoons chili powder

2 teaspoons ground cumin

2 teaspoons ground coriander

1 teaspoon salt

1 cup warm water

½ cup chopped fresh cilantro

PROCESS

Heat the oil in a wok or other wide, deep pan. Add the cumin seeds, then add the onion when the cumin starts to sizzle. Fry both of them together, stirring often. Add the eggplant and continue to stir for a few minutes more. Add the potatoes, zucchini, tomatoes, and green pepper. Stir the mixture for another few minutes and then add all the seasonings (turmeric through salt). Add the water, cover, and let the mixture cook over medium heat for 15 minutes. When all the vegetables are tender, add the cilantro.

NEPALI POTATO-FILLED FLATBREAD WITH SPICY TOMATO CHUTNEY

BY GABRIEL HECK, COURTESY OF REAP

Pillows of flatbread stuffed with garlicky potatoes and slathered with spicy chutney—Nepali comfort food at its best. Serve this dish on its own as a snack, or make it part of a larger Nepali meal. Make the chutney in advance (store in the refrigerator) to cut down on preparation time.

SERVES 4 // VEGAN // APPETIZER

INGREDIENTS

CHUTNEY:

2 medium tomatoes, diced (1½ cups)

1 teaspoon oil

½ teaspoon cayenne (optional)

¼ teaspoon salt

2 tablespoons chopped fresh cilantro

FLATBREAD:

1 cup sifted whole-wheat flour, plus more for rolling

1 cup sifted all-purpose flour

¾ cup plus 2 tablespoons water

1 medium potato, parboiled

¼–⅓ cup oil, divided

1 teaspoon mashed fresh ginger

1 clove garlic, mashed

½ teaspoon salt

PROCESS

CHUTNEY: Liquefy the tomato in a blender. Pour into a wok or skillet along with the oil, cayenne (if desired), and salt. Cook over medium heat until the mixture begins to simmer. Remove from the heat and stir in the cilantro. Set aside to cool to room temperature.

FLATBREAD: In a mixing bowl, combine the whole-wheat and white flours. Gradually add the water and knead into a pliable dough. Cover the bowl with a damp cloth and set aside.

In a separate mixing bowl, mash the potato, then add 1 teaspoon of the oil and the ginger, garlic, and salt. Mix well and set aside.

Divide the dough into 8 equal pieces. Using your hands, roll each piece into a ball on a floured surface. Form each ball into a bowl shape, fill the bowl with a portion of the mashed potato mixture, then seal the potato inside the dough by pinching the dough shut around it. Form each one into a ball again with your hands. On a floured surface, roll each potato-filled ball into a large, thin circle.

Very lightly oil the surface of each circle with a portion of the remaining oil, then fold each circle in half to form a semicircle. Very lightly oil the surface of each semicircle, and then fold each in half again to form a quarter circle. Roll the quarter circles out into large, thin triangles. In a skillet or on a griddle, fry each triangle in ½ teaspoon of the remaining oil, adding oil as needed. Turn the flatbread over as necessary, lightly browning both sides. Serve warm with spicy tomato chutney.

POTATO, KALE, AND SAUSAGE SOUP
BY HEIDI ACCOLA OF ROOTS & SHOOTS FARM

Onions, sausage, garlic, and kale lend big flavor to this warming and deeply satisfying soup. The sausage gives it a rich, meaty flavor, while the kale is earthy and sweet. This dish may convert even the most kale-adverse!

SERVES 8–10 // MEAT // MAIN DISH

INGREDIENTS

12 ounces spicy sausage, chopped or crumbled

¾ cup diced onion

2 tablespoons minced garlic

8 cups chicken broth

2 medium potatoes, cut in half, then into ¼-inch slices

4 cups chopped kale (or spinach)

⅓ cup whipping cream

PROCESS

Fry the sausage in a stockpot over medium heat until browned and cooked through. Remove from the pot and set aside. Add the onions and cook over medium heat until almost translucent, 2–3 minutes. Add the garlic and cook 1 minute. Add the broth, potatoes, and kale, and simmer 15 minutes. Stir in the cooked sausage and cream and simmer 4 minutes. Serve warm.

STUFFED POTATO SURPRISE
BY KEEGAN THOMPSON, COURTESY OF REAP

Keegan developed this recipe at the age of six. The "surprise" is the spicy layer of beans hiding in the potato skin under the flesh.

SERVES 1 // VEGETARIAN // SIDE DISH

INGREDIENTS

½ baked Yukon Gold potato

¼ cup cooked or canned black beans

1–2 tablespoons mild salsa

½ ounce grated cheese of choice

PROCESS

Scoop out the potato flesh with a spoon, being careful not to damage the skin, and set it aside. Fill the potato skin with the beans and top with salsa. Put the potato flesh back in the skin on top of the beans and salsa. Top with grated cheese and a little more salsa if desired. Serve at room temperature, or heat to serve warm.

UNKY DAVE'S POTATO SALAD

BY DEBRA SHAPIRO/FAIRSHARE CSA COALITION

With the added contrast of crunchy carrots and tender peas, this dish isn't your average potato salad.

SERVES 6 // VEGAN // SIDE DISH

INGREDIENTS

1½ pounds unpeeled potatoes (any color), diced

4 cloves garlic, peeled and sliced

3 tablespoons olive oil

1½ cups frozen peas

4 carrots, peeled and diced

3 tablespoons Dijon mustard

¼ cup balsamic vinegar

Salt and freshly ground black pepper to taste

PROCESS

Preheat an oven to 400°. Combine the potatoes, garlic, and olive oil in a shallow baking dish and toss to coat the vegetables well with oil. Roast until the potatoes are lightly browned and tender, about 30 minutes. Meanwhile, place the peas in a colander. Place the carrots in a pot with water to cover, bring to a boil, and cook for about 2 minutes. Pour the carrots and hot water over the peas to thaw them, rinse with cool water, and drain well. When the potatoes are done, transfer them to a bowl and let cool slightly. Combine the mustard and vinegar and pour over the potatoes. Add the peas and carrots, season with salt and pepper, and mix well. This dish is best if eaten at room temperature. It will keep for at least a week in the refrigerator.

APPLE RADISH SALAD

BY AMYE TEVAARWERK

This remarkably simple salad balances the sweetness of apples with the heat of radishes in a combination that will keep them guessing—and coming back for seconds. It's a delicious foil for rich grilled meats, especially pork. Kohlrabi or young turnips can also be used in place of radishes.

SERVES 4 // VEGETARIAN // SIDE DISH

INGREDIENTS

DRESSING:

¼ cup oil

Juice from 1 orange or lemon (or 2 limes)

1 teaspoon Dijon mustard

1 teaspoon honey, or or more to taste

Leaves from 1–2 sprigs fresh thyme

Salt and ground black pepper to taste

SALAD:

2 Granny Smith apples, sliced or julienned

1 bunch radishes, sliced or julienned

PROCESS

Combine all the dressing ingredients in a small bowl and whisk to combine. In a large bowl, combine the apples and radishes. Drizzle with dressing and toss to combine. Depending on the sweetness of the apples, you may need to adjust the amount of honey.

FISH TACOS (RADISH)

BY JAMIE DECARIA OF SAVORRA.COM

Jamie's whole family loves this tasty fish taco—adapted from a Bobby Flay grilling recipe. She incorporates radishes and kohlrabi—two perennial "what do I do with this?" CSA vegetables. If you don't have either of those, cabbage works great too, as does anything with a pungent crunch. Jamie usually doubles the recipe because it's equally tasty on day 2.

SERVES 4 // FISH/SEAFOOD // MAIN DISH

INGREDIENTS

¼ cup safflower oil

Juice from 1 lime

1 tablespoon chili powder

¼ cup finely chopped fresh cilantro

1 pound tilapia fillets, or other white, flaky fish

SALSA BLANCA:

½ cup mayonnaise

½ cup plain yogurt or sour cream

½ teaspoon salt

8 flour tortillas

GARNISHES:

1 pound radishes, shredded

1 pound kohlrabi, peeled and shredded

½ cup coarsely chopped fresh cilantro

PROCESS

Whisk together the first 4 ingredients (oil through cilantro) in a shallow baking dish and place the fish on top, turning to coat. Let marinate for 15–30 minutes. Meanwhile, move an oven rack to the top third of the oven and preheat the broiler. Prepare the Salsa Blanca: whisk together the mayonnaise, yogurt, and salt in a small bowl. Set aside.

Once the fish is done marinating, broil it for 5–7 minutes, then flip to the other side and broil another 5 minutes, until the fish flakes easily with a fork. Remove from the oven and use a fork to flake all the fish into bite-size pieces. To serve, divide the fish among the tortillas and top with the garnishes, Salsa Blanca, and other sauces (such as tomato salsa and hot pepper sauce) if desired.

RADISH, TURNIP, AND SMOKED TROUT SALAD WITH WASABI VINAIGRETTE

BY PATRICIA MULVEY AND LAURA GILLIAM
OF LOCAL THYME

This substantial salad features peppery radishes and turnips dressed in a sweet and spicy wasabi vinaigrette. If you are not a fan of wasabi, you can easily omit it; or you can add more if you like a very spicy dressing.

SERVES 4 // FISH/SEAFOOD // MAIN DISH

INGREDIENTS

1 head lettuce, leaves torn

4 radishes, halved and sliced

1 turnip, peeled, quartered, and thinly sliced

4 ounces smoked trout

2 teaspoons wasabi powder

2 teaspoons water

1 tablespoon minced garlic scapes

1½ tablespoons honey

1½ tablespoons rice vinegar

1 tablespoon soy sauce or tamari

⅓ cup orange juice

¼ cup toasted sesame oil

1 tablespoon sesame seeds, toasted

PROCESS

Toss the lettuce, radishes, and turnip together in a salad bowl. Remove the trout flesh from the skin and crumble into the salad bowl. In a small bowl, make a dressing: whisk together the wasabi powder and water; stir in the garlic scapes, honey, vinegar, and soy sauce; add the orange juice and stir well; and slowly pour in the sesame oil in a steady stream, whisking constantly. Pour the desired amount of dressing over the salad, toss well, and sprinkle with sesame seeds.

CURRIED RUTABAGA STEW

BY ANNIE WEGNER LEFORT

Fragrant with warm spices, this stew adds bright flavor to cold winter days. This adaptable recipe can be served over fragrant basmati rice as a main dish, or pureed and served as an elegant soup. It also works well prepared with other root vegetables.

SERVES 6 // VEGAN // MAIN DISH

INGREDIENTS

3 tablespoons coconut or other oil

1 large onion, diced

3 cloves garlic, peeled and minced

½ teaspoon ground ginger

2–3 tablespoons green curry paste diluted in 1–2 tablespoons water or broth

⅛ teaspoon chili powder

2 medium rutabagas, peeled and diced small

1 small carrot, peeled and sliced

2 red bell peppers, seeded and diced

¾ teaspoon sea salt

1½ teaspoons brown sugar

1 cup red lentils

2 cups vegetable broth, or more as needed (can substitute water for additional broth)

Chopped fresh cilantro

Plain whole-milk yogurt (optional)

PROCESS

In a large stockpot over medium heat, heat the oil (if using coconut oil, heat until melted). Add the onion, garlic, and ginger and cook over medium heat until soft and fragrant, 6–8 minutes. Add the diluted curry paste and chili powder. Stir well and cook for 1–2 minutes. Add the rutabaga, carrot, and pepper and cook for 2–3 minutes. Add the salt and sugar, mixing thoroughly. Stir in the lentils and broth. Bring to a boil, then reduce the heat to a simmer. Cook, covered, 20–30 minutes, or until all the vegetables and lentils are tender. Serve garnished with cilantro and yogurt (if desired).

MIDWEST VEGGIE BAKE (RUTABAGA)

BY ROSEMARY LEGGETT, COURTESY OF REAP

A mild, fresh cheese forms the creamy base of this Scottish-inspired casserole. Add a simple green salad to make it a meal.

SERVES 6 // VEGETARIAN // SIDE DISH

INGREDIENTS

1 pound rutabaga, peeled and thinly sliced

1 pound carrots, peeled and thinly sliced

1 pound white potatoes, peeled and diced

3 tablespoons butter

1 teaspoon salt

1 teaspoon ground black pepper

4 ounces quark (or substitute 2 ounces cottage cheese mixed with 2 ounces yogurt)

1–2 cups grated melting cheese

PROCESS

Preheat an oven to 400°. Place the rutabaga in a large stockpot with water to cover, bring to a boil, and cook for 10 minutes. Add the carrots and cook for 10 minutes more. Add the potatoes and cook for an additional 20 minutes. Drain and mash the vegetables with the butter, salt, and pepper. Gradually add the quark and mix by hand, or blend with an electric mixer on low speed if a smoother consistency is desired. Spread the mixture into a casserole dish and cover with the grated cheese. Bake for about 15 minutes, or until the top is golden and crusty.

RUTABAGA BISQUE
BY EDITH THAYER

Pale gold and creamy, rutabaga bisque has a richness that belies its earthy origins. This simple soup is delicious served plain, or garnished with frilly chervil leaves, fresh croutons, or even grilled shrimp. Smoked paprika adds intriguing flavor as well as bright color to this dish, so it is worth seeking out.

SERVES 6-8 // VEGETARIAN // SIDE DISH

INGREDIENTS

1 tablespoon butter

1 medium yellow onion, coarsely chopped

2 medium celery stalks, coarsely chopped

Salt to taste

1½ pounds rutabaga, peeled and coarsely chopped (about 4¼ cups)

3 cups chicken or vegetable broth

2 cups half-and-half

2½ teaspoons high-quality smoked paprika

½ teaspoon ground white pepper (or more to taste)

PROCESS

Melt the butter in a large stockpot over medium heat. Add the onion and celery and season generously with salt. Cook, stirring occasionally, until the vegetables are tender but not browned, about 5 minutes. Add the rutabaga and broth, bring to a boil, then reduce the heat to low and simmer until the rutabaga is tender when pierced with a fork, 30–40 minutes. Add the half-and-half, paprika, and pepper and stir to combine. Puree the soup with an immersion blender until smooth. Taste and season with more salt and pepper as needed. To serve, ladle into soup bowls and sprinkle with a bit of additional paprika.

CREAM OF SALSIFY SOUP
BY PATRICIA MULVEY AND LAURA GILLIAM OF LOCAL THYME

Cooked, pureed salsify has an intriguing, subtle flavor and the creamy texture of a potato—two features that make it the perfect star of this rich, silky soup.

SERVES 4 // VEGETARIAN // SIDE DISH

INGREDIENTS

2 tablespoons unsalted butter

1 cup chopped onion

1 stalk celery, chopped

4 cloves garlic, minced

12 ounces salsify, peeled and sliced

6 cups chicken or vegetable broth

1 teaspoon dried thyme

1 bay leaf

½ cup half-and-half

Salt and ground black pepper to taste

PROCESS

Melt the butter in a stockpot. Sauté the onion and celery until tender, 5–6 minutes. Add the garlic and stir for 1 minute, then add the salsify, broth, and herbs. Bring to a boil, skimming off any foam that rises to the surface. Reduce the heat to a simmer and cook until the vegetables are tender, about 20 minutes. Discard the bay leaf and puree the soup. Return the soup to the pot, stir in the half-and-half, and simmer until warmed through. Season with salt and pepper.

Salsify oxidizes to an unappetizing gray color once peeled, unless you place it into acidulated water. Have a bowl of cold water with a splash of vinegar or citrus near your work space, and submerge your peeled or sliced salsify as you prep it. Drain it when you are ready to cook.

MAPLE-ROASTED SALSIFY

BY PATRICIA MULVEY AND LAURA GILLIAM OF LOCAL THYME

Here's a way to serve vegetables to even the pickiest eaters. The maple syrup caramelizes in the oven and practically turns the salsify into candy!

SERVES 4 // VEGAN // SIDE DISH

INGREDIENTS

2 pounds salsify, peeled, quartered lengthwise, and cut into 2-inch pieces

2 tablespoons canola oil

⅓ cup maple syrup

Salt and ground black pepper to taste

PROCESS

Preheat an oven to 400°. Toss the salsify with the oil and syrup, sprinkle with salt and pepper, and spread in a single layer on a parchment- or aluminum foil-lined baking sheet (use 2 baking sheets if necessary). Place the sheet(s) in the oven and roast the salsify, stirring occasionally, until tender and caramelized, 35–45 minutes.

TRUFFLED SALSIFY PUREE

BY PATRICIA MULVEY AND LAURA GILLIAM OF LOCAL THYME

A drizzle of truffle oil gives this simple side dish a decadent twist.

SERVES 4 // VEGETARIAN // SIDE DISH

INGREDIENTS

2 pounds salsify, peeled and chopped

4 cups whole milk

1 teaspoon dried herbs of choice

3 cloves garlic

Dash freshly grated nutmeg

2 tablespoons butter

Truffle oil

Salt and ground black pepper to taste

PROCESS

Combine the salsify with the milk, herbs, garlic, and nutmeg in a large, heavy pot. Simmer until the salsify is tender, about 20 minutes. Strain off the cooking liquid and reserve for later use. Puree the salsify by passing it through a food mill or ricer back into the pot. Stir over low heat for 3–5 minutes. Stir in the butter and add a little of the reserved cooking liquid to achieve the desired consistency. Drizzle with truffle oil and season with salt and pepper.

AMARETTO SWEET POTATOES
BY LISA WIESE

Almond-flavored amaretto and Wisconsin maple syrup join sweet potatoes in a decadent holiday dish that's deceptively simple. Try skipping the marshmallows next year with this sophisticated dish, or serve it any time of year as dessert with a glass of Amontillado sherry.

SERVES 6 // VEGETARIAN // SIDE DISH

INGREDIENTS

3 large sweet potatoes, peeled and cut into bite-size pieces

½ cup maple syrup

½ cup amaretto

Salt (optional)

2 tablespoons butter

PROCESS

Preheat an oven to 325°. Spread the sweet potatoes in a 1½-quart baking dish. In a small bowl, mix together the maple syrup and amaretto. Pour over the sweet potatoes, stirring to coat. Sprinkle with salt (if desired) and dot with butter. Bake, covered, for 45 minutes, or until the sweet potatoes are easily pierced with a fork.

CURRIED VEGETABLE STEW (SWEET POTATO)
BY JEANETTE PACHA

Make this hearty stew on the weekend and enjoy satisfying lunches in the week ahead. Serve with brown rice, quinoa, or naan.

SERVES 8–10 // VEGAN // MAIN DISH

INGREDIENTS

2 tablespoons olive oil

2 cups chopped onion

2 cloves garlic, minced

2 tablespoons minced fresh ginger

1 tablespoon Indian curry powder

1 pound cauliflower, cut into florets (about 1½ cups)

2 waxy potatoes, diced into ½-inch cubes (about 1½ cups)

3 carrots, chopped (about 2 cups)

1 fennel bulb, sliced

3 sweet potatoes, peeled and diced into ½-inch cubes (about 2 cups)

2 cups fresh green beans, snapped

4 cups vegetable or chicken broth

2 tablespoons agave nectar or honey

4 whole cloves

1 cinnamon stick

1 (15-ounce) can chickpeas, drained and rinsed

Salt to taste

½ cup chopped fresh cilantro

2 tablespoons chopped fresh mint

PROCESS

Heat the oil in a large stockpot. Add the onion and cook for 3 minutes, until it begins to soften. Add the garlic and ginger and cook for 3 minutes, stirring frequently. Add the curry powder and cook for 2 minutes more, continuing to stir. Add the vegetables, broth, and agave nectar; place the cloves and cinnamon in a tea ball or tie in some cheesecloth (for easy retrieval) and add them to the pot. Bring to a boil, reduce the heat, and simmer uncovered for about 10 minutes. Add the chickpeas and cook for 10 minutes more. Remove from the heat. Remove the cloves and cinnamon, season with salt, and serve sprinkled with cilantro and mint.

SWEET POTATO AND ZUCCHINI BREAD
BY ALEXANDRA STAUB

Sweet potato, ground walnuts, and applesauce stand in for less healthy fats in this delicious quick bread. Our tester loved it, describing it as not-too-sweet, but moist and delicious. She plans to add this recipe to her regular rotation and is hoping for a bumper crop of zucchini this year.

YIELDS 1 LOAF // VEGETARIAN // DESSERT

INGREDIENTS

2 cups whole-wheat flour

1½ teaspoons ground cinnamon

1 teaspoon baking soda

¼ teaspoon baking powder

¼ teaspoon salt

1 cup brown sugar

6 tablespoons vegetable oil

6 tablespoons applesauce

3 large eggs

1 teaspoon vanilla extract

1½ cups grated zucchini

1½ cups peeled, grated sweet potato

1 cup ground walnuts (whirl in a food processor to grind)

PROCESS

Preheat an oven to 350°. Butter and flour a 9 × 5-inch loaf pan or use a silicone pan. Sift the first 5 ingredients (flour through salt) into a bowl. In a separate, larger bowl, beat the sugar, oil, applesauce, eggs, and vanilla to blend. Mix in the zucchini and sweet potato. Add the dry ingredients and ground walnuts and stir well.

Pour the batter into the prepared pan. Bake until a toothpick inserted into the center comes out clean, 60–80 minutes. Cool completely before slicing. This bread keeps in the refrigerator for several days.

BUTTER-GLAZED TURNIPS AND THEIR GREENS
BY DEBRA SHAPIRO/FAIRSHARE CSA COALITION

This effortless recipe allows the sweet earthiness of root vegetables to shine. It works equally well with rutabagas, kohlrabi, or carrots.

SERVES 4-6 // VEGETARIAN // SIDE DISH

INGREDIENTS

Salt for cooking water

1–2 pounds turnips, peeled and diced into 1-inch cubes

3 tablespoons butter

Greens from the turnips, or about ¾ pound spinach, stems removed

Salt and freshly ground black pepper to taste

PROCESS

Fill a large pot with water, add some salt, and bring it to a boil over medium-high heat. Drop the turnips into the water and cook until they're crisp-tender, 10–12 minutes. Drain. Melt the butter in a large, deep skillet and add the boiled turnip cubes. Cook, stirring occasionally, until they begin to brown. Add the greens, cover, and cook until the greens wilt. Remove the lid and let the moisture steam off. Season with salt and pepper and serve hot.

KOHLRABI, SNAP PEA, AND TURNIP LETTUCE WRAPS WITH CHOICE OF MEAT

BY PATRICIA MULVEY AND LAURA GILLIAM OF LOCAL THYME

Pat's kids will eat ANYTHING if she lets them wrap it in a leaf of lettuce, especially if they can dip it in a flavorful sauce. Kids (and adults!) everywhere are sure to enjoy these fun and tasty wraps too.

SERVES 4 // MEAT // MAIN DISH

INGREDIENTS

Leaves from 1 head lettuce (butterhead works well)

DIPPING SAUCE:

¼ cup hoisin sauce

1 tablespoon lime juice

1 tablespoon soy sauce or tamari

1 teaspoon toasted sesame oil

1 tablespoon warm water

FILLING:

2 tablespoons toasted sesame oil, divided

1 pound ground meat of choice (chicken, pork, lamb, turkey)

2 cloves garlic, minced

1 kohlrabi, peeled and diced into ¼-inch cubes

1 turnip, peeled and diced into ¼-inch cubes

½ pound sugar snap peas, stems and strings removed, cut into ¼-inch slices

⅓ cup soy sauce or tamari

½ cup dry-roasted peanuts or other nuts (optional)

Asian sweet chile sauce (optional, for those who like their wraps spicy)*

*Asian sweet chile sauce can be found in the ethnic food aisle of most grocery stores, and in Asian specialty markets.

PROCESS

Arrange the lettuce leaves on a platter and set aside.

DIPPING SAUCE: Stir together the hoisin sauce, lime juice, soy sauce, sesame oil, and water until well blended. Divide the sauce among 4 individual dipping bowls.

FILLING: In a large skillet, heat 1 tablespoon of the sesame oil over medium heat. Add the meat and garlic and cook, stirring and breaking up the meat, until the meat is cooked through. Using a slotted spoon, transfer the cooked meat to a clean bowl and set aside. Wipe the skillet with a paper towel.

Heat the remaining tablespoon of sesame oil in the skillet. Add the kohlrabi and stir-fry for 1–2 minutes, then add the turnip and stir-fry 3–4 minutes longer. Add the sugar snap peas and continue stir-frying for 2 minutes more, until the peas become darker green but are still crisp. Return the meat to the skillet and pour in the soy sauce, stir-frying until well blended and heated through. Transfer the filling to a serving bowl and sprinkle with peanuts (if desired). Set out the lettuce leaves, filling, dipping sauce, and sweet chile sauce (if desired) for individual wrap assembly.

YUKON GOLD AND TURNIP MASH WITH SOUR CREAM

BY PATRICIA MULVEY AND LAURA GILLIAM OF LOCAL THYME

This modest mash is hearty enough to be a meal on its own; add a simple salad and a glass of wine and turn your meal into a feast.

SERVES 4-6 // VEGETARIAN // SIDE DISH

INGREDIENTS

Salt for cooking water

1 turnip, peeled and diced

1 pound Yukon Gold potatoes,
peeled and diced

1 bay leaf

3 tablespoons unsalted butter

3 tablespoons sour cream

Salt and ground black pepper to taste

PROCESS

Bring a pot of water to a boil and add some salt. Add the turnip, potato, and bay leaf. Boil until the vegetables are tender, about 20 minutes. Drain off the water, discard the bay leaf, return the vegetables to the pot, and set over a warm burner. Add the butter and stir the vegetables to help evaporate any excess moisture. When the steam begins to subside, mash the vegetables, stir in the sour cream, and season with salt and pepper. Serve hot.

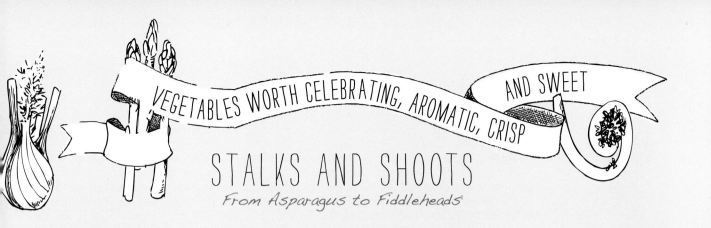

STALKS AND SHOOTS
From Asparagus to Fiddleheads[1]

Aromatic, crisp, and sweet, stalks and shoots are vegetables worth celebrating. Asparagus and fiddleheads have deep, earthy flavors that are complex and sweetly intriguing. They are delicious alone or as accents to rich foods like eggs, mushrooms, and cheeses. Succulent celery and fragrant fennel have bold flavor from tip to root: their stalks are used as flavor bases and accents in countless recipes; their seeds are used as spices; and their leaves are used as herbs. Even the roots of celery are edible (see "Root Vegetables: Celeriac" on page 8).

Crunchy stalk vegetables, such as celery and fennel, are thick stems that support leaves and flowers while the plant grows. Crisp by nature, these stems are made of strong, fibrous cells and have structures that carry water and nutrients from leaves to roots. Shoots, such as asparagus, are tender rather than sturdy. They are newly emerged plants that have not yet developed tough fibers, leaves, or flowers. Both crunchy stalks and tender shoots are pleasantly juicy, thanks to their high water content.

Selection.   Look for stalk vegetables that are smooth and blemish-free. If possible, choose celery and fennel with leaves intact. Make sure that asparagus tips are tightly closed, and that fiddleheads are small, bright green, and firm.

Storage.   Stalks and shoots should be stored loosely wrapped in the vegetable drawer of the refrigerator. Keep celery stalks together in bunches until ready to use. Alternatively, celery can be stored upright in water to be kept crisp: cut stalks free from their base and stand them cut side down in a sturdy, water-filled container. Sturdy celery and fennel can be stored for up to two weeks, but tender asparagus and fiddleheads should be used as soon as possible, since they begin losing stored sugars almost immediately after harvest.

Preparation.   Most stalks and shoots merely need to be cleaned and trimmed, but asparagus with tough skin, or stalks with thick fibers, can be peeled. Fibrous celery and bigger fennel bulbs may be tenderized by running a peeler lightly over particularly heavy ridges. Alternatively, slice very fibrous stalks crosswise into thin pieces with a sharp knife or mandoline.

Revive tired stalk vegetables in an ice-water bath.

> *Respecting the dignity of a spectacular food means enjoying it at its best. Europeans celebrate the short season of abundant asparagus as a form of holiday. In the Netherlands the first cutting coincides with Father's Day, on which restaurants may feature all-asparagus menus and hand out neckties decorated with asparagus spears.*
>
> **—BARBARA KINGSOLVER,** *Animal, Vegetable, Miracle*

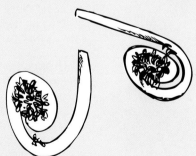

---

1   Although rhubarb is technically a stalk vegetable, it is most often used as a fruit substitute. Therefore, we feature it in the "Sweet Fruits" section (see page 123).

ASPARAGUS

Green.   A species of perennial herbaceous plants, asparagus is harvested as a shoot before it flowers. Tenderness is determined by the age of the vegetable, not the size. Look at the budlike tips of the spears to determine freshness; if they are starting to open, they are past their prime. The woody bottom of the asparagus spear can be either snapped off or trimmed with a knife.

White.   Green asparagus that is blanched, or covered with soil or paper during growth to prevent chlorophyll from developing, becomes white asparagus. It is a harbinger of spring in parts of Europe, where entire restaurant menus are planned around it. But in the United States, white asparagus is not as popular, possibly because the labor required for production makes it an expensive specialty. It is rare or nonexistent in farmers' markets, and during the brief window when it's available in grocery stores, it is often no longer fresh. If you find it, ask when it was picked and how it was stored. If it has been harvested recently and kept cold, it is worth trying. White asparagus should be peeled from about an inch below the tip all the way to the bottom, as even the freshest spears will have a tough and bitter skin. It is best with a simple dressing of butter and lemon or fresh Hollandaise sauce.

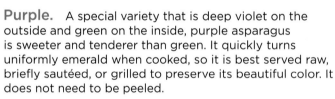

Purple.   A special variety that is deep violet on the outside and green on the inside, purple asparagus is sweeter and tenderer than green. It quickly turns uniformly emerald when cooked, so it is best served raw, briefly sautéed, or grilled to preserve its beautiful color. It does not need to be peeled.

CELERY

Common.   A member of the parsley family (Apiaceae or Umbelliferae), crunchy celery is a popular staple both raw and cooked. Choose tight bunches with firm stalks and fresh leaves, if attached. Along with onions and carrots, celery is often used as a flavor base for soups, stews, and sauces. Celery leaves are delicious in salads or used as an herb. Add chopped celery to any of the slaws on page 167.

Chinese.   With skinny stalks and lots of leaves, Chinese celery resembles common celery's wild ancestors. It is stronger in flavor than common celery, though, and it works well as an herb or an aromatic addition to stir-fries, soups, or stews. Most recipes call for the leaves, but the tough stems are also edible. Blanch these or slice them thin before using. Use Chinese celery in place of common celery in "Creamy Celery and Potato Soup" (page 13).

Celery has been around for literally thousands of years, yet rarely does it earn an honored place on the American table. But celery can take center stage in soups and salsa and can even be marinated, braised, and grilled. Even better, celery tends to be very cheap, making for a delicious and highly economical meal. Use a paring knife or peeler to remove the toughest outer strings from the stalks. The leaves are edible, too, although the flavor is very strong, so use them in moderation and taste as you go. Celery hearts—paler, tenderer, and less stringy than outer stalks—are the best parts to use raw.

FENNEL

Crisp and sweetly scented, fennel is most often used for its white, bulbous lower stem, but its feathery leaves and thin green stems should be saved. Remove and reserve the fronds for use in salads, as a garnish, or as an herb. Use the green stems and the tough outer layers of the bulb to flavor broths, roasted poultry, or fish (discard before serving). To serve fennel raw, remove the core and slice the bulb thin. For thicker slices suitable for cooking, keep the core intact to hold sections together. To enhance fennel's characteristic licorice flavor, cook it with crushed fennel seeds or an anise-based liquor like Ricard Pastis or Pernod Anise. Fennel can even be used in desserts. Serve fresh slices with soft goat cheese, figs, and dessert wine, or candy it to serve alone or in lemony desserts.

FIDDLEHEAD FERN

The new, tightly curled coils of any type of fern are called fiddleheads, although ostrich ferns are the only types that should be eaten. Fiddleheads are foraged wild plants with a chewy texture and a flavor that mimics a cross between asparagus and green beans. They are most prized for their appearance. Buy them from a reputable source, and look for small vegetables that are still springy. Trim the tail ends just past the circular shape. Any fuzz or scales can be removed by rubbing fiddleheads between your hands. They are best after boiling, and they must be cooked for at least five minutes to eliminate bitterness and irritating compounds. If using them in a recipe where they will be stir-fried or sautéed, they should be parboiled. Substitute parboiled fiddleheads for the asparagus in "Asparagus and Saffron Risotto with Shrimp" (page 53) or "Cream of Asparagus and Jerusalem Artichoke Soup with Dill" (page 28).

STALKS AND SHOOTS
Storage and Usage Guide

VEGETABLE	STORAGE AND PRESERVATION				USAGE SUGGESTIONS							
	IDEAL CONDITIONS	PICKLE	FREEZE	DEHYDRATE	EDIBLE GREENS*	RAW	STEAM	BRAISE	BOIL/ BLANCH	GRILL	ROAST	SAUTÉ
ASPARAGUS	wrapped, refrigerated	•	•	•		•	•	•	•	•	•	•
CELERY												
common	wrapped, refrigerated	•	•	•	•	•		•				•
Chinese	wrapped, refrigerated		•	•	•	•			•			•
FENNEL	wrapped, refrigerated	•	•	•	•	•		•	•	•	•	•
FIDDLEHEAD FERN	wrapped, refrigerated						•	•	•			

*For more information, see "Leafy Greens" on page 157.

MASTER RECIPE: FOUR-WAY RISOTTO

Although risotto may seem like a challenging dish to make, the basic technique requires merely stirring and a little patience. Customize this creamy basic recipe with vegetable, herb, cheese, or meat add-ins or toppings for an impressive side or main dish. Stalk vegetables, like celery and fennel (added at the aromatics stage), and shoots, like asparagus (added at the add-ins stage), add fresh flavor to risottos and are particularly good paired with seafood.

THE BASICS

Broth: chicken, seafood, vegetable (seasoned to taste)

Fat: oil or butter

Aromatics: finely diced onions, shallots, garlic, celery, fennel, carrots (any combination)

Rice: Arborio or other Italian short-grain

Wine: dry white or red (red will turn the dish pink)

Add-ins and toppings: herbs and spices, vegetables, seafood, meats, cheeses, herbs, cream, butter

Seasoning: salt and pepper

PROCESS

Heat the **broth** and keep warm on the stove. Heat the **fat** in a large saucepan or skillet. Sauté the **aromatics** until softened. Stir in the **rice** and toss to coat in oil, continuing to stir until fragrant and toasted (1–2 minutes). Add the **wine**, stir, and boil until almost all the liquid has evaporated. Add ½ cup of warm **broth** and stir gently until the liquid is mostly absorbed. Repeat this process, adding broth ½ cup at a time and stirring until absorbed, until the rice is cooked al dente, about 25 or more minutes (taste a grain to check, or cut a grain in half and look for a small white dot in the center). Remove from the heat, stir in any **add-ins**, such as herbs, butter, and cheese, and allow to rest for a few minutes. **Season** to taste. Add **toppings** if desired, and serve immediately.

Note. The amount of liquid required to cook the rice will vary depending on the type of rice, its moisture content, and the heat of the liquid. It's best to warm more liquid than you think you will need in case your rice is very thirsty, and know that you might have some left over (save this for reheating leftover risotto). It's fine to stretch broth with water; it will not affect the flavor of the finished dish.

VARIATIONS

ASPARAGUS AND SAFFRON RISOTTO WITH SHRIMP

By Patricia Mulvey and Laura Gilliam

SERVES 4

4–6 cups chicken or vegetable broth

2 tablespoons olive oil

1 cup finely diced onion

1½ cups Arborio rice

1 cup white wine, warmed with 1 pinch crumbled saffron steeped in it for 5 minutes

ADD AFTER COOKING:

½ pound asparagus, chopped

2 tablespoons butter

1 teaspoon lemon juice

Salt and ground black pepper to taste

TOP WITH:

1 pound cooked shrimp, peeled and deveined

FENNEL AND SAUSAGE RISOTTO

By Patricia Mulvey and Laura Gilliam

SERVES 4

4–6 cups chicken or vegetable broth

2 tablespoons olive oil

1 cup finely diced onion

1 fennel bulb, finely diced

1½ cups Arborio rice

1 cup white wine

ADD AFTER COOKING:

1 pound bulk Italian sausage, cooked, drained, and crumbled

½ cup grated Pecorino Romano

Salt and ground black pepper to taste

TOP WITH:

1 tablespoon chopped fennel fronds

SWEET CORN, RED ONION, AND MASCARPONE RISOTTO

By Beth Fortune

SERVES 4

4–6 cups vegetable broth

2 tablespoons olive oil

½ cup finely diced red onion

1½ cups Arborio rice

1 cup white wine

ADD AFTER COOKING:

1 cup fresh corn kernels (reserve some for topping)

4 ounces mascarpone

Salt and ground black pepper to taste

TOP WITH:

Snipped chives and reserved corn

SHELL PEA, GREEN ONION, MINT, AND FETA RISOTTO

By Patricia Mulvey and Laura Gilliam

SERVES 4

4–6 cups vegetable broth

2 tablespoons olive oil

1 cup finely diced onion

1½ cups Arborio rice

1 cup white wine

ADD AFTER COOKING:

1 cup shelled peas

⅓ cup finely chopped green onion (reserve some for topping)

¼ cup chopped fresh mint (reserve some for topping)

4 ounces feta

Salt to taste

TOP WITH:

Reserved chopped herbs

IDEA STARTERS

Spring onion, garlic, asparagus, sautéed mushrooms, Parmesan

Leek, garlic, pumpkin, rosemary, goat cheese; topping: pumpkin seeds

Leek, garlic, chard, thyme, fontina

Shallot, garlic, corn, shiitake; toppings: cooked pancetta, chives

Cipolline onion, garlic, tomato, zucchini, corn, oregano, Parmesan

Onion, butternut squash, sage, Parmesan; topping: pistachio nuts

Leek, roasted beet, beet greens, blue cheese; topping: walnuts

SERVING SUGGESTIONS

◆ Serve with a salad for a simple, hearty meal.

◆ Serve in small portions as an appetizer.

◆ Mix leftover chilled risotto with an egg, form into cakes or balls with a cube of mozzarella in the center, roll in breadcrumbs, and fry for *arancini*.

◆ Stuff into steamed cabbage, escarole, chard, or other leaves.

◆ Use as a soup thickener.

COMMUNITY RECIPES

ASPARAGUS CASHEW PILAF
BY HEIDI ACCOLA OF ROOTS & SHOOTS FARM

Pilaf is a rice-based dish popular in India and the Middle East. Many consider pilaf to be rice's crowning form. This one incorporates the fresh taste of asparagus with cashews for crunch.

SERVES 6–8 // VEGETARIAN // SIDE DISH

INGREDIENTS

¼ cup butter

2 ounces whole-grain spaghetti, broken into 1-inch pieces

1 cup minced onion

1 tablespoon minced garlic

1¼ cups jasmine rice

2¼ cups chicken or vegetable broth

Salt and ground black pepper to taste

1 pound asparagus, cut into ½-inch pieces

½ cup cashew halves (or more)

PROCESS

Melt the butter in a medium pot over medium-low heat. Increase the heat to medium and stir in the spaghetti, cooking until coated with the butter and lightly browned, about 3 minutes. Add the onion and garlic and cook for 2 minutes, or until tender. Stir in the rice and cook for about 5 minutes. Pour in the broth and season with salt and pepper. Bring the mixture to a boil, then reduce to a simmer. Cover and cook for 20 minutes, or until the rice is tender and the liquid has been absorbed.

Meanwhile, steam the asparagus until bright green and crisp-tender (about 10 minutes in a steamer basket; 3–5 minutes in a pan with a bit of boiling water). When the rice is finished, fluff with a fork, stir in the asparagus and cashews, and serve immediately.

ASPARAGUS PASTA SOUP
BY HEIDI ACCOLA OF ROOTS & SHOOTS FARM

The asparagus sings in this quick pasta soup that highlights the vegetable's fresh flavor. It's particularly lovely in the spring when asparagus is at its peak and when nights are still cool enough for something rich and warm.

SERVES 6–8 // VEGETARIAN // SIDE DISH

INGREDIENTS

1 tablespoon olive oil

1 bunch asparagus, sliced (3–4 cups)

6 cups vegetable or chicken broth

1 teaspoon grated lemon peel

4 ounces whole-grain angel hair pasta, broken into small pieces

3 large egg yolks

PROCESS

Heat the oil in a large stockpot or Dutch oven over medium-high heat. Add the asparagus and cook for 1 minute. Add the broth and lemon peel; increase the heat to high and bring the mixture to a boil. Stir in the pasta and cook for 2 minutes. Reduce the heat to low.

In a small bowl, beat the egg yolks with an electric mixer on low. Scoop out 1 cup of the hot soup and slowly add it to the eggs while mixing. Pour the egg mixture into the soup, whisking vigorously to blend. Return the soup to a simmer over medium heat and cook for 1 minute.

FETA PASTA SALAD (ASPARAGUS)

BY ASHLEY RAMAKER

Colorful feta pasta salad is delicious with grilled chicken on a hot summer day. Try it prepared with diced cucumber, summer squash, or snap beans when asparagus is not in season.

SERVES 8 // VEGETARIAN // SIDE DISH

INGREDIENTS

1 pound cavatappi or other small pasta

1 pound asparagus, cut into bite-size pieces

1 cup diced tomato

1 green bell pepper, diced

1 (2¼-ounce) can sliced black olives

4 tablespoons olive oil

2 tablespoons balsamic vinegar

Salt and ground black pepper to taste

1 cup crumbled feta

PROCESS

Cook the pasta according to the package directions, then drain, rinse, and set aside. Sauté or steam the asparagus until crisp-tender, then rinse under cold water to stop the cooking process. Mix the pasta and vegetables together. Drizzle the oil and vinegar over the salad and toss to coat; taste and adjust the oil-vinegar ratio as desired. Season with salt and pepper. Add the feta and mix well. Chill for at least 30 minutes before serving. Serve cold.

HAM AND ASPARAGUS WITH PASTA

BY JODY BARRY, COURTESY OF REAP

This dish is a meal in itself, covering the vegetable, grain, dairy, and protein food groups in one easy preparation. It makes a quick lunch or dinner for chilly spring days.

SERVES 6 // MEAT // MAIN DISH

INGREDIENTS

1 pound asparagus, cut into 1½-inch pieces

2–3 tablespoons olive oil

3 tablespoons butter

1 small onion, diced

2 cloves garlic, minced

1 teaspoon crushed red pepper

¼ teaspoon hot pepper sauce (optional)

½ cup shredded Parmesan or smoked Swiss cheese

1 pound ham, diced into 1-inch cubes

Salt to taste

¼ teaspoon ground black pepper

3 cups mostaccioli or elbow macaroni, cooked and drained

PROCESS

In a large skillet, sauté the asparagus in the oil and butter for 7–8 minutes. Add the onion and garlic and sauté until the asparagus is crisp-tender, 2–3 minutes more. Add the crushed red pepper and hot pepper sauce (if desired). Stir for 1 minute to bring out the flavor of the red pepper. Add the cheese and ham and mix well. Season with salt and pepper. Pour over the hot pasta and toss to coat.

PAN-FRIED ASPARAGUS

BY HEIDI ACCOLA OF ROOTS & SHOOTS FARM

Simpler is better with fresh asparagus—many people simply steam or roast it. Pan-frying is part steaming and part sautéing, which gives you the browned edges of roasted asparagus without the hassle of heating up the oven. This dish is infused with garlicky goodness.

SERVES 4 // VEGETARIAN // SIDE DISH

INGREDIENTS

1 pound asparagus

1 tablespoon butter

1 tablespoon olive oil

¼ teaspoon coarse salt

¼ teaspoon ground black pepper

3 cloves garlic, minced

PROCESS

Dry the asparagus thoroughly so it doesn't cause the oil to splatter during cooking. Melt the butter in a skillet over medium-high heat. Stir in the olive oil, salt, and pepper. Cook the garlic in the butter and oil for 1 minute, but do not brown. Add the asparagus and cook for 10 minutes, turning to ensure even cooking. The asparagus will begin to char and blister when it is ready. Serve hot.

TOASTED ORZO WITH SPRING VEGETABLES (ASPARAGUS)

BY JEANETTE PACHA

Toasting the orzo and roasting the vegetables in this recipe add a pleasant nuttiness and depth to the finished dish. Fresh herbs can be substituted for dried: just double the quantity, omit them from the roasting step, and stir them into the orzo and roasted vegetables before the dish is baked.

SERVES 6–8 // VEGETARIAN // MAIN DISH

INGREDIENTS

1 pound asparagus, cut into bit-size pieces

3 bell peppers, diced

1 bunch green onions, minced

1 cup halved grape tomatoes

1 small zucchini, diced

1 clove garlic, minced

1–2 teaspoons each dried thyme, basil, and oregano

Salt and ground black pepper to taste

3 tablespoons olive oil, divided

1 cup orzo

2 cups vegetable or chicken broth

½ cup pine nuts, toasted

½–1 cup crumbled feta

PROCESS

Preheat an oven to 400°. Toss the vegetables, garlic, herbs, salt, and pepper with 2 tablespoons of the oil. Spread in a 13 × 9-inch baking dish and roast for 25–30 minutes, or until the vegetables are tender and beginning to char. Adjust the seasonings as desired.

Meanwhile, heat the remaining tablespoon of oil in a large pan over medium heat and sauté the orzo until browned, 5–8 minutes. Add the broth, cover, and cook over medium heat until the liquid is absorbed, about 10 minutes. Let stand for 10 minutes, then fluff with a fork.

Mix the orzo into the roasted vegetables and sprinkle with pine nuts and cheese. Cover with aluminum foil and bake for 20 minutes. Remove the foil and bake for an additional 5–10 minutes, or until browned.

FENNEL AND FETA BURGERS

BY ANGELA BOOTZ

With fresh fennel and garlic added, these burgers share a flavor profile with good Italian sausage. Increase the resemblance by adding toasted, ground fennel seeds and crushed red pepper to the mixture, or go Greek by adding oregano. This mixture also makes excellent meatballs.

SERVES 6 // MEAT // MAIN DISH

INGREDIENTS

1 pound ground beef or ground turkey

1 fennel bulb, cut into ½-inch pieces

2–3 cloves garlic, minced

1 cup crumbled feta, divided

¼ teaspoon salt

¼ teaspoon ground black pepper

Other herbs and spices as desired (optional)

6 hamburger buns

Lettuce, tomato slices, and condiments

PROCESS

Place the first 7 ingredients (ground beef through herbs) in a medium bowl, reserving some of the feta, and mix well. Form the mixture into 6 patties. Cook the patties on a grill or in a skillet over medium-high heat until cooked through (15–20 minutes). Sprinkle the remaining feta on top of the cooked patties. Serve on hamburger buns with lettuce, tomato slices, and condiments of your choice.

GRILLED SHRIMP, FENNEL, AND WHITE BEAN SALAD

BY AMYE TEVAARWERK

With shrimp and fennel cooked on the grill, this salad is a delightful combination for warm spring days or Indian summer nights. It's a great dinner party first course, since the fennel and shrimp can be cooked a day ahead and kept in the refrigerator. Substitute 2 cups cooked white beans, or boiled fresh fava or lima beans when in season, for canned. If your fennel has its fronds intact, chop some of the feathery leaves and sprinkle them on the salad at serving time for vivacious color and a fresh anise note.

SERVES 2-4 // FISH/SEAFOOD // MAIN DISH

INGREDIENTS

Juice and grated peel from 1 lemon

1–2 sprigs fresh thyme, leaves stripped and roughly chopped

¼ cup extra-virgin olive oil, plus more for coating the fennel

1 (15-ounce) can cannellini or other white beans, drained

1 large or 2 medium fennel bulbs, cored and sliced into ¼-inch strips*

⅓ pound large, deveined shrimp*

1 small white onion, finely diced

Salt and ground black pepper to taste

Leafy greens

*If the fennel and shrimp are small enough to slip through the grill grates, place them on skewers before cooking.

PROCESS

Heat a grill to medium hot. Whisk together the lemon juice and peel, thyme, and oil in a bowl. Add the beans to the lemon mixture. Brush the fennel with olive oil and grill, turning occasionally, until slightly browned on both sides. Remove from the grill and add to the bean mixture.

Grill the shrimp until pink and opaque, turning once to heat evenly (this will take only a few minutes). Add the shrimp and onion to the bean and fennel mixture. Toss to combine, and season with salt and pepper. Serve over a bed of leafy greens.

ITALIAN SAUSAGE, ZUCCHINI, AND FENNEL BAKE
BY PEG CARLSON

Fresh fennel, aromatic herbs, and tender zucchini shine in this delicious layered dish. Try it on its own as a lightened-up lasagna alternative, or serve atop a nest of angel hair pasta. It's a great use for larger zucchini, but any summer squash can be used. To adapt it for vegetarian diets, substitute Italian seitan for the sausage.

SERVES 4-6 // MEAT // MAIN DISH

INGREDIENTS

½ pound Italian sausage, chopped

½ cup chopped onion

2 cloves garlic, minced

½ cup chopped fennel

1 quart home-canned (or 2 [14-ounce] cans) diced tomatoes

3 tablespoons balsamic vinegar

1 tablespoon sugar

3 tablespoons minced fresh basil

1 tablespoon minced fresh oregano

Salt and ground black pepper to taste

2 large zucchini, cut in half, then into ¼-inch slices (about 6 cups)

1 tablespoon olive oil

2 cups shredded low-fat mozzarella

PROCESS

Preheat an oven to 350°. In a large sauté pan, brown the sausage, then add the onion, garlic, and fennel and cook until the vegetables are wilted (about 5 minutes). Meanwhile, in a large pot, heat the tomatoes, balsamic vinegar, sugar, herbs, salt, and pepper. Simmer for about 15 minutes. Add the sausage mixture and set aside, keeping warm.

In a sauté pan over medium heat, sauté the zucchini slices in a small amount of oil for about 2 minutes on each side. Drain the zucchini on paper towels. Repeat until all the zucchini is sautéed, adding more oil if necessary.

Spray an 8 × 8-inch baking dish with nonstick cooking spray. Layer one third of the zucchini in the bottom of the pan, spread on one third of the tomato-sausage mixture, and sprinkle with one third of the mozzarella. Repeat to create 3 layers, finishing with the cheese. Bake for 30 minutes, covered with aluminum foil. Remove the foil and bake for 10 minutes more. Let rest about 5 minutes before serving.

VERITABLE VEGETABLE SANDWICHES (FENNEL)

BY ROBIN TIMM, COURTESY OF REAP

Give these sandwiches some real personality with one of the suggested garnishes: purslane will contribute a snappy, lemony flavor, and nasturtiums a dramatic splash of color.

SERVES 4–8 // VEGAN // MAIN DISH

INGREDIENTS

¼ cup olive oil, divided

2 Chinese or Japanese eggplants, cut into ¼-inch slices (or 1 common eggplant, diced)

1 large summer squash, cut into ¼-inch slices

1 fennel bulb, sliced lengthwise

1 Walla Walla sweet or red onion, sliced

2–3 cloves garlic, finely sliced

1 pound firm tofu, cut into ¼-inch slices

1 teaspoon dried oregano

½ teaspoon coarse salt

Freshly ground black pepper to taste

½ cup sliced Thai basil leaves

Bread of your choice: sourdough, rye, crusty whole-wheat, sesame hard roll, etc.

Balsamic vinegar to taste

Purslane leaves or nasturtium flowers and leaves

PROCESS

Preheat an oven to 400°. Spread a thin layer of olive oil (about 1 tablespoon) over the bottom of a large roasting pan or rimmed baking sheet. Spread the eggplant, squash, fennel, onion, garlic, and tofu into the pan in a single layer. Drizzle the remaining olive oil over the vegetables and tofu. Sprinkle with oregano, salt, and pepper. Roast until the vegetables are crisp-tender, about 20 minutes, stirring occasionally. Remove the pan from the oven. Sprinkle the basil over the vegetables; cover the pan with aluminum foil, allowing the basil to steam for a few minutes. Remove the foil; pile a portion of the roasted vegetables and tofu onto your favorite sandwich bread. Sprinkle with balsamic vinegar and purslane or nasturtiums.

Some of the most common fresh shell beans are:

◆ **Fava beans.** Whether called broad beans, English beans, or fava beans, these are a buttery springtime treat. They do require a bit of extra work because they have a thick skin around the bean that must be removed after they are shelled. To do this, first cut the tips off the pods. Then squeeze the pods open at the seam and pull out the beans. Blanch the beans for thirty to sixty seconds (no more), then cool and peel off the skins. Enjoy skinned favas right away or cook them a bit more. Fresh favas are subtle, so take care not to overcook or over-season them.

CAUTION: A very small percentage of people, usually of Mediterranean descent, have an enzyme deficiency that can lead to severe and potentially fatal anemia upon exposure to fava beans. Be assured that, since the condition is inherited, people with favism are usually well aware of the issue by the time they show up to your house for a dinner party. Nevertheless, it's always a good idea to ask about food allergies before planning menus for guests.

◆ **Fresh lima beans.** Fresh lima beans, or butter beans, are quite different from the frozen or canned versions many of us grew up with. They may be speckled or green, small or large. They require less cooking than other fresh shell beans, but they must be fully cooked. With a creamy texture and an earthy, vegetal flavor similar to favas, they are excellent in starring roles. It may be easiest to remove limas from their pods by carefully cutting the pods open with scissors.

◆ **Green soy beans or edamame.** Green soy beans are grown specifically to be enjoyed fresh. They are deliciously sweet and simple to prepare. Boil whole pods until just tender, drain, and sprinkle with a little coarse salt. Serve them whole, and eat them by popping the beans out one at a time, with either the fingers or teeth. (Be sure to serve them with an extra dish to discard empty pods.) Or shell the blanched beans and add them to tofu dishes, salads, or any dish in which they will not be overcooked. Like fava beans, soy beans are safe to eat after brief cooking.

Snap. Variously called green beans, string beans, filet, or French beans, snap beans are harvested young, before the beans within the pods develop. They vary in size from the petite haricot vert to the hearty Blue Lake, and in color from pale yellow to deep purple. Speckled red and purple varieties lose color when they're cooked, regardless of any alchemy the cook may attempt. They need only to have the stems snipped off before cooking; modern varieties are usually stringless.

Yard-long. Yard-long beans, or Chinese long beans, are not related to snap beans, although they look like extra-long green beans (usually closer to a half-yard than a full thirty-six inches). They are a subspecies of black-eyed peas that are harvested for their pods. In flavor they are similar to shell beans, and in texture they are dense and solid, rather than crisp. Look for thin beans with no lumps—the beans within the pods should

not be developed. Avoid those that are excessively thick, dry, or limp. Yard-long beans are used in Sichuan-style dry-sautéed beans, a popular restaurant dish. Because of their texture, they are delicious fried, whether stir-fried, sautéed, or pan- or deep-fried. Yard-long beans are also ideal for braising, as they stand up well to strong or rich flavors. To prepare, merely cut them to the length desired.

SUBLIME WHEN FRESH FROM THE FIELD

KERNELS, LEGUMES, AND PODS
From Beans to Sugar Peas

Sex is good, but not as good as fresh sweet corn.
—GARRISON KEILLOR

Ahem. We couldn't have said it better ourselves. Fresh sweet corn, peas, and beans just hours from the field are sublime. They are tender and high in natural sugars, with flavors that can ruin a person for anything less.

Fresh corn, English peas, shell beans, and edible pods (like snap beans, sugar peas, and okra) have the benefits of youth. They are picked during windows of peak tenderness and sugar content. When these windows close, sugars begin to turn into starches, seed coats get thicker, and beans develop inside the pods. Maturity has its perks, of course. Dried seeds, such as beans and corn, are nutrient storehouses that keep for up to a year. Cooked, they are wonderfully versatile and nutritious.

Selection. Look for firm and plump pea and bean pods, okra, and ears of corn. Avoid pods and husks with browning at the cut ends, and dryness and shriveling at the tips. For corn, look for fresh green husks and pale silk.

Dried beans should be as fresh as possible. Check the packing dates on packaged beans, or buy in bulk from stores with high turnover. Choose dried beans with uniform color and size, with minimally cracked seed coats and no pinholes caused by insects.

Storage. Except for dried beans and corn, all vegetables in this category should be refrigerated and used quickly.

◆ **Corn, okra, and bean pods.** Keep these in a basket or loosely wrapped in a paper bag in the warmest part of the refrigerator, between 40° and 45°, if possible. Stir them around to redistribute them daily, and use them within a few days.

◆ **English peas, sugar peas, and green beans.** Keep these loosely wrapped in the vegetable drawer of the refrigerator.

◆ **Dried beans and corn.** Store these in an airtight container in a dry, cool place.

If corn, fresh beans, or peas need to be stored for more than a few days, it's best to blanch and freeze them rather than keep them in the refrigerator.

To freeze corn kernels, fresh beans, or peas: Blanch until just tender, then cool and dry. Freeze them in a single layer on a baking sheet with space around individual pieces. Once frozen, they can be packed into a container.

Preparation. Keep fresh shell beans and peas in their pods until ready to use. All shell beans, except for soy and fava beans, must be fully cooked. Cook corn, peas (English and sugar), and snap beans briefly to preserve their flavor and tenderness. Chinese long beans and okra are versatile and can be cooked briefly or at length.

ABOUT KERNELS, LEGUMES,

BEAN

Dried shell. There are hundreds of sizes, shapes, colors, patterns, and textures of cultivated beans, from tiny green mung beans to red-and-white-speckled Christmas lima beans. Because of their low cost, high nutritional value, and long storage time, beans are the second-most important food source on the planet, after grains. As proof of their importance in the ancient world, consider the names of four prominent Roman families: Fabius (from fava bean), Lentulus (lentil), Piso (pea), and Cicero (chickpea).

Dried beans can last for a year or more if stored properly. They are rich in complex carbohydrates, protein, and fiber and should be a staple in most pantries. Look for specialty dried beans at farmers' markets: they are a low-cost, low-risk way to try something new. For tips on cooking dried beans, see "Master Recipe: Four-Way Beans and Greens" in the recipe section on page 66.

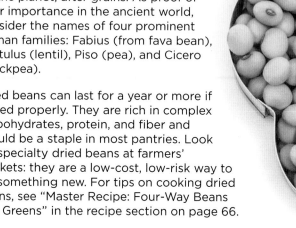

Fresh shell. Called shellies in the South, fresh shell beans were once a household staple but are now hard to find outside farmers' markets and home gardens. Their mellow flavor and tender texture make them worth the extra work required to remove them from their pods. Fresh shell beans are still moist, so they cook much more quickly than dried beans. Look for shell bean pods that appear plump and full. A hint of yellow is normal, but entirely yellow pods are past their prime. For colorful varieties like cranberry beans, choose pods that are subdued in color, because these beans are more likely to be tender and sweet. Except for soy and fava beans, fresh shell beans should never be consumed raw or undercooked, as most types contain proteins that interfere with digestion and can cause symptoms similar to food poisoning. Proper cooking disables or removes these compounds. Fresh beans should be cooked gently, at a simmer rather than a boil, to prevent breakage and t

Fresh shell beans are still much more quickly than dri

CORN

Sweet. Called maize outside the United States, fresh sweet corn is a treat that needs little adornment. Choose ears that feel heavy, with green stems and husks and lots of pale silk. Avoid ears that have been in the sun all day or are warm to the touch, as heat hastens the conversion of sugar to starch. Corn is ideally served the day it is picked, but if you must store it, leave the husks on. It is best cooked simply, either boiled or grilled. Do not add salt to the cooking water and avoid overcooking.

Baby. Baby corn is a labor-intensive specialty: tiny ears that are picked by hand just as the silk appears. They can be lower ears plucked from a plant with the top ear kept intact to grow to full-size, or they can be grown as a specialty crop. Both field corn (grown as animal feed) and sweet corn plants can produce delicious baby corn. If you find it, make sure it looks fresh, with soft leaves and greenish silk that has not dried or turned brown. Avoid storing it, but if you must, keep it in the husk and refrigerate it. Since the cobs are edible, preparation is simple: steam cleaned, trimmed ears for just a few minutes, and then serve them whole or sliced. Baby corn is delicious eaten the Southeast Asian way: as an edible skewer with seasoned pork or shrimp wrapped around it and steamed.

Popping. Popcorn was probably the first type of corn to be cultivated; remains of cobs at archaeological sites in Peru suggest that it was eaten as early as 4,700 B.C.E. Although it is usually white or yellow, popcorn kernels can also be red, blue, or variegated. Corn can be popped in an air popper, on a stovetop in a large, covered kettle with a little oil, or in a special container for the microwave. Two tablespoons of un-popped kernels yields about four cups popped corn.

OKRA

The seedpod of a plant that yields large, hibiscus-like flowers, okra evokes a strong reaction in those who object to its characteristic sliminess. This mucilage, which helps the plant and seeds retain water, can be downplayed by frying or balanced by acidic preparations like tomato sauces. It is useful as a thickener in soups, such as gumbo, and it adds body to low-fat dishes. Okra is very mild, so it easily absorbs surrounding flavors in recipes. It is highly perishable; choose firm and bright green or red pods, and use them within a day or two.

PEA

English. Sometimes called green peas or shelling peas, these staples of the frozen-food aisle are an exciting find when they're fresh. They have a very short shelf life and are best enjoyed the day they are picked. (It's best to avoid bagged, shelled "fresh peas" in the grocery store for this reason.) They can be used in any pea recipe, or briefly steamed and simply seasoned to show off their freshness.

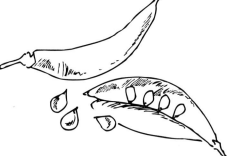

Sugar. Sugar snap and snow peas are the most popular of the edible-podded sugar peas. Like others in this category, they are at their sweetest and most tender when freshly harvested, losing more sugar the longer they are stored. Choose unwrinkled snow peas with no browning. If the shriveled blossoms are intact at the stem end, they will be a good indicator of freshness. For sugar snap peas, look for plump pods and dry stems. Avoid limp and flabby vegetables of either variety. Both will need to be de-stringed. Snap the stem end and pull to remove the string along the seam. Test a few peas to see if the opposite side also has a tough string, and if necessary remove it as well. Both snow and sugar snap peas can be eaten raw, but they may benefit from brief blanching to enhance the flavor. Avoid overcooking both types.

KERNELS, LEGUMES, AND PODS
Storage and Usage Guide

VEGETABLE	STORAGE AND PRESERVATION				USAGE SUGGESTIONS					
	IDEAL CONDITIONS	PICKLE	FREEZE	DEHYDRATE	RAW	STEAM	BRAISE	BOIL	SAUTÉ	FRY
BEAN										
dried shell	airtight container, cool and dry						•	•		
fresh shell	basket or loose paper bag, warm refrigeration (40°–45°)		•			•	•	•	•	
snap	basket or loose paper bag, warm refrigeration (40°–45°)	•	•	•	•	•		•	•	
yard-long	basket or loose paper bag, warm refrigeration (40°–45°)	•					•			•
CORN										
sweet	basket or loose paper bag, warm refrigeration (40°–45°)	•	•		•	•		•	•	
baby	basket or loose paper bag, warm refrigeration (40°–45°)	•	•			•		•	•	
popping	airtight container, cool and dry									
OKRA	basket or loose paper bag, warm refrigeration (40°–45°)	•	•			•	•		•	•
PEA										
English	wrapped, refrigerated		•	•	•	•		•		
sugar	wrapped, refrigerated		•		•	•		•	•	

MASTER RECIPE: FOUR-WAY BEANS AND GREENS

Dried shell beans are nutritional powerhouses that, when cooked and combined with greens, make a super meal. Preparing dried beans takes some planning, but once your dish is finished you'll have a storable, easy meal that will reheat in minutes. Beans and greens are convenient for busy cooks because they are prepared in a single pot, with just one main cooking step: put the ingredients in the pot and simmer until tender! Many beans benefit from presoaking, as they cook faster after their seed coats are hydrated. See the facing page for more specifics on how to cook dried beans.

THE BASICS

Beans, presoaked if necessary (see the cooking tips on the facing page)

Liquid: water or broth

Aromatics and flavorings: chopped onions, garlic, celery, carrots, bell pepper, ham hocks, dried herbs and spices

Add-ins: other vegetables, fresh herbs, cooked meat, fat, dairy (sour cream, grated cheese) (optional)

Greens, chopped

Seasoning: salt and pepper

PROCESS

Cover the **beans** with 2–3 inches of cooking **liquid**. Add the **aromatics and flavorings** (but do not salt). Bring just to a boil, skimming off any foam that rises to the surface, then reduce to a simmer. Cook until the beans are tender, adding additional cooking liquid if the level drops too low. Stir in any **add-ins** (if desired), such as other vegetables, cooked meat, sour cream, or grated cheese, and simmer until tender. Drain off the excess cooking liquid if necessary (to serve as a stew or side dish). Stir in the **greens** and cook until wilted. **Season** to taste.

VARIATIONS

By Patricia Mulvey and Laura Gilliam

BRAISED LENTILS WITH SWISS CHARD

SERVES 6

2 cups lentils (no need to presoak)

Water to cover the lentils

1 onion, diced

4 carrots, diced

1 bell pepper, diced

2 cloves garlic, minced

2 bay leaves

1 bunch Swiss chard, chopped

Salt and ground black pepper to taste

NAVY BEANS WITH SAGE, SAUSAGE, TOMATOES, AND KALE

SERVES 6

1 pound navy beans

8 cups water

6 cloves garlic, minced

1 large sprig sage

6 Italian sausages, browned, drained, and crumbled

1 pound tomatoes, seeded and chopped

1 bunch kale, center stems removed, leaves chopped

Salt and ground black pepper to taste

BLACK-EYED PEAS WITH HAM HOCKS AND COLLARD GREENS

SERVES 4

2 cups black-eyed peas (no need to presoak)

6 cups chicken broth

1 onion, chopped

4 cloves garlic, minced

1 ham hock

1 dash hot pepper sauce

1 teaspoon cider vinegar

1 bunch collard greens, center stems removed, leaves chopped

Salt and ground black pepper to taste

   Note.   Remove the ham hock when the beans are tender; cut the meat from the bone and return to the pot.

GREAT NORTHERN BEANS WITH ESCAROLE

SERVES 4

½ pound Great Northern beans

Water to cover the beans

6 cloves garlic, lightly smashed

1 bay leaf

1 ounce Parmesan rind

4 tablespoons extra-virgin olive oil

1 pound escarole, chopped

Salt and ground black pepper to taste

TOP WITH:

Grated Parmesan

IDEA STARTERS

Kidney beans, jalapeño, garlic, bell pepper, chili powder; add-ins: corn, cabbage, cilantro, sour cream

Chickpeas, pork fatback, carrot; add-ins: tomato, parsley, spinach

Black beans, leek; add-ins: pumpkin, arugula

Navy beans, onion, garlic, carrot, thyme; add-ins: smoked sausage, broccoli rabe

Red beans, onion, celery, green bell pepper, Creole seasoning; add-ins: cooked andouille sausage, parsley, collard greens

Cranberry beans, garlic, smoked paprika; add-ins: cooked clams, kale

SERVING SUGGESTIONS

◆ Toss with pasta, rice, or other grains.

◆ Stuff into tortillas and top with cheese for burritos or enchiladas.

◆ Layer with tortillas, cheese, sour cream, and salsa for a tortilla casserole.

◆ Add additional cooking liquid along with the greens to create a soup.

DRY BEAN COOKING TIPS

◆ **Sort.** Spread beans in a single layer and pick out any rocks or shriveled beans.

◆ **Presoak.** Either soak beans in water overnight (then cook beans in soaking water, adding more as necessary) or quick soak by bringing beans and water to a boil for 1 minute, then turning off the heat; soak for 1–2 hours and proceed with cooking. (This step is optional; it is most important for beans that have been stored for long periods of time, and for beans with very hard seed coats, like chickpeas. Softer beans, like lentils and split peas, do not need to be presoaked.)

◆ **Cover with water.** Use three times as much water as beans (e.g., 1 cup water for $1/3$ cup beans, 3 cups water for 1 cup beans, etc.).

If you are in a hurry to cook dried beans, use a pressure cooker—presoaked beans may cook in as little as 15 minutes, and unsoaked beans in 45 minutes to an hour. Add beans, water, and any desired flavorings to the cooker all at once. Follow the manufacturer's directions, and be aware that pressure-cooked beans may have more liquid left after cooking than traditionally boiled beans.

BEAN TROUBLESHOOTING

◆ **Hard beans.** Beans may be too old or dehydrated. Discard batch and try again. If the problem persists across multiple batches of beans, it may be a result of hard water. Try cooking in distilled or deionized water.

◆ **Unevenly cooked beans.** Heat may be uneven. Try using a slow cooker or oven instead of cooking on the stovetop. Or, some of the beans in the batch may be older or more dehydrated than others. Try presoaking so both old and fresh beans cook in the same amount of time.

◆ **Mushy, disintegrating beans.** Shorten cooking time, or add molasses or 1 tablespoon vinegar toward the end of cooking time to help beans retain their shape. Reduce temperature; vigorously boiling water may agitate the beans too much. Try using a slow cooker or oven instead of cooking on the stovetop. Or try presoaking.

CRANBERRY BEANS WITH PENNE, GARLIC, CARROTS, AND ROSEMARY

BY TERESE ALLEN

Terese adapted this from a Deborah Madison recipe, probably one from The Savory Way. *It is dynamite. If the beans are dried, add them when you start the ham.*

SERVES 4 // MEAT // MAIN DISH

INGREDIENTS

4 cups rabbit or chicken broth

1 ham shank, cut into 3–4 pieces (about 1½ pounds bone in)

3 pints fresh cranberry beans, shelled (1½–2 cups)

1½ cups chopped carrots

3 cloves garlic, minced

4–6 sprigs rosemary

Ground black pepper to taste

8 ounces penne

Freshly grated Parmesan

PROCESS

Combine the broth and ham shank pieces in a deep saucepan. Bring to a simmer and cook until the meat is tender, about 45 minutes, skimming any foam from the top as needed. Remove the meat pieces; let cool. Add the cranberry beans, carrots, garlic, and rosemary sprigs to the cooking liquid. Return to a simmer and cook gently until the beans are tender, 20–30 minutes.

Meanwhile, remove the meat from the bones. Remove the fat from the meat and discard. Chop the meat into small

chunks. When the beans are tender, toss the meat into the mixture, grind in some pepper, remove from the heat, and let it cool completely. It is best if you let the mixture sit in the refrigerator overnight.

To serve, cook the pasta in boiling water until al dente. Meanwhile, reheat the bean-ham mixture. Divide the pasta among four 4 bowls and ladle the bean mixture over the pasta. Sprinkle with grated Parmesan and serve immediately.

FRESH GARDEN SUPER SALAD (BEAN)

BY DIANE WIPPERFURTH

Salads make for quick and easy meals, no stove required. Toss whatever vegetables or fruits you have on hand for a salad that moves through the seasons with you.

SERVES 4-6 // VEGETARIAN // SIDE DISH

INGREDIENTS

1 cup chopped green beans

2 tablespoons oil of choice

1 tablespoon vinegar of choice

1 cup halved cherry tomatoes

1 cucumber, finely chopped

½ medium onion, finely chopped

1 cup chopped kale or Swiss chard

4 ounces feta, crumbled

4 tablespoons raw or roasted pumpkin seeds

PROCESS

Steam the green beans until tender and bright green, about 5 minutes. Submerge them in cold water to stop the cooking process, drain, and cool. Combine the oil and vinegar and shake or whisk until combined. Add the remaining ingredients (tomatoes through pumpkin seeds) and the cooled beans to a large salad bowl. Toss with the oil and vinegar shortly before serving.

GARDEN SOUP WITH BEETS AND GREEN BEANS
BY DIANE WIPPERFURTH

Colorful and bright, this soup can be enjoyed year-round with produce fresh from the garden or with frozen tomatoes and greens saved from the summer's harvest. If beet greens aren't available, try chard (chopped stems included). Fresh herbs can also be used instead of dried; just add them toward the end of cooking.

SERVES 4 // VEGAN // SIDE DISH

INGREDIENTS

2 tablespoons grape seed or olive oil

3 cloves garlic, minced

1 small onion, chopped

3–4 tomatoes, peeled and chopped

2 carrots, chopped

2 stalks celery, chopped

1 beet, chopped

1 cup cut green beans

1 (15-ounce) can beans of choice (black, cannellini, pinto, etc.)

1–2 teaspoons dried oregano

1–2 teaspoons dried basil

½ cup finely chopped beet greens

Salt and ground black pepper to taste

PROCESS

Heat the oil in a large stockpot. Add the garlic and onion and cook until translucent, about 5 minutes. Add the next 8 ingredients (tomatoes through basil), cover with water (about 6 cups), and bring to a boil. Reduce the heat and cook, covered, until the vegetables are tender, about 25 minutes. Add the beet greens and cook a bit longer, until the greens are tender, about 5 minutes. Season with salt and pepper.

HUMMUS WITH A TWIST (BEAN)
BY MARLEY AND DARCY CREWS-HILL, COURTESY OF REAP

Surprise! The twist in this hummus is horseradish.

YIELDS 3 CUPS // VEGAN // APPETIZER

INGREDIENTS

¾ cup dried chickpeas, soaked overnight and then cooked

2 cloves garlic, minced

2 teaspoons soy sauce or tamari, or to taste

Juice from 1 lemon

3 heaping tablespoons tahini

2 tablespoons chopped fresh parsley

3 tablespoons extra-virgin olive oil

1 tablespoon horseradish, or to taste

PROCESS

Place all ingredients in a food processor. Blend until the consistency is smooth and creamy. Let it rest for a few minutes. Store in the refrigerator for up to 2 weeks.

GREEN BEAN AND TOMATO CHUTNEY SALAD

BY ALYSSA HENRY

As is often the case, a serendipitous combination of leftovers led to the creation of this savory salad. It has now become one of Alyssa's favorite recipes, despite her general lack of enthusiasm for green beans. It is a great side dish for grilled meats, and a popular dish for potlucks.

SERVES 6–8 // VEGETARIAN // SIDE DISH

INGREDIENTS

TOMATO CHUTNEY AND BEANS:

½ cup cider vinegar

1 teaspoon ground celery seed

⅛ teaspoon ground cloves

⅛ teaspoon ground allspice

⅛ teaspoon ground cinnamon

¼ teaspoon paprika

Dash cayenne

1 tablespoon sugar

1 teaspoon salt

2 pounds tomatoes (about 4 large), seeded and chopped

1 medium onion, diced

1 pound green beans

DRESSING:

¼ cup packed fresh basil

¼ cup garlic-infused olive oil

2 tablespoons white wine vinegar

2 tablespoons balsamic vinegar

1 teaspoon Dijon mustard

Salt and ground black pepper to taste

TOPPING:

4 ounces fresh goat cheese

PROCESS

Combine the vinegar and the next 8 ingredients (celery seed through salt) in a medium saucepan and simmer over medium heat for 2–3 minutes to activate the spices. Add the tomatoes and onion, bring to a boil, then reduce the heat and continue to simmer, uncovered, stirring occasionally, until the sauce is thickened and the liquid is reduced, about 20 minutes.

Meanwhile, steam the green beans until crisp-tender, 5–8 minutes; when done, submerge the beans in a bowl of cold water to stop the cooking process, then drain and allow them to dry a bit.

When the tomato sauce is thick and much of the liquid reduced, remove it from the heat and strain with a sieve or fine colander (you can save the drained liquid for another use if desired, such as an additive to soup or dressing). Allow the chutney to cool slightly while you make the dressing. (The green beans can be steamed and the tomato chutney made a day ahead of time and stored separately in the refrigerator until ready to make the salad.)

Place the dressing ingredients in a blender or food processor and puree; toss the beans with the tomato chutney and dressing in a serving bowl. Top the salad with crumbled goat cheese and serve cold or at room temperature.

LENTIL AND SAUSAGE SOUP (BEAN)

BY ASHLEY RAMAKER

Memories of a childhood favorite inspired Ashley to create this delectable version of lentil soup. Here, an intriguing blend of herbs and spices adds depth to rustic lentils, with spicy kielbasa contributing main-dish heartiness. Ashley recommends serving the soup with a slice of crusty bread and a glass of red wine.

SERVES 8–10 // MEAT // MAIN DISH

INGREDIENTS

1 pound lentils (about 2½ cups)

2 onions, diced

5 carrots, peeled and sliced

8 stalks celery, sliced

½ teaspoon salt

½ teaspoon ground black pepper

1 teaspoon dried tarragon

1 teaspoon dried thyme

½ teaspoon ground cumin

2 tablespoons olive oil

¼ cup tomato paste

3 quarts chicken broth

3 tablespoons red wine

2 bay leaves

1 pound kielbasa, quartered and diced

Salt and ground black pepper to taste

Grated Parmesan

PROCESS

In a large bowl, cover the lentils with boiling water and allow them to sit for 15 minutes. Drain. In a large stockpot over medium heat, sauté the onions, carrots, celery, salt, pepper, tarragon, thyme, and cumin in the oil until the vegetables are tender, about 20 minutes. Add the tomato paste, broth, red wine, and bay leaves, and stir well. Add the lentils and bring to a boil. Reduce the heat and allow the soup to simmer gently, covered, for 1 hour. Add the kielbasa and simmer for an additional 30 minutes. Remove the bay leaves and season with salt and pepper. Serve topped with grated Parmesan.

SQUASH, WHITE BEAN, AND KALE SOUP

BY RACHEL WOLF

Hearty and satisfying, this soup makes the most of big winter flavors. It is particularly delicious with lacinato kale.

SERVES 4 // VEGETARIAN // MAIN DISH

INGREDIENTS

1 medium onion, chopped

2 tablespoons butter, ghee, coconut oil, or bacon fat

2 cloves garlic, minced

1 quart slightly undercooked white beans (2 cups dry or 2 [15-ounce] cans)

1 medium winter squash, diced

4 cups broth

Salt to taste

1 large bunch kale (about 12 medium to large leaves), stemmed and chopped

1 small bunch fresh sage (8–10 leaves), chopped; or a generous pinch dried sage

6 slices cooked bacon, chopped (optional)

PROCESS

In a large stockpot, sauté the onion in the fat until translucent, about 5 minutes. Add the garlic and cook for 1 minute more. Add the cooked white beans, squash, and broth. Stir, add salt, and bring to a simmer. Cook until the squash is tender, 15–25 minutes. Remove about 2 cups of the soup and puree until smooth. Return the puree to the pot, add the kale and sage, and stir. Cover and simmer until the kale is tender, 5–10 minutes. Serve topped with bacon (if desired).

SUNNY CHICKPEA AND RICE SALAD WITH MARINATED TOFU (BEAN)

BY BETSY LEVINE, COURTESY OF REAP

Chickpeas and lemon are natural companions in this sunny salad. With rice, lots of protein, and plenty of veggies, you won't need much else to round out the meal. Follow it with fresh fruit for dessert if you want something sweet.

SERVES 5–6 // VEGAN // MAIN DISH

INGREDIENTS

TOFU MARINADE:

¼ cup extra-virgin olive oil

¼ cup water

½ cup red wine vinegar

2–3 teaspoons salt

1 tablespoon plus 1 teaspoon dried basil

½ teaspoon ground black pepper

1 teaspoon dried oregano

1 pound extra-firm tofu, squeezed dry and crumbled

DRESSING:

⅓ cup fresh lemon juice (from 2 medium lemons)

3–4 cloves garlic, minced

⅓ cup extra-virgin olive oil

Salt and ground black pepper to taste

SALAD:

4 cups cold cooked brown rice

2 cups cooked or canned chickpeas

2 cups seeded, diced tomatoes

1 cup chopped cucumber

½ cup chopped fresh parsley

⅓ cup chopped fresh dill or 3 teaspoons dried dill

3–4 green onions, sliced

PROCESS

TOFU MARINADE: In a small bowl, mix together the olive oil, water, red wine vinegar, salt, basil, pepper, and oregano. Add the crumbled tofu and mix well. Set aside, letting the tofu marinate for at least 30 minutes, stirring occasionally.

DRESSING: In a small bowl, stir together the lemon juice, garlic, olive oil, salt, and pepper until combined.

SALAD: In a large bowl, combine the rice, chickpeas, tomato, cucumber, parsley, dill, and green onion. Toss to mix well. Add the tofu mixture and dressing to the salad. Mix thoroughly and served chilled or at room temperature.

CHILLED CORN SALAD WITH BASIL DRESSING

BY SUMMER LEI SHIDLER, COURTESY OF REAP

This attractive salad is perfect for barbecues, picnics, and other outdoor meals.

SERVES 4 // VEGAN // SIDE DISH

INGREDIENTS

1 cup chopped fresh basil

¼ cup diced Vidalia onion

¼–½ cup olive oil

Dash sea salt

2 cups corn kernels (cut from 2–3 ears of corn)

PROCESS

Combine the basil, onion, olive oil, and salt in a blender or food processor and blend until smooth. In a medium pot, combine the basil mixture and corn and cook, covered, over medium heat for 5 minutes, stirring occasionally. Transfer to a nonreactive bowl and refrigerate, covered, for 30 minutes or overnight. Serve chilled.

CORN PUDDING

BY DEBRA SHAPIRO/FAIRSHARE CSA COALITION

Corn pudding is comfort food at its finest. This take on a classic dish has a soufflé-like texture that highlights two summer stars: corn and tomatoes. For meat lovers, this dish is delicious with the addition of bacon or ham: dice about 5–6 slices of bacon and fry it with the onions (use a little less oil), or add about 1 cup of diced ham.

SERVES 6-8 // VEGETARIAN // SIDE DISH

INGREDIENTS

6–8 ears corn (to yield about 4 cups kernels)

½ tablespoon oil or butter

1 cup diced onion

1 clove garlic, minced or pressed

2 eggs

1 cup whole milk, evaporated milk, or soy milk (or use part whipping cream or half-and-half)

2 cups grated cheese, divided

1 cup fresh breadcrumbs, divided

Salt and freshly ground black pepper to taste

1 medium tomato or 10 cherry tomatoes, sliced

Paprika

PROCESS

Preheat an oven to 350°. Cut the corn kernels off the cob and into a large bowl; extract the corn milk by scraping the cobs with the back of the knife. Melt the butter (or heat the oil) in a skillet and cook the onion and garlic until they are softened but not browned, about 5 minutes. Add the onion mixture to the corn, then stir in the eggs, milk, and most of the cheese and breadcrumbs. Season with salt and pepper. Mix well and spread into a greased 13 × 9-inch baking dish. Top with the tomato slices, the rest of the breadcrumbs, and the rest of the cheese. Sprinkle with paprika and bake for about 45 minutes, or until golden brown and firm.

CORN SALSA

BY DEBRA SHAPIRO/FAIRSHARE CSA COALITION

Colorful, easy, and delicious, this corn salsa is more than just a dip for chips. Try it over grilled chicken, on turkey burgers, or in fish tacos. Once you make it, you will undoubtedly find that it's good on just about everything. For an added smoky flavor, try grilling the corn and roasting the jalapeño(s).

SERVES 8–10 // VEGAN // CONDIMENT

INGREDIENTS

Salt for cooking water

2 cups corn kernels (cut from 4–5 ears)

1½ cups chopped red onion

1–2 jalapeños, finely chopped (depending on your taste and their heat)

1 bunch fresh cilantro, chopped

2–4 tablespoons rice vinegar or lime juice

Chopped tomatoes (optional)

Canned black beans, drained and rinsed (optional)

Pinch each salt and sugar

PROCESS

Fill a pot with water, bring it to a boil, add salt, and add the corn. Bring the water back to a boil, skimming off any corn silk that rises to the surface. Boil the corn for 2 minutes, then drain in a colander and rinse with cold water to stop the cooking process. Toss the corn, onion, jalapeños, cilantro, and tomatoes or black beans (if desired) together in a bowl and season with the rice vinegar or lime juice. Taste on a chip and add salt and/or a pinch or two of sugar if necessary.

SUMMER CORN CHOWDER

BY LIZ BOYLE

Silky and satisfying, this chowder is deceptively quick. And, with less cream than other versions, the sweet flavor of fresh corn is the star. It is particularly delicious paired with grilled shrimp and a chilled Chardonnay.

SERVES 4 // MEAT // SIDE DISH

INGREDIENTS

4 slices bacon, chopped

3–4 cups corn kernels (cut from 6–8 ears)

½ cup chopped onion

½ cup chopped carrot

½ cup chopped celery

1 cup diced yellow or green zucchini

1 cup diced Yukon Gold potatoes (½-inch cubes)

3 cups (or more) low-salt chicken broth (see page 268 in "Pantry Basics" for Liz's homemade broth)

½ cup whipping cream

½ teaspoon ground cumin

¼ teaspoon cayenne (optional)

Salt and ground black pepper to taste

2 tablespoons chopped fresh chives

PROCESS

Sauté the bacon in a large pot over medium-high heat until crisp. Using a slotted spoon, transfer the bacon to paper towels to drain. Pour off all but about 2 tablespoons of the drippings. Add the corn, onion, carrot, celery, zucchini, and potatoes to the drippings in the pot; sauté 5 minutes. Add 3 cups of broth and simmer, uncovered, over medium heat until the vegetables are tender, about 20 minutes.

Transfer 2 cups of the soup to a blender and puree until smooth. Return the puree to the pot. Stir in the cream, cumin, and cayenne (if desired). Bring the chowder to a simmer, thinning with more broth or milk if too thick. Season with salt and pepper. Ladle the chowder into bowls and sprinkle with the bacon and chives.

ELOTE (CORN)

BY BARBARA WRIGHT/FAIRSHARE CSA COALITION

A common street food in Mexico, elote is dressed-up corn on the cob. This recipe also works well when prepared on a grill; you can grill the corn in the husk to keep the kernels tender, or husk the corn first so it gets nice and charred.

SERVES 4-6 // VEGETARIAN // SIDE DISH

INGREDIENTS

4 ears corn, cut in 2- to 3-inch sections

⅔ cup finely grated Parmesan or other hard white cheese

¼ teaspoon paprika

¼ teaspoon salt

Dash cayenne (optional)

⅓ cup mayonnaise

PROCESS

Cook the corn in boiling water until just tender, 2–3 minutes. Remove from the water and lay on a kitchen towel to drain. While the corn is cooking, mix the cheese and seasonings and mound them on a plate. Put the mayonnaise on the plate next to the cheese mixture. Holding the bottom and tapered tip of the cob, roll the corn in the mayonnaise and then in the cheese mixture. Serve quickly so it stays hot.

SPICY SUMMER SQUASH AND CORN QUESADILLAS

BY IZZY DARBY

These quesadillas are packed with fresh summer produce. Serve them with salsa and guacamole for an exciting lunch option. Or try them with "Vegetarian Pozole" (page 110) for a satisfying vegetarian dinner.

SERVES 4-6 // VEGAN // MAIN DISH

INGREDIENTS

2–3 tablespoons olive oil, divided

1 onion, diced

1 clove garlic, minced

1 red bell pepper, diced

Kernels from 1 ear corn

1 small zucchini, diced

1 summer squash, diced

½ jalapeño, minced (optional)

¼ cup salsa

2 teaspoons ground cumin

½ teaspoon chili powder

Juice from 1 lemon

1 teaspoon salt, or to taste

8 (6-inch) flour tortillas

1–2 cups nondairy (or regular) cheese

PROCESS

In a medium skillet, heat 1 tablespoon of the olive oil over medium heat. Add the onion and garlic and sauté for 5–6 minutes, until the onion is translucent. Add the remaining vegetables, olive oil, salsa, spices, and lemon juice. Cook for 10–12 minutes, stirring often and adding a splash of water if necessary to loosen the mixture. Season with salt.

Heat a large skillet coated with a bit of oil and add a tortilla. Top with 2 tablespoons cheese, ⅓ cup of the vegetable mixture, a bit more cheese, and another tortilla. Flatten with a spatula and cook for 3–4 minutes on each side, or until the tortillas are lightly browned and the cheese is melted. Repeat with the remaining tortillas.

SWEET CORN AND RED PEPPER CRUSTLESS QUICHES
BY NICOLE BRAYTON

These mini quiches are elegant entrées for a summer brunch, and a great way to use grilled corn leftover from a barbecue. Since they are baked and served in individual ramekins rather than in a crust, they are also a lighter alternative to conventional quiche.

SERVES 8 // VEGETARIAN // MAIN DISH

INGREDIENTS

2 teaspoons olive oil

2 medium red bell peppers, diced

8 green onions, finely chopped

1½ cups cooked corn kernels (boiled or grilled)

1 tablespoon fresh oregano, or ½ tablespoon dried oregano

2 teaspoons ground cumin

½ teaspoon chili powder

½ teaspoon salt

12 large eggs

¼ cup milk

¾ cup grated pepper jack cheese

¼ cup grated Asiago cheese

1 plum tomato, sliced

Cilantro sprigs

PROCESS

Preheat an oven to 375°. Coat 8 (6-ounce) ramekins with nonstick spray and set on a baking sheet.

In a nonstick skillet, heat the oil over medium heat. Add the red peppers, green onions, and corn. Cook for a few minutes, stirring often, until the vegetables are tender. Remove from the heat and stir in the oregano, cumin, chili powder, and salt. Let cool.

Whisk the eggs and milk together. Add the pepper jack cheese and cooled vegetables and stir well. Divide among the ramekins. Top each with a tomato slice and sprinkle with Asiago. Bake for 30–35 minutes, or until set, brown, and puffy. Garnish with sprigs of cilantro.

TERIYAKI CORN ON THE COB
BY FUMIKO MIYAZAKI, COURTESY OF REAP

Like "Elote" (facing page) in Mexico and grilled corn at American fairs, corn on the cob is a festival favorite in Japan. Fumiko's homemade teriyaki blend is much subtler than most commercial sauces, lending just a touch of flavor to enhance the delicious corn.

SERVES 6 // VEGETARIAN // SIDE DISH

INGREDIENTS

⅓ cup soy sauce

⅓ cup sake

1 tablespoon sugar

1 tablespoon butter

6 ears corn

PROCESS

Combine the soy sauce, sake, sugar, and butter in a small saucepan over medium heat. Cook for about 1 minute. Continue stirring or swirling the sauce until the sugar dissolves. Set aside.

Cook the corn briefly either by soaking the unhusked ears in water and placing them on a grill, or by submerging the husked ears in boiling water for 3–5 minutes. Husk the cooked corn (if necessary), brush it with the soy sauce-sake marinade, and return to the grill or place under a broiler. Turn the corn every minute or so and brush on more marinade. The corn will be done when the kernels start to separate and become blackened on the edges.

VEGGIE-FIED CORNBREAD

BY ERIN WILICHOWSKI

Cornbread is controversial. Savory or sweet, everyone has a recipe and an opinion. This cornbread pairs sweet corn with moist zucchini for a bread that's filled with good-for-you vegetables and tastes terrific. Adjust the amount of sugar for your own sweet or savory preference.

SERVES 9 // VEGETARIAN // SIDE DISH

INGREDIENTS

1 cup grated zucchini

1 cup all-purpose flour

¾ cup cornmeal

1½ teaspoons baking powder

½ teaspoon baking soda

½ teaspoon salt

2–4 tablespoons brown sugar

1 cup buttermilk

1 egg

2 tablespoons molasses

3 tablespoons butter, melted

Kernels cut from 2 ears corn (about 1 cup)

PROCESS

Preheat an oven to 400°. Lightly grease or butter an 8 × 8-inch baking pan. Squeeze out the excess moisture from the zucchini by pressing it against the sides of a colander or wringing it in a kitchen towel.

In a large bowl, whisk together the flour, cornmeal, baking powder, baking soda, salt, and brown sugar. Add the buttermilk, egg, molasses, and butter and stir until just combined. Add the zucchini and corn and stir to combine. Pour the batter into the prepared pan and spread evenly. Bake for 25–30 minutes, until a toothpick comes out clean and the bread springs back when pressed lightly.

OVEN-ROASTED OKRA

BY PATRICIA MULVEY AND LAURA GILLIAM OF LOCAL THYME

This recipe is easy as pie, and just about as good. It's also healthier than the traditional fried okra preparation.

SERVES 4 // VEGAN // SIDE DISH

INGREDIENTS

1 bunch okra, cut into 1-inch pieces (or kept whole if baby-size)

Olive oil

Kosher salt to taste

PROCESS

Preheat an oven to 400°. Toss the okra with a little olive oil, spread it in a single layer on a rimmed baking sheet, and season well with kosher salt. Roast for 12–15 minutes (shaking the sheet once halfway through the cooking time), until the okra becomes slightly browned on the edges.

PAN-FRIED OKRA WITH INDIAN SPICES

BY PATRICIA MULVEY AND LAURA GILLIAM OF LOCAL THYME

Okra is especially adept at soaking up surrounding flavors. In this easy side dish, cumin, ginger, and coriander give it a classic Indian flair.

SERVES 1 // VEGETARIAN // SIDE DISH

INGREDIENTS

1 tablespoon butter

2 large okra, sliced

Dash ground cumin

Dash ground ginger

Dash ground coriander

Salt and ground black pepper to taste

PROCESS

Melt the butter in a small skillet. Add the okra and spices and sauté until the okra is soft, 15–20 minutes. Season with salt and pepper and serve.

SOUTHERN-STYLE FRIED OKRA

BY PATRICIA MULVEY AND LAURA GILLIAM OF LOCAL THYME

Laura likes to plant okra among her flower beds so she can enjoy fresh okra during the summer. The plants are admittedly rather spindly, but the beautiful flowers and steady supply of okra for the kitchen make up for it!

SERVES 2 // VEGETARIAN // SIDE DISH

INGREDIENTS

Canola or peanut oil for frying (about 1 cup)

4–5 ounces okra, cut crosswise into ½-inch slices

¼ cup buttermilk

½ cup cornmeal

½ teaspoon baking powder

¼ teaspoon cayenne

½ teaspoon kosher salt

¼ teaspoon freshly ground black pepper

½ teaspoon sugar

PROCESS

Pour about an inch of oil into a medium pot and heat over medium-high heat until the temperature reaches 375°.

Meanwhile, place the sliced okra in a medium bowl and stir in the buttermilk. In another medium bowl, whisk together the cornmeal, baking powder, cayenne, salt, black pepper, and sugar. Using a slotted spoon, lift the okra from the buttermilk and place it into the cornmeal mixture. Use your fingers to toss the okra so it's well coated.

When the oil is hot, lift up the okra a few pieces at a time, using your hands or a slotted spoon. Gently shake the okra over the bowl, letting the excess cornmeal fall back into the bowl. Place the okra gently into the oil and fry until brown and crisp, 4–5 minutes. Briefly drain on a towel-lined plate and serve immediately.

CORNUCOPIA SALAD (PEA)

BY MARGOT LEE, COURTESY OF REAP

A little bit of chopping, and this robust salad is ready to serve. And with two sources of protein, it makes a complete meal.

SERVES 4 // VEGETARIAN // MAIN DISH

INGREDIENTS

SALAD:

1 bunch arugula, torn

1 bunch butterhead lettuce, torn

½ pound sugar snap peas, strings removed

1 cup cooked black beans

1 cup diced buffalo mozzarella

8 cherry tomatoes, halved

Kernels from 1 ear cooked corn

¼ cup diced orange or red bell pepper

DRESSING:

2 tablespoons red wine vinegar

2 tablespoons balsamic vinegar

2 tablespoons lime juice

1 tablespoon grated lime peel

¼ cup minced red onion

2 tablespoons chopped fresh basil

1 tablespoon minced parsley

1 tablespoon Dijon mustard

½ teaspoon salt

1 teaspoon freshly ground black pepper

2 tablespoons chopped roasted red bell pepper

2 tablespoons water

6 tablespoons olive oil

6 tablespoons canola oil

PROCESS

Toss all the salad ingredients together in a large bowl. Make the dressing by whisking together all ingredients except the oils. Add the oils a little at a time, mixing well, until the consistency is smooth and thick. Drizzle over the salad and toss to mix.

MIXED VEGETABLE KORMA (PEA)

BY SHAILEENA JIWANI, COURTESY OF REAP

Korma is a creamy, rich stew originating in South and Central Asia. In this version, vegetables flavored with fragrant spices float in a sauce made from yogurt and ground nuts. Your kitchen will smell fantastic while this dish is cooking!

SERVES 4–5 // VEGETARIAN // MAIN DISH

INGREDIENTS

2 tablespoons canola oil (or any kind of cooking oil)

1 large onion, chopped

1 teaspoon grated ginger

1 clove garlic, grated

1–1½ large tomatoes, chopped

Salt to taste

¼ cup yogurt

3–4 teaspoons finely ground cashews (or peanuts)

1 teaspoon ground cumin

¼ teaspoon ground turmeric

Paprika to taste

1 teaspoon ground coriander

3–4 new potatoes, chopped

½ cup peas

A few baby carrots, halved

A few mushrooms, halved

A few cauliflower florets

Whipping cream

Finely chopped fresh cilantro

PROCESS

Heat the oil in a skillet with a fitted lid. Add the onion and sauté until lightly browned, about 7 minutes. Add the ginger and garlic and continue to sauté for a few minutes. Add the tomatoes, salt, yogurt, cashews, and spices (cumin through coriander). Stir until the tomatoes are tender. Add the rest of the vegetables (potatoes through cauliflower) and a little water to make a creamy consistency. Cover the skillet and cook for about 15 minutes, or until all the vegetables are tender. Add a drizzle of cream and give a gentle stir. Garnish with cilantro.

PINK AND GREEN SPRING PASTA (PEA)

BY DAWN BIEHLER, COURTESY OF REAP

Dawn created this dish with the bounty of a spring CSA delivery. Substitute late-season ingredients (such as zucchini and parsley) for the basil and peas if your beets arrive in the fall.

SERVES 4–5 // VEGAN // MAIN DISH

INGREDIENTS

3 tablespoons plus 1 teaspoon olive oil, divided

5 medium beets, diced into ½-inch cubes

1 pound penne or farfalle

¼ cup lime juice, plus 1 teaspoon additional if using the beet stems and greens (see below)

1 teaspoon balsamic vinegar

¾ teaspoon salt

⅛ teaspoon ground black pepper

2 cloves garlic, minced

Stems and greens from the beets (above), cut into 2-inch strips (optional)

¼ cup slivered fresh basil leaves

⅓ cup chopped toasted walnuts

¾ pound sugar snap peas, stems removed and cut into bite-size pieces

Freshly grated Parmesan (optional)

PROCESS

Preheat an oven to 375°. Lightly grease a baking sheet with 1 teaspoon of the olive oil. Spread the diced beets on the sheet and bake for 25 minutes, or until fork tender, turning over with a spatula after 10 minutes. Remove from the oven and set aside.

While the beets are baking, prepare the pasta according to the package directions. In a small bowl, prepare a dressing by combining 2 tablespoons of the olive oil, ¼ cup of the lime juice, and the vinegar, salt, pepper, and garlic. Whisk together and set aside.

If using the beet stems and greens, sauté them in a skillet with the remaining oil over low to medium heat, stirring often to ensure even cooking, until the leaves are bright green, 4–6 minutes. Remove from the heat, sprinkle with the remaining lime juice, and stir.

When the pasta is al dente, drain it and transfer to a large bowl. Add the beets, basil, walnuts, and peas and toss to combine evenly. Whisk the dressing again and immediately pour it over the pasta mixture. Stir to coat all ingredients thoroughly with the dressing. Divide the beet stems and greens (if using) among individual serving bowls and spoon the pasta over the greens. Grate Parmesan over the top (if desired) and serve.

FRUITS EATEN AS VEGETABLES

From Bell Peppers to Winter Squash

It's true that, botanically, tomatoes are fruits—organs that grow from the plant's ovary and surround its seeds with fleshy walls. Bell peppers, cucumbers, eggplants, and squash are fruits in this sense as well. Most cooks (and the Supreme Court), however, prefer to categorize produce by how it is used, rather than botanically, so they consider these "fruits" to be vegetables. It's helpful to keep the botanical definition in mind as a reminder that all members of this group have similar characteristics. As well as having seeds and fleshy walls, they are typically sweet, juicy, and mild.

Most in this category belong to one of two taxonomic groups: the nightshade family (Solanaceae), which includes tomatoes, tomatillos, peppers, and eggplants (also potatoes and tobacco), and the gourd family (Cucurbitaceae), which includes cucumbers, summer squash, winter squash, and watermelon.[1]

> *Botanically speaking, tomatoes are the fruit of a vine, just as are cucumbers, squashes, beans, and peas. But…all these are vegetables…usually served at dinner in, with, or after the soup, fish, or meats which constitute the principal part of the repast, and not, like fruits generally, as dessert.*
>
> —U.S. SUPREME COURT,
> Nix v. Hedden, 149 U.S. 304 (1893)

Selection. Choose firm, plump vegetables with no soft spots. Make sure skins are dry and stems, if attached, look fresh and green. Additionally:

◆ **Bell peppers.** Choose those with plump, bright green stems. As green peppers ripen, they turn from green to red, so multicolored peppers are perfectly fine as long as they appear to be otherwise fresh.

◆ **Cucumbers.** Scratch the skin of cucumbers to verify that they are unwaxed. Check for bruising or wrinkling.

◆ **Eggplants.** Choose those that are shiny and heavy, with no bronze spots or pits. Check the fuzzy cap for mold.

◆ **Summer squash.** Choose small- to medium-size vegetables with shiny skin and no pitting. Some bruising and scratching is to be expected on more delicate varieties; this should not affect the quality.

◆ **Tomatillos.** Choose those that are dry and hard with tight-fitting husks. Check for signs of mold or moisture.

◆ **Tomatoes.** Choose tomatoes based on when you wish to serve them. Soft, ripe vegetables will need to be used the same day, while harder tomatoes will ripen in a few days. Look for fresh-looking stems and leaves, if they are still attached. At farmers' markets, tasting a sample is the best way to assess quality. Do not buy refrigerated tomatoes.

◆ **Winter squash.** Look for indicators of maturity and freshness in winter squash. These include tough skin that cannot be scratched with a fingernail, bright colors, and rock-hard flesh.

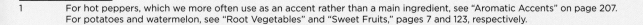

1   For hot peppers, which we more often use as an accent rather than a main ingredient, see "Aromatic Accents" on page 207. For potatoes and watermelon, see "Root Vegetables" and "Sweet Fruits," pages 7 and 123, respectively.

Storage. Many of the vegetables in this category originate in warm climates and are particularly susceptible to chilling injury. Unfortunately, they also deteriorate quickly when they are too warm. Cucumbers, eggplants, and summer squash are best stored at about 55°, so choose the coolest part of the kitchen or the warmest part of the refrigerator, and wrap them loosely in a paper bag or kitchen towel. Bell peppers and tomatillos can be loosely wrapped and refrigerated normally, and tomatoes should be kept at room temperature out of direct sunlight. Winter squash should be stored in a cool, dark, well-ventilated area. Unless cut, they should not be refrigerated.

Cucumbers, eggplants, summer squash, and tomatoes can be pre-salted to remove some moisture. This technique is helpful for recipes in which extra water will be detrimental, such as salsas, fried foods, and doughs. To pre-salt, cut or shred the vegetable as desired, sprinkle with coarse salt, and let stand on an absorbent material, such as paper towels, or in a strainer for thirty minutes. Rinse all but tomatoes. Pat away the excess moisture (or squeeze gently) and proceed with the recipe. Pre-salting increases the firmness of cooked eggplant and reduces the amount of oil it absorbs in fried preparations.

Preparation. Except for eggplant and winter squash, all fruits eaten as vegetables can be eaten raw. Only thick-skinned cucumbers, eggplants, and winter squash need peeling, although tomatoes are sometimes peeled for cooking. All eggplants will become dull after cooking, although slender Asian types will keep a little more purple color than others. Brief cooking of bell peppers, summer squash, and tomatillos will preserve their vibrant colors.

Often the most challenging aspect of cooking with winter squash is getting to its flesh, as breaking the skin of these hard, slippery vegetables can be difficult. There are several methods to use, depending on the toughness of the squash and the sturdiness of your knife:

◆ **Cutting.** Use a heavy knife or cleaver, and work on a stable surface. Knock the stem off, and then whack the knife blade into the squash. Using a rubber mallet or a rolling pin, tap at the knife where the blade meets the handle until the squash splits. Clean the interior, and then cut the squash into smaller chunks as desired. Peel either before or after cooking.

◆ **Microwaving.** If the squash will fit in your microwave, poke a few slits through the skin and cook the squash on high power until it is just tender enough to cut, usually about four minutes. Cut and clean the squash, and proceed with the recipe.

◆ **Baking.** Heat an oven to 350°. Prick the skin in a few places and cook the squash until a knife easily pierces the skin, then remove it from the oven and allow it to cool. Peel and cut the squash or scoop the flesh from the skin, and proceed with the recipe.

◆ **Smashing.** For large, hard squash, sometimes smashing is the only way to open it safely. Line the floor (and sides of cabinets, if they are near) with clean paper, then drop the squash onto the paper. (This can also be done on clean paper outdoors.) Clean out the seeds, cook the chunks, and scoop the flesh from the rind when it is soft.

ABOUT THE VEGETABLES

BELL PEPPER

Although they are relatives of chiles, sweet or bell peppers are mild members of the Capsicum genus that do not produce capsaicin, the "heat" in hot peppers. Bell peppers can be yellow, orange, red, green, purple, or white. Generally, red peppers are the sweetest, although flavor is affected by growing and post-harvest storage conditions. Bell peppers are versatile and delicious raw or cooked. In Creole cuisine, equal parts bell pepper, onion, and celery form the sautéed flavor base known as the "holy trinity" upon which many dishes are built.

CUCUMBER

Crisp, mild, and refreshing, cucumbers are prized in many cuisines for their cool crunch. Common cucumbers, the type usually found in grocery stores, are bred to withstand the rigors of shipping. They have thick, sometimes wax-coated skin, prominent seeds, and a strong flavor. Pickling varieties are smaller and have thinner skins to allow brine to penetrate. English (or hothouse) cucumbers are long and slender, with a mild flavor and underdeveloped seeds. Japanese and Persian cucumbers are similar: both are small, slender, and thin-skinned, with a sweet, delicate flavor and small seeds. Lemon cucumbers, named for their appearance, are yellow and similar in size and shape to the citrus fruit. In flavor they are delicate and somewhat sweet. They are particularly attractive alternating with tomato slices in a "stacked" salad. Peeling and seeding are optional with most cucumbers; typically only common varieties require it.

> To seed a cucumber, cut it in half lengthwise and run the bowl of a spoon from one end to the other. The seeds will dislodge, leaving a smooth, rounded trough in the center of each slice.

EGGPLANT

Although the big, purple varieties may be most familiar, eggplants can be as small as a marble or as large as a football, and they can have white, green, magenta, or dark purple skin (even orange, but these are rare outside home gardens). In the 1800s, European settlers brought small, round, mostly white ornamental varieties to the United States, Australia, New Zealand, and Canada; their resemblance to goose or hen eggs inspired the name "eggplant."

All eggplants have spongy flesh consisting of many air pockets between the cells. When cooked, the air pockets collapse and the flesh becomes pleasantly dense: creamy in some, meaty in others. In general, long, thin eggplants, usually called Chinese or Japanese, are mild in flavor and hold their form better than others after cooking. Green-skinned versions are usually sweet; small, green Thai eggplants are unique in that they are dense, not airy, with mild, crunchy, sesame-like seeds. White eggplants come in all shapes and sizes; in general, they have thick skin that may need to be peeled. Large, dark purple eggplants, the most common type sold in conventional markets, tend to have thicker skin and, when cooked, an especially meaty texture. Peel eggplants based on personal preference and the thickness of a particular vegetable's skin.

SUMMER SQUASH

From slender zucchini to scalloped pattypan and curvy yellow crookneck to spherical Eight Ball, in colors from deep green to pale yellow and every variation in between, there are many different-looking vegetables that fit under the "summer squash" umbrella. They all have similar properties: thin skins and pale, delicate flesh that softens easily when cooked. In general, smaller squash have a milder flavor and fewer seeds than larger squash; extremely large vegetables can become bitter and woody and should be avoided. "Baby squash" refers to any variety picked very small; these are usually quite mild. Squash blossoms have a subtle flavor and are edible both raw and cooked. They are often stuffed with a cheese mixture, dipped in batter, and fried.

TOMATILLO

The papery-husked tomatillo is, as its name implies, a relative of the tomato. It has been cultivated in Mexico and Guatemala even longer than the tomato, and it is most commonly used in recipes from those regions. Under the dull husk, tomatillos are usually bright green (they can also be yellow, red, or purple) and firm, with thick skin and a water-soluble, sticky coating that helps them stay fresh for several weeks. They have a tart, refreshing flavor and lots of small seeds. They are high in pectin, so they make a pleasantly thick sauce when pureed. Look for plump tomatillos with dry, tight-fitting husks, as they grow into their husks as they mature.

TOMATO

Ripe, aromatic tomatoes are a summer treat, whether tiny cherries or hearty heirlooms. Today's farmers grow thousands of cultivars, in a huge range of colors, shapes, and sizes. For American markets, tomatoes tend to fall into a few main categories. Slicing or globe tomatoes are the familiar red supermarket varieties, often sold "on the vine." Beefsteak tomatoes are large and irregularly shaped, with thin skin and hearty flavor. They are fragile and less often sold commercially. Plum tomatoes such as Roma are elongated red vegetables with thicker walls and fewer seeds; they are best for cooking. The heirloom tomato category covers a range of varieties, from the green-and-yellow-striped Green Zebra to the gold-and-red-marbled Striped German. Heirlooms vary in flavor and texture as much as they do in appearance, so farmers' market samples are a great way to get familiar with local varieties. Cherry or grape tomatoes are small with round or elongated shapes. Mini-heirlooms are also available, in as many colors, sizes, and shapes as their full-size relatives.

> Don't be afraid of heirloom tomatoes that stay green at the top, a trait called "green shoulders." The gene that creates this condition was suppressed from modern commercial varieties to create uniformly colored tomatoes, but researchers now know that might have been a mistake, since the green shoulder gene is also responsible for superior flavor.

Tomatoes are best when they have stayed on the vine until they have nearly ripened (some farmers pick them a bit early to avoid splitting). They will become fully ripe and soft at room temperature within a couple of days, or more quickly if loosely wrapped in a paper bag. They should never be refrigerated, as they will lose flavor and become mealy. If tomatoes have been refrigerated, however, allowing them to come to room temperature for a day or two will improve their quality.

> To peel a tomato for cooking, cut a small X in the skin at the bottom (opposite the stem end). Drop it into boiling water for thirty to sixty seconds, or until the skin starts to crack. Remove the tomato, cool, and peel off the skin.

WINTER SQUASH

Thin-skinned. Delicata is the most common of the thin-skinned squash. It is an oblong squash with cream-colored skin and green stripes, and its relatively small size is ideal for a meal for one or two. It has butter-yellow flesh with a flavor similar to butternut squash, corn, and sweet potatoes. The thin skin can be left on or lightly peeled, leaving the stripes in place for an elegant presentation. Its green stripes will turn orange as it ages, but the flavor will not degrade as long as it doesn't dry out.

Medium-skinned. Acorn, buttercup, butternut, kabocha, sweet dumpling, and turban are medium-skinned squash. They can be tough to cut and are good candidates for softening in the microwave or oven before cutting (be sure to pierce the skin first). Medium-skinned squash have dry, starchy flesh with a fine texture and mild sweetness. Baking squash concentrates its flavor, while steaming gives it a lighter texture and emphasizes sweetness. Steaming also dilutes the flavor a bit, so it's best for richly flavored varieties like buttercup and kabocha.

Cooked, pureed squash freezes very well. It makes an excellent quick side dish or soup, as well as a useful addition to sauces, soups, and stews in need of more color, flavor, or thickening.

Hard-skinned. Hubbard squash, pumpkins, and spaghetti squash can be the most difficult to cut, but they are worth the extra effort. Hubbards are a group of squash that vary in size and color, from five to fifty pounds, with skin that can be bluish, gray, orange, or various shades of green. They are either teardrop or toy top shaped (i.e., pointy on both ends) and have smooth, starchy flesh. Large pumpkins are usually bred to be ornamental and, while edible, do not have much flavor. Pie and cheese pumpkins have thicker flesh and more flavor than those bred for decorating porches. Spaghetti squash neatly turns stringiness, a flaw in other squash, into a remarkable asset. When cooked, the flesh of spaghetti squash separates easily into pastalike strands; larger specimens create sweeter and thicker strands than do smaller ones. The flesh is mild, lightly sweet, and somewhat bland and is a great foil for strongly flavored accompaniments. Bake chunks of large squash cut side down to retain flavor and moisture.

> *It was time to take the pumpkin out of the pot and eat it. In the final analysis, that was what solved these big problems of life. You could think and think and get nowhere, but you still had to eat your pumpkin. That brought you down to earth. That gave you a reason for going on. Pumpkin.*
>
> —ALEXANDER MCCALL SMITH,
> *The No. 1 Ladies' Detective Agency*

FRUITS EATEN AS VEGETABLES
Storage and Usage Guide

VEGETABLE	STORAGE AND PRESERVATION				USAGE SUGGESTIONS							
	IDEAL CONDITIONS	PICKLE	FREEZE	DEHYDRATE	RAW	STEAM	BRAISE	BOIL	GRILL	ROAST	SAUTÉ	FRY
BELL PEPPER	loosely wrapped, refrigerated	•	•	•	•	•	•	•	•	•	•	•
CUCUMBER	loose paper bag, warm refrigeration (45°–55°)	•		•	•						•	
EGGPLANT	loose paper bag, warm refrigeration (45°–55°)	•				•	•			•	•	•
SUMMER SQUASH	loose paper bag, warm refrigeration (45°–55°)	•	•		•	•	•	•	•		•	•
TOMATILLO	loosely wrapped, refrigerated	•	•	•	•			•		•	•	•
TOMATO	room temperature	•	•	•	•		•	•	•	•	•	•
WINTER SQUASH	room temperature	•	•	•		•	•	•	•	•	•	•

MASTER RECIPE: FOUR-WAY CHILLED SOUP

Chilled soups are refreshing treats on hot summer days, and with the help of a blender (or food processor) and refrigerator, they are ready to serve with minimal effort. Soups made from raw vegetables, such as traditional gazpacho, are often thickened with bread. Cooked root vegetables and fruits with creamy flesh, like melon, can also serve as thickeners, giving the soup a uniform, silky texture. Ajo blanco, a popular Spanish cold soup sometimes called white gazpacho, uses ground raw nuts to form a rich base in which to showcase chopped fresh vegetables and fruits. There are endless combinations of vegetables and fruits that work well in chilled soups—try our variations, play with our idea starters, or, if you're feeling adventurous, experiment to find your own favorites.

THE BASICS

Vegetables and fruits (raw if soft and juicy; cooked if firm and crunchy), roughly chopped; or ground raw nuts

Aromatics and flavorings: herbs, spices, oil, vinegar, salt and pepper

Liquid: water, broth, juice, buttermilk, wine or sparkling wine

Thickener: stale bread (optional)

Garnishes: fresh herbs, chopped or finely diced fresh vegetables or fruits, pesto, crème fraîche

PROCESS

Puree the chopped **vegetables and fruits** (or nuts), the **aromatics and flavorings**, half to three quarters of the **liquid**, and the **thickener** (if desired) in a blender or food processor. Adjust the consistency with the remaining liquid and adjust the flavoring as desired. Most chilled soups are best when thoroughly chilled before serving; extra time in the refrigerator also helps to meld the flavors. Serve with **garnishes** of choice.

VARIATIONS

BEST GAZPACHO EVER

By John Walker

SERVES 8-10

4 pounds tomatoes, peeled and seeded

1 large English cucumber

6 cloves garlic

1 large yellow or white onion

2 fresh chiles, seeds removed for less heat

1 red bell pepper

1 green bell pepper

1 tablespoon olive oil

Juice from 1 lemon

1 tablespoon red wine vinegar

Salt and ground black pepper to taste

3 cups tomato juice

6 slices whole-wheat bread

CHILLED ROASTED PEPPER AND BEET SOUP WITH FRESH HERBS

By Danielle Pacha

SERVES 6-8

2 red bell peppers, roasted and peeled

1 pound beets, cooked and peeled

1½ cups apple cider or orange juice

Salt and ground white pepper to taste

2½ cups buttermilk

STIR IN AFTER PUREEING:

2 tablespoons minced fresh dill

3 tablespoons minced chives

AJO BLANCO

By Patricia Mulvey and Laura Gilliam

SERVES 4-6

2 cups almonds, ground

6 tablespoons olive oil

¼ cup sherry vinegar

4 cloves garlic, peeled

5 cups ice water

1 pound French bread, sliced with crusts removed, thoroughly hydrated

ADD AS GARNISH:

3 cups grapes, halved

Note. To hydrate the bread: Soak for 5 minutes in 4 cups of water, then drain.

FRUIT GAZPACHO

By Barbara Wright

SERVES 4-6

Flesh from 1 ripe cantaloupe

1 bunch red or green grapes

1 medium cucumber, peeled

1 yellow tomato

¼ cup fresh basil

¼ teaspoon ground cardamom

Splash white wine

2 cups cranberry juice (or more or less as desired)

ADD AS GARNISH:

Sour cream or plain yogurt

Fresh herbs

Crusty bread croutons

Note. Blend everything but the juice to form a slurry, then swirl in the juice to reach the desired consistency.

IDEA STARTERS

Peach, tomato, garlic, white grape juice; garnishes: cilantro, avocado

Cucumber, green onion, sparkling wine, yogurt; garnishes: basil, mint

Blanched shell peas, butterhead lettuce, sautéed shallot, broth; garnishes: mint, chives

Steamed carrot, ginger, curry powder, carrot juice, coconut milk; garnish: cilantro

Boiled potato, sautéed leek, cream; garnish: chives

Corn, roasted garlic, roasted poblano, cumin, buttermilk

SERVING SUGGESTIONS

◆ Use tomato-based soup as a killer Bloody Mary mix.

◆ Freeze in an ice pop tray.

◆ Drizzle over salad for a fresh dressing.

◆ Make into ice cubes for fancy drinks.

COMMUNITY RECIPIES

FAST AND FABULOUS FAJITAS (BELL PEPPER)

BY STARR AMRIT TROLL, COURTESY OF REAP

Starr's fajitas, a complete lunch or light dinner in one quick recipe, substitute teriyaki sauce and tamari for traditional Mexican spices.

SERVES 4 // VEGETARIAN // MAIN DISH

INGREDIENTS

2 tablespoons canola oil

2 red onions, coarsely chopped

1 clove garlic, minced

1 pound extra-firm tofu, diced into 1-inch cubes

2 tablespoons teriyaki sauce

1 tablespoon soy sauce or tamari

2 small bell peppers (1 yellow, 1 green), seeded and diced

2 small or 1 large summer squash, peeled, seeded, and diced

1 (15-ounce) can black beans, drained and rinsed

2 tablespoons chopped fresh basil

4 whole-grain tortillas

1 cup grated melting cheese, divided

Sour cream

Hot pepper sauce or salsa

PROCESS

Heat the oil over medium-high heat in a large skillet. Add the onions and cook, stirring occasionally, for about 3 minutes. Add the garlic and cook for 1–2 minutes more. Add the tofu, teriyaki sauce, and tamari and cook, stirring regularly, for 3–5 minutes. When the liquid has evaporated and the tofu is beginning to brown, add the peppers and squash. Cook until the vegetables are soft, about 5 minutes. Remove from the heat, stir in the beans and basil, and set aside.

Heat an ungreased large skillet over medium-high heat. Place a tortilla in the skillet and sprinkle ¼ cup of the cheese onto one half. Spoon one fourth of the tofu-vegetable mixture over the cheese and fold the unfilled side of the tortilla over the filling. Prepare a second tortilla on the other side of the skillet in the same manner. Cook until the tortillas are perfectly browned on both sides, about 3 minutes per side. Repeat with the remaining ingredients. Serve immediately, topped with sour cream and hot pepper sauce or salsa.

JODI'S HUMMUS WITH RED BELL PEPPER AND BASIL

BY JODI SAMUELS, COURTESY OF REAP

Jodi loves chickpeas, but she dislikes tahini and garlic—two staples in traditional hummus. She developed her own variation with roasted red bell pepper, basil, lemon, and spices. Mild, nutty chickpeas, the core ingredient in hummus, pair well with a wide range of flavors, so go ahead and experiment with your own hummus creations.

YIELDS 3 CUPS // VEGAN // APPETIZER

INGREDIENTS

1 (15-ounce) can chickpeas, drained and rinsed

1 red bell pepper, roasted and sliced; or 3 ounces commercially roasted red peppers

½ teaspoon extra-virgin olive oil

Juice and pulp from ¼ lemon

2 teaspoons dried basil

6 leaves fresh basil

2 teaspoons ground cumin

2 teaspoons ground coriander

Sea salt and freshly ground black pepper to taste

PROCESS

Combine all ingredients in a food processor in the order listed. Process on low speed until smooth, stopping to scrape the sides of the bowl as needed. Serve spread on bruschetta, crackers, raw vegetables, or pita. This hummus can be stored in the refrigerator for up to 2 weeks.

HOLY SHIZA CHICKPEA AND RED BELL PEPPER PIZZA

BY IZZY DARBY

In this vegan pizza, cashews blended into the sauce cleverly stand in for the cheese. Nutritional yeast, which is different from baker's yeast and available in health food stores, adds savory flavor. The sauce can be modified to make a delicious spaghetti sauce by adding ¼ cup of water.

SERVES 8 // VEGAN // MAIN DISH

INGREDIENTS

TOMATO-CASHEW SAUCE:

½ cup raw cashews

1 small ripe tomato, chopped

1 tablespoon tomato paste

Juice from 1 lemon

1 tablespoon nutritional yeast

½ teaspoon salt, or to taste

PIZZA:

1 prepared whole-wheat pizza dough

Cornmeal

2 tablespoons olive oil, divided

1 onion, sliced

1 red bell pepper, sliced

½ cup grape tomatoes, halved

¼ cup cooked or canned chickpeas

PROCESS

TOMATO-CASHEW SAUCE: Blend all ingredients in a food processor or blender, adding water as needed to keep it loose. You want it to be a thick, spreadable pizza sauce.

PIZZA: Preheat an oven to 450°. With floured hands, stretch out the pizza dough by bouncing it in a circular motion on your hands, or by simply rolling it out on a floured counter. Sprinkle cornmeal on a pan or preheated pizza stone and lay the dough on top. Bake for 5–6 minutes, or until the dough starts to become firm and crusty.

Heat 1 tablespoon of the olive oil in a skillet and add the onion and pepper. Sauté for 6–7 minutes, until the vegetables are browned and soft.

TO ASSEMBLE: Spread 1 cup of sauce evenly on the crust and top with the sautéed vegetables, tomatoes, and chickpeas. Drizzle with the remaining tablespoon of olive oil and return the pizza to the oven for 15–20 minutes, checking often to be sure it doesn't burn.

VEGETABLE SAUTÉ (BELL PEPPER)

BY BARBARA WRIGHT/FAIRSHARE CSA COALITION

You can make a sensational sauté with whatever you happen to have on hand. Once you've mastered the technique, you can adapt it to accompany any meal by varying the sauce and seasonings. Use Barbara's suggested flavor combinations, or try some of your own.

SERVES 2 // VEGAN // SIDE DISH

INGREDIENTS

Clarified butter or olive oil

1 cup protein (tofu, chicken, shrimp, etc.), cut into bite-size pieces (optional)

6 cups chopped vegetables of choice

Sauce and seasonings of choice

Herbs of choice

PROCESS

Melt a small amount of clarified butter or olive oil in a skillet over medium heat and sauté the protein until cooked through. Remove from the skillet and set aside. Add a bit more butter or oil if necessary and sauté the firmer vegetables (e.g., carrots, broccoli) first until they begin to soften. Add the aromatics (onions, garlic), then the softer vegetables (e.g., spinach, zucchini, asparagus). Add the sauce, seasonings, and cooked protein. Cook until the sauce is reduced; remove from the heat when all the vegetables are tender. Always add the herbs last.

SUGGESTED COMBINATIONS:

- Carrots, onions, garlic, green and red bell peppers, celery, and spinach with tomato sauce; top with plain yogurt mixed with herbs and garlic.

- Chicken or shrimp, green and red bell peppers, garlic, and canned artichoke hearts with white wine and whipping cream.

- Bacon, chicken, onions, garlic, green and red bell peppers, and green olives; top with grated sharp cheese.

MEXICAN BELL PEPPER CASSEROLE

BY EDITH THAYER

In the summer when peppers are abundant, this savory casserole saves the day. It makes an excellent brunch dish. Poblano or Anaheim chile peppers can be substituted for part of the bell peppers if more kick is desired.

SERVES 4-6 // VEGETARIAN // MAIN DISH

INGREDIENTS

2 tablespoons butter and/or olive oil, plus more for greasing the baking dish

1½ cups thinly sliced onion

2 cloves garlic, minced

1 teaspoon salt

1 teaspoon ground cumin

1 teaspoon ground coriander

½ teaspoon ground mustard

¼ teaspoon ground black pepper

¼ teaspoon cayenne

About 3 cups thinly sliced red, yellow, or green bell peppers

2 tablespoons all-purpose flour

4 ounces Colby, grated

4 large eggs

1½ cup sour cream

Smoked paprika

PROCESS

Butter a deep 8 × 8-inch baking dish. Preheat an oven to 375°. Heat the butter and/or olive oil in a heavy skillet. Sauté the onion and garlic with the salt and spices for a few minutes. When the onion is translucent, add the bell peppers and sauté over low heat for about 10 minutes. Sprinkle in the flour, mix well, and sauté until there is no extra liquid, about 7 minutes. Spread half of the pepper mixture in the bottom of the baking dish and top with half of the cheese. Repeat these layers.

Mix together the eggs and sour cream, blending well. Pour the mixture over the peppers and cheese and sprinkle with paprika. Cover and bake for 25–30 minutes; uncover and bake for 15 minutes more.

MOUHAMARA (RED BELL PEPPER AND WALNUT SPREAD)

BY DANIELLE PACHA

Mouhamara is an easy make-ahead dip that tastes even better the day after you make it. Garnish with walnuts right before serving. To create fatayer mouhamara, a delectable Syrian snack, spread mouhamara on little rounds of fresh pizza dough and bake for about 10 minutes.

Pomegranate molasses can be found in Middle Eastern markets, at specialty food stores, or online. It can also be made by boiling 4 cups pomegranate juice, $\frac{1}{2}$ cup sugar, and 1 tablespoon lemon juice for 60–75 minutes until it is reduced to about $1\frac{1}{2}$ cups.

SERVES 8 // VEGAN // APPETIZER

INGREDIENTS

2 cloves garlic

2 cups loosely packed toasted walnuts, divided

2 large red bell peppers, seeded, roasted, and coarsely chopped; or 1 (12-ounce) jar roasted red peppers, drained

¾ cup fresh breadcrumbs

½–1 tablespoon pomegranate molasses (or more to taste)

1 tablespoon lemon juice

1 teaspoon ground cumin

1 hot chile pepper, minced (seeds retained for more heat); or ½–1 teaspoon cayenne

1 tablespoon tahini

¼–½ cup extra-virgin olive oil

Salt to taste

PROCESS

Whirl the garlic cloves in a food processor until finely chopped. Add 1½ cups of the walnuts and the next 7 ingredients (bell peppers through tahini) and process until smooth, scraping the sides of the bowl as necessary. Taste and adjust the seasonings as desired. Restart the processor and slowly pour the olive oil through the chute until the consistency is thick and creamy. Season with salt. Spoon the spread into a serving dish and set aside.

Chop the remaining ½ cup of walnuts and sprinkle over the spread. Serve at room temperature with pita chips or as a garnish to Mediterranean entrées.

SUMMER'S BOUNTY ENCHILADA CASSEROLE (BELL PEPPER)

BY ALYSHA WITWICKI

Layering tortillas in this casserole, instead of blanching them in oil and rolling them, makes enchiladas a snap. This is a versatile recipe in which you can substitute hot peppers according to your own sensitivity, and bell peppers and summer squash according to what's in season. It's also a great way to use leftover cooked beans and rice; just substitute about 2 cups of beans for one can.

SERVES 8–10 // VEGETARIAN // MAIN DISH

INGREDIENTS

1 tablespoon canola oil

1 medium onion, diced

1 red bell pepper, seeded and diced

1 jalapeño, seeded and finely diced

1 banana pepper, seeded and finely diced

1 medium zucchini, halved lengthwise and diced

3 cloves garlic, minced

1 (15-ounce) can black beans, drained and rinsed

2 cups cooked brown rice

1 medium tomato, diced

2 cups enchilada sauce, divided

½ cup minced fresh cilantro

⅔ cup crumbled feta

Salt and ground black pepper to taste

18 (6-inch) corn tortillas

1 cup shredded Monterey Jack

Sour cream and salsa

PROCESS

Preheat an oven to 450°. Heat the oil in a large skillet over medium-high heat. Add the onion, bell pepper, jalapeño, and banana pepper and cook until slightly softened, about 5 minutes. Add the zucchini and garlic and cook for about 4 minutes more. Stir in the black beans, rice, and tomato and cook until warm.

Transfer the pepper-zucchini mixture to a large mixing bowl. Mix in ½ cup of the enchilada sauce, the cilantro, and the feta. Season with salt and pepper.

To make the casserole, spread ½ cup of the enchilada sauce in the bottom of a 13 × 9-inch baking dish. Lay 6 tortillas over the sauce and trim to fit as needed (you may have to cut some of them in half, depending on the shape of your dish). Spread half of the filling over the tortillas. Repeat with another layer of 6 tortillas and the rest of the filling. Add one more layer of tortillas on top. Spread the remaining cup of enchilada sauce over the casserole. Sprinkle the cheese on top.

Cover the casserole with aluminum foil and bake for 20 minutes. Remove the foil and bake for an additional 5 minutes, or until the cheese begins to brown. Let cool for at least 5 minutes before serving. Garnish with sour cream and salsa.

SOUR CREAM CUCUMBER SALAD

BY DEBRA SHAPIRO/FAIRSHARE CSA COALITION

The cooling combination of sour cream and cucumbers makes this an excellent accompaniment to a spicy meal.

SERVES 6 // VEGETARIAN // SIDE DISH

INGREDIENTS

3 medium cucumbers, peeled (if desired) and thinly sliced

1 small red or white onion, thinly sliced

1 teaspoon coarse salt

1 tablespoon white vinegar

¼ cup sour cream

½–1 tablespoon sugar

Ground black or white pepper to taste

PROCESS

Place the cucumber and onion slices in a colander, sprinkle with salt, and toss to coat evenly. Let stand 20–30 minutes. Drain the liquid, pat the vegetables dry with a paper towel, and place the vegetables in a bowl. Mix the vinegar, sour cream, and sugar and pour over the cucumbers and onions. Season with pepper. Mix well and chill for at least 30 minutes.

REFRESHING CUCUMBER SALSA

BY JODI BUBENZER

In the early spring, Jodi waits impatiently, tortilla chips at the ready, for her first cucumbers to come in. Once, this salsa was just a way to use up extras. Now it is a colorful herald of warmer weather and the lazy days of summer. Not to mention, it tastes darn good on a chip.

YIELDS ABOUT 6 CUPS // VEGAN // CONDIMENT

INGREDIENTS

2 cucumbers, peeled, seeded, and finely diced

3 medium tomatoes, finely diced

1 medium red onion, finely diced

1–2 jalapeños, finely diced (optional)

1 garlic clove, minced

1 bunch cilantro, chopped

⅓ cup rice vinegar

2 tablespoons each chopped fresh oregano and parsley

1–2 tablespoons chopped fresh thyme

Salt and ground black pepper to taste

PROCESS

Mix all the ingredients in a large bowl. Let stand for about 15 minutes to allow the flavors to meld. Adjust the seasonings if necessary.

AUNT CAROL'S REFRIGERATOR PICKLES (CUCUMBER)

BY HEIDI ACCOLA OF ROOTS & SHOOTS FARM

Easy and delicious, these pickles come together in only a few minutes and last for weeks. Plus, refrigerator pickles need no steamers, special jars, or vacuum-tight lids. This type of pickle is not shelf stable and must be kept in the refrigerator.

YIELDS 1 GALLON // VEGAN // CONDIMENT

INGREDIENTS

1½ quarts water

2 cups white vinegar

½ cup (5 ounces) pickling salt*

1 tablespoon mustard seeds

2 large onions, sliced

1–2 heads garlic, cloves peeled

8 heads dill (or 4 tablespoons dill weed or dill seed)

5 pounds pickling cucumbers

Chile peppers, minced (optional)

*Kosher salt works too, but make sure to weigh it to ensure that the volume is correct, as it is usually denser than pickling salt. It may also take longer to dissolve, so you may have to let the brine boil longer.

PROCESS

In a large stockpot, combine the water, vinegar, salt, and mustard seeds to create a brine. Bring to a boil on the stove. While heating, layer the slices from 1 onion on the bottom of a large, nonreactive container. Add the cloves from 1 head of garlic, 4 heads of dill, and the cucumbers. When the brine has reached a vigorous boil, let it cool slightly and pour it over the cucumbers. Add the remaining onion slices, garlic, and dill on top. Add the chile peppers (if desired). Let the mixture stand at room temperature for 1 day, then move to the refrigerator. Lasts for at least 4 months.

ELAINE'S SWEDISH CUCUMBERS

BY TRACY EVANS

Tracy learned to make this quick pickle over fifty years ago from her mother, Elaine, who still brings it to church suppers and potlucks. It's a nice way to use cucumbers that may have lingered on the vine a bit too long and become a little bitter or yellowed.

SERVES 4-8 // VEGAN // CONDIMENT

INGREDIENTS

2–3 medium cucumbers, sliced (can use yellowed cucumbers)

1 medium red, white, or yellow onion, sliced

Salt to taste

⅓ cup white or cider vinegar

⅓ cup sugar

⅓ cup water

10–12 whole black peppercorns

PROCESS

Layer the cucumber and onion slices in a nonreactive container, sprinkling salt between the layers. Let stand for 1–2 hours at room temperature. Create a brine by heating the remaining ingredients on a stove or in a microwave until the sugar dissolves. Let cool. Pour the brine over the cucumbers and refrigerate until chilled.

SESAME NOODLE SALAD WITH CUCUMBERS

BY MARY SPIKE

Here, an excess of ordinary cucumbers becomes a savory picnic standout. Serve this Asian-inspired salad alone, or as a bed for marinated, grilled chicken thighs or flank steak.

SERVES 8-10 // VEGAN // SIDE DISH

INGREDIENTS

16 ounces spaghetti, broken into thirds

4 tablespoons soy sauce

3 tablespoons toasted sesame oil

2 tablespoons vegetable oil or light olive oil

6 tablespoons lime juice

Dash cayenne

3 cucumbers, seeded and thinly sliced

2 carrots, grated; or 6 radishes, thinly sliced (optional)

3 green onions, minced

3 tablespoons finely chopped fresh cilantro

3 tablespoons toasted sesame seeds

PROCESS

Cook the pasta according to the package directions, drain, rinse with cold water, and set aside. Meanwhile, prepare a dressing by whisking together the soy sauce, oils, lime juice, and cayenne. When the noodles are cool, toss with the dressing to coat. Stir in the cucumbers, additional vegetables (if desired), green onions, cilantro, and sesame seeds.

EGGPLANT LASAGNA

BY IZETTA SCHOENROCK, COURTESY OF REAP

Browned, breaded slices of eggplant stand in for lasagna noodles in this satisfying layered casserole.

SERVES 9–12 // VEGETARIAN // MAIN DISH

INGREDIENTS

1 egg

¼ cup milk

¾ cup all-purpose flour

½ teaspoon salt

½ teaspoon ground black pepper

2 medium eggplants, cut into ¾-inch slices

½ cup oil, divided

1 large onion, chopped

1 medium zucchini, sliced

1½ cups corn kernels

½ green bell pepper, seeded and chopped

½ red bell pepper, seeded and chopped

4 medium tomatoes, peeled

2 (8-ounce) cans tomato sauce

1 tablespoon sugar

1 teaspoon dried oregano

1¼ cups water, divided

1½ tablespoons cornstarch

1½ cups grated mozzarella

PROCESS

Preheat an oven to 350°. In a medium bowl, beat the egg and milk together. In a separate bowl, combine the flour, salt, and pepper. Dip each slice of eggplant in the egg mixture, drain, and then dip in the flour mixture, turning to coat evenly. Heat a small amount of the oil in a skillet over medium-high heat and brown the eggplant slices in batches. When all slices are browned, set aside on paper towels to drain.

Add more oil to the skillet if necessary and sauté the onion until translucent, about 5 minutes. Add the next 8 ingredients (zucchini through oregano) and 1 cup of the water, bring to a boil, and simmer for 10 minutes. Mix the cornstarch with the remaining ¼ cup of water and add it to the vegetable mixture. Cook, stirring, 5 minutes more to thicken.

Line the bottom of a 13 × 9-inch baking dish with half of the eggplant slices. Cover the eggplant with half of the vegetable mixture, then repeat these layers. Bake for 30 minutes. Remove from the oven, sprinkle with cheese, and continue baking for another 10 minutes, or until the cheese is browned and bubbling.

SLOW COOKER RATATOUILLE (EGGPLANT)

BY AMANDA STRUCKMEYER

A vibrant mix of vegetables mingles perfectly in the gentle heat of a slow cooker. Fill your cooker to the brim with in-season vegetables—just make sure you can get the lid on! This rustic French classic makes for a delicious vegetarian main dish. Stir in some pesto after cooking, top with grated Parmesan for additional flavor, and serve over rice or quinoa.

SERVES 8 // VEGAN // MAIN DISH

Slow cookers make quick work of preparing hearty meals. Assemble the ingredients in just a few minutes earlier in the day and let the slow cooker work its magic; you'll have time to spare for other activities—and a piping hot dish ready for dinner.

INGREDIENTS

8 cups chopped eggplant, tomato, zucchini, onion, or any other in-season vegetable(s)

½ cup water or broth

2 tablespoons olive oil

1 tablespoon dried Italian seasoning

2 cloves garlic, minced

½ teaspoon crushed red pepper

Salt and ground black pepper to taste

Chopped fresh herbs (optional)

PROCESS

Place the vegetables in a 4-quart slow cooker. Add the water or broth, oil, Italian seasoning, garlic, and crushed red pepper and stir well. Cook on low for 5–6 hours. Season with salt and pepper. Garnish with fresh herbs (if desired).

PHOTO BY LESLIE DAMASO FOR
DRIFTLESS APPETITE BLOG

EGGPLANT TORTANG TALONG (OMELET)

BY LESLIE DAMASO OF DRIFTLESS APPETITE BLOG

When Leslie was a child, her grandmother served this Filipino eggplant omelet with garlic fried rice. And Leslie hated it. Now an adult with a more refined palate, she can't get enough of it, and she often serves it as a quick weeknight supper. The eggplant is roasted or grilled, then pressed into a fan shape, dipped in egg, and fried. Look for long, thin eggplants for this dish; they are usually called Japanese eggplants but they sometimes have other names.

SERVES 2 // VEGETARIAN // MAIN DISH

INGREDIENTS

2 Japanese eggplants

2 eggs

1 clove garlic, minced

Salt and ground black pepper to taste

1 tablespoon chopped fresh chives, divided

1 tablespoon olive oil

PROCESS

Preheat an oven to 400°. Bake the eggplants until soft (10–15 minutes), then place them under a broiler to char the skin (the eggplants may also be grilled until soft and charred, about 5 minutes). Set aside to cool.

Meanwhile, beat the eggs in a bowl. Add the garlic, salt, pepper, and most of the chives. Peel the eggplants and press them with a fork until thin and fan shaped. Heat a cast-iron skillet over medium heat and add the oil. Place the flattened eggplants in the egg mixture and let soak for a few seconds, then fry in the oiled skillet until golden brown. Garnish with the remaining chives and serve.

FETTUCCINE WITH EGGPLANT, TOMATO, AND BLUE CHEESE
BY HEATHER WORKMAN

This pasta recipe has made an eggplant lover out of Heather's fiancé. Using a little of the pasta cooking water in the sauce is a restaurant trick that works; the starch from the cooked pasta adds body and a velvety texture to the finished dish.

SERVES 2–4 // VEGETARIAN // MAIN DISH

INGREDIENTS

½ large eggplant, diced into ¾-inch cubes

2 tablespoons olive oil, divided

Salt for cooking water

¼–⅓ pound fettuccine

¼ medium or large red onion, thinly sliced

1 medium clove garlic, minced

2 tablespoons sherry vinegar or other wine vinegar

1 large Roma tomato, diced

½ cup tomato sauce

2–3 large white button mushrooms, diced

Crushed red pepper to taste (¾ teaspoon provides a good kick)

Handful fresh basil leaves, sliced into thin strips

1 tablespoon minced fresh flat-leaf parsley

4 ounces blue cheese (plus more for topping), cut or crumbled into small chunks

1–1½ tablespoons extra-virgin olive oil

Kosher salt and freshly ground black pepper to taste

PROCESS

Preheat an oven to 400°. Toss the eggplant with 1 tablespoon of the olive oil and spread in a single layer on a small baking sheet. Roast for 20 minutes, or until the eggplant is brown and tender.

Bring a large pot of water to a boil. Generously salt the water and add the fettuccine. Slightly undercook the pasta, 1–2 minutes less than the package directions suggest.

While the pasta is cooking, heat a large sauté pan and cook the onion in the remaining tablespoon of olive oil until golden. Add the garlic, stir, and cook for 1 minute. Add the vinegar to deglaze the pan (scrape the bottom with a wooden spoon while stirring). Add the roasted eggplant, tomato, tomato sauce, mushrooms, crushed red pepper, and most of the basil (reserve a few strips for topping). Heat until just simmering.

Using a pair of tongs, transfer the fettuccine directly into the sauce and toss gently; reserve the pasta water. Add the parsley, blue cheese, and extra-virgin olive oil to the pasta and sauce, tossing again to combine. Add 2–4 tablespoons of the reserved pasta water and allow the dish to cook for 1–2 minutes; the cheese should melt down and mix with the liquid to create a luxurious sauce. Taste and adjust the seasonings as necessary with salt, pepper, and/or more crushed red pepper. Serve hot, with the remaining basil and additional blue cheese on top.

SUMMER VEGETABLE FRITTERS (EGGPLANT)

BY DANIEL FOX OF THE MADISON CLUB

Fritters are an easy and fun way to serve summer vegetables, either as an appetizer or as a snack. We've included instructions for baking as well as frying for those who want a healthier option. Try adding a dash of cayenne to the flour for a little more kick, or serve these with your favorite fresh salsa.

SERVES 6–8 // VEGETARIAN // APPETIZER

INGREDIENTS

½ cup all-purpose flour

Pinch each fresh thyme, ground black pepper, paprika, and ground allspice (or more to taste)

2–3 medium zucchini or yellow squash, or 1 eggplant, cut lengthwise into ¼-inch slices

2 large eggs, beaten

2½ cups panko

Oil for frying (canola, vegetable, soybean, or grape seed) (omit if baking)

Salt to taste

PROCESS

Mix the flour with the herbs and spices. Toss the vegetables in the flour mixture. Remove the vegetables, shake off the excess flour, and dip into the egg. Drain off the excess egg and coat completely in the panko. If necessary, dip the vegetables again in the flour, egg, and panko until thoroughly coated.

TO FRY: Pour the oil into a large skillet to cover the bottom ¼ inch deep and heat on medium-high. The oil should be hot enough to slowly brown the breaded vegetables but not so hot that it begins smoking. Fry the vegetables in small batches until golden brown. Have a tray lined with paper towels ready to hold the fried vegetables when they finish cooking.

TO BAKE: Preheat an oven to 400°. Arrange the coated vegetables in a single layer on a baking sheet and bake until the vegetables are softened and the crumbs are brown, about 25 minutes, turning over halfway through the cooking time.

After cooking, season immediately with salt.

BAKED ZUCCHINI CAKES (SUMMER SQUASH)

BY KARIS KUCKLEBURG

Karis was determined to recreate the zucchini cakes she had enjoyed at a restaurant. We think she's done it; in fact, we're betting hers are better than the original. Suitable as an appetizer or as a vegetarian main dish, these cakes are good eaten plain, with Greek-style yogurt, or, as Karis suggests, with ranch dressing.

SERVES 4 // VEGETARIAN // APPETIZER

INGREDIENTS

3 cups coarsely grated zucchini (about 2 medium)

½ teaspoon salt

1 cup panko

½ cup freshly grated Parmesan

1 egg

4 green onions, thinly sliced

¼ cup finely chopped red bell pepper

1½ teaspoons Old Bay seasoning (or substitute given here)

1 teaspoon Dijon mustard

1 tablespoon mayonnaise

⅛ teaspoon crushed red pepper

OLD BAY SUBSTITUTE:

¼ teaspoon paprika

¼ teaspoon salt

¼ teaspoon garlic powder

⅛ teaspoon ground black pepper

⅛ teaspoon onion powder

⅛ teaspoon cayenne

⅛ teaspoon dried oregano

⅛ teaspoon dried thyme

PROCESS

Preheat an oven to 400°. Squeeze the grated zucchini in a clean kitchen towel until it is fairly dry and you have about 2 cups after removing it from the towel. Place the zucchini and the remaining ingredients in a bowl; mix well.

Form the dough into 12 (2-inch) patties and place them on a baking sheet coated with cooking spray. Bake for 10 minutes, then turn each cake over and bake for another 10 minutes.

These cakes are a great way to use up leftover cooked summer or winter squash, or even carrots, kohlrabi, or turnips. Use tender vegetables like summer squash raw or cooked; sauté, steam, or microwave shredded root vegetables until soft. Squeeze out the excess moisture, and proceed with the recipe as written.

FRIED "BILLY CLUB" SUMMER SQUASH WITH PESTO, BACON, AND GOAT CHEESE

BY JILL HAUGH, COURTESY OF REAP

Prolific summer squash plants will produce vegetables the size of billy clubs unless harvested frequently. Most growers prefer to pick the vegetables when they're fairly small, but if you encounter a giant, try it in this recipe.

SERVES 2–3 // MEAT // MAIN DISH

INGREDIENTS

3–4 pieces uncured turkey bacon

2 tablespoons olive oil

1 large sweet onion, thinly sliced

Salt

1 massive zucchini or other summer squash (or 4 smaller ones), cut into ¼-inch slices

1 tablespoon ground herbes de Provence (savory, fennel seeds, basil, thyme)

2–3 tablespoons pesto

1–2 cups cherry tomatoes

Crackers

2–3 ounces fresh goat cheese, crumbled

Freshly ground black pepper to taste

PROCESS

In a large skillet, fry the bacon over medium-high heat until crisp. Remove from the skillet and set aside to drain on a paper towel. Break it into crumbles when cool.

Without wiping the skillet, add the olive oil, the sliced onion, and a pinch of salt and cook over medium-high heat. When the onion is starting to caramelize (about 15 minutes), toss in the zucchini and the herbs. Brown the zucchini slices on both sides, then add the pesto, the crumbled bacon, tomatoes, and a pinch of salt. Stir everything together over medium heat until the tomatoes split. Serve topped with crumbled crackers, goat cheese, and pepper.

FRIED STUFFED SUMMER SQUASH BLOSSOMS

BY KIMIKO MIYAZAKI, COURTESY OF REAP

Harvesting squash blossoms is a great way to keep a vigorously producing plant in check. These crispy little morsels make fantastic appetizers. Try serving them with marinara sauce for dipping.

SERVES 3-4 // VEGETARIAN // APPETIZER

INGREDIENTS

½ cup finely grated zucchini

½ cup finely grated fontina or other cheese

¼ cup breadcrumbs (either plain or seasoned)

Several fresh basil leaves, finely chopped

Pinch each salt and ground black pepper

20 summer squash blossoms

1 egg, beaten

¼ cup milk

1 cup all-purpose flour

Oil for frying

Cayenne (optional)

PROCESS

Press the grated zucchini into a colander to squeeze out the excess liquid. In a large bowl, combine the drained zucchini, cheese, breadcrumbs, basil, salt, and pepper. Open each of the blossoms (carefully—they are delicate!) and push aside or pull out the stamen. Using a small spoon, fill each flower with the zucchini mixture. Pinch and twist the ends shut.

In a small dish, combine the egg and milk. Place the flour in a second dish. Cover the bottom of a skillet with about ½ inch of oil and heat over medium-high heat until the oil runs like water (it should be about 365°). Dip the blossoms into the egg mixture, dredge with flour, and fry for about 2 minutes on each side, working with about 3–5 at a time, depending on the size of your skillet. When the blossoms are crisp and golden, remove them from the oil and drain on a paper-towel-lined plate. Sprinkle lightly with cayenne (if desired) and serve immediately.

GRILLED ZUCCHINI CURLS (SUMMER SQUASH)
BY TERESE ALLEN

Grilling does something delicious to zucchini; that is, the caramelizing of the surface sweetens the slight bitterness of the vegetable. The squash is sliced into long, thin planks and then cooked just long enough to soften them, whereupon they can be rolled into fun-loving curls.

SERVES 2–4 // VEGAN // SIDE DISH

INGREDIENTS

1 small to medium zucchini (green or golden, or use a combination), sliced lengthwise into ⅛-inch planks

Extra-virgin olive oil or lemon-flavored olive oil

Sea salt and freshly ground black pepper to taste

Grated peel from 1 lemon

PROCESS

Prepare an outdoor grill or heat a stovetop griddle (ridged side up) over a medium flame until very hot, about 10 minutes. Brush both sides of each zucchini plank with olive oil and sprinkle with salt, pepper, and lemon peel. Lay the zucchini across the hot grill or griddle and cook on both sides until grill marks show and the zucchini is fully pliable (but not limp), 3–4 minutes per side. Adjust the heat as the zucchini cooks so you get nice dark grill marks without any burning. Use tongs to transfer each zucchini slice to a plate, rolling them up and piling them against each other attractively.

SASSY SUMMER SQUASH
BY ANN HARSTE

Simple, fun, and delicious, this recipe is especially good with homemade salsa (we recommend "Tomatillo Salsa Verde" on page 109). Ann says mild salsa can be substituted for the hot, but she notes the result will be less "sassy."

SERVES 3–4 // VEGETARIAN // SIDE DISH

INGREDIENTS

1 tablespoon butter

2 medium zucchini or other summer squash, seeded and cut into ½-inch slices

8 ounces cherry tomatoes, quartered

½ cup hot salsa

2–4 ounces crumbled feta

Freshly ground black pepper to taste

PROCESS

Melt the butter in a small sauté pan over medium-high heat. Add the zucchini and sauté a few minutes, until it starts to soften. Add the tomatoes and salsa and simmer for about 10 minutes, until the salsa is reduced and thickened. Transfer to a serving dish and sprinkle generously with feta. Season with pepper.

SUNBURST SUMMER SQUASH AND SEITAN SAUTÉ

BY AMANDA GRAMLICH

This simple one-pan dish is one of Amanda's favorites. It's bursting with fresh summer flavors like pattypan squash, tomatoes, and basil, and packed with protein for a vegan main course. Vegetables can be swapped in and out to your heart's (and stomach's) content.

SERVES 6 // VEGAN // MAIN DISH

INGREDIENTS

1 tablespoon olive oil

1 Spanish or other sweet onion, chopped

6 cloves garlic, roughly chopped

1 package Italian-style seitan, crumbled

6 small pattypan squash, thinly sliced

2 cups fresh fava beans, shelled and blanched; or 1 (15-ounce) can, drained and rinsed

2 (15-ounce) cans diced tomatoes

1 teaspoon sea salt

1 teaspoon dried oregano

1 teaspoon crushed red pepper

Handful fresh basil leaves, sliced into thin strips

Grated Parmesan or other cheese

PROCESS

Heat the olive oil in a medium stockpot or large heavy-bottomed pot over medium-low heat until warm, then add the onion. Sauté for about 5 minutes, then add the garlic and cook for 3 minutes more. Add the seitan and allow it to brown, stirring occasionally. Add the squash to the sauté mixture along with the beans, tomatoes, salt, oregano, and crushed red pepper. Allow the mixture to simmer until it is bubbly and the squash is cooked but not mushy, about 5 minutes. Add most of the basil and turn off the heat. Serve warm with grated Parmesan and the remaining fresh basil.

SUPER-FRESH RATATOUILLE (SUMMER SQUASH)

BY IZZY DARBY

Use only young, sweet vegetables for this ratatouille, since their flavor is essential to the dish. Ratatouille is excellent tossed with pasta, as a sandwich filling, as a side dish, or over creamy polenta as a main course. A skinny eggplant can also be used in place of one or two of the squash.

SERVES 4-6 // VEGAN // MAIN DISH

INGREDIENTS

¼–½ cup olive oil, divided

1 onion, chopped

1–2 cloves garlic, minced

1 large or 2 small zucchini, chopped

2–3 medium yellow squash, chopped

2 medium tomatoes, chopped

1 cup Sungold tomatoes, halved

1 cup vegetable broth

1 bay leaf

Salt and ground black pepper to taste

¼ cup chopped fresh basil

PROCESS

In a large pot with a fitted lid, heat 1 tablespoon of the oil over medium heat. Add the onion and garlic and cook until soft, about 5 minutes. Remove from the heat.

In a large skillet, heat 1½ tablespoons of the oil and sauté the zucchini and squash in batches until browned, adding extra oil as necessary. As the batches are browned, add them to the onion mixture.

Add all the remaining ingredients except the basil to the onion-squash mixture. Return the pot to the heat, cover, and cook for 20–25 minutes, stirring occasionally.

Remove the bay leaf and adjust the seasonings as necessary. Sprinkle in the chopped basil and cook for an additional 1–2 minutes, until the basil is wilted. Serve immediately or chill for a delicious cold lunch.

ZUCCHINI CARPACCIO (SUMMER SQUASH)

BY SARA SITZER

Sara and her husband learned this recipe in a cooking class while on their honeymoon in Italy. They've been making it ever since, adjusting it to suit their tastes as time passes. It is delicious on an antipasto platter with salty cheeses and cured meats, or as a side dish for grilled meats. This simple recipe is a reminder that humble ingredients can make for a spectacular dish when they are handled with grace. We look forward to seeing what recipes Sara brings us from future anniversary trips.

SERVES 2 // VEGETARIAN // SIDE DISH

INGREDIENTS

1 medium zucchini

Salt

1 garlic clove, minced

3 tablespoons pine nuts

3 tablespoons extra-virgin olive oil

Juice from ½ lemon

Honey to taste

PROCESS

Slice the zucchini paper-thin using a cheese slicer or mandoline. Salt lightly and spread on paper towels, taking care not to break the slices. Let them sit for about 20 minutes, blotting off excess liquid as necessary. Arrange the zucchini in a thin layer in a shallow serving dish. Top the slices with the garlic and nuts. Drizzle with olive oil and lemon juice, cover, and let the zucchini marinate in the refrigerator for at least 30 minutes. Just before serving, drizzle a little honey on top of the zucchini.

This dish can be prepared the day before and left to marinate overnight, leaving only the drizzling of the honey for the serving day. The longer it marinates, the more delicious it becomes!

ZUCCHINI CINNAMON PANCAKES (SUMMER SQUASH)

BY BETH VAN DE BOOM

These simple pancakes are a great way to serve vegetables for breakfast. Since there is no added sugar in the pancakes, be sure to use mild, sweet zucchini. Top with toasted walnuts for an added nutritional boost.

SERVES 2-4 // VEGETARIAN // MAIN DISH

INGREDIENTS

2 eggs

1 teaspoon cinnamon

Dash sea salt

2 cups shredded zucchini

Butter or ghee

Maple syrup or honey

PROCESS

In a medium bowl, whisk together the eggs, cinnamon, and salt. Stir in the zucchini. Drop the batter by spoonfuls onto a hot, greased griddle. Cook for about 3 minutes, or until the centers of the pancakes start to become firm. Flip the cakes over gently and cook on the other side for about 2 minutes, or until the pancakes spring back when pressed lightly on top. Serve topped with butter or ghee and maple syrup or honey.

ZUCCHINI CORN FRITTERS (SUMMER SQUASH)

BY BARBARA WRIGHT/FAIRSHARE CSA COALITION

These fritters feel indulgent while filling you with nothing but summer goodness. This recipe is a great way to use any oddly shaped or large zucchini.

SERVES 8-10 // VEGETARIAN // APPETIZER

INGREDIENTS

2 cups all-purpose flour

1 tablespoon baking powder

½ teaspoon ground cumin

½ cup sugar

½ teaspoon salt, or more to taste

Freshly ground black pepper to taste

2 eggs, beaten

1 cup milk

¼ cup butter, melted

2 cups grated zucchini

1½ cups corn kernels

1 cup finely shredded Cheddar

Oil for frying

PROCESS

In a large bowl, stir together the flour, baking powder, cumin, sugar, salt, and pepper. In a small bowl, whisk together the eggs, milk, and butter. Whisk the wet ingredients into the dry ingredients. Stir in the zucchini, corn, and cheese; mix well.

Fill the bottom of a cast-iron skillet with about ½ inch of oil. Heat the oil over medium-high heat and then drop the batter by tablespoonfuls into the hot oil. Fry in batches, adding more oil as necessary, until the fritters are puffy, crisp, and golden brown, turning once with tongs (about 60–90 seconds per side). Remove to drain on paper towels.

ZUCCHINI FRITTERS TOPPED WITH EGGS (SUMMER SQUASH)

BY JEAN SCHNEIDER OF TOKEN CREEK ECO-INN

Poached eggs perched on golden fritter foundations look elegant and impressive. Jean serves this dish to her guests along with a salad of greens and tomatoes dressed in a light vinaigrette. Zucchini can be watery, so be sure to wring it out well for this recipe. The strands should be very dry before forming the fritters.

SERVES 6 // VEGETARIAN // MAIN DISH

INGREDIENTS

1 pound zucchini, coarsely grated

1 teaspoon salt

1 large egg

½ cup chopped onion (optional)

½–1 bunch fresh chives or green onions, finely chopped

½ cup all-purpose flour

¼ teaspoon ground black pepper

Salt to taste

½ cup sunflower oil or olive oil

1 dozen fresh eggs

PROCESS

Place the zucchini in a colander and toss with 1 teaspoon of salt. Let it sit for 10 minutes, then squeeze out the excess water, pressing it against the sides of the colander or wringing it in several layers of paper towel or a dishcloth until it's very dry. Whisk the egg in a large bowl and mix in the zucchini, onion (if desired), chives, flour, pepper, and salt.

Heat the oil in a large skillet over medium-high heat. Drop the batter into the skillet, creating mounds with about 2 tablespoons of batter each; flatten the mounds with a spatula. Cook until brown, then turn over and brown the other side (2–4 minutes per side). Remove from the skillet and drain on a paper towel-lined plate. Sprinkle with sea salt.

Poach the fresh eggs. Place each fritter on a plate, top with one poached egg, and serve immediately.

ZUCCHINI STEW (SUMMER SQUASH)

BY MICHELE ZINDARS, COURTESY OF REAP

Michele's grandmother used to make this recipe with vegetables she picked from her own garden. Whenever she served it she would say at the end of the meal, "Well, that was pretty good, if I do say so myself!"

SERVES 5 // MEAT OR POULTRY // MAIN DISH

INGREDIENTS

1 pound lean ground beef or ground turkey

1 large onion, chopped

1 teaspoon salt

½ teaspoon ground black pepper

3 large tomatoes, diced

2 large potatoes, diced

2 cups corn kernels

4 medium zucchini, diced into 1-inch cubes

PROCESS

Sauté the ground beef and onion together in a Dutch oven over medium heat, breaking up the meat as it cooks. When the meat is thoroughly browned, drain off any fat and season with salt and pepper. Add the tomatoes and continue heating. Add the potatoes and let simmer until the potatoes are soft and easy to pierce, about 15 minutes. Add the corn and zucchini and continue to simmer until they are tender, about 3 minutes. Do not overcook.

ZUCCHINI WITH GARLIC AND LEMON (SUMMER SQUASH)

BY BARBARA WRIGHT/FAIRSHARE CSA COALITION

Peeling stripes into the zucchini before slicing it gives this festive dish an attractive presentation.

SERVES 4 // VEGAN // SIDE DISH

INGREDIENTS

2 medium zucchini

3 tablespoons butter or olive oil

1 clove garlic, minced

¼ cup minced red bell pepper

¼ teaspoon grated lemon peel

2 tablespoons lemon juice

Salt and ground black pepper to taste

PROCESS

Peel the zucchini with a vegetable peeler, removing only half of the skin in a striped pattern. Cut the zucchini in half lengthwise, then slice the halves into semicircles. Heat the oil in a sauté pan over high heat until shimmering. Add the garlic and cook until it is fragrant but not brown. Add the zucchini and red pepper and sauté by shaking the pan until the squash begins to soften, 5–7 minutes. Add the lemon peel and lemon juice. Cook for 1 minute more. Season with salt and pepper and serve immediately.

TOMATILLO SALSA VERDE

BY BARBARA WRIGHT/FAIRSHARE CSA COALITION

Salsa verde can be found in nearly every taqueria in Mexico City, and lately in a lot of places in the United States as well. Roasting the tomatillos give this salsa a complex fresh, rich, and smoky flavor. In the summer, try grilling the tomatillos.

YIELDS 3 CUPS // VEGAN // CONDIMENT

INGREDIENTS

1½ pounds tomatillos, husked

½ cup chopped white onion

½ cup fresh cilantro leaves

1 tablespoon fresh lime juice

¼ teaspoon sugar

2 jalapeño or serrano peppers (or more for a hotter salsa), seeded and chopped

Salt to taste

PROCESS

Cook the tomatillos following one of two methods:

Roasting method: Cut the tomatillos in half and place them cut side down on an aluminum foil-lined baking sheet. Place the sheet under a broiler for 5–7 minutes to lightly blacken the skin.

Boiling method: Place the tomatillos in a pot and cover with water. Bring to a boil and simmer for 5 minutes. Remove the tomatillos with a slotted spoon.

Place the tomatillos, onion, cilantro, lime juice, sugar, and peppers in a food processor or blender and pulse until all ingredients are finely chopped and mixed. Season with salt. Chill for at least 1 hour.

TRIPLE T CHILI (TOMATILLO)

BY PATRICIA MULVEY AND LAURA GILLIAM OF LOCAL THYME

The three Ts in this chili are Turkey, Tomatillo, and Tomato. If we could suggest a fourth T, it would be Tasty!

SERVES 6 // POULTRY // MAIN DISH

INGREDIENTS

2 tablespoons olive oil

1 cup chopped red onion

1 green bell pepper, seeded and chopped

Dash salt

6 cloves garlic, minced

1 pound ground turkey

3 tablespoons chili powder

1 teaspoon ground coriander

1 teaspoon ground cumin

2 bay leaves

¾ pound tomatillos, husked and quartered

1 pint cherry tomatoes, halved

1 (28-ounce) can cannellini beans

1 tablespoon cider vinegar

2 cups chicken broth

½ pound zucchini or pattypan squash, chopped

4 green onions, sliced

2 tablespoons chopped fresh cilantro

Salt and ground black pepper to taste

PROCESS

Heat a large, sturdy stockpot over medium-high heat. Add the oil and heat until shimmering. Add the onion, pepper, and salt. Stir until the liquid is released from the vegetables and evaporates, about 8 minutes. Add the garlic and sauté for 30 seconds. Add the turkey and cook, breaking it up with a spoon, until it is no longer pink. Sprinkle in the spices, add the bay leaves, and stir well. Add the tomatillos, tomatoes, beans, vinegar, and broth. Bring to a boil, reduce the heat, and simmer for 15–20 minutes, skimming off any foam that rises to the surface. Stir in the zucchini, green onions, and cilantro, and simmer until the zucchini is tender, about 8 minutes. Season with salt and pepper and serve.

VEGETARIAN POZOLE (TOMATILLO)
BY SHELLY FLORES

Pozole, or posole, is a Mexican soup traditionally served with pork or chicken. In this delicious vegetarian version, chewy, fluffy hominy is the star. Shelly dry-roasts her tomatillos in a cast-iron skillet to reduce the tartness of the soup; they can also be coated in olive oil and roasted in the oven.

SERVES 4-6 // VEGETARIAN // SIDE DISH

INGREDIENTS

1 large sweet onion, finely diced

4 cloves garlic (or more), minced

4–6 cups vegetable broth, divided

1 tablespoon dried oregano, crumbled to release flavor

½–1 teaspoon crushed red pepper

6 tomatillos (roasted if desired), finely chopped in a food processor

1–2 plum tomatoes, diced (optional)

2 (15-ounce) cans hominy

Salt to taste

1 teaspoon sugar (optional)

Toasted and salted pumpkin seeds

Crumbled feta

Finely shredded cabbage

Hominy is dried corn that has been soaked in an alkaline solution to improve its flavor, increase its nutritional value, and make it easier to grind. Canned hominy can be found in the canned bean or Mexican section of the grocery store.

PROCESS

Sauté the onion and garlic in ½ cup of the broth for 5 minutes. Add the oregano and pepper and sauté for about 2–3 minutes more. Add the tomatillos, tomatoes (if desired), 4–5 cups of broth, and the hominy. Simmer for 20 minutes. Add more broth if necessary to achieve the desired consistency. Taste and add salt as needed. Add the sugar if the soup is too tart. Serve topped with pumpkin seeds, feta, and shredded cabbage.

CHILLED CHERRY TOMATO SOUP TOPPED WITH AVOCADO, CUCUMBER, AND BASIL OIL

BY JAMIE BAKER OF PRIMROSE VALLEY FARM

Fresh tomatoes are perfect for a chilled tomato soup. Sungold tomatoes will make this no-cook summer delight extra delicious.

SERVES 4-6 // VEGAN // SIDE DISH

INGREDIENTS

SOUP:

18 ounces cherry tomatoes, cut in half
(about 2½ cups; for the best flavor, use two varieties)

¼ red onion, chopped

1 tablespoon balsamic vinegar

1 teaspoon minced garlic

2 cups tomato juice

Coarse salt and ground black pepper to taste

GARNISHES:

3 tablespoons chopped fresh basil

¼ cup extra-virgin olive oil

1 avocado, peeled and diced

½ cucumber, peeled, seeded, and diced

PROCESS

SOUP: Place the tomatoes in the bowl of a food processor and process until chopped. Add the onion, vinegar, garlic, and tomato juice and whirl briefly to blend. Season with salt and pepper. Chill for 30 minutes before serving.

GARNISHES: Whirl the basil and olive oil in a blender or food processor until smooth (the basil should be finely chopped, creating small green flecks throughout the oil); set aside. In a small bowl, combine the avocado and cucumber and set aside.

TO ASSEMBLE: Pour the soup into mugs. Drizzle a little basil oil over the soup just before serving and then top with the avocado-cucumber mixture.

FARMERS' MARKET OVERSTUFFED LASAGNA (TOMATO)

BY ANDREA H. NELSON, COURTESY OF REAP

A traditional lasagna brimming with fresh veggies!

SERVES 6-8 // MEAT // MAIN DISH

INGREDIENTS

SAUCE:

3 tablespoons olive oil

2–3 cloves garlic

1 large onion, finely chopped

1½–2 pounds tomatoes, crushed

1 tablespoon dried basil (or more to taste)

1 teaspoon dried oregano (or more to taste)

Salt and ground black pepper to taste

½ teaspoon crushed red pepper (optional)

Flour or cornstarch (optional)

FILLING:

1 pound ground beef

1 egg

12 ounces ricotta

1 pound garlic herb lasagna noodles, cooked al dente

1 pound spinach, chopped

12 ounces mozzarella, grated

½ cup grated Parmesan

4 tablespoons butter (optional)

PROCESS

SAUCE: In a large sauté pan with a fitted lid, swirl the olive oil to lightly coat the bottom. Add the garlic and onion and sauté over medium-high heat until the onion is translucent, about 5 minutes. Add the crushed tomatoes and reduce the heat. Add the basil, oregano, salt, pepper, and crushed red pepper (if desired). Cover and simmer, stirring occasionally, until the flavors are well blended. If the sauce seems runny, add some flour or cornstarch to thicken it.

FILLING: Preheat an oven to 375°. Brown and drain the ground beef; set aside. In a small bowl, beat the egg into the ricotta and set aside.

TO ASSEMBLE: In a 13 × 9-inch baking dish, spread a little of the sauce to cover the bottom. Lay down a layer of lasagna noodles. Spread about a third of the sauce on top of the noodles. Cover the sauce with a third of the beef, then a third of the spinach and a third of the ricotta mixture. Repeat these layers two more times, reserving some of the sauce for the top. Add a fourth layer of noodles and cover with the remaining sauce. Sprinkle with mozzarella and Parmesan and dot with butter (if desired).

Bake the lasagna for 45 minutes, or until bubbly. Remove from the oven and let stand for 15 minutes before serving.

GUATEMALAN CHILAQUILES (TOMATO)

BY KARA SPARKS, COURTESY OF REAP

Not to be confused with Mexican chilaquiles (a layered casserole dish), Guatemalan chilaquiles are cheese-stuffed, egg-battered, golden-crisp tortilla pockets served with a spicy tomato sauce. The chilaquiles are quite mild on their own, and you can add as much or as little sauce as you like. They are delicious served with rice and black beans.

SERVES 4 // VEGETARIAN // MAIN DISH

INGREDIENTS

SPICY TOMATO SAUCE:

2 large tomatoes

1 small serrano pepper

½ teaspoon ground cumin

½ medium white onion

CHILAQUILES:

6 large eggs

2 tablespoons vegetable oil, divided

½ cup cheese curds, sliced

1 large red bell pepper, thinly sliced

8 flour tortillas

PROCESS

Make the spicy tomato sauce by roughly chopping all ingredients and pureeing them in a blender or food processor until completely liquefied. Set aside.

Beat the eggs in a medium bowl. Heat 1 tablespoon of the oil in a skillet over medium heat. Put one eighth of the cheese and red pepper in the middle of each tortilla. Fold in the sides and roll the tortillas into tight cylinders (they should look like egg rolls). Using tongs, dip the rolled tortillas in the egg, coating the entire outside thoroughly and being careful not to let them open. Fry the coated tortillas in the hot oil, turning occasionally to brown them on all sides. When thoroughly browned, set aside on paper towels to drain. Repeat until all the chilaquiles are cooked, adding additional oil to the pan as needed. Serve topped with the spicy tomato sauce.

SLOW-ROASTED TOMATOES

BY SHERRY MINKUS

Oven-roasting tomatoes concentrates their sugars and is good for both preserving bumper crops and enhancing the flavor of those that are not at their peak. In fact, this recipe can even save a batch that's been refrigerated. Use roasted tomatoes in salads, pizzas, pastas, and any other recipe in place of fresh or sun-dried tomatoes.

YIELDS ABOUT 4 CUPS // VEGAN // CONDIMENT

INGREDIENTS

Olive oil or nonstick spray

Fresh Roma tomatoes (about 15 to fill a single baking sheet), halved

PROCESS

Preheat an oven to 250°. Lightly coat a baking sheet with olive oil or with nonstick spray. Arrange the tomato halves on the prepared sheet, cut side up. Bake for about 1 hour, until the tomatoes are roasted and the edges are crisp and dry. Remove from the oven and let cool. Freeze the roasted tomatoes in a single layer on the baking sheet. When they are frozen, remove them to freezer bags and seal. To serve, chop and add to prepared pasta sauce, put on homemade pizza, etc.

HEIRLOOM SPICED TOMATO PRESERVES

BY EMILY TAYLOR LAZAR

One of the highlights of Emily's childhood was her grandmother's summer garden bursting with tomatoes. To this day, she thinks of those summer afternoons with her smiling grandmother whenever she bites into a ripe tomato. These preserves capture the fruit's vibrant flavor as well as its versatility. With sugar and spices, your friends and family might not be able to guess the star ingredient. Serve atop biscuits, bread, or waffles. Or spread onto a peanut butter sandwich or grilled cheese for a new twist on an old favorite.

YIELDS 5-6 CUPS // VEGAN // CONDIMENT

INGREDIENTS

3 pounds ripe tomatoes (to yield 3½ cups crushed)

1 package fruit pectin

4¼ cups sugar, divided

1½ teaspoons grated lemon peel

¼ cup fresh lemon juice

¼ teaspoon ground cloves

½ teaspoon ground cinnamon

½ teaspoon ground allspice

PROCESS

Scald the tomatoes by dropping them, in small batches, into a large pot of boiling water for about 15 seconds per batch, followed by plunging them immediately into cold water. Once they have cooled, peel the tomatoes. Crush the peeled tomatoes in a large mixing bowl.

Mix the pectin with 2¼ cups of the sugar. Transfer the crushed tomatoes to a pot and bring to a simmer over medium heat. Stir in the pectin-sugar mixture and continue to simmer, uncovered, for 10 minutes. Add the lemon peel, lemon juice, remaining sugar, and spices to the cooked tomatoes and mix well. Bring to a full boil, stirring constantly, and allow to boil for at least 1 minute. Remove from the heat, let cool for a few minutes, and skim off any foam. Can the preserves in appropriately sanitized canning jars using the instructions provided by the pectin packaging. Store for up to one year and refrigerate after opening.

> Foam will appear on the surface of the preserves as they thicken, and if left in place it could compromise the luxurious texture. Most cooks either skim it off with a ladle, or prevent it from forming in the first place by adding a teaspoon of butter or oil along with the pectin.

HOT HERBED TOMATO CHEESE BROIL

BY FRIEDA SCHOWALTER BARKEI, COURTESY OF REAP

Cheddar and tomato are natural companions, but these open-face sandwiches can be canvases for creating your own melted masterpiece. You can add or subtract ingredients as you wish, or start over with your own fresh ideas.

SERVES 4 // VEGETARIAN // MAIN DISH

INGREDIENTS

4 slices white, whole-wheat, or rye bread

4 tablespoons mayonnaise, butter, or margarine

1 tablespoon hot pepper sauce

2–3 medium red or yellow tomatoes, cut into ¼-inch slices

Salt and ground black pepper to taste

6 tablespoons chopped fresh mixed herbs (parsley, chives, basil), divided

2 ounces mild or sharp white Cheddar, thinly sliced

PROCESS

Toast the bread until medium brown. Spread with mayonnaise and dot sparingly with hot pepper sauce. Cover the slices of toast with tomato slices and season gently with salt and pepper. Liberally sprinkle the chopped herbs over the tomatoes (about 1 tablespoon per sandwich). Place the cheese on top and add the remaining herbs over the cheese. Place the sandwiches on a baking sheet or aluminum foil and broil until the cheese melts and starts to bubble. Serve with soup or salad, or cut each one diagonally into 4 pieces for an appetizer.

RAW SUMMER VEGETABLE TOMATO SAUCE
BY DANIEL FOX OF THE MADISON CLUB

Versatile and colorful, this puree makes an excellent bruschetta topping, omelet filling, or pasta sauce. Keep the texture coarse and use it to top pizzas, or make a fine puree and serve as a dip with grilled bread slices. It even makes an excellent soup shooter for summer brunches: just serve it chilled in a shot glass with a small dollop of crème fraîche or Greek-style yogurt.

YIELDS 4 CUPS // VEGAN // CONDIMENT

INGREDIENTS

2 large heirloom tomatoes, cored

1 small to medium yellow or red bell pepper, seeded

4 green onions, roughly chopped

1 medium to large cucumber, roughly chopped

15 pitted Kalamata or mixed country olives

3 cloves garlic, finely minced

10 large fresh basil leaves (lemon, opal, Hawaiian)

Pinch sugar

Splash sherry vinegar or red wine vinegar

10 seedless grapes (green, red, Concord)

1 small chile pepper (serrano, jalapeño, Anaheim)

¼ cup extra-virgin olive oil

1 small zucchini, diced

Salt and ground black pepper to taste

PROCESS

Combine the tomatoes, bell pepper, green onions, cucumber, olives, garlic, basil, sugar, vinegar, grapes, and chile pepper in a blender and pulse to chop. The sauce's consistency is entirely up to you. For a finer sauce, pour the olive oil very slowly into the blender while it is running. For a coarser sauce, place the vegetable mixture in a bowl and pour the olive oil over it very slowly while constantly whisking by hand. Continue mixing until the oil is entirely incorporated. Remove the sauce from the blender and fold in the diced zucchini; season to taste with salt and pepper. (Depending on the ripeness and acidity of the tomatoes, you can adjust the seasoning of the sauce with different ratios of sugar, salt, black pepper, and vinegar.)

WISCONSIN CANICULE SALAD (TOMATO)
BY MARK VOSS, COURTESY OF REAP

Mark learned the word "canicule" (heat wave) while traveling in France one summer. He used it to describe this impromptu salad because it's perfect peak-of-summer picnic fare. Assemble the salad a couple of hours before you plan to serve it to allow sufficient chilling time.

SERVES 6-8 // FISH/SEAFOOD // MAIN DISH

INGREDIENTS

9 cups water, divided

Salt for cooking water

1 cup wild rice

3 cups quinoa

3 mild yellow shallots, finely chopped

½ cup plus 3 tablespoons extra-virgin olive oil, divided

1 yellow bell pepper, chopped

1 red bell pepper, chopped

1 large Walla Walla sweet onion, chopped

1 large Cherokee Purple or other heirloom tomato, or 6 cherry tomatoes, chopped or halved as appropriate

1½ cups chopped hickory nuts

½ cup sliced fresh basil leaves

½ cup chopped fresh flat-leaf parsley

Juice from 1 lemon

Salt and freshly ground black pepper to taste

4 smoked trout fillets, skinned, boned, and flaked

PROCESS

Bring 3 cups of salted water to a boil and add the wild rice. Reduce the heat, cover, and simmer for 1 hour, or until tender. In a second pot, bring 6 cups of salted water to a boil and add the quinoa. Reduce the heat, cover, and simmer for 10 minutes, or until tender.

Meanwhile, in a small skillet over medium heat, sweat the shallots in 3 tablespoons of the olive oil until translucent. In a large bowl, combine the peppers, onion, tomato, nuts, basil, parsley, lemon juice, salt, pepper, and the remaining olive oil with the flaked trout. When the grains are cooked, add the wild rice to the quinoa, then add the shallots and the vegetable-nut mixture and gently combine. Allow the mixture to sit for 15 minutes for the flavors to combine. Chill for 1–2 hours before serving.

MEXICAN-STYLE WINTER SQUASH
BY SUNSHINE BUCHHOLZ

Flavorful and amazingly easy, this recipe is a great use for corn (frozen from the summer's harvest) and home-canned salsa. Any sweet winter squash can be substituted for butternut. This recipe makes an excellent dip for chips, filling for enchiladas or quesadillas, or side dish.

SERVES 4 // VEGAN // SIDE DISH

INGREDIENTS

1 medium butternut squash (about 1 pound)

2 tablespoons extra-virgin olive oil

3–5 green onions (both white and green parts), cut into ¼-inch pieces

1 (15-ounce) can black beans, drained and rinsed

Kernels from 1–2 ears of corn (about 2 cups)

1 jar salsa

PROCESS

Pierce the squash with a fork and microwave on high power for 5 minutes. Let stand for 5 minutes. Cook for another 3–5 minutes, or until soft. Remove the squash from the microwave and let cool. Cut open the squash, remove the seeds, and scoop out the flesh. If a very smooth texture is desired, puree in a blender or with a hand mixer. Set aside.

In a deep pot, heat the olive oil over medium heat. Add the onions and cook 2–3 minutes, or until soft. Add the black beans, corn, and salsa and heat, stirring occasionally, for about 5 minutes. Add the squash and gently stir until all ingredients are mixed. Heat until warmed through. The recipe can be modified by adding additional vegetables or diced cooked chicken.

GINGER CRANBERRY STUFFED WINTER SQUASH

BY APRIL YUDS OF LOTFOTL FARM

April's husband never thought he liked squash until he tried this stuffed preparation. The ginger adds a zingy flavor that complements the sweet acorn squash and sweet-tart cranberries.

SERVES 2 // VEGETARIAN // SIDE DISH

INGREDIENTS

1 acorn squash

2 tablespoons butter, melted

2 tablespoons brown sugar

2 tablespoons sunflower seeds

2 tablespoons minced fresh ginger

2–4 tablespoons dried cranberries

2 (¼-inch) slices yellow onion

Salt and ground black pepper to taste

PROCESS

Preheat an oven to 375°. Cut the squash in half; scoop out and discard the seeds. Divide each ingredient equally between the two halves in the following order: drizzle the butter inside each squash half, then sprinkle in the brown sugar, sunflower seeds, ginger, and cranberries. Top each half with a slice of onion and season with salt and pepper to taste. Cover the squash with aluminum foil, set on a baking sheet to catch any drips, and bake until the squash is tender, 45–60 minutes.

CONFETTI WINTER SQUASH SOUP

BY CARA JENKINS

Deliciously rich and not too sweet, this creamy soup is a showcase for winter squash. Try it at the end of summer, when bell peppers are abundant and winter squash is starting to come in, or in midwinter with bounty frozen from the previous summer. If using frozen peppers or squash, just add them with the broth, as they will already be soft.

SERVES 6-8 // VEGETARIAN // SIDE DISH

INGREDIENTS

2 delicata or other winter squash

2 tablespoons olive oil, plus more for roasting the squash

2 medium to large leeks, finely chopped

½ cup diced celery

1–2 red bell peppers, diced

3–4 cups chicken or vegetable broth

Juice from ½ lemon

½ cup half-and-half

Salt and ground black pepper to taste

PROCESS

Preheat an oven to 400°. Halve and seed the squash. Place the halves cut side up in a 13 × 9-inch baking dish and fill the dish with ¼ inch of water. Drizzle the squash with olive oil, cover, and bake until soft, 30–40 minutes. When it's cool enough to handle, scoop out the flesh and set aside.

In a stockpot, heat 2 tablespoons of olive oil over medium heat and sauté the leeks until they begin to soften, 5–7 minutes. Add the celery and peppers and cook until soft, another 5 minutes. Add the broth and squash flesh and simmer for about 10 minutes. Add the lemon juice and coarsely puree the soup with an immersion blender. Stir in the half-and-half and adjust the consistency with more broth or half-and-half if necessary. Season with salt and pepper.

DECADENT WINTER SQUASH PASTA

BY KRISTJÁN BURMEISTER

This hearty pasta dish features the sweetness of winter squash, carrots, and onions, with fresh notes from preserved summer tomatoes and basil pesto. Most winter squash can be substituted for butternut in this recipe; if using a variety that is too hard to peel and dice, precook the squash and add the flesh with the tomatoes.

SERVES 3–4 // MEAT // MAIN DISH

INGREDIENTS

½ pound Italian sausage, chopped or crumbled

1 tablespoon olive oil

½ large butternut squash, peeled and diced

4 medium carrots, diced

1 teaspoon dried herbs of choice

Salt and ground black pepper to taste

1 medium onion, diced

3 cloves garlic, minced

½–1 cup white wine

6–8 cups peeled and quartered frozen tomatoes, thawed (canned are OK, but use less)

Smoked paprika to taste

1 pound penne or other tube-shaped pasta

3 tablespoons basil pesto

Fontina or goat cheese

PROCESS

In a large skillet with a fitted lid, cook the sausage over medium heat until browned, 5–8 minutes. Remove the sausage from the skillet and set aside on paper towels to drain. Add the olive oil to the skillet; add the squash and carrots with the herbs, salt, and pepper. Cover and cook until the vegetables begin to soften, about 5 minutes. Add the onion, and when it's translucent (about 5 minutes), add the garlic and cook for 1 minute, until fragrant. Add the wine, reserved sausage, tomatoes, and smoked paprika. Simmer, covered, for 10–15 minutes. The squash and carrots should still be somewhat firm at the end of the cooking process.

Meanwhile, cook the pasta according to the package directions. Drain the pasta and stir in the pesto. Serve topped with the vegetable sauce and a sprinkling of shaved fontina or a dollop of goat cheese.

SUMMER AND WINTER SQUASH "ENCHILADAS"
BY ALYSSA HENRY

Although it may seem unlikely that summer and winter squash could coexist in the same season, they do. This is because winter squash is named for its longevity in storage rather than its growing season. This recipe makes good use of late-summer squash bumper crops and makes a delicious main course. Serve with Spanish-style rice, beans, and margaritas.

SERVES 6–8 // VEGETARIAN // MAIN DISH

INGREDIENTS

2 tablespoons olive oil

1 large onion, diced

2 medium bell peppers (any color), seeded and diced

2 cloves garlic, minced

1½ tablespoons chili powder

1 tablespoon ground cumin

1 medium butternut squash, peeled, seeded, and finely diced

1 teaspoon garlic salt

4 medium summer squash (yellow crookneck, zucchini, and/or pattypan), diced

Dash crushed red pepper

1 (4-ounce) can mild diced green chiles (or use fresh)

3–4 tablespoons chopped fresh cilantro

12 (8-inch) flour tortillas

1 pound pepper jack cheese, shredded

Sour cream and pico de gallo

PROCESS

Preheat an oven to 350°. Heat the olive oil in a large skillet over medium-high heat. When the oil runs like water, add the onion, bell peppers, garlic, chili powder, and cumin to the skillet. Sauté for 2 minutes, until the vegetables start to soften. Add the butternut squash and garlic salt. Continue sautéing, stirring frequently, for another 5 minutes, until the squash begins to soften. Add the summer squash, crushed red pepper, and chiles and continue cooking until a brown crust begins to develop on the bottom of the skillet. Cover the skillet and reduce the heat slightly. Cook, stirring occasionally, until the vegetables are soft and the flavors melded, 10–15 minutes, then remove the lid and allow any remaining liquid to simmer off (about 5 minutes). When the mixture is dry, remove from the heat and stir in the cilantro. (The squash filling can be made a day ahead and stored in the refrigerator until ready to fill the tortillas.)

Fill each tortilla with about ⅓ cup of the squash mixture and roll up, leaving the ends open. Place the filled tortillas seam side down on a rimmed baking sheet (you may need two sheets). Sprinkle the enchiladas generously with the cheese. Bake until the cheese is bubbly and golden, 10–15 minutes. Serve topped with sour cream and salsa or pico de gallo.

SPAGHETTI SQUASH WITH RED PEPPER CREAM (WINTER SQUASH)

BY BARBARA WRIGHT/FAIRSHARE CSA COALITION

Named for its long, thin strands of noodlelike flesh, spaghetti squash is a good alternative to pasta, potatoes, or rice. Plus, it's easy to prepare and tastes great with just a drizzle of olive oil, salt, and pepper. This creamy red pepper sauce highlights the sweetness of the squash.

SERVES 6–8 // VEGETARIAN // SIDE DISH

INGREDIENTS

SQUASH:

1 large spaghetti squash

1 tablespoon olive oil

Salt and ground black pepper to taste

RED PEPPER CREAM:

2 large red bell peppers, seeded and halved

3 tablespoons extra-virgin olive oil, plus more for roasting the peppers

2 tablespoons minced garlic

¼ cup chopped fresh basil

2 cups half-and-half

¼ cup grated Pecorino Romano

4 tablespoons butter

Salt and ground black pepper to taste

PROCESS

SQUASH: Preheat an oven to 400°. Cut the squash in half lengthwise and scoop out the seeds. Place the squash halves in a baking dish, cut side up; drizzle with olive oil and sprinkle with salt and pepper. Cover and bake until the skin is easily pierced with a fork, 30–40 minutes. Let cool, then remove the strands of flesh with a fork.

RED PEPPER CREAM: Preheat a broiler. Place the bell pepper halves cut side down on an aluminum foil-lined baking sheet and lightly coat them with olive oil. Grill under the broiler until the skin is blackened and the flesh has softened slightly, about 8 minutes. Place the peppers in a paper bag, a resealable plastic bag, or a ceramic bowl covered with a plate to cool for about 45 minutes (this process will help loosen the skin). Remove the skin from the peppers and cut the peppers into small pieces.

In a skillet, cook and stir the garlic, basil, and peppers in the olive oil over medium heat for 10 minutes. Place the mixture in a blender and puree to the desired consistency. Return the puree to the skillet and reheat to a boil. Reduce the heat and stir in the half-and-half and cheese; simmer, stirring, until the cheese melts. Add the butter and stir until melted. Season with salt and pepper. Simmer for a few minutes more. Serve ladled over the spaghetti squash.

SWEET CURRY WINTER SQUASH FRITTERS
BY LEEANN ZIEGLER

These fritters are excellent party snacks. Serve with Greek-style yogurt or raita to balance the heat if you've used a healthy dose of cayenne. They are also delicious with homemade pickles and chutneys (try "Aunt Carol's Refrigerator Pickles" on page 96 or the tomato chutneys on pages 37 and 70). LeeAnn notes that they freeze well and can be reheated in a toaster oven.

SERVES 4-6 // VEGETARIAN // APPETIZER

INGREDIENTS

1 small winter squash (any variety)

2–3 tablespoons olive oil

1 egg, beaten

1 medium yellow onion, minced

6 tablespoons all-purpose flour

5 tablespoons cornmeal

½ teaspoon baking powder

½ teaspoon curry powder

¼ teaspoon paprika (or more to taste)

⅛ teaspoon cayenne (optional)

½ teaspoon kosher salt

Freshly ground black pepper to taste

Vegetable oil for frying

PROCESS

Preheat an oven to 350°. Slice the squash lengthwise into halves and place cut side down in a roasting pan. Fill the pan with about ¼ inch of water, cover with aluminum foil, and roast for 30–60 minutes. Halfway through the roasting time, remove the foil, turn the squash cut side up, and drizzle with olive oil. Roast until the flesh is completely tender and soft. Scrape the squash flesh into a bowl and let it cool (you should have about 1 cup of cooked squash). Mix the egg into the squash and add the onion.

In another bowl, combine all the dry ingredients and seasonings (flour through pepper) and mix well. Adjust the seasonings until the dry mix smells the way you'd like it to taste, or a little more intense. Mix the dry ingredients into the squash mixture and stir until everything is well incorporated.

Cover the bottom of a wok or cast-iron skillet with about ½ inch of vegetable oil and heat over medium heat. Drop heaping teaspoonfuls of the squash mixture into the oil and fry for 1–2 minutes. Flip the fritters after they turn golden brown around the edges, then remove after about 1 minute more; place them on a cooling rack set inside a rimmed baking sheet lined with paper towels to drain. Add more oil to the pan as needed, allowing the oil to come up to temperature before adding more squash mixture.

THREE SISTERS WINTER SQUASH ENCHILADAS
BY CARA JENKINS

To Native Americans, the Three Sisters are corn, climbing beans, and squash, planted together in a technique called companion planting. The corn plant provides a structure for the bean vines to climb, the bean plant adds needed nitrogen to the soil, and the low-growing squash vines act as natural mulch, retaining moisture in the soil and blocking weeds and pests. Additionally, corn and beans together form a balanced diet. Cara was inspired to develop this recipe by a friend who plants a Three Sisters garden every year. Feel free to adapt this recipe to what your garden (or farmer) grows; you can use nearly any type of winter or summer squash, precooked fresh or dried beans instead of canned (about 2 cups), and fresh tomatoes and chiles in the summertime. Garnish with sour cream and chopped cilantro, if desired.

SERVES 6-8 // VEGETARIAN // MAIN DISH

INGREDIENTS

½ cup butter

4 cloves garlic, minced, divided

½ cup all-purpose flour

¼ cup chili powder

2 cups tomato sauce

2 cups beef or vegetable broth

2 tablespoons olive oil

½ teaspoon ground cumin

¼–½ teaspoon dried oregano

4 cups butternut squash, diced into ½-inch cubes

1 (15-ounce) can diced tomatoes

1 (4-ounce) can diced green chiles

1 (15-ounce) can black beans, drained and rinsed

½–1 cup fresh or frozen corn kernels

4 ounces cream cheese

Salt and ground black pepper to taste

10–12 (6-inch) flour tortillas

2 cups shredded Cheddar or Monterey Jack cheese

PROCESS

ENCHILADA SAUCE: Melt the butter in a saucepan over medium heat, add half of the minced garlic, and cook until fragrant, about 30 seconds. Add the flour and chili powder, whisking to combine well. Cook for 2–3 minutes, stirring constantly, then whisk in the tomato sauce and broth. Cook until thickened and bubbly, 3–4 minutes. Simmer over low heat while preparing the filling for the enchiladas.

FILLING: Heat the olive oil in a large skillet over medium heat. Add the remaining minced garlic and cook until fragrant, about 30 seconds. Add the cumin and oregano and cook for an additional 30 seconds. Add the squash and cook, stirring frequently, until it is almost soft, 10–15 minutes. Add the tomatoes, chiles, beans, and corn and cook until the squash is completely soft, about 5 minutes more. Reduce the heat and add the cream cheese, stirring until everything is well combined. Season with salt and pepper.

TO ASSEMBLE: Preheat an oven to 350° and lightly grease a 13 × 9-inch baking dish. Place about ⅓ cup of filling in the center of each tortilla, roll up the tortillas, and place them seam side down in the prepared dish. Cover with the enchilada sauce, sprinkle with cheese, and bake for 20 minutes, or until the cheese is melted and the sauce is bubbly.

MOTHER NATURE'S CANDY

SWEET FRUITS

From Apples to Watermelon

Brightly colored, meltingly soft or refreshingly crisp, and perfectly sweet-tart, fruits are delicious by design. Most vegetables are best when they are young, but fruit is most appealing when it reaches maturity. This is no coincidence; fruit at the peak of ripeness has seeds that are fully developed and ready for dispersal. Seed dissemination often depends on a little help from animal friends, and plants recruit animal labor with ripe fruit's enticing qualities: alluring scents and sweetness make it tempting to eat, and vivid colors ensure that it's easy to find amid dense green foliage.

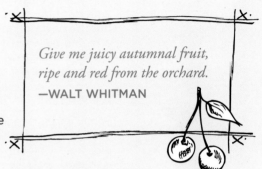

> *Give me juicy autumnal fruit, ripe and red from the orchard.*
> —WALT WHITMAN

Fruit tastes better when it's allowed to mature on the parent plant, even if it will ripen further after picking. Think of the flavor of a fragile, fragrant peach allowed to reach its juicy potential on the tree, and compare it to that of a hard, imported specimen. Immature fruits, while better able to withstand the rigors of packing and shipping, have not fully converted their starches to sugars. Additionally, they may have compounds that make them tart, tannic, or astringent—qualities in nature that render them unappealing to would-be eaters while in the early stages of their life cycle.

Selection.   For apples, pears, and quinces, pick firm fruits with no bruising or browning. Check berries for mold, soft spots, or discoloration. Choose firm cherries and grapes with upright stems, and ask for a sample to check quality, as they will not ripen any further. Melons should be heavy for their size, without any cracks in their skins. They will be fragrant when ripe, and the stem end will give to slight pressure. Peaches, plums, nectarines, and apricots should be ripe at the time of purchase, yielding slightly when gently squeezed. Check the stem ends of these fruits and avoid any with still-green skin.

Storage.   Fragile fruits, like berries, will keep for as little as a few days, while hearty fruits, like apples, may keep for as long as a few months. Do not wash fruits until just before using. Ideally, berries should be stored in a single layer on a paper towel. Melons can be kept at room temperature or refrigerated until ready to use. To maximize storage life after ripening, refrigerate fruit in the coldest part of the refrigerator.

> Apples and pears may turn brown after slicing. To slow this process, dip slices in water with some lemon juice added.

Preparation.   Some fruits will ripen faster if placed in a loosely closed paper bag (never plastic) with another piece of ripe fruit. Check the storage guide below to see which fruits are good candidates for paper-bag ripening. These fruits will also ripen on their own at room temperature, it will just take a little longer.

All melons should be thoroughly washed before slicing to prevent dragging bacteria from the surface down into the flesh.

APPLE

There are several thousand named apple varieties, which fall into roughly four groups: cider, eating, cooking, and dual-purpose (for both eating and cooking). Most of the apples available commercially and in farmers' markets are eating apples, like Fuji, and dual-purpose apples, like Granny Smith. These varieties have fairly consistent flavor profiles, but the flavor of an individual apple can be affected by when it was harvested or even where it was growing on the tree. Be sure to try samples offered at the farmers' market to choose your favorite on a given day.

To determine whether an apple is suitable for baking, wrap a few slices in aluminum foil and bake for fifteen minutes, or microwave on high power in a covered container for two to three minutes. A good baking apple should keep its shape as well as taste good after cooking.

APRICOT

Filmishmish, meaning "in apricot season," is a common Arabic expression, usually uttered to convey an unlikely occurrence (similar in spirit to "when pigs fly"). One encounters apricot season more often than flying pigs, but it is indeed short, so nab the ripe stone fruits while you can. When fully ripe, they are soft and quite delicate. Hard apricots will soften if stored in a paper bag, but they will not develop more flavor. Avoid purchasing fruits tinged with green, as they will never ripen. Apricots are rich in pectin, which makes them a popular choice for jam and gives them a satisfying texture when dried.

BERRY

Blackberry. There are hundreds of species of blackberries native to the Americas. Wild or cultivated, they taste best when the color becomes dull and very dark. Frozen blackberries sometimes turn red, but this cosmetic change does not affect quality.

To freeze berries, place them on a paper-towel-lined baking sheet in a single layer with space between the fruits. When they have frozen solid, move them to an airtight container. Except for cranberries, frozen berries become mushy when thawed, so use them for smoothies, purees, and cooked dishes.

Blueberry. Although they are popular today, blueberries have been cultivated only since the 1920s. Before then, they were gathered from the wild plants that thrive in the wooded and mountainous regions of North America. Choose blueberries that are still covered in their characteristic bloom—a dusty, whitish substance that protects the berry against sun damage.

Cranberry. Because cranberries are very high in acid, they both store well and taste seriously tart. Some cooks stock up at Thanksgiving and find that their refrigerated cranberries are still good at Christmas; they also freeze well and remain firm after thawing. Cranberries contain a high level of pectin, so they thicken easily into sauce when cooked.

Currant. These small red, black, or white berries grow in grapelike clusters, but on bushes rather than vines. They are very tart, with black currants having the most intense flavor, and white the mildest. The "currant" most familiar to American consumers is the dried Zante currant, but its name is misleading: it is technically a type of raisin made from an unrelated species—the Black Corinth grape (see "Grape: Champagne" on the facing page). True currants are mainly made into preserves.

Elderberry.   Purple-black elderberries are best when cooked, and they are usually made into jam, syrup, wine, candy, tea, sauce, or pastries. Their white flowers are edible as well, whether made into syrups, added to pancake batters, fried as fritters, eaten raw, or brewed as tea. Both berries and flowers are consumed medicinally for their anti-inflammatory and immune-boosting properties. Do not consume red elderberries or elderberry leaves, as they are toxic.

Gooseberry.   Beautiful little gooseberries are round fruits about a half-inch in diameter, with translucent skin in shades of green, amber, pink, or purple. They pack a serious pucker and are mainly used in baked desserts and sauces.

Mulberry.   Mulberries resemble long, skinny blackberries. They are small and fragile and can be white, red, or black. Red varieties tend to be more tart, and black fruits more flavorful. The leaves of the white mulberry tree have long been used in China to feed silkworms.

Raspberry.   Although red varieties are by far the most common, raspberries can also be pale yellow or dark purple. Of the three, yellow berries have the mildest flavor, and purple the most intense; wild raspberries are more flavorful than any of their cultivated counterparts. Raspberries are related to blackberries, and boysenberries (which are mostly used for commercial jam) are a cross between the two. Raspberries are very fragile, so check packaged fruits carefully for mold.

Strawberry.   The "straw" in strawberry likely stems from the word *strew,* meaning "to spread," perhaps in reference to the runners the plant sends out as it grows. Look for strawberries with bright, fresh-looking green tops and light-colored seeds as indicators of freshness.

CHERRY

Like peaches and plums, cherries are stone fruits. There are two basic cultivated types: sweet and sour. Sour cherries are typically sweetened (although they don't have to be) and used in baked goods and jams or preserved through dehydration. If sweet cherries are not devoured before they can be cooked, they, too, can be used in baked goods, frozen treats, and jams. A cherry pitter is a tool that quickly removes seeds; it is not essential, but it makes short work of a tedious step in cooking with these fruits. Ideally, cherries should be ripe when purchased, so ask for a taste if possible.

GRAPE

Green, red, and black.   Table, seedless, or common grapes are grapes grown for eating rather than winemaking. Green grapes are sweet and low in acid, red grapes are crisp and sweet-tart, and black grapes are very juicy with moderate acidity. Be sure to ask for a sample to make sure grapes are ripe, as they will not ripen further after picking.

Champagne.   While their name evokes thoughts of winemaking, champagne grapes (also called Black Corinth grapes) are not used to make the sparkling beverage. Rather, they are most likely named for the tiny wine bubbles they resemble. They are diminutive, very sweet, seedless grapes that make an excellent edible garnish for champagne flutes and cheese boards. They are also good when dried and are commonly marketed as Zante currants (see "Berry: Currant" on the facing page).

Concord.   The flavor of Concord grapes will be familiar to any grape jelly or juice fan. They are deep purple, almost black, with a protective dusty bloom similar to that of blueberries (see above). They have a thick skin and a slippery, pulpy interior, and may be seedless or not.

Muscat.   Floral-scented muscat grapes range in color from white to black, and they can be eaten fresh, dried for raisins, or made into sparkling or dessert wines. They are deliciously sweet and juicy.

GROUND CHERRY

Also called cape gooseberries, or husk cherries, ground cherries are related to tomatoes and tomatillos. They are small, orange, sweet-tart berries enclosed in a lacy, papery husk (similar to that of tomatillos). The berries should be consumed when they are yellow-orange rather than pale yellow, and they can be eaten raw or baked into desserts. Because of their high pectin content, they make excellent jams. Try them in "Lemon Verbena Ground Cherry Compote" (page 129).

MELON

Cantaloupe.   Ripe cantaloupes have a flowery fragrance that is most apparent in farm-fresh fruits, since they have not been subjected to mold-inhibiting commercial sprays. Cantaloupes will soften and become juicier after picking, but their sugar content will not increase. Selecting a cantaloupe based on scent is thus a good way to ensure that it is optimally sweet.

Crenshaw.   Large crenshaw melons are completely yellow when ripe. They have dense orange flesh with a sweet, pleasantly spicy flavor. Green-skinned, unripe crenshaw melons are also useful in cooking, as they make excellent pickles.

> Want to choose the best melon? Look for a melon that is fragrant, heavy for its size, and free of soft spots and blemishes. The fruit should also have a smooth indentation where the stem was attached, as ripe melons detach naturally and easily from the vine.

Honeydew.   Honeydews have smooth rinds that change color from pale green to white to creamy yellow as they mature. Inside, honeydews can be pale green, pale gold, or even orange. When ripe, they are very sweet and soft.

Watermelon.   Although watermelons can weigh as much as sixty pounds, mini versions, from five to eight inches in diameter, are currently popular. These baby watermelons have a thicker rind and a longer shelf life than larger varieties. Yellow- and orange-fleshed varieties are grown in addition to the familiar red, and the flavor of all three is fairly consistent. A creamy yellow spot on the rind of a watermelon marks where the fruit touched the ground while growing; it is an indicator of ripeness at harvest.

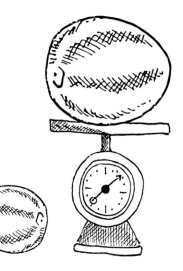

PEACH/NECTARINE

Peaches and their subspecies nectarines have similar flavor profiles, although nectarines have smooth skin and are a little firmer when ripe. Both are considered "freestone" if the flesh can be removed easily from the pit, and "cling" if not. The flesh is either white or orange. Peaches and nectarines ripen at the stem end first, so avoid any fruit with green near the stem, as it will remain unripe. They will soften and get juicier with the paper-bag ripening method, but their flavor and sugars will not develop further.

> A serrated peeler will make short work of peeling a peach. Alternatively, drop the fruit in boiling water for about a minute, and then cool it in ice water. The skin should slip right off (tomatoes can be peeled in the same way). Cut cling peaches in half and remove the pit before peeling.

PEAR

Common. The exception to the ripening rule, pears are best when picked unripe. When allowed to ripen on the tree, they become mushy. For that reason, pears should be purchased several days before you plan to serve them. They will ripen in a paper bag within a few days, or more slowly in an open container at room temperature. Petite Forelle and Seckel pears are good for snacking or poaching whole, and they are beautiful around a Thanksgiving turkey. Round Comice pears have a rich flavor and juicy texture that makes them delicious raw, especially with cheese. Red and green Bartletts and brown Boscs are good for both eating raw and cooking.

Asian. Also called apple pears, crunchy Asian pears are more similar in texture to an apple than a traditional pear when ripe. They are sweet, with a mild pear or melon flavor. There are more than twenty-five varieties of Asian pears. The Yali variety has a short and broad pear shape, while the rest are nearly spherical. All but Korean pears are best peeled. They are most often served raw, although they can be cooked. They will take longer to soften than traditional pears. Asian pear is often an ingredient in Korean barbecue marinades, as the fruit has enzymes that help tenderize the meat.

PLUM

Although dark purple plums with golden flesh are probably the most familiar, plums can be green, yellow, red, or purple with flesh in the same color range. Generally, plums are characterized by sweet, juicy flesh and tart skin. Dried, they are traditionally called prunes, although that name has fallen out of favor with marketers lately. If prunes are mysteriously missing from your market, look instead for dried plums, since they are the same thing.

PLUOT

As its name would indicate, a pluot is a cross between a plum and an apricot. Such hybrids can also be plumcots or apriums, depending on their heritage, but 75% plum-25% apricot pluots are the most common. Most varieties are sweeter than both plums and apricots, and they range in color from greenish yellow to dark purple. Choose pluots that are firm but yield to gentle pressure. Use pluots in "Fruit of the Season Clafouti" (page 152) or in place of plums in "Balsamic Ginger Baked Plums" (page 151).

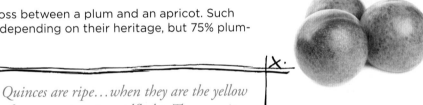

Quinces are ripe…when they are the yellow of canary wings in midflight. They are ripe when their scent teases you with the snap of green apples and the perfumed embrace of coral roses. But even then quinces remain a fruit, hard and obstinate…until they are simmered, coddled for hours above a low, steady flame. Add honey and water and watch their dry, bone-colored flesh soak up the heat, coating itself in an opulent orange, not of the sunrises that you never see but of the insides of tree-ripened papayas, a color you can taste.

—MONIQUE TRUONG, *The Book of Salt*

QUINCE

Quinces look like squat, bumpy, yellow pears. Raw, the flesh is white and hard, with an astringent, dry taste. Cooked, the flesh becomes flavorful, soft, and fragrant, and most varieties will turn pink or red. Quince paste is popular in both Mediterranean and Mexican cuisines, and it is particularly delicious with salty cheese.

RHUBARB

Although technically a stalk vegetable, rhubarb is most often cooked with sugar in desserts, syrups, and preserves. In fact, it's called pieplant in some parts of the country. It also adds brightness to savory dishes; it is particularly good served with game. Look for rhubarb stalks that are firm and crisp with glossy skin. Peel stalks that are particularly stringy. Rhubarb leaves are poisonous and should never be eaten.

SWEET FRUITS
Storage and Usage Guide

FRUIT	STORAGE AND PRESERVATION				USAGE SUGGESTIONS				
	IDEAL CONDITIONS*	PAPER-BAG RIPENING METHOD	FREEZE	DEHYDRATE	RAW	JUICE	JAM	PIE	SORBET
APPLE	room temperature or refrigerated	•		•	•	•	•	•	•
APRICOT	room temperature or refrigerated	•	•	•	•	•	•	•	•
BERRY									
blackberry	refrigerated		•	•	•	•	•	•	•
blueberry	refrigerated		•	•	•	•	•	•	•
cranberry	refrigerated		•	•		•	•	•	•
currant	refrigerated		•	•		•	•	•	•
elderberry	refrigerated		•	•		•	•	•	•
gooseberry	refrigerated		•	•		•	•	•	•
mulberry	refrigerated		•	•	•	•	•	•	•
raspberry	refrigerated		•	•	•	•	•	•	•
strawberry	refrigerated		•	•	•	•	•	•	•
CHERRY	refrigerated		•	•	•	•	•	•	•
GRAPE									
green, red, black	refrigerated		•	•	•	•			
champagne	refrigerated		•	•	•	•		•	•
Concord	refrigerated		•	•	•	•	•	•	•
muscat	refrigerated		•	•	•	•	•	•	•
GROUND CHERRY	kept in husk, refrigerated		•	•	•	•	•	•	•
MELON									
cantaloupe	room temperature or refrigerated		•		•	•	•		•
crenshaw	room temperature or refrigerated		•		•	•	•		•
honeydew	room temperature or refrigerated		•		•	•			•
watermelon	room temperature or refrigerated		•		•	•			•
PEACH/NECTARINE	room temperature or refrigerated	•	•	•	•	•	•	•	•
PEAR									
common	room temperature or refrigerated	•	•	•	•	•	•	•	•
Asian	room temperature or refrigerated			•	•	•	•	•	•
PLUM	room temperature or refrigerated	•	•	•	•	•	•	•	•
PLUOT	room temperature or refrigerated	•		•	•	•	•	•	•
QUINCE	room temperature or refrigerated		•				•	•	•
RHUBARB	refrigerated		•	•			•	•	•

*For fruits that may be stored both at room temperature and refrigerated, refrigeration extends the shelf life. Fruits in this category should not be refrigerated until fully ripe.

MASTER RECIPE: FOUR-WAY COMPOTE

A compote is a simple stewed dish of fresh or dried fruits softened in sweetened liquid. It is very quick to pull together, and very versatile. Preparing fruit in this way allows for many variations—for example combining frozen berries with dried apples and cranberries, or mixing cubes of cooked pumpkin with pear slices. It's also a good way to improve dried or under-ripe fruits. Feel free to play around with the amount and types of sweeteners until you find the sweet-tart balance that suits your taste.

THE BASICS

Fruit: fresh, frozen, or dried, peeled or hulled and cut into cubes if necessary

Liquid: juice, wine, brandy (optional)

Sweetener: sugar, maple syrup, honey, agave nectar

Flavorings: herbs, spices, citrus

Add-ins: vinegar, citrus, liqueur, nuts, candied citrus peel

PROCESS

Place the **fruit** in a saucepan with the **liquid** (if desired). Firmer fruits, such as apples, require about ¼ cup of liquid per cup of fruit, while juicy fruits may be cooked without any additional liquid. Dried fruits require soaking overnight in 4½ cups liquid per cup of fruit. Add **sweetener** as desired and heat over medium heat, stirring frequently. Stir in additional **flavorings**, such as vanilla beans, cloves, or sprigs of rosemary. Reduce the heat and simmer gently until the fruit just begins to release its juices, or until tender. Stir in any **add-ins**, such as liqueur or nuts. Serve warm, or chill to serve cold.

VARIATIONS

By Patricia Mulvey and Laura Gilliam

CRANBERRY MAPLE COMPOTE

SERVES 4

2 cups fresh cranberries

½ cup dried cranberries

1 cup maple syrup

½ cup maple sugar

WARM APPLE COMPOTE

SERVES 4

3 cups diced baking apples

⅔ cup apple juice

1 tablespoon sugar

Seeds from ½ vanilla bean

1 cinnamon stick

1 pinch salt

STIR IN AFTER COOKING:

1 tablespoon Calvados apple brandy or other fruit brandy

STRAWBERRY RHUBARB GINGER COMPOTE

SERVES 4

1 pound strawberries

½ pound rhubarb, chopped

6 tablespoons sugar

1½ tablespoons minced crystallized ginger

STIR IN AFTER COOKING:

2 teaspoons lemon juice

LEMON VERBENA GROUND CHERRY COMPOTE

SERVES 4

1 pint ground cherries

½ cup water

⅓ cup sugar

Seeds from ¼ vanilla bean

1 tablespoon orange liqueur

3 leaves lemon verbena, lightly crushed (discard after cooking)

Note. Adapted from a recipe in Food and Wine *(July 2006).*

IDEA STARTERS

Raspberry, molasses, basil; add-in: aged balsamic vinegar

Cranberry, sugar, ginger; add-in: candied orange peel

Dried cranberry, dried cherry, chai tea, honey

Roasted butternut squash, apple, dried cherry, apple cider, maple syrup

Plum, honey, cardamom; add-in: grated lemon peel

Mulberry, tomatillo, honey, habanero, coriander seed

Black currant, honey; add-in: crème de cassis

Cherry, water, brown sugar, vanilla; add-ins: brandy, toasted almonds

Concord grape, raisins, water, agave nectar, cinnamon, cloves

Peach, rum, brown sugar, vanilla; add-in: candied ginger

Blackberry, orange juice, sugar, cinnamon, cloves

SERVING SUGGESTIONS

◆ Serve over pound cake or spread on toast, waffles, or pancakes.

◆ Use as a pie or pastry filling.

◆ Top with a crumbly streusel and bake until crisp.

◆ Pair sweet-savory compotes with roasted meats, such as pork, turkey, or game.

◆ Use to dress up ice cream or cheesecake, or stir into fresh ricotta or plain Greek-style yogurt.

◆ Use as a sandwich spread.

◆ Stir into warm oatmeal for a decadent breakfast.

◆ Make parfaits with layers of compote, granola, and yogurt.

APPLE WALNUT PASTA WITH BLUE CHEESE SAUCE

BY HEATHER WORKMAN

A few days of unseasonably cool weather in the midst of a hot Texas summer made Heather long for a real Midwestern fall. The hot days returned, but not before she had captured the flavors of autumn in this comforting dish.

SERVES 4-6 // VEGETARIAN // MAIN DISH

INGREDIENTS

Salt for cooking water

⅔ pound cavatelli or other tube-shaped pasta

2 tablespoons extra-virgin olive oil

3 small Gala or Cortland apples, julienned

3 small shallots, thinly sliced

Kosher salt and freshly ground black pepper to taste

1 teaspoon dried thyme, sage, and/or tarragon

6 ounces blue cheese, crumbled

½ cup toasted walnuts, coarsely chopped

Aged Emmentaler or other grating cheese (optional)

PROCESS

Bring a large pot of water to a boil, salt generously, and add the pasta. Slightly undercook the pasta, 1–2 minutes less than the package directions suggest.

While the pasta is cooking, heat the oil in a medium skillet over medium heat. Add the apples and shallots and cook, stirring often, until the apples are lightly browned and fragrant and the shallots are translucent, 4–5 minutes. Season with salt and pepper and toss in the herb(s). Keep warm over low heat.

When the pasta is ready, add the crumbled blue cheese to the apple-shallot mixture. Using a large slotted spoon or spider (a skimming tool with a flat mesh basket on a long handle), transfer the pasta directly from the water to the top of the blue cheese, allowing some of the cooking water to come along (this step will help create a silky, creamy sauce with the blue cheese). Toss to combine.

When the cheese has melted and the sauce is evenly distributed, spoon the pasta into serving dishes and top with the toasted walnuts and grated cheese (if desired).

FALL PUMPKIN PASTA WITH APPLES AND SAGE

BY SARAH MURRAY

Sweet-tart apples, like Granny Smith, are delicious in this unusual pasta recipe, and fresh sage adds savory depth. Serve as a main dish with a hearty fall beer, or as a side dish with turkey or grilled pork.

SERVES 2-4 // VEGETARIAN // MAIN OR SIDE DISH

INGREDIENTS

1 package fresh pumpkin pasta

1 teaspoon olive oil (optional)

1–2 tablespoons butter

1 medium yellow onion, coarsely chopped

2½–3 cups chopped apples

¼ cup chopped fresh sage leaves

Salt and ground black pepper to taste

Grated Parmesan

PROCESS

Cook the pasta according to the package directions. If it is done before the toppings, toss it with the olive oil (to keep the pieces from sticking together) and set aside.

Heat the butter in a medium skillet over medium-high heat. When the butter is melted, add the onion and sauté until it begins to soften, 5–7 minutes. Add the apples and sauté for another 3–4 minutes. Add the sage and sauté until the apples are soft but not falling apart.

Combine the pasta with the apple-onion mixture in a large bowl and season with salt and pepper. Top each serving with grated Parmesan.

GOAT CHEESE, SWEET ONION, APPLE, AND BRANDY STUFFED CHICKEN

BY ASHLEY RAMAKER

These dressed-up chicken breasts are a perfect dinner party main course. Ashley likes to serve them with roasted sweet potatoes and parsnips and a tossed green salad, but she warns that this combination may lead to friends frequently "just stopping by" at future mealtimes.

SERVES 4 // POULTRY // MAIN DISH

INGREDIENTS

1 tablespoon butter

1 tablespoon olive oil

1 tablespoon sugar

1 large apple, chopped

1 medium sweet onion, sliced

⅓ cup brandy

4 boneless, skinless chicken breasts

3 ounces goat cheese

Salt and ground black pepper to taste

PROCESS

Lightly grease a baking dish and set aside. Preheat an oven to 350°. Heat the butter and oil over medium heat in a large skillet. Add the sugar, apple, onion, and brandy; stir and bring to a simmer. Continue to simmer, stirring occasionally, until the liquid is absorbed and the onion is tender, 15–20 minutes. Set aside.

Place the chicken breasts into separate plastic bags and pound with a meat tenderizer until the chicken is about ¼ inch thick. Remove the chicken from the bags and spread one quarter of the goat cheese onto each chicken breast. Mound ¼ cup of the apple mixture over the goat cheese in the center of each chicken breast, reserving ½ cup of the mixture for later. Fold in the sides of the chicken over the apple mixture and secure with toothpicks. Place the chicken in the prepared dish and season with salt and pepper. Bake for 30–40 minutes, until the chicken is white throughout or a thermometer inserted into the center reaches 165°. Top with the remaining apple mixture.

OATMEAL WITH FRUIT AND STREUSEL TOPPING (APPLE)
BY CINDY THORNE, COURTESY OF REAP

Decked-out oatmeal with a decadent nutty topping—a perfect one-dish meal for busy mornings.

SERVES 4 // VEGETARIAN // MAIN DISH

INGREDIENTS

STREUSEL TOPPING:

½ cup whole-wheat flour

¼ cup brown sugar

½ teaspoon ground cinnamon

¼ cup unsalted butter, diced

OATMEAL:

4 cups cooked oatmeal (still warm)

⅓ cup protein powder (optional)

Honey

2 bananas, sliced

2 apples, sliced

¼ cup chopped pecans

PROCESS

STREUSEL TOPPING: In a small bowl, mix together the flour, sugar, and cinnamon. Cut in the butter, mixing until thoroughly combined and crumbly. You will have more than you need—store the excess in the refrigerator for later use.

OATMEAL: Stir together the oatmeal and protein powder (if desired). Divide evenly among 4 bowls and drizzle each with honey. Distribute the banana and apple slices evenly among the bowls. Sprinkle about 1 tablespoon of the streusel topping and 1 tablespoon of pecans over each bowl of oatmeal and fruit.

SCOTCH APPLE PIE
BY LOUISE J. ELBAUM, COURTESY OF REAP

With a crumbly topping rather than a crust, Scotch apple pie is healthier and simpler to make than a regular pie. Louise always makes extras when apples are in season and keeps them in her freezer for last-minute desserts.

SERVES 12 // VEGETARIAN // DESSERT

INGREDIENTS

6–7 baking apples, peeled, cored, and sliced

1 cup all-purpose flour

½ cup butter, softened

1 cup chopped pecans

1 cup brown sugar, divided

Vanilla ice cream or whipped cream

PROCESS

Preheat an oven to 450°. Layer the apples in a 9-inch pie pan. In a medium bowl, combine the flour, butter, pecans, and ¾ cup of the brown sugar and mix together until they resemble wet sand. Sprinkle the remaining ¼ cup of brown sugar over the apples, adjusting the amount of sugar to the sweetness of the apples. Pat the topping over the apples, covering the edges thoroughly. Bake for 30 minutes. Reduce the oven temperature to 350° and continue baking for a few minutes more, until the top is browned and the apples are a little bubbly. Cool and serve topped with vanilla ice cream or whipped cream.

To freeze: Line the pie pan with aluminum foil, butter or lightly oil the foil, then put in the apples and proceed with the recipe. Underbake the pie slightly, cool, cover the top with aluminum foil, and freeze the pie in the pie pan. When solid, remove the pan, seal the foil around the pie, wrap it in plastic, and store it in the freezer until ready to serve. Reheat at 350° until hot and bubbly.

TUSCANY BREAD PUDDING WITH APPLES AND NUTS

BY AMANDA DAVIS, COURTESY OF REAP

A special Tuscany loaf baked by Amanda's favorite baker inspired her to create this delectable dessert.

SERVES 10 // VEGETARIAN // DESSERT

INGREDIENTS

½ cup butter, melted

¾ cup sugar

4 eggs, beaten

3 cups milk

1 tablespoon vanilla extract

½ teaspoon ground nutmeg

½ teaspoon ground cinnamon

6 cups diced day-old Tuscany bread

½ cup golden raisins

2 tart apples, grated

½ cup dried cranberries

1 cup hickory nuts

Whipping cream

PROCESS

Preheat an oven to 325°. Butter a 13 × 9-inch baking dish. In a large bowl, beat together the butter, sugar, eggs, milk, vanilla, nutmeg, and cinnamon until well blended. Stir in the bread cubes, fruits, and nuts, mixing to coat thoroughly. Pour into the prepared baking dish. Bake until a knife inserted into the center comes out clean, 40–50 minutes. Serve hot with cream.

APRICOT DUTCH BABY

BY LEE DAVENPORT

Lee has nothing against pancakes or waffles, but if she wants something REALLY special on the weekend she makes a Dutch Baby. Dutch Babies are beautifully puffy and golden when finished; before you pull yours from the oven, make sure everyone is gathered around the table so they can appreciate it in all its glory, as it will lose its puff fast!

SERVES 4-6 // VEGETARIAN // MAIN DISH

INGREDIENTS

3 eggs

⅔ cup whole milk

⅔ cup all-purpose flour

¼ cup sugar

¼ teaspoon ground cinnamon

2–4 apricots, pitted and sliced

2½ tablespoons butter

Powdered sugar

PROCESS

Preheat an oven to 425° and place a 10-inch cast-iron skillet inside while it's heating. Whisk together the eggs, milk, flour, sugar, and cinnamon. Stir in the apricots. Remove the hot skillet from the oven and melt the butter in it, swirling to coat the entire surface evenly. Pour in the batter and return the skillet to the oven. Bake for 20–25 minutes, until the Dutch Baby is puffed and golden. Cut into wedges and serve with a dusting of powdered sugar.

BOOZY BAKED APRICOTS

BY LEE DAVENPORT

Unless you can pick a sun-ripened apricot straight from the tree, the best way to coax maximum flavor out of this fruit is to bake it. Honey is a perfect match for the tartness of apricots and bourbon gives them a decadent flair. Serve these on Greek-style yogurt for breakfast or with vanilla ice cream for an easy, elegant dessert.

SERVES 4-6 // VEGETARIAN // CONDIMENT

INGREDIENTS

2 tablespoons honey

2 tablespoons bourbon or water

1 pound apricots, halved and pitted (about 8–12)

2 teaspoons chopped lemon thyme (optional)

PROCESS

Preheat an oven to 350°. Whisk together the honey and bourbon or water. Put the apricots in a baking dish and drizzle with the honey mixture. Bake until the fruit softens and releases its juices, 25–35 minutes. Remove from the oven and stir in the lemon thyme (if desired). Store in the refrigerator for up to a week.

LAMB AND CHICKPEA STEW WITH APRICOTS

BY BETH FORTUNE

Although it's not traditional, Beth adds harissa, a Tunisian pepper paste, to this Moroccan-style stew. She notes that if you, too, decide to add a little spice, stir it in a little at a time, tasting after each addition, until you reach the level of heat you desire. With a slow cooker and about 30 minutes of prep time earlier in the day, you'll have this succulent stew ready for dinner with very little effort. Serve on a bed of couscous or quinoa for a fragrant, filling meal.

SERVES 8 // MEAT // MAIN DISH

INGREDIENTS

2 pounds lamb shoulder or leg, diced

¼ cup all-purpose flour

1 teaspoon salt, plus more to taste

½ teaspoon ground black pepper, plus more to taste

1 teaspoon ground cinnamon

½ teaspoon ground coriander

3 tablespoons oil, divided

1 small onion, chopped

2 cups beef broth, divided

1 (1-inch) piece fresh ginger, peeled and chopped

1 (4-inch) cinnamon stick

1½ cups dried apricots, halved or quartered

2 cups chopped carrots (about 3)

1 (15-ounce) can chopped tomatoes, juice reserved

2 cups cooked chickpeas; or 1 (15-ounce) can chickpeas, drained and rinsed

Fresh lemon juice to taste

Harissa paste to taste* (optional)

¼ cup sliced toasted almonds

½ cup torn fresh parsley or cilantro leaves

> *Harissa can be found in Middle Eastern markets, at specialty food shops, or online. Spice level varies from brand to brand, so be sure to start with a little and taste as you go.

PROCESS

Pat the lamb dry with a paper towel. Combine the flour, salt, pepper, ground cinnamon, and coriander in a bowl or plastic bag. Toss the lamb in the flour mixture until it is evenly coated, then shake off the excess flour. Heat 2 tablespoons of the oil in a large sauté pan until shimmering. Add the lamb to the pan, making sure there is space between the cubes (you may need to cook the meat in two batches). Sear the meat until it is golden brown on all sides, then transfer to a slow cooker.

> Dehydrating is a convenient way to preserve summer fruits for use in other seasons. Apricots are especially good for dehydrating because their high pectin level keeps them moist and chewy. Many commercially dried apricots have sulfites added to preserve their color, but you can choose to omit this preservative when dehydrating at home.

When all the meat is seared, add the remaining oil to the pan and heat until shimmering. Add the onion and sauté until golden brown. Transfer the onion to the slow cooker. Add ½ cup of the broth to the pan and heat until bubbling. Scrape the pan with a wooden spoon to release any browned bits from the bottom, and add the heated broth to the slow cooker. Add the remaining broth, ginger, cinnamon stick, apricots, carrots, tomatoes, and chickpeas to the slow cooker and stir to combine. Cover and cook for 5 hours on high, or 8–10 hours on low.

When the stew is finished, taste and add more salt, the lemon juice, and the harissa (if desired). Serve with a sprinkling of almonds and parsley or cilantro leaves.

APPLE CRANBERRY CRISP PIE
BY EDITH THAYER

This pie brings together two fall favorites—apples and cranberries—in a pie with the crunchy top of a crisp. The cranberries add a tart zing to the sweet apples. It's even better with ice cream.

SERVES 8 // VEGETARIAN // DESSERT

INGREDIENTS

1 (10-inch) single piecrust

¾ cup sugar

2 tablespoons all-purpose flour

1 teaspoon ground cinnamon

¼ teaspoon salt

4 apples, peeled and thinly sliced (5 cups)

1½ cups fresh or frozen cranberries, halved

TOPPING:

½ cup rolled oats

⅓ cup firmly packed brown sugar

⅓ cup all-purpose flour

¼ cup butter

PROCESS

Preheat an oven to 425°. Line a 10-inch pie pan with the piecrust. Crimp or flute the edge of the crust. In a large bowl, combine the sugar, flour, cinnamon, and salt. Mix well. Add the apples and cranberries and stir to combine. Spoon into the crust-lined pan.

In a separate bowl, combine the topping ingredients; mix with a fork or pastry blender until crumbly. If the topping seems too soft, add a bit more flour. Sprinkle over the apple-cranberry mixture. Cover the edges of the crust with a piecrust shield if you have one, or use strips of aluminum foil to prevent the edges from getting too brown. Bake the pie for 35–45 minutes, or until the apples are tender and the topping is golden brown.

BERRY SALAD WITH MAPLE-BALSAMIC VINAIGRETTE

BY MARGIE MICHICICH

With strawberries, blueberries, and goat cheese, this salad is perfect for an Independence Day picnic; just toss in the dressing right before serving. Margie makes her own croutons with stale French bread tossed with olive oil and salt and toasted in a skillet. Almonds or walnuts could also be substituted.

SERVES 4 // VEGETARIAN // SIDE DISH

INGREDIENTS

MAPLE-BALSAMIC VINAIGRETTE:

¼ cup extra-virgin olive oil

2 tablespoons balsamic vinegar

1 tablespoon maple syrup

½ teaspoon Dijon mustard

Pinch salt

SALAD:

3 cups mixed baby salad greens

2 tablespoons Maple-Balsamic Vinaigrette (or to taste)

1 cup quartered fresh strawberries (6–8 whole berries)

½ cup fresh blueberries

1 ounce goat cheese, crumbled (about 2 tablespoons)

2 tablespoons croutons

PROCESS

MAPLE-BALSAMIC VINAIGRETTE: Combine all ingredients in a sealable container, cover securely, and shake until emulsified; or whisk vigorously in a small bowl. Taste and adjust the seasonings, adding more maple syrup and/or salt as desired. Store covered in the refrigerator.

SALAD: Toss the salad greens with a portion of the vinaigrette in a medium bowl. Scatter the strawberries, blueberries, goat cheese, and croutons over the greens. Serve immediately.

BLACKBERRY RASPBERRY PIE

BY MARY E. WILHELM, COURTESY OF REAP

At the height of summer, when berries of all types are in abundance, make sure to collect or purchase extras for freezing. You'll be glad that you did when, later in the year, you get to enjoy this summery pie.

SERVES 8 // VEGETARIAN // DESSERT

INGREDIENTS

1⅓ cups plus ½ tablespoon sugar, divided

2 tablespoons quick-cooking tapioca

2 tablespoons cornstarch

2 cups frozen lightly sweetened raspberries

2 cups frozen unsweetened blackberries

1 (9-inch) double piecrust

2 tablespoons butter or margarine, diced

1 tablespoon milk

½ tablespoon ground cinnamon

Vanilla ice cream

PROCESS

Preheat an oven to 350°. In a large mixing bowl, combine 1⅓ cups of the sugar, the tapioca, and cornstarch. Add the berries, tossing gently until coated. Let stand for 15–30 minutes, or until the fruit is partially thawed.

Line a 9-inch pie pan with the bottom portion of the piecrust. Transfer the berry mixture into the crust and dot with butter. Cover the fruit with the top portion of the pie crust and trim, seal, and flute the edges. Cut slits in the top and brush with milk. Combine the cinnamon with the remaining sugar and sprinkle over the crust.

To prevent over-browning, cover the edges of the pie with aluminum foil. Bake for 50 minutes. Remove the foil and bake for 20–25 minutes more, or until the pastry is golden and the filling is bubbly. Cool on a wire rack and serve with vanilla ice cream.

MARVELOUS MULBERRY PIE

BY AMY SINNER

Not sure if you've seen a mulberry before? You may discover them under your feet. Mulberries often stain sidewalks with dark purplish splotches that look like spilled red wine. The berries are sweet with a little tartness. Substitute other berries like raspberries, blueberries, or blackberries if you can't find mulberries; grated lemon peel will add a bit of that zingy mulberry tartness.

SERVES 8 // VEGETARIAN // DESSERT

INGREDIENTS

1 (9-inch) double piecrust

4 cups fresh mulberries

¾ cup sugar

¼ cup all-purpose flour

¼ teaspoon ground cinnamon

1 teaspoon grated lemon peel (optional)

2–4 teaspoons lemon juice

2 tablespoons butter

PROCESS

Preheat an oven to 425°. Line a 9-inch pie pan with the bottom portion of the piecrust, covering the bottom and sides of the pan. Place the berries, sugar, flour, cinnamon, and lemon peel (if desired) in a large bowl, tossing to coat the berries. Pour the mixture into the crust-lined pan. Sprinkle the fruit with lemon juice and dot with butter. Place the top portion of the crust over the fruit mixture, pressing the edges of the top and bottom crusts together to seal. Cut 4–6 slits in the top crust to allow steam to escape. Bake for 35–40 minutes, or until the top is golden brown.

MID-MORNING ENERGY BARS (BERRY)

BY NORA VRAKAS, COURTESY OF REAP

Nora developed these bars to provide a healthy alternative to the office candy bowl. They're chock-full of protein, whole grains, and other goodies; we bet they keep her going through mid-morning and beyond.

SERVES 30 // VEGETARIAN // SNACK

INGREDIENTS

1 cup peanut butter

1 cup honey

1 cup milk or soy milk

4 eggs, beaten

2 tablespoons orange extract

2 scoops soy protein powder

5 cups instant oatmeal

½ cup oat bran

½ cup flaxseed meal

2 tablespoons ground cinnamon

2 tablespoons grated orange peel

1 cup dried mixed berries

1 cup chopped nuts

1 cup chocolate chips

1 cup unsweetened flaked coconut

PROCESS

Preheat an oven to 350°. Grease a 14 × 11-inch baking dish. Warm the peanut butter, honey, and milk in a saucepan over low heat and stir to combine. Cool slightly, then add the eggs, orange extract, and protein powder. Set aside to cool completely.

Meanwhile, combine all the remaining ingredients (oatmeal through coconut) in a large bowl. Add the cooled peanut butter mixture and mix well. Lightly pat the mixture into the prepared pan. Bake 20–25 minutes, or until the edges are slightly brown. Avoid overbaking, as the bars can dry out easily. Remove from the oven, cool slightly, and cut into squares.

MIKAYLA'S BLUEBERRY PIE

BY MIKAYLA FLYTE, COURTESY OF REAP

The inspiration for this recipe dates back to before Mikayla was born, when her parents planted some blueberry bushes. Picking (and eating) fresh berries became the highlight of Mikayla's summers, and at the age of five she developed this delectable pie.

SERVES 8 // VEGETARIAN // DESSERT

INGREDIENTS

1 (9-inch) double piecrust

¾ cup sugar

½ cup all-purpose flour

6 cups fresh blueberries

1 tablespoon lemon juice

1 tablespoon butter or margarine

PROCESS

Preheat an oven to 425°. Line a 9-inch pie pan with the bottom portion of the piecrust. Mix together the sugar and flour in a large bowl. Stir in the blueberries. Spoon the berry mixture into the crust-lined pan. Sprinkle with lemon juice and dot with butter. Cover the blueberries with the top portion of the piecrust. Seal and flute the edges and cut slits in the top. Cover the edges of crust with aluminum foil to prevent over-browning. Bake for 20–25 minutes, remove the foil, and bake for an additional 15 minutes, until golden brown.

MULBERRY LIQUEUR

BY MARGE PITTS, COURTESY OF REAP

Mulberry-infused vodka is lovely and festive when mixed with Champagne or sparkling water. For more mouthwatering party drinks, see the "Cocktails" section on page 249.

YIELDS 1 QUART // VEGAN // BEVERAGE

INGREDIENTS

1 cup mulberries

½ cup sugar

Vodka to cover the berries

PROCESS

Put the berries into a clean quart-size jar and add the sugar. Fill the jar with vodka, cover tightly, and put it in a dark place. In several weeks your mulberry liqueur will be ready. Give the jar a good shake, then strain the liqueur into another container. Press the mulberries against the strainer to squeeze out all the juice, then discard the solids. This liqueur makes a refreshing high ball with lemonade or soda.

Clean the mulberries by putting them in a colander and immersing them in a bowl of cold water. Remove whatever floats to the surface. Drain and give the berries another rinse. Jiggle as much water as you can through the colander.

PEANUT BUTTER AND RASPBERRY SANDWICH
BY ANTHONY DUPRÉ, COURTESY OF REAP

This recipe, contributed by Anthony at the age of three, contains good advice for aspiring young cooks: moms and dads make excellent kitchen helpers!

SERVES 1 // VEGAN // MAIN DISH

INGREDIENTS

1 slice bread, toasted

1 tablespoon peanut butter

1 handful fresh raspberries

PROCESS

Have your mom or dad help you cover one slice of toasted bread with the peanut butter. Take a handful of raspberries and place them on half of the covered bread. Fold over and eat immediately.

STRAWBERRY MERINGUE SHORTCAKES
BY MELISSA JAMES, COURTESY OF REAP

Making meringue takes some planning, but the technique is easy, and the baked shells store well in an airtight container (three to four days at room temperature, or longer in the freezer). The frozen shells defrost at room temperature in just minutes. Keep a stash of these on hand for impromptu desserts.

SERVES 8 // VEGETARIAN // DESSERT

INGREDIENTS

MERINGUE SHELLS:

3 egg whites

1 teaspoon vanilla

¼ teaspoon cream of tartar

Dash sea salt

1 cup superfine sugar

FILLING:

1 quart fresh strawberries, sliced

3 tablespoons water

Sugar to taste

Balsamic vinegar to taste (optional)

Whipped cream

8 whole fresh strawberries

PROCESS

MERINGUE SHELLS: Let the egg whites stand in a large mixing bowl for about 1 hour, or until room temperature. Preheat an oven to 300°. Line a baking sheet with brown paper and trace 8 (3-inch) circles on the paper. Add the vanilla, cream of tartar, and sea salt to the egg whites. Beat with an electric mixer on medium speed until soft peaks form. Add the sugar, 1 tablespoon at a time, beating on high speed until very stiff peaks form and the sugar is almost dissolved (about 7 minutes). Using the back of a tablespoon, spread the meringue mixture over the circle outlines, building up the sides. Bake for about 35 minutes. Turn off the oven and allow the shells to dry in the oven with the door closed for 1 hour.

FILLING: In a large bowl, combine the sliced strawberries with the water and sugar. Stir in some balsamic vinegar (if desired). Let the filling macerate while the meringue shells are drying.

TO ASSEMBLE: When the shells are dried, remove them from the paper. Fill the shells with the strawberry filling and top with whipped cream. Garnish with a fresh strawberry.

STRAWBERRY PIZZA

BY DEBRA SHAPIRO/FAIRSHARE CSA COALITION

A delicious twist on strawberry shortcake, this pizza is a big hit with kids, especially if they get to help make it. Have them roll out the dough or pat it into a big heart shape. For a more grown-up version, this pizza easily becomes a tart. Just press the dough into a tart pan with a removable bottom and bake as instructed. Take care in slicing the berries, and arrange them in concentric circles with the pointed ends facing out: the result should look like a flower. Drizzle with a balsamic glaze, pomegranate molasses (see page 94), or melted chocolate.

SERVES 12 // VEGETARIAN // DESSERT

INGREDIENTS

2 cups all-purpose flour

1 tablespoon baking powder

½ teaspoon salt

½ cup cold butter

¾ cup milk

2 tablespoons butter, melted

2 tablespoons sugar

1 (8-ounce) package cream cheese, softened

3 tablespoons powdered sugar

4 cups sliced strawberries

PROCESS

Preheat an oven to 400°. Measure the flour into a large bowl. Whisk in the baking powder and salt. Slice the cold butter into the bowl and work into the flour with a pastry blender, a knife, or your hands, until you have a mealy mixture. Add the milk and mix with a fork until the dough clumps. Turn the dough out onto a floured surface and knead lightly to make a smooth ball. Cut the dough in half, roll each piece into a 9-inch circle, and place on a baking sheet. Brush the circles with the melted butter and sprinkle with the sugar. Bake for about 12 minutes, or until firm and browned. Cool.

Meanwhile, mix the cream cheese and powdered sugar. To assemble, spread each round with the sweetened cream cheese and arrange the strawberries on top. Cut each pizza into wedges to serve.

CHERRY TOFU BREAKFAST BREAD

BY JOLENE ZIEBART, COURTESY OF REAP

In this hearty bread, tofu both enriches the texture and ups the protein. Take a slice for a quick breakfast on the go, or serve it warm as part of a leisurely brunch.

YIELDS 1 LOAF // VEGETARIAN // SIDE DISH OR DESSERT

INGREDIENTS

¾ cup soft tofu

1 cup sugar

¼ cup oil

1 teaspoon vanilla

½ teaspoon almond extract

1 cup all-purpose flour

1 cup whole-wheat flour

½ teaspoon baking powder

½ teaspoon baking soda

¼ teaspoon ground nutmeg

¼ teaspoon salt

1 cup chopped pitted tart red cherries, either fresh or thawed frozen (including any juice)

⅓ cup milk

2 tablespoons wheat germ

½ cup chopped walnuts (optional)

½ cup dried cherries (optional)

Superfine sugar

PROCESS

Preheat an oven to 350°. Butter or oil an 8 × 4-inch loaf pan. Blend the tofu in a blender or food processor until smooth and creamy. Add the sugar, oil, vanilla, and almond extract and process until thoroughly mixed. Set aside.

Sift the flours, baking powder, baking soda, nutmeg, and salt into a large bowl. Add the tofu mixture, chopped cherries with their juice, milk, wheat germ, and the walnuts and dried cherries (if desired). Mix only until just blended. Pour the batter into the loaf pan and sprinkle the top with superfine sugar. Bake for 1 hour, until the bread is firm and golden on top. Cool slightly on a wire rack before slicing.

MICHIGAN DOUBLE-CHERRY COBBLER

BY MARY BILYEU, COURTESY OF REAP

This cobbler highlights two different sour cherries: Montmorency, the popular baking staple, and Balaton, a newer variety. You can substitute other cherries as well, but stick with sour or tart cherries for the best result.

SERVES 6-8 // VEGETARIAN // DESSERT

INGREDIENTS

4 cups pitted fresh cherries (2 cups Montmorency, 2 cups Balaton recommended)

¾ cup sugar

2 tablespoons cornstarch

1 teaspoon vanilla extract

1 teaspoon almond extract

1½ cups whole-wheat pastry flour

2 teaspoons baking powder

1 teaspoon salt

6 tablespoons butter or shortening

1 egg

⅓ cup vanilla soy milk

¼ cup brown sugar

½ teaspoon cinnamon

Vanilla ice cream or whipped cream

PROCESS

Preheat an oven to 400°. Grease a 12 × 7-inch glass baking dish. In a large bowl, combine the cherries, sugar, cornstarch, and extracts and mix well; pour into the prepared baking dish. In the same bowl, combine the flour, baking powder, and salt. Blend in the butter with a fork until the flour is moistened and forms pea-size lumps. Whisk together the egg and soy milk, then pour over the flour mixture and mix gently. Drop the batter over the cherries and spread to the edges of the dish, covering the fruit as much as possible.

Combine the brown sugar and cinnamon; sprinkle over the batter. Bake for 30–35 minutes, or until the fruit is bubbling and the topping is golden. Serve warm with ice cream or whipped cream.

OAT SCONES WITH DRIED FRUIT AND LAVENDER (CHERRY)

BY DOROTHY REYES, COURTESY OF REAP

Lavender lends a magical flavor and fragrance to baked goods, and these scones are no exception. They are definitely worthy of a special occasion.

SERVES 8-10 // VEGETARIAN // SNACK OR DESSERT

INGREDIENTS

⅔ cup butter, melted

⅓ cup buttermilk

1 egg

1½ cups quick-cooking oats

¼ cup brown sugar

1½ cups all-purpose flour

1 tablespoon baking powder

1 teaspoon cream of tartar

½ cup dried cherries

½ cup dried golden currants

¼ cup minced fresh mint

1 tablespoon dried lavender buds

PROCESS

Preheat an oven to 425°. Lightly grease a baking sheet. Mix together the butter, buttermilk, and egg in a small bowl. In a medium bowl, mix together the oats, sugar, flour, baking powder, and cream of tartar. Add the butter-egg mixture and mix just until the dough is moist. Stir in the remaining ingredients (cherries through lavender) and mix slightly. If the dough seems too dry, add more buttermilk. Shape the dough into a ball. Pat out on the prepared sheet to form an 8-inch circle. Bake for 12–15 minutes, or until lightly brown. Cut into 8–10 wedges and serve warm with butter and jam.

CHICKEN VERONIQUE (GRAPE)

BY PATRICIA MULVEY AND LAURA GILLIAM OF LOCAL THYME

Pat first encountered this classic French dish in culinary school. She remembers thinking at the time, "Chicken with grapes in cream sauce? How odd." But after tasting it her reaction immediately changed to "Wow, sublime!"

SERVES 4 // POULTRY // MAIN DISH

INGREDIENTS

4 boneless, skinless chicken breasts

2 tablespoons chopped fresh tarragon, divided

Salt and ground black pepper to taste

¼ cup unsalted butter

½ cup chopped shallots

1½ cups halved grapes (seeded if necessary)

1 cup dry white wine

1 cup whipping cream

PROCESS

Pound the chicken breasts to an even thickness. Sprinkle the chicken with ⅓ of the tarragon and some salt and pepper. Melt the butter in a large skillet. Add the chicken breasts and sear until browned, turning once to brown both sides (about 4–5 minutes per side). Remove the chicken from the skillet and set aside on a plate.

Add the shallots and remaining tarragon to the chicken drippings in the skillet. Sauté over medium-high heat until the shallots are wilted, about 5 minutes. Add the grapes and wine, scraping up any browned bits from the bottom of the skillet. Stir in the cream and return the chicken to the skillet. Simmer until the sauce thickens and the chicken is cooked through (10–15 minutes more). Adjust the seasonings and serve.

SMOOTHIE SUBTERFUGE (GRAPE)

BY HEIDI ACCOLA OF ROOTS & SHOOTS FARM

Looking to get more greens in your diet? Heidi swears by this smoothie. The greens are naturally sweetened with fruit and honey for a light and refreshing drink. Experiment with different berry and fruit juice combinations to vary the flavor; grapes will make it extra sweet. If frozen berries are used, eliminate the ice cubes.

SERVES 4 // VEGETARIAN // MAIN DISH

INGREDIENTS

1 cup berries of choice

1 cup fruit juice of choice

1 cup chopped greens (spinach, Swiss chard or kale)

1 cup plain yogurt

1 tablespoon honey

6–8 ice cubes

PROCESS

Combine all ingredients in a high-powered blender and puree until smooth. Pour into individual glasses and serve immediately.

CONCORD GRAPE STREUSEL PIE
BY TERESE ALLEN, ORIGINALLY PUBLISHED IN *EDIBLE MADISON*

If a peanut butter and jelly sandwich is the only thing that comes to mind when you think of Concords, go visit Cindy Secher of Carandale Farms at the Dane County Farmers' Market. She inspired Terese to create this recipe.

SERVES 8 // VEGETARIAN // DESSERT

INGREDIENTS

1 quart Concord grapes, stems removed

½ cup honey

⅓ cup all-purpose flour

⅓ cup brown sugar

⅓ cup quick-cooking oats

¼ teaspoon salt

3 tablespoons cold butter, cut into small pieces

2½ tablespoons cornstarch

2 tablespoons water

1 (10-inch) deep-dish piecrust, unbaked or prebaked

PROCESS

FILLING: Pop the pulp out of each grape by squeezing it gently; the pulp will come out in one small ball wherever there is a break in the skin. Place the skins in a medium bowl, add the honey, and set this mixture aside.

Place the pulp in a small saucepan (do not add any water). Bring to a simmer; simmer for 5–7 minutes, stirring occasionally. Place the hot pulp in a fine-mesh strainer set over the skins. Rub the pulp through the strainer and discard the seeds. Let the pulp and skins cool for at least 1 hour, stirring occasionally (this will bring out the deep color).

TOPPING: Combine the flour, brown sugar, oats, and salt in a food processor. Process for 20 seconds. Add the butter and pulse until the mixture looks crumbly. Refrigerate the mixture until you're ready to bake the pie.

TO ASSEMBLE AND BAKE: Preheat an oven to 400°. Mix the cornstarch with the water and stir into the filling. Line a 10-inch pie pan with the crust and pour the filling into the crust. Sprinkle the topping evenly over the filling. Place the pie on an aluminum foil-lined baking sheet and bake for 15 minutes. Reduce the heat to 350° and continue baking until it is set in the middle, 30–40 minutes more. Cool the pie to room temperature.

MIXED GREENS WITH APPLES, GRAPES, AND WALNUTS
BY PATRICIA MULVEY AND LAURA GILLIAM OF LOCAL THYME

This easy salad comes together in minutes. Walnut oil gives the dressing a depth of flavor that belies its simplicity.

SERVES 4 // VEGAN // SIDE DISH

INGREDIENTS

3 tablespoons walnut oil

3 tablespoons cider vinegar

1 teaspoon Dijon mustard

1 tablespoon chopped fresh tarragon

Salt and ground black pepper to taste

5 ounces mixed greens

2 apples, cored and chopped

1½ cups grapes

½ cup walnuts, toasted

PROCESS

In a small bowl, make a dressing by whisking together the walnut oil, vinegar, mustard, and tarragon; season with salt and pepper. In a salad bowl, toss together the greens, apples, grapes, and walnuts. Drizzle the dressing over the salad and toss well.

SALTED MELON

BY PATRICIA MULVEY AND LAURA GILLIAM OF LOCAL THYME

Sweet melons become even sweeter when served with a light sprinkling of salt. The addition of mint in this recipe brightens the flavor even more.

SERVES 2 // VEGAN // SIDE DISH

INGREDIENTS

1 Charantais, cantaloupe, or honeydew melon

Pinch sea salt

2 teaspoons minced fresh mint

PROCESS

Scoop the seeds out of the melon and slice it into sections. Sprinkle each section with a little salt and mint. Serve immediately.

SUMMER MELON DESSERT

BY BARBARA WRIGHT/FAIRSHARE CSA COALITION

This cool summer dessert is refreshing, simple, and beautiful. You can easily scale up the recipe by doubling, tripling, etc., all of the ingredients. It will also work with unequal proportions of melons, as long as you preserve the ratio of total melon to the remaining ingredients.

SERVES 4 // VEGETARIAN // DESSERT

INGREDIENTS

1 cup diced seeded watermelon

1 cup diced cantaloupe or muskmelon

1 cup diced honeydew

⅓–½ cup honey

Juice from 1 lime

¼ cup chopped fresh mint

PROCESS

Place the diced melon in a bowl. Drizzle with the honey, then with the lime juice. Sprinkle on the mint. Chill for at least 1 hour in the refrigerator. Toss gently. Serve in clear, stemmed glasses.

WATERMELON BITES WITH BLUE CHEESE AND CANDIED WALNUTS

BY PATRICIA MULVEY AND LAURA GILLIAM OF LOCAL THYME

These colorful bites look lovely arranged on an appetizer platter. They make great finger food, especially when skewered with toothpicks for easy grabbing.

SERVES 4-8 // VEGETARIAN // APPETIZER

INGREDIENTS

4 cups bite-size watermelon cubes

2 slices prosciutto, cut into thin strips (optional)

¼ cup crumbled blue cheese

¼ cup candied walnuts (plain toasted nuts may be substituted)

PROCESS

Place the watermelon cubes on in a single layer a platter. Drape each melon cube with some strips of prosciutto (if desired) and top with a small piece of blue cheese and one candied walnut.

SWEET AND SAVORY WATERMELON SALAD

BY JAMIE DECARIA OF SAVORRA.COM

In this simpler version of a restaurant favorite, Jamie combines sweet and savory ingredients to create a sophisticated salad in just a few easy steps. It sounds like an odd combination, but the sweet, juicy watermelon cools off the heat from the spicy pepper nicely. Perfect for the end of summer!

SERVES 8 // VEGETARIAN // SIDE DISH

INGREDIENTS

Juice from 1 lime

¼ cup olive oil

1 tablespoon rice vinegar

½ tablespoon honey

Salt to taste

8 cups diced watermelon

1 jalapeño, seeded and minced

¼ cup finely chopped fresh mint

2 tablespoons minced fresh chives

PROCESS

In a large, nonmetallic bowl, whisk together the first 5 ingredients (lime juice through salt). Toss in the watermelon, jalapeño, and herbs and fold gently to combine. Refrigerate for 2 hours to allow the flavors to develop.

WATERMELON JALAPEÑO SALSA

BY PATRICIA MULVEY AND LAURA GILLIAM OF LOCAL THYME

Pat based this recipe on a Dorie Greenspan original. She seconds Dorie's claim that it's "great on everything you grill," and on almost everything else as well. Feel free to increase the amount of honey to temper the heat of the Sriracha sauce if you wish. If spicy Sriracha is not your thing, substitute a little tomato juice in its place.

SERVES 6 // VEGETARIAN // CONDIMENT

INGREDIENTS

3½ tablespoons Sriracha sauce

2½ tablespoons rice vinegar

3½ tablespoons olive oil

1 teaspoon honey

1 green or purple bell pepper, seeded and diced

2 cups diced watermelon

2 jalapeños, seeded and diced (optional)

2 tablespoons chopped fresh cilantro

Salt and ground black pepper to taste

PROCESS

Whisk the Sriracha sauce, vinegar, oil, and honey in a large bowl. Stir in the bell pepper, watermelon, jalapeños (if desired), and cilantro and season with salt and pepper.

GRILLED PEACHES AND PROSCIUTTO
BY LEE DAVENPORT

This recipe is Lee's take on the classic melon and prosciutto appetizer. These can be enjoyed alone or as a topping for a simple green salad.

SERVES 4 // MEAT // APPETIZER

INGREDIENTS

2 ripe yet firm peaches, halved and pitted

Neutral oil (such as canola)

4 slices prosciutto, cut in half

PROCESS

Brush the cut sides of the peaches with the oil. Grill on a medium-hot grill until the peaches have grill marks and are soft but not falling apart, about 5 minutes. Cool until you can comfortably handle them. Cut each half in half again and wrap each quarter with a ½ slice of prosciutto. Serve immediately.

PEACH AND GINGER SALSA
BY PATRICIA MULVEY AND LAURA GILLIAM OF LOCAL THYME

Soy sauce and sesame oil give this deeply flavorful salsa an Asian flair. It is delicious served on seafood or grilled meats.

SERVES 4 // VEGAN // CONDIMENT

INGREDIENTS

2 cups diced peaches

¼ cup finely diced red bell pepper

¼ cup thinly sliced green onions

3 tablespoons lime juice

2 tablespoons chopped fresh mint

1 tablespoon minced jalapeño

2 teaspoons minced fresh ginger

½ teaspoon minced garlic

2 tablespoons soy sauce or tamari

2 teaspoons toasted sesame oil

PROCESS

Combine all ingredients in a sealable container. Mix well and chill until ready to use.

PEACH BOY BAIT

BY LEE DAVENPORT

Legend has it that this dessert was named by its creator, a teenage county fair contestant, for its boy-luring abilities. This version is adapted from a recipe in Cook's Country *that was based on the original. Boy Bait works well with almost any kind of fruit, although peach is Lee's favorite.*

SERVES 12 // VEGETARIAN // DESSERT

INGREDIENTS

2 cups all-purpose flour

1 tablespoon baking powder

1 teaspoon salt

1 cup (2 sticks) unsalted butter, softened

¾ cup packed light brown sugar

¾ cup white sugar, divided

3 large eggs

1 cup buttermilk

2 peaches, one chopped into small pieces and one sliced for the top

¼ teaspoon ground cinnamon

¼ teaspoon ground ginger

¼ teaspoon ground nutmeg

PROCESS

Preheat an oven to 350°. Grease and flour a 13 × 9-inch baking dish. Whisk together the flour, baking powder, and salt in a medium bowl. In a separate bowl, combine the butter, the brown sugar, and ½ cup of the white sugar; beat with an electric mixer on medium-high speed for about 2 minutes, or until fluffy. Add 1 of the eggs, beating until just incorporated; scrape the sides of the bowl and repeat with the remaining 2 eggs. Reduce the mixer speed to medium and beat in one third of the flour mixture until incorporated. Beat in half of the buttermilk. Beat in half of the remaining flour mixture, then the remaining milk, and finally the remaining flour mixture. Fold in the chopped peach and spread the batter into the prepared pan.

Arrange the peach slices over the top of the batter. Stir together the remaining ¼ cup of the white sugar and the spices in a small bowl and sprinkle over the peach slices. Bake until a toothpick inserted in the center comes out clean, 45–50 minutes.

PEACH RELISH

BY PATRICIA MULVEY AND LAURA GILLIAM OF LOCAL THYME

Adapted from a recipe by Sheila Lukins in her U.S.A. Cookbook, *this delightful relish often adorns turkey sandwiches and grilled meats at Pat's house.*

SERVES 12 // VEGAN // CONDIMENT

INGREDIENTS

6–8 peaches, peeled and finely diced (about 6 cups)

3 tablespoons lemon juice, divided

1 red bell pepper, seeded and finely diced

¼ cup minced red onion

2 teaspoons minced jalapeño, or more to taste

1 tablespoon minced fresh ginger

1 tablespoon minced crystallized ginger

1 teaspoon salt

¼ teaspoon ground allspice

1 cup golden raisins

1 cup cider vinegar

PROCESS

Combine the peaches, 2 tablespoons of the lemon juice, and all the remaining ingredients (bell pepper through vinegar) in a large, heavy saucepan. Bring to a boil, reduce the heat to medium, and simmer for 30 minutes. Cool to room temperature, then stir in the remaining tablespoon of lemon juice. The relish will thicken as it cools. Refrigerate, covered, for up to 4 weeks.

WHITE WINE MACERATED PEACHES
BY PATRICIA MULVEY AND LAURA GILLIAM OF LOCAL THYME

Serve these refreshing peaches, and a little of their soaking liquid, in chilled wine glasses for a memorable last course in a summer meal.

SERVES 6 // VEGAN // DESSERT

INGREDIENTS

6 peaches, peeled and sliced

¼ cup sugar to taste

1 vanilla bean

1 bottle dry white wine

PROCESS

Place the sliced peaches in a narrow, deep container (such as a food-safe plastic storage container) and sprinkle with sugar. With the tip of a sharp knife, slice open the vanilla bean and scrape the seeds into the container with the peaches. Pour the wine over the peaches and stir well. Cover and chill for at least 3 hours. Stir several times during chilling, adjusting the sweetness as necessary.

FALL SALAD WITH PEARS, WALNUTS, AND BLUE CHEESE
BY LEE DAVENPORT

Green salads are excellent when they contain a mixture of sweet, salty, and crunchy ingredients. By varying these three basic components, you can create an endless number of tasty salads.

SERVES 4 // VEGETARIAN // SIDE DISH

INGREDIENTS

¾ pound arugula or other salad greens, torn

1 small shallot, minced

2 tablespoons cider vinegar

¼ cup walnut, sunflower, or olive oil

¼ teaspoon salt

2 ripe but firm pears, thinly sliced

½ cup crumbled blue cheese

½ cup walnuts, toasted

PROCESS

Put the arugula in a large bowl. Whisk together the next 4 ingredients (shallot through salt) and add to the greens. Toss until well coated. Top with the sliced pears, blue cheese, and walnuts and serve immediately.

APPLE AND PEAR PIE WITH MAPLE SYRUP AND TOASTED WALNUTS

BY BARBARA ESTABROOK, COURTESY OF REAP

This classic pie embodies the best of fall, enhancing naturally sweet fruits with maple syrup and traditional spices.

SERVES 8 // VEGETARIAN // DESSERT

INGREDIENTS

PIE:

1 (9-inch) double piecrust

3½ cups peeled, sliced apples

1½ cups peeled and sliced firm, ripe pears

⅔ cup sugar

2 tablespoons all-purpose flour

1½ teaspoons ground cinnamon

¼ teaspoon ground mace

⅓ cup maple syrup

1 teaspoon butter (cut into small pieces)

TOPPING:

3 tablespoons butter

3 tablespoon maple syrup

¼ cup firmly packed light brown sugar

½ cup chopped toasted walnuts

Vanilla ice cream (optional)

PROCESS

PIE: Preheat an oven to 425°. Line a 9-inch pie pan with the bottom portion of the piecrust. In a large bowl, combine the apple and pear slices. Whisk the sugar, flour, cinnamon, and mace together in a small bowl. Add to the fruit mixture and toss to coat. Spoon the fruit mixture into the pie pan, mounding it slightly toward the center. Pour the maple syrup over the fruit mixture and dot with butter. Place the top portion of the crust over the filling; trim and flute the edges. Cut several ½-inch slits into the top crust. Bake for 45 minutes. Remove from the oven and place on a wire rack. Maintain the oven temperature at 425°.

TOPPING: Melt the butter in a small saucepan over low heat. Add the maple syrup and sugar, stirring constantly until the sugar dissolves (1–2 minutes). Stir in the toasted walnuts. Remove from the heat and spoon over the top of the piecrust, spreading evenly.

Return the pie to the oven for 3–4 minutes, or until the topping bubbles slightly. Serve warm or cold, topped with ice cream (if desired).

SWEET POTATO AND PEAR LATKES
BY EDITH THAYER

This twist on traditional latkes pairs rich, earthy sweet potatoes with succulent pears. The result is a latke with a complex flavor and a strikingly bright orange color.

SERVES 4-5 // VEGETARIAN // MAIN DISH

INGREDIENTS

1 pound sweet potatoes, peeled

1–2 firm pears, cored

½ medium onion, skin removed

2 eggs

⅓ cup whole-wheat breadcrumbs

¼ teaspoon ground cinnamon

Salt to taste

¼ cup dried cranberries

½ cup chopped pecans or walnuts

Sour cream or unsweetened applesauce

PROCESS

Preheat an oven to 450° and place 2 nonstick baking sheets in the oven. Grate the sweet potatoes, pears, and onion in a food processor and set aside. In a large bowl, beat the eggs, breadcrumbs, cinnamon, and salt. Stir in the sweet potato-onion mixture. Stir in the cranberries and nuts. Mix until blended.

Remove the hot baking sheets from the oven and spray thoroughly with cooking spray. Spoon the latke mixture onto the sheets, forming 2- to 3-inch patties. Bake until golden brown, turning once with a spatula, about 10 minutes per side. Watch closely so they don't burn. Serve with sour cream and/or warm applesauce.

BALSAMIC GINGER BAKED PLUMS
BY DANIELLE PACHA

Whip up this dessert on late-summer evenings when you first notice the hint of a chill in the air. It combines the best of late summer—sweet, ripe fruit—with welcome harbingers of fall—warm, spicy sauce and toasted walnuts.

SERVES 6 // VEGAN // DESSERT

INGREDIENTS

½ cup water

½ cup balsamic vinegar

6 tablespoons brown sugar, divided

½ teaspoon ground ginger

½ teaspoon vanilla extract

Freshly ground black pepper to taste

6 plums, halved and pitted

Mascarpone, whipped cream, or crème fraîche (optional)

⅓ cup chopped toasted walnuts

PROCESS

Preheat an oven to 400°. Combine the water, vinegar, 4 tablespoons of sugar, ginger, vanilla, and a few grinds of pepper in a small bowl, stirring well to dissolve the sugar. Place the plums cut side up in a shallow baking dish. Pour the vinegar mixture over the plums and sprinkle evenly with the remaining 2 tablespoons of sugar. Bake until the plums are tender and juicy, 25–30 minutes. Ladle the pan juices over the plums one or two times during the baking process.

Remove the plums with a slotted spoon and set aside in a nonreactive bowl. Pour the vinegar mixture into a small saucepan and bring to a boil over high heat. Reduce the heat to medium-high and cook, stirring frequently, until the syrup is reduced and beginning to thicken, about 5 minutes. Pour the syrup over the plums and toss to coat evenly. Serve in individual dessert cups with a dollop of mascarpone, whipped cream, or crème fraîche (if desired) and a sprinkling of walnuts.

FRUIT OF THE SEASON CLAFOUTI (PLUM)

BY TERESE ALLEN, ORIGINALLY PUBLISHED IN *EDIBLE MADISON*

Clafouti is a dreamy, dense French custard cake baked with berries or other fresh fruit. With no crust to make and no frosting to spread, it is also one of the simplest of summer desserts.

SERVES 8 // VEGETARIAN // DESSERT

INGREDIENTS

3 extra-large eggs, beaten

2 cups half-and-half

2 tablespoons berry liqueur
(try "Mulberry Liqueur" on page 139)

2 teaspoons vanilla extract

1 cup all-purpose flour

½ cup sugar

¼ teaspoon salt

2 cups summer fruit (blueberries, blackberries, pitted plum halves, pitted cherries, etc.)

2 tablespoons butter, cut into small pieces

Powdered sugar or lightly sweetened whipped cream

PROCESS

Preheat an oven to 350°. Butter and flour a large, deep glass pie pan or a 10-inch ceramic quiche dish. Use a whisk or electric mixer to combine the eggs, half-and-half, liqueur, and vanilla in a medium bowl until the mixture is smooth.

Whisk the flour, sugar, and salt in another bowl. Whisk the wet mixture into the dry mixture until there are no lumps. Pour the batter into the pie pan, scatter the fruit over the batter, and dot with butter.

Bake until a toothpick inserted near the center comes out clean, 40–45 minutes. Cool to lukewarm or room temperature. Sift the powdered sugar over the entire clafouti, or add a dollop of whipped cream to each serving.

SPICED PLUM BUTTER

BY LEE DAVENPORT

Apple is the most familiar fruit butter, but lots of other fruits can be turned into "butters" too. The name refers to the consistency of the spread. Fruit butters are a great way for a beginner to delve into preserve-making because they can be cooked to the desired consistency without having to set. They also contain less sugar than jams or jellies.

YIELDS ABOUT 4 CUPS // VEGAN // CONDIMENT

INGREDIENTS

10 cups chopped plums

2 cups sugar

Juice and grated peel from 1 lemon

2 teaspoons ground cinnamon

½ teaspoon freshly grated nutmeg

1 cup water

PROCESS

Place all the ingredients in a heavy saucepan and bring to a boil. Reduce the heat to low, cover, and cook until the plums are soft, about 20 minutes. Puree with an immersion blender or food processor. Return the mixture to low heat and continue cooking, stirring occasionally, until the desired consistency is reached (this may take several hours). When finished, transfer the plum butter into an airtight container and store in the refrigerator, or place into sterile jars and process in a water bath canner (according to the manufacturer's directions) to store at room temperature.

BAKED CHICKEN BREASTS WITH QUINCE

BY LEE DAVENPORT

In this unusual recipe, adapted from Uncommon Fruits and Vegetables: A Commonsense Guide *by Elizabeth Schneider, a delectable sweet-tart sauce made from quinces, apple juice, and white wine dresses golden baked chicken.*

SERVES 4 // POULTRY // MAIN DISH

INGREDIENTS

4 medium quinces, peeled, cored, and quartered

1 cup apple juice or cider

1 cup white wine

2 tablespoons sugar

¼ cup all-purpose flour

½ teaspoon salt

4 chicken breasts

2 tablespoons butter

1 tablespoon olive oil

2 teaspoons ground coriander

Ground black pepper to taste

PROCESS

Preheat an oven to 375°. Combine the quinces, apple juice, wine, and sugar in a large pot. Cover and cook at a simmer over medium-low heat until the quinces are tender, about 30 minutes. Uncover and continue cooking until the sauce is reduced to about 1 cup. Set aside.

Combine the flour and salt in a shallow dish and dredge the chicken breasts in this mixture, covering both sides. Heat the butter and oil in a large skillet and brown the chicken, cooking about 4–6 minutes per side. You may need to cook the chicken in batches, depending on the size of your skillet. Sprinkle the chicken breasts with coriander and pepper on both sides and transfer to a baking dish. Spoon the quince mixture over the chicken and bake for 15 minutes. Baste the chicken with some of the cooking liquid and continue baking for 15 minutes more. The chicken should be golden brown and the juices should run clear when pierced with a knife.

REFRESHING QUINCE AND CRANBERRY MOCKTAIL

BY DANIELLE PACHA AND LEE DAVENPORT

Full-fledged cocktails have nothing on this fantastic mocktail. For an extra-special presentation, freeze the cranberries in the ice cubes before adding them to the pitcher.

YIELDS 1 QUART // VEGAN // BEVERAGE

INGREDIENTS

3 cups base beverage: club soda, sparkling water, tonic water, or lemon-lime soda

1 cup "Spiced Quince and Cranberry Syrup" (by Lee Davenport, page 154), or more or less to taste

Frozen cranberries (optional)

Ice cubes

PROCESS

Stir together the base beverage and syrup in a large pitcher. Taste and add more syrup (or more base) to adjust the sweetness if necessary. Add a handful of frozen cranberries (if desired) and fill the pitcher with ice. Serve in tall, chilled glasses.

SPICED QUINCE AND CRANBERRY SYRUP

BY LEE DAVENPORT

If you can set aside some time to make this syrup, you'll have the key ingredient for quick, fancy drinks. This ruby-red syrup can be used with sparkling water for homemade soda, or in cocktails. Using whole spices, which you can remove easily after cooking, will ensure that the color of the syrup is not muddied. Feel free to get creative with the spicing.

YIELDS 4-6 PINTS // VEGAN // CONDIMENT

INGREDIENTS

1 tablespoon mixed whole spices and flavorings (e.g., allspice, cloves, orange peel, cardamom)

1 pound quinces (about 3–4), cut into quarters

4 cups water

2 cups sugar

4 cups cranberries

PROCESS

Secure the spices in a tea ball or some cheesecloth and combine them with the quinces, water, and sugar in a slow cooker or pot and cook until the quinces are very soft and ruby red: if you are using a slow cooker, cook on low overnight or for 6–8 hours; if cooking in a pot on the stove, bring to a boil, reduce to a simmer, and cook for 2–4 hours. Remove and discard the spices and strain the syrup into a large stockpot. Add the cranberries and bring to a boil. Reduce the heat to medium and cook the cranberries in the syrup until they begin to pop and release their juices, about 15 minutes. Strain the syrup and pour it into jars with fitted lids. Store the jars in the refrigerator.

Note: you can reserve and puree the strained solid fruit (quinces and cranberries) for another use.

RHUBARB BREAD

BY EDITH THAYER

Baking with rhubarb is surely one of the rites of spring. The bright red stalks, brown sugar, buttermilk, and nuts make for a moist and delicious quick bread that sings of the season.

YIELDS 2 LOAVES // VEGETARIAN // SIDE DISH

INGREDIENTS

1½ cups packed brown sugar

⅔ cup canola or safflower oil

1 cup buttermilk

1 egg

1 teaspoon vanilla extract

2½ cups all-purpose flour

1 teaspoon baking soda

1 teaspoon salt

1½ cups chopped rhubarb (if you don't have enough rhubarb you can add some strawberries or other fruit)

½ cup chopped nuts

½ cup sugar

1½ tablespoons grated orange peel

1 tablespoon butter, softened

PROCESS

Preheat an oven to 350°. Grease 2 (8 × 4-inch) loaf pans. In a large bowl, combine the brown sugar, oil, buttermilk, egg, and vanilla and beat well. In a separate bowl, mix the flour with the baking soda and salt. Add to the liquid mixture and blend until just combined, being careful not to over-mix. Fold in the rhubarb and nuts. Divide the batter between the two pans.

Combine the sugar, orange peel, and butter and blend well with a fork. Sprinkle over the batter. Bake until a knife inserted in the center of the loaves comes out clean, about 1 hour. Let the bread rest in the pans 10 minutes, and then turn out onto racks. Cool slightly before slicing.

RHUBARB COFFEE CAKE

BY EDITH THAYER, ADAPTED FROM "DONNA'S RECIPES," CHANNEL 3000

Using a base that's similar to her "Rhubarb Bread" (facing page), Edith adds extra fruit and a streusel topping, turning this version into a sweet coffee cake. In order to whip up this cake in a hurry, Edith prepares the ingredients the night before she plans to serve it. She keeps the wet and dry ingredients separate, then combines them just before baking, allowing her plenty of time to have a fresh, warm coffee cake ready for her book club on a workday evening. She serves the cake with lightly sweetened whipped cream.

SERVES 12–15 // VEGETARIAN // DESSERT

INGREDIENTS

BATTER:

¾ cup brown sugar

¾ cup white sugar

⅔ cup canola oil

1 egg

1 cup buttermilk

½ teaspoon ground cinnamon

1 teaspoon baking soda

1 teaspoon salt

1 teaspoon vanilla extract

2½ cups all-purpose flour

3 cups diced rhubarb

STREUSEL TOPPING:

⅓ cup sugar

¼ cup all-purpose flour

⅓ cup rolled oats

½ cup chopped walnuts

½ teaspoon ground cinnamon

¼ cup butter

PROCESS

Preheat an oven to 325°. Butter a 13 × 9-inch baking dish. To make the batter, combine the sugars, oil, and egg in a large bowl and beat well with an electric mixer. Add the buttermilk, cinnamon, baking soda, salt, and vanilla. Beat well. Add the flour and mix just until blended. Stir in the rhubarb. Spoon the batter into the baking pan.

In a small bowl, combine the dry streusel ingredients (sugar through cinnamon) and mix well. Cut the butter into the dry ingredients until the mixture is crumbly. Sprinkle evenly on top of the batter. Bake for 35–45 minutes, or until lightly browned and set in the middle.

RHUBARB SHRUB

BY ANNA THOMAS BATES, ORIGINALLY PUBLISHED IN *EDIBLE MADISON*

Shrubs are vinegar-based drinks that date back to Colonial days. They are typically lightly sweetened and flavored with fruit.

SERVES 3 // VEGAN // BEVERAGE

INGREDIENTS

1 pound rhubarb stalks, diced

⅔ cup sugar

2 tablespoons cider or other fruit vinegar

PROCESS

Add the rhubarb and sugar to a medium saucepan and warm over low heat, stirring occasionally until the rhubarb begins to release its juices and the sugar dissolves. Cover and increase the heat to medium-low. Cook until the rhubarb is very soft, about 6 minutes.

Strain through a fine-mesh sieve, pressing to get all the liquid from the rhubarb fibers. Add the vinegar to the strained liquid and stir to incorporate, then chill.

To serve, add 1 part shrub to 3 parts cold water or seltzer water (⅓ cup shrub to 1 cup water), or to taste. Add ice and serve very cold.

PHOTO BY JIM KLOUSIA © 2012 FOR *EDIBLE MADISON*

LETTUCE IS ONLY THE BEGINNING

LEAFY GREENS
From Amaranth to Watercress

When leafy greens are in season, lettuce is only the beginning. Bountiful CSA boxes packed with various types of glorious green leaves can elicit a hint of anxiety in even the most seasoned member, particularly in the spring. Fortunately for cooks, for all their differences, there are two basic principles that apply to most leafy greens.

> If a leaf seems too bitter, sour, or astringent to eat alone, try adding it to other ingredients as an accent; a small amount of a flavor that seems overpowering alone can contribute a surprising depth to a dish, adding contrast and allowing other flavors to sing.

> *Lettuce is like conversation; it must be fresh and crisp, so sparkling that you scarcely notice the bitter in it.*
> —CHARLES DUDLEY WARNER

First, nearly any young, tender leaf can be eaten raw. Young greens are generally mild and tender, and babies of all types add subtle spice and interest to mixed salads. Second, nearly any mature, sturdy leaf can be cooked, even lettuce. Mature greens are generally dense, savory, and pleasantly bitter; they are at their best when cooked with garlic in quick sautés, shredded and stirred into soups or stews, or braised to melting tenderness.

Depending on their type, leafy greens have a wide range of flavors, from sweet and herbaceous to earthy and bitter. Many are related to one another, however, and their collective attributes may help the cook approach even unfamiliar varieties with confidence. Take the vast Brassica genus. Many leafy greens fall into this group, including arugula, choys, cabbages, collard greens, mustards, and kales, as well as some non-leafy cruciferous vegetables, like broccoli and cauliflower, and roots like rutabagas and turnips. All brassicas have some level of sweetness and a peppery, mustardy bite, with each vegetable's heat falling somewhere on a continuum. On the mild end are kale and broccoli, and at the sharp or hot end are mustard greens. Most cultivated brassicas, like green and red cabbage, fall somewhere in the middle-to-mild end of the scale. Thus, even if you

> Relationships matter! Because genus is such a strong indicator of flavor, particularly among brassicas, we've included taxonomic labels in the storage and usage guide at the end of this chapter. Some greens are related at the larger level of family, as we point out in the text below.

have never cooked bok choy, you can safely assume that it will be mild with a bit of a mustardy bite, and since it's related to cabbage, that it's a good substitute for cabbage and probably shouldn't be overcooked.

Other common classifications are lettuces (Lactuca), which are typically mild and sweet, and chicories (Cichorium)—including escarole, frisée, radicchio, and cultivated dandelion greens—which have sturdy leaves and assertive bitterness. Amaranth, chard, lamb's quarters, and spinach belong to distinct categories in the amaranth family (Amaranthaceae), and they are excellent substitutes for one another in recipes. A few leafy greens, most notably wild greens, belong to none of the above groups. These should be tasted to determine their qualities.

COMMON GROUPS *of* LEAFY GREENS

lettuces   chicories   amaranths

Selection. Brassicas and lettuces will be sweeter and milder in the cooler part of the growing season. Leafy greens should look perky and vibrant. If they are sold bundled, take a peek at the interior leaves to make sure there is no spoilage, and loosen them from bundles after purchase. Avoid leafy greens that have been sitting out on hot or sunny days or otherwise exposed to high temperatures, as they will deteriorate much more quickly than those that have been kept cool.

Storage. Unlike most other vegetables, leafy greens (with the exception of fragile baby greens) should be washed when they get home to revive them and extend their storage life. Fill a clean sink with tepid water, add the greens, and swish them around a little. Let them soak for about five minutes, then gently lift them out and spin dry. If they seem particularly dirty, you may need to repeat the process once or even twice more. If your greens have insects nestled in their leaves (evidence that they are truly organic), add lemon juice or salt to the soaking water, and then rinse thoroughly before spinning dry.

Loosely wrap greens in plastic or cloth and store them in the coldest part of the refrigerator, away from fruits that continue ripening after harvest (like apples, pears, and most tropical fruits), but don't let them freeze.

Preparation. Leaves with thin, tender stems, like spinach, do not need to be de-stemmed, but tough center stems should be removed from larger leaves, like curly kale. If leaves tear away from the stems easily, or if the stems are very thick and fibrous, the stems should probably be removed. With or without stems, tear or chop greens into bite-size pieces, as desired.

Greens for cooking freeze easily. For ease of use, coarsely chop them, then blanch them just until they are limp (this kills bacteria that cause spoilage). Allow them to dry and then freeze them in sealed, one-cup bundles.

ABOUT LEAFY GREENS

AMARANTH

Also known as Chinese spinach, amaranth is a plant most often used in ornamental landscaping in the United States. Edible forms vary in appearance from small mounds with green and magenta leaves (sometimes found in salad mixes), to tall, emerald-green bunches (usually found in Caribbean markets). All varieties have a similar flavor profile: earthy and spinachlike, not hot or bitter. Small leaves are good in salads (mixed with other greens), and larger leaves, stems, and stalks are delicious cooked. Use amaranth in "Polenta with Nuts and Greens" (page 179) or "Greens Quiche" (page 179), or as a substitute for spinach.

ARUGULA

Arugula, or rocket, is a tender, spicy green that has grown in popularity in recent years. Its flavor is comparable to that of radishes, with a similar bite and a slight bitterness. Wild arugula is a variety with slimmer, prettily jagged leaves and a hotter flavor. Arugula can be eaten raw or wilted. It balances other flavors well, whether sweet, salty, rich, or acidic. It requires thorough washing before use.

BROCCOLI RABE

Broccoli rabe, or rapini, is an assertive green more closely related to turnips than to broccoli. It is decidedly bitter and balances salty, spicy, and strong flavors well. It is often served with pasta, chile, and garlic. Choose broccoli rabe carefully: avoid bunches that are yellowing, and check for any hint of old-cabbage smell. Check the cut ends to make sure the stalks are smooth and green, with no separating fibers or white core. It should always be cooked. Use broccoli rabe in place of kale in "Navy Beans with Sage, Sausage, Tomatoes, and Kale" (page 66) or in place of collard greens in "Sautéed Collard Greens" (page 180).

CABBAGE

Common. Green or red, fresh cabbage is pleasantly sweet, slightly spicy, and satisfyingly crunchy. It has been recognized since ancient times—the Roman statesman Cato the Elder proclaimed that cabbage "surpasses all other vegetables" for its medicinal qualities—and remains a popular vegetable worldwide today. Cabbage is infamous for its odiferous qualities when overcooked, but quick cooking will minimize these sulfurous scents.

> The act of slicing cabbage releases enzymes that can create harsh flavors, especially when combined with acidic dressings. To slow their activation, soak sliced cabbage in cold water and spin it dry before dressing. This step also hydrates the shreds and makes them crisper.

Napa. Napa (also known as celery cabbage or Chinese cabbage) has thick, white central stalks that are as valued for eating as its pale green leaves. Heads can be either long and slim or squat and rounded. It has a mild flavor and a crisp texture. It can be used raw in salads as long as it is very fresh; older heads are good for cooking. Unlike common cabbage, it does not develop strong odors or flavors with long cooking times, so it is excellent for braises and Asian-style stews. This is the type of cabbage used for Korean kimchi.

Savoy. With ruffled, deeply veined jade-green leaves, savoy cabbage is almost too pretty to eat. Its leaves have a delicate texture and a milder flavor than common cabbage. It makes a lovely wrapper for stuffed cabbage leaves and a nice textural addition to slaws. Like common cabbage, it should not be overcooked.

CHARD

Whether uniform green or rainbow-stemmed, chard (also called Swiss chard or silverbeet) is a widely palatable hearty green. This beet relative has leaves with a mild, spinachlike flavor and edible stems. Green, red-ribbed, and Rainbow chard (a mixture of various colored varieties) are interchangeable in recipes. Before cooking, remove the leaves from the stems and slice or chop each component separately, as stems require a slightly longer cooking time than leaves. Chard can be eaten raw, but it is a sturdy green and therefore should be shredded before being added to salads.

CHICORY

Escarole. Pleasantly bitter escarole (also called broad-leaved endive or Batavian endive) is similar in appearance to lettuce, but with much chewier leaves that are delicious cooked. The pale leaves in the heart of the head are less bitter and can be used in place of frisée in recipes. Look for heads in which the leafy core is compact—sprawling leaves indicate increased bitterness.

Frisée. Frisée (also called curly endive or curly chicory) is the same plant as escarole, but with wildly curling leaves. Commercially, it is sometimes deprived of light while growing to produce small, pale yellow heads (a process called blanching—not to be confused with blanching in cooking). Its leaves are often used as an accent in lettuce mixes, but it also stands up well to cooking.

Radicchio. Most commonly an addition to salad mixes, radicchio is the Italian name for all chicories. The variety most familiar in the United States is Chioggia, the type that grows in round, red and white heads. Raw, radicchio adds a pleasant bite to mixed-green salads. Cooked, it turns from red to rich brown and develops a mellow, earthy flavor. Cut the heads into quarters, brush with olive oil, and grill, or add chopped radicchio to soups, stews, and braises to intensify the color and depth of flavor.

CHINESE BROCCOLI

Chinese broccoli (also called Chinese kale or kai-lan), is like two vegetables in one. It has large, chewy, collardlike leaves and juicy, kohlrabi-like stalks. It usually has small white flowers. It is not as bitter as broccoli rabe, but it is a good stand-in. Choose bunches with no off smell, as Chinese broccoli will start to deteriorate before it looks bad. Check the cut end to make sure it has no white core. Larger stalks may need to be peeled. Blanching before stir-frying or other cooking will keep Chinese broccoli juicy and preserve its sweetness. Use Chinese broccoli in "Polenta with Nuts and Greens" (page 179) or in place of collard greens in "Sautéed Collard Greens" (page 180).

CHOY

Bok choy and baby bok choy. The assortment of leafy greens that go by the name "choy" can cause some confusion; and it's little wonder, for the Cantonese *choy* (or *choi*) means simply "vegetable." Add the similarly nonspecific *bok*, meaning "white," and there's a lot of room for interpretation. Bok choy, also called Chinese cabbage, is the Chinese vegetable most commonly found in Western markets. The wide white stems, connected at the base in a bulblike manner, are juicy, crisp, and mild, more similar to celery than cabbage. The dark green leaves have a mild cabbage flavor. Baby bok choy has the same characteristics but is tenderer. Separate the stems from the leaves before cooking, as the leaves cook very quickly. Avoid overcooking.

> Bok choy isn't just for cooking. It's refreshing and delicious when raw, too. Toss the tender leaves and crunchy stalks with a little sesame oil, vinegar, and green onions for a quick salad.

Choy sum. Choy sum, or flowering cabbage, looks like a taller, slimmer, slightly leafier version of bok choy. It sometimes has small yellow flowers. Its stalks are as juicy and crisp as bok choy, with a hint of radish flavor. The leaves have a pleasant bitterness, and the yellow flowers have a mustardy bite that works well in salads.

Gai choy. Gai choy, or Chinese mustard, is similar in shape to bok choy, with apple-green stems and leaves with ragged edges. It is less juicy than either bok choy or choy sum, and both leaves and stems have a peppery, mustardy bite.

Hon tsai tai. A relative of bok choy and Chinese broccoli, hon tsai tai is a leafy green with edible slender purple stalks and yellow flowers. It has a mild broccoli flavor and can be cooked or used in salads when young. It is delicious stir-fried and simply dressed with oyster sauce, or it can be added to recipes in place of bok choy or other cooked greens.

Many greens thrive in cooler temperatures, yielding the tastiest leaves in the spring and fall. Some farmers even wait to harvest hearty greens like kale until after the first frost, since frost exposure intensifies the sweet flavor. Overwintered spinach is an especially popular cool-weather crop—cold-tolerant varieties planted in the fall, protected with mulch (and additional insulation if necessary) through the winter, and harvested in the early spring after active growth has resumed.

Tatsoi. Also known as rosette bok choy or (less elegantly) as Chinese flat cabbage, tatsoi is an attractive plant with thin green stems topped with glossy, round, deep green leaves. It has different characteristics depending on its maturity when harvested; tender, young leaves are often added to baby lettuce mixes. When young, the lollipop-shaped leaves are juicy with a hint of cabbage flavor. More mature bundles have a firm texture and a prominent cabbage flavor that mellows with cooking.

GREENS

Beet, radish, rutabaga, and turnip. Fresh leaves from these root vegetables are sturdy and are delicious cooked. They reflect the flavor of their roots: beet greens are mild and chewy and can be used in place of chard in recipes; radish, rutabaga, and turnip greens have more bite and bitterness and can be substituted for assertive greens like arugula, escarole, and mustard greens in recipes.

Carrot, celeriac, parsley root, and salsify. Grasslike salsify leaves and greens from carrots, celeriac, and parsley root have strong herbaceous flavors and are best used as accents in cooked dishes or salads.

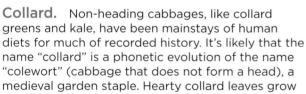

Collard. Non-heading cabbages, like collard greens and kale, have been mainstays of human diets for much of recorded history. It's likely that the name "collard" is a phonetic evolution of the name "colewort" (cabbage that does not form a head), a medieval garden staple. Hearty collard leaves grow on a slim central stem. They have a chewy texture and a toothsome cabbage flavor. Look for bunches that have been kept cold, and store them in the coldest part of the refrigerator. Separate the leaves from the stems for cooking. In the South, collard greens are subjected to prolonged cooking, usually in bacon fat, until they form a soft mass. They are also delicious cooked to medium-firm or sliced thin and sautéed. They are versatile, working well with either simple seasoning or pungent flavors, like curry or chiles.

GREENS (CONTINUED)

Dandelion.   Dandelion greens add spice and complexity to both salads and cooked dishes. The slender, saw-toothed leaves (hence "dandelion" from *dent de lion*, meaning "lion's tooth") have a bit of a bite. Cultivated dandelion greens, which most CSAs offer, are members of the Chicorium genus and a different species than either foraged dandelions or the yellow-flowered lawn pest. They have a red or white central rib and are sold either young and tender or mature and assertive. Add smaller leaves to mixed-green salads, or use them in salads with warm dressings that will wilt the leaves. Larger leaves are delicious cooked in soups or served with grains or beans. To reduce bitterness, blanch the leaves before proceeding with the recipe.

Mustard.   Mustard greens are the leaves of brown mustard plants. They are large, frilly, and pale green, with a slightly fuzzy texture. Taste mustard greens before use; the heat and bitterness vary, depending on the plant and its growing conditions. Use small, tender leaves to add punch to salads, or de-stem and thinly slice larger leaves for cooking. They add delicious depth to soups and braises when stirred in during the last half-hour of cooking time. Long-cooked greens will lose some heat, but will maintain some bitterness.

KALE

Curly.   Happily, curly kale in the United States has moved beyond its decorative duty lining salad bars and buffets. Mild, chewy, and filling, kale is a versatile green that's delicious raw (especially when its leaves are small and tender), lightly cooked, or braised until soft. It can be seasoned simply or paired with bold flavors. Small leaves do not need to be de-stemmed, and large leaves pull away easily from the center rib. Unlike many other greens, curly kale maintains much of its volume after cooking.

Lacinato.   A green with many names, lacinato kale also goes by Tuscan kale, black kale, cavolo nero, and even dinosaur kale. Whatever it's called, it is delicious when cooked: earthy, dense, and savory, with no bitterness. It pairs exquisitely with rich flavors like cheese or nut oils, and stands up to long cooking. Its center ribs must be removed before use, a process usually best accomplished by cutting the leaves away from the stems with a knife. Avoid searing it or cooking it without moisture, as it scorches easily.

Ornamental.   Ruffled ornamental kale, or salad savoy, is pretty enough for a flower arrangement, but modern cultivated types are tasty as well. For all but the tiniest leaves, remove the central stem before use. Steam or blanch to soften, and then add them to salads or cooked dishes. Steamed ornamental kale makes a beautiful bed for poached or steamed seafood or vegetable dishes.

> While it may seem odd to massage your greens, a rubdown does wonders to tenderize kale for salads. Massaging kale is easy to do, if a little messy. De-stem, chop, and wash the leaves well. In a large bowl, rub your dressing into the kale, taking care to get your hands on each leaf. You'll notice visible changes as you do this: the leaves will darken and become silky as the kale's tough cellulose structure breaks down. Taste as you go— if it's still bitter, it could use a little more massaging.

Russian.   Russian kales have names like Red Russian, Ragged Jack, White Russian, and Red Ursa. A different species from other kales, Russian cultivars have flat, scallop-edged leaves similar to turnip tops. Russian kale has a succulent, imposing flavor and a chewy texture. It works well in robust, savory dishes. Large leaves should be de-stemmed before cooking; tiny leaves with stems intact are good salad garnishes.

LAMB'S QUARTERS

Often called wild spinach, lamb's quarters are small bunches of blue-green leaves, some of which have brilliant magenta or violet undersides. The leaves are spinachlike in flavor, with fresh, herbaceous notes in raw leaves, and an earthy, nutty flavor when cooked. Smaller leaves can be eaten stems and all, but larger leaves should be de-stemmed. Use lamb's quarters in "Smoothie Subterfuge" (page 143) or "Greens Quiche" (page 179), or as a substitute for spinach.

LETTUCE

Butterhead.   Butter, Boston, or Bibb, these lettuces form loose heads of large, softly ruffled leaves in colors that vary from bright yellow-green to magenta-tipped emerald. Leaves are tender rather than crisp, and the flavor is mild and sweet. These leaves make excellent wrappers or lettuce cups because of their size and pliability.

Crisphead.   Familiar iceberg and other related varieties are known for their crisp, watery leaves and sturdiness. Because these lettuces are particularly sensitive to heat, they may be hard to find at farmers' markets, but if they appear they will be more flavorful than supermarket varieties. They add crunch and bulk to mixed lettuce salads, and nothing beats them for a classic wedge salad.

Looseleaf.   Loose bunches of leaves connected at the base, these lettuces are also known as bunching or cutting lettuces. Although there are a number of cultivars grown, they are most often called simply green or red leaf lettuce. Look for ruffled leaves that range in color from brilliant chartreuse to burgundy, or from emerald to bronze-tipped green. Oak leaf lettuces in all colors also fall into this category. Looseleaf lettuces are typically mild, sweet, and crisp.

Romaine.   Romaine or cos types of lettuce form long, upright heads of crisp leaves with a prominent center stem. Farmers' market varieties range from the familiar crisp, tall, green heads to squat, fluffy bright green versions, and even a burgundy-freckled beauty called Flashy Trout's Back. Romaine leaves are sturdy and plump, with a mild, savory flavor.

> When preparing lettuce for a salad, tear the lettuce into bite-size pieces by hand; don't cut it with a knife. Cutting damages the leaves and hastens browning along the cut edge. Tear gently, though, because lettuce leaves bruise easily.

Stem.   Stem lettuce (or celtuce or asparagus lettuce) is popular in Asian markets, where the leaves take a back seat to the thick, juicy stem. The leaves are similar to romaine and can be used raw or cooked. The stem should be peeled down to the juicy core, then used raw or cooked. Raw, the stem has a sweet lettuce flavor and the dense, crunchy texture of a broccoli stem. Cooked, it remains pleasantly crunchy and turns bright green. It is a delicious addition to stir-fries or accompaniment to seafood, and in China the stems are often used for pickles. Brown leaf scars at the stem are normal and do not affect quality.

MÂCHE

These tender green rosettes, also known as corn salad or lamb's lettuce, are popular on restaurant menus, thanks to their soft succulence and pretty leaves. They grow in small clusters that make a lovely garnish for cooked dishes, or a fluffy bed for roasted poultry or meats. Mâche is very mild in flavor, and it wilts easily. Mix it with other salad greens to add fluff and mild sweetness, or use it alone for simple salads. Mâche would be a nice component in "Mixed Greens with Apples, Grapes, and Walnuts" (page 144) and "Beet, Orange, and Blue Cheese Salad" (page 18).

MINER'S LETTUCE

Miner's lettuce (also called winter purslane or Indian lettuce) is very high in vitamin C and is named for its use by miners to prevent scurvy during the California Gold Rush. It has small, heart-shaped leaves wrapped around tiny pink or white flowers. It has a mild, peppery flavor, and it is typically eaten raw in salads, although it can be cooked like spinach. Use miner's lettuce in place of watercress in "Watercress, Onion, and Goat Cheese Tart" (page 192) or combine it with the arugula in "Arugula, Watermelon, and Goat Cheese Salad" (page 169).

MIZUNA

A Japanese green with a pleasant, mustardy bite, mizuna has attractive, jagged leaves. It appears frequently in commercial salad mixes, where it adds a peppery accent. In bunches, mizuna also makes an attractive garnish for meat and fish dishes. Larger leaves are best when briefly cooked. Use mizuna in "Wheat Berry and Beet Salad with Maple-Balsamic Vinaigrette" (page 20) or "Dressing-in-the-Bowl Supper Salad" (page 183).

NETTLE

Mild, fresh-flavored foraged plants, nettles are excellent in sauces and soups; they can also be used in salads if they are finely minced. Be sure to wear gloves and take care when gathering or preparing fresh nettles—they are covered in fine, hollow bristles, each filled with a cocktail of chemicals that will irritate exposed skin (hence the moniker "stinging nettle"). Blanching, freezing, or very finely chopping the leaves removes this toxic compound, making the nettles safe to eat.

PURSLANE

A wild green once commonly eaten in the United States, purslane's popularity is back on the rise. It is a medium-green or yellow-green plant with thick, small, oval leaves. It has a mild, fresh flavor with a pleasant tartness and a slightly mucilaginous texture. Cultivated purslane is quite mild in flavor. Foraged late-summer purslane has thick stems that are too tart to eat, and it produces, and sheds, many small black seeds (these are edible and tasty). The taste and texture of purslane is variable, so taste it before using. It can be briefly cooked or eaten raw. Use purslane as a garnish in "Veritable Vegetable Sandwiches" (page 60).

SORREL

Cultivated. In its cultivated form, sorrel is known as common, garden, or broad-leafed sorrel. It has long, bright green, tissue-thin leaves that add a pleasant, almost citruslike sour brightness to salads. When cooked, it collapses almost instantly into a pureelike texture that, with its flavor softened by a little cream or butter, makes an excellent companion to cooked meat or fish. Sorrel is quite nice wilted; stir thinly sliced leaves into cooked pasta, bean, or grain dishes after they have been removed from the heat, or sprinkle them over hot chicken, fish, or meat.

Wild. A catchall name, wild sorrel covers several plants that have an acidic kick. Sheep sorrel, or sour grass, has small, narrow leaves and a subtle, fruity, acidic flavor. It is an interesting addition to salads and is similar to cultivated sorrel when cooked. Curly dock and broadleaf dock are sorrel relatives that grow wild nearly everywhere in the United States. They are coarser and bitterer than cultivated sorrels, so they are best cooked. Wood sorrel resembles clover and is related to other sorrels only in flavor. Its tiny, lobed leaves add a bright punch to salads and make a pretty garnish. It is best used raw or wilted.

SPINACH

Cultivated since the fourth century C.E. (or earlier), spinach was called the "prince of vegetables" by the twelfth-century Moorish agriculturist Ibn al-'Awwām. It is still prized for its mild flavor and deep green color. When cooked, spinach reduces in volume by about three-quarters. Tender young leaves are popular for salads.

WATERCRESS

The most common of the mustardy cresses, watercress has small, pungent leaves that add a kick to both raw and cooked dishes. It is available in both cultivated and wild varieties. Take care in foraging or buying wild forms; these semiaquatic plants flourish in contaminated streams, absorbing pollutants as they grow. Watercress is versatile: add it to salads, simple sandwiches, or grilled foods for its peppery bite; or add it to soups, stir-fries, sauces, or pasta to balance bland, sweet, or salty ingredients.

LEAFY GREENS
Storage and Usage Guide

VEGETABLE	STORAGE AND PRESERVATION		USAGE SUGGESTIONS					
	IDEAL CONDITIONS	FREEZE	GENUS	FLAVOR/TEXTURE	RAW	STEAM	BRAISE	SAUTÉ
AMARANTH	washed, dried, loosely wrapped, refrigerated	•	Amaranthus	earthy, tender	•	•		•
ARUGULA	washed, dried, loosely wrapped, refrigerated		Brassica	hot, bitter	•	•		•
BROCCOLI RABE	washed, dried, loosely wrapped, refrigerated	•	Brassica	bitter		•	•	•
CABBAGE								
common	loosely wrapped, refrigerated	•	Brassica	mild, spicy-sweet	•	•	•	•
napa	loosely wrapped, refrigerated	•	Brassica	mild, juicy	•	•	•	•
savoy	loosely wrapped, refrigerated	•	Brassica	mild, sweet	•	•	•	•
CHARD	washed, dried, loosely wrapped, refrigerated	•	Beta	mild	•	•	•	•
CHICORY								
escarole	loosely wrapped, refrigerated	•	Cichorium	bittersweet, chewy	•	•	•	•
frisée	loosely wrapped, refrigerated	•	Cichorium	bittersweet, chewy	•	•	•	•
radicchio	loosely wrapped, refrigerated	•	Cichorium	bitter, crunchy	•	•	•	•
CHINESE BROCCOLI	washed, dried, loosely wrapped, refrigerated		Brassica	succulent		•	•	•
CHOY								
bok choy	loosely wrapped, refrigerated	•	Brassica	mild, juicy		•	•	•
choy sum	loosely wrapped, refrigerated	•	Brassica	juicy, slightly spicy, bitter		•		
gai choy	loosely wrapped, refrigerated	•	Brassica	peppery, mustardy		•		
hon tsai tai	loosely wrapped, refrigerated	•	Brassica	mildly mustardy, broccoli-like	•	•		
tatsoi	loosely wrapped, refrigerated	•	Brassica	cabbagelike	•	•		
GREENS								
beet, radish, rutabaga, turnip	washed, dried, loosely wrapped, refrigerated	•	Beta, Raphanus, Brassica	chewy, slightly bitter	•	•	•	•
carrot, celeriac, parsley root, salsify	loosely wrapped, refrigerated		various	strong, herbaceous	•	•		•
collard	washed, dried, loosely wrapped, refrigerated	•	Brassica	savory, cabbagelike		•	•	•
dandelion	washed, dried, loosely wrapped, refrigerated	•	Cichorium	spicy, bitter	•	•		•
mustard	washed, dried, loosely wrapped, refrigerated	•	Brassica	assertive, tannic, bitter	•	•		•
KALE								
curly	washed, dried, loosely wrapped, refrigerated	•	Brassica	mild, chewy	•	•	•	•
lacinato	washed, dried, loosely wrapped, refrigerated	•	Brassica	earthy, dense		•	•	•
ornamental	washed, dried, loosely wrapped, refrigerated	•	Brassica	mild, chewy		•	•	•
Russian	washed, dried, loosely wrapped, refrigerated	•	Brassica	juicy, assertive	•	•	•	•
LAMB'S QUARTERS	loosely wrapped, refrigerated		Chenopodium	savory, herbaceous	•	•		•

LEAFY GREENS
Storage and Usage Guide (Continued)

VEGETABLE	STORAGE AND PRESERVATION		USAGE SUGGESTIONS					
	IDEAL CONDITIONS	FREEZE	GENUS	FLAVOR/TEXTURE	RAW	STEAM	BRAISE	SAUTÉ
LETTUCE								
butterhead	washed, dried, loosely wrapped, refrigerated		Lactuca	mild, sweet, tender	•	•		•
crisphead	washed, dried, loosely wrapped, refrigerated		Lactuca	mild, crunchy, watery	•	•		•
looseleaf	washed, dried, loosely wrapped, refrigerated		Lactuca	mild, savory, sweet	•	•		•
romaine	washed, dried, loosely wrapped, refrigerated		Lactuca	mild, savory, crunchy	•	•		•
stem	washed, dried, loosely wrapped, refrigerated		Lactuca	mild, crunchy	•	•	•	•
MÂCHE	loosely wrapped, refrigerated		Valerianella	mild, soft	•			
MINER'S LETTUCE	loosely wrapped, refrigerated		Claytonia	mild, peppery	•	•		•
MIZUNA	loosely wrapped, refrigerated		Brassica	mildly mustardy, savory	•	•	•	•
NETTLE	loosely wrapped, refrigerated	•	Urtica	mild, fresh	•	•		•
PURSLANE	loosely wrapped, refrigerated		Portulaca	mild, tart, savory	•	•		•
SORREL								
cultivated	loosely wrapped, refrigerated		Rumex	acidic, fresh	•	•		•
wild	loosely wrapped, refrigerated		various	acidic, fresh	•	•		•
SPINACH	washed, dried, loosely wrapped, refrigerated	•	Spinacia	mild, sweet	•	•		•
WATERCRESS	loosely wrapped, refrigerated		Nasturtium	peppery	•	•	•	•

MASTER RECIPE: FOUR-WAY SLAW

Slaw, or coleslaw, is a satisfying salad made from shredded (or sometimes sliced or chopped) hearty vegetables. Traditional slaw features shredded cabbage, but other firm, crunchy vegetables and fruits (e.g., carrots, turnips, parsnips, and apples) make excellent additions or variations. Slaws can be dressed with any number of dressings, from traditional vinaigrettes to creamy concoctions flavored with interesting herbs and spices. By varying the dressing, you can adapt your slaw to accompany any meal.

THE BASICS

DRESSING:

Acid: vinegar, citrus

Sweetener: sugar, honey, agave nectar (optional)

Flavorings: herbs, spices

Seasoning: salt and pepper

Fat: oil, sour cream, buttermilk, yogurt, mayonnaise

SALAD:

Vegetables (and fruits), shredded, sliced, or chopped

Aromatics and flavorings: green onions, fennel fronds, herbs

Garnishes: eggs, nuts, seeds, ramen noodles (optional)

PROCESS

To prepare a vinaigrette dressing: Whisk together the **acid, sweetener** (if desired), **flavorings**, and **seasoning**. Drizzle in the **fat** (oil) while continuing to whisk until combined. Adjust the seasoning as desired.

To prepare a creamy dressing: Whisk together the **fat, sweetener** (if desired), **flavorings**, and **seasoning**. Whisk in the **acid** a little at a time.

To assemble the salad: Place the **vegetables** (and fruits) in a large salad bowl. Toss with the **dressing** and **aromatics and flavorings**, and adjust the seasoning as desired. Add **garnishes** (if desired) and serve.

VARIATIONS

MISS CHERIEZEE'S FABOO SLAW

By Cherie St. Cyr

SERVES 6-8

DRESSING (VINAIGRETTE):

2 tablespoons balsamic vinegar

1 teaspoon agave nectar (or sugar, honey, or maple syrup)

Favorite spices to taste

Salt and ground black pepper to taste

¼ cup olive oil

Splash toasted sesame oil

SALAD:

½ small head each green and red cabbage, shredded or chopped

2 kohlrabi bulbs, shredded

2 fennel bulbs, finely chopped

4 green onions, minced

1–2 tablespoons finely chopped fresh cilantro

1–2 tablespoons finely chopped fennel fronds

ADD AS GARNISH:

¼ cup slivered almonds, toasted (optional)

CHUNKY COLESLAW

By Lisa Wilson Krause

SERVES 6-8

DRESSING (VINAIGRETTE):

2–4 tablespoons white wine vinegar or rice vinegar

1 tablespoon celery seed

1½ tablespoons finely chopped parsley

Salt and ground black pepper to taste

¼ cup olive oil

SALAD:

½ head green cabbage, or ¼ head each red and green cabbage, shredded

1 green bell pepper, coarsely chopped

3 medium carrots, peeled and sliced into rounds

6 green onions, finely minced

ADD AS GARNISH:

2 tablespoons sunflower seeds

1 (3½-ounce) package ramen noodles, crushed

ENSENADA SLAW

By Patricia Mulvey and Laura Gilliam

SERVES 4

DRESSING (CREAMY):

½ cup mayonnaise

4 or more dashes hot pepper sauce

Salt and ground black pepper to taste

4 teaspoons lime juice

SALAD:

½ head cabbage, shredded

1 bunch broccoli stems, peeled and shredded

PARSNIP AND APPLE SLAW WITH CREAMY PARSLEY DRESSING

By Edith Thayer

SERVES 4-6

DRESSING (CREAMY):

¾ cup sour cream

1½ teaspoons sugar

3 tablespoons minced red or yellow onion

3 tablespoons chopped fresh parsley

Salt and ground black pepper to taste

1½ tablespoons lemon juice

SALAD:

3–4 medium parsnips, peeled and shredded

2 medium apples (unpeeled), cored and finely diced

¼ cup dried cranberries

ADD AS GARNISH:

¼ cup pine nuts or slivered almonds

Note. Refrigerate at least 2 hours before serving to allow the parsnips to soften.

IDEA STARTERS

Rice wine-chile-ginger vinaigrette, napa cabbage, green onion

Caesar dressing, kale; garnishes: hard-cooked eggs, toasted pumpkin seeds

Soy sauce-molasses vinaigrette, red cabbage, carrot, green bell pepper, red onion, Thai basil; garnish: toasted peanuts

Sherry-ginger vinaigrette, cucumber, carrot, red bell pepper, kohlrabi; garnish: toasted almonds

Lemon-yogurt vinaigrette, sweetheart cabbage, cucumber, onion, jalapeño, mint

Lime-cilantro vinaigrette, carrot, daikon, Swiss chard, onion

Cider-mustard vinaigrette, savoy cabbage, celery, fennel

Lemon-honey vinaigrette, kohlrabi, apple, onion

SERVING SUGGESTIONS

◆ Bring to picnics and potlucks (slaw travels well).

◆ Add to barbecue sandwiches.

◆ Serve as a versatile side.

◆ Toss with cooked grains and beans for a one-dish meal.

◆ Toss with pasta for a quick pasta salad.

COMMUNITY RECIPIES

ARUGULA, WATERMELON, AND GOAT CHEESE SALAD
BY EDITH THAYER

Spicy arugula and sweet watermelon combine perfectly in this salad, united by creamy goat cheese. It's a delicious, cooling addition to barbecue menus and a combination that's sure to become a favorite. Edith uses fresh goat cheese with apricots and lavender honey, but any goat cheese can be used—or feta can be substituted if desired.

SERVES 4 // VEGETARIAN // SIDE DISH

INGREDIENTS

1 bunch arugula (about 4 cups)

4 cups diced seeded watermelon

½ cup goat cheese

½ cup pecans, toasted (optional)

Pomegranate or raspberry vinaigrette to taste

PROCESS

Tear the arugula and put it on a platter. Top with the watermelon, then crumble or put dabs of goat cheese on top and sprinkle with the pecans. Top individual servings with dressing.

REBECCA'S COUSCOUS WITH ARUGULA, ALMONDS, AND FETA
BY PATRICIA MULVEY AND LAURA GILLIAM OF LOCAL THYME

When Pat's friend Rebecca Walsh made this fabulous dish for a party at least a dozen years ago, Pat instantly recognized its potential for variation. Retaining the basic components of couscous, arugula, almonds, feta, mint, and capers, she sometimes adds chickpeas, oven-roasted cherry tomatoes, and even leftover grilled chicken or meat for a heartier main-dish entrée. Quick, portable, and endlessly flexible, it's a great dish to share at potlucks.

SERVES 6 // VEGETARIAN // SIDE DISH

INGREDIENTS

2 cups chicken or vegetable broth

1 tablespoon olive oil

1 teaspoon salt, plus more to taste

1 cup couscous

1 bunch arugula, chopped

½ pint cherry tomatoes, halved

½ cup chopped toasted almonds

4 ounces feta, crumbled

¼ cup chopped mint

¼ cup capers

3 tablespoons lemon juice

2 tablespoons extra-virgin olive oil

Ground black pepper to taste

PROCESS

In a small pot, bring the broth, oil, and 1 teaspoon of salt to a boil. Stir in the couscous, cover tightly, remove from the heat, and allow the couscous to steam until tender, about 5 minutes. Fluff the couscous thoroughly with a fork as soon as it finishes cooking. Fold in the next 8 ingredients (arugula through olive oil), allowing the arugula to wilt a bit in the heat of the couscous, then season with salt and pepper. Serve hot, cold, or at room temperature.

STRAWBERRY ARUGULA SALAD

BY PATRICIA MULVEY AND LAURA GILLIAM OF LOCAL THYME

Something about ripe summer fruit mixed with crisp leafy greens is just so refreshing! Fall and winter salads with dried fruits are certainly delicious, but nothing beats the amazing flavor of local strawberries. For the dressing, be sure to use a relatively sweet vinegar. If you don't have an aged balsamic vinegar, add a little honey or sugar to the dressing.

SERVES 4 // VEGETARIAN // SIDE DISH

INGREDIENTS

1 head lettuce, torn into bite-size pieces

1 bunch arugula, torn into bite-size pieces

1 pint strawberries, halved

⅓ cup sliced toasted almonds

3 ounces feta, crumbled

3 tablespoons aged balsamic vinegar

1 teaspoon Dijon mustard

1 teaspoon poppy seeds

½ teaspoon sea salt

Freshly ground black pepper to taste

½ cup extra-virgin olive oil

PROCESS

Place the lettuce, arugula, and strawberries in a large salad bowl and top with the toasted almonds and crumbled feta.

In a small bowl, whisk together the vinegar, mustard, poppy seeds, salt, and pepper. Add the olive oil in a slow stream while whisking. Toss the salad with the dressing immediately before serving.

CABBAGE SOUP

BY HEIDI ACCOLA OF ROOTS & SHOOTS FARM

Hearty and satisfying, this cabbage soup is a cinch to make. If the last cabbage soup you had was on the infamous cabbage soup diet, give this healthy, yes, but delicious soup a try.

SERVES 8–10 // VEGAN // SIDE DISH

INGREDIENTS

½ medium head cabbage, chopped

2 cups chopped tomatoes (fresh, frozen, or canned)

½ head cauliflower, cut into small florets

1 cup chopped green beans (can be fresh, frozen, or canned)

1 large onion, sliced or chopped

4 cloves garlic, sliced or crushed

2 large carrots, sliced

4 tablespoons chopped fresh herbs such as parsley, marjoram, or oregano (or 2 tablespoons dried)

8 cups broth

Salt and pepper to taste

PROCESS

Place the vegetables and herbs in a large stockpot. Pour in the broth and bring to a boil over high heat, then reduce the heat to low. Simmer until the vegetables are tender, about 15 minutes. Season with salt and pepper.

CABBAGE RAMEN NOODLE SALAD

BY DEBRA SHAPIRO/FAIRSHARE CSA COALITION

Versions of this popular, crunchy salad have long graced picnic tables at family reunions. For a more colorful salad, add carrots, red bell peppers, or snow peas in addition to the cabbage.

SERVES 10–12 // VEGAN // SIDE DISH

INGREDIENTS

SALAD:

2 (3-ounce) packages ramen noodles, crushed (discard the flavor packets)

1 cup blanched slivered almonds

2 tablespoons sesame seeds

2 tablespoons vegetable oil

1 bunch green onions (and/or garlic scapes), chopped

1 head napa or other cabbage, thinly sliced (about 10 cups)

DRESSING:

½ cup sugar

2 tablespoons vegetable oil

2 tablespoons toasted sesame oil

⅓ cup cider vinegar

2 tablespoons soy sauce

PROCESS

In a cast-iron or other heavy skillet, brown the ramen noodles, almonds, and sesame seeds in the vegetable oil. The sesame seeds will start popping. When everything is toasted, mix in the green onions, remove from the heat, and let cool. Combine the cabbage with the noodle-nut mixture in a large bowl.

Whisk together the dressing ingredients in a small bowl. Pour the dressing over the salad and toss everything together. Serve immediately.

SAUTÉED CABBAGE OVER BROWN RICE WITH TOASTED WALNUTS AND PARMESAN

BY KARI SPELTZ

This surprisingly simple recipe is a reminder of just how delicious cabbage can be. Brown rice and toasted walnuts add depth of flavor and nutty chewiness, making this dish a fine main course. Kari loves it with a hearty lager, and our tester described it as great comfort food on a winter day.

SERVES 4 // VEGETARIAN // MAIN DISH

INGREDIENTS

1 medium sweet onion, chopped

2–3 cloves garlic, minced

3 tablespoons olive oil, divided

2 tablespoons butter

1 medium cabbage, shredded (about 8 cups)

¼ teaspoon crushed red pepper (use more to make spicier, or omit)

Salt and ground black pepper to taste

Cooked brown rice (about 4 cups)

½ cup chopped walnuts, toasted

Grated Parmesan to taste

PROCESS

Place the onion and garlic in a large sauté pan (with tall sides). Add 1 tablespoon of the olive oil and the butter. Sauté over medium heat until the onion and garlic soften, 3–5 minutes. Add the cabbage and drizzle with the remaining olive oil (at first the cabbage will seem to fill the pan to overflowing, but as it heats it will cook down). Mix in the crushed red pepper, salt, and black pepper. Continue to cook over medium heat until the cabbage wilts and turns bright green, 5–8 minutes. Serve over brown rice, topped with toasted walnuts and grated Parmesan.

TANGY RED CABBAGE AND BEETS WITH BEEF
BY BARBARA WRIGHT/FAIRSHARE CSA COALITION

With bright green dill against the vibrant purple-red of the beets and cabbage, this dish is a real eye catcher. Serve it alone or toss it with cooked pasta or grain for a one-pot meal.

SERVES 4 // MEAT // MAIN DISH

INGREDIENTS

¾ pound flank steak

Salt and ground black pepper to taste

3 tablespoons vegetable oil

1 teaspoon caraway seeds

1 pound red cabbage, shredded (about 6 cups)

1 beet, grated

¼ cup cider vinegar

4 teaspoons sugar

¾ cup water

2 tablespoons chopped fresh dill (optional)

PROCESS

Season the flank steak with salt and pepper and set aside. In a large skillet, heat the oil over medium-high heat until almost smoking. Add the steak and cook, turning once, for 8 minutes (for medium-rare); transfer to a cutting board and tent with aluminum foil.

Add the caraway seeds to the skillet and cook over medium-high heat for 1 minute. Add the cabbage and beet and cook, stirring, until wilted, about 5 minutes. Add the vinegar, sugar, and water. Reduce the heat to medium-low and cook, stirring occasionally, until the cabbage is tender, about 10 minutes; season with salt and pepper.

Slice the steak thinly against the grain, adding any remaining juices to the cabbage mixture. Divide the cabbage-beet mixture among 4 plates and top with the steak and dill.

HEIDI'S SWISS CHARD SOUP
BY HEIDI ACCOLA OF ROOTS & SHOOTS FARM

Swiss chard stars in this zesty soup. Chard is sturdier than spinach but has a subtler flavor than other hearty greens like collards, turnip greens, or kale.

SERVES 4-6 // VEGETARIAN // SIDE DISH

INGREDIENTS

1 tablespoon olive oil

1 green onion (both white and green parts), chopped

3–4 cloves garlic or 4 garlic scapes or 1 small bunch green garlic, minced

1 bunch Swiss chard, stems chopped and leaves sliced

6 cups chicken or vegetable broth

1 teaspoon grated lemon peel

3 egg yolks

Salt to taste

PROCESS

Heat the oil in a stockpot over medium heat. Add the onion and garlic and cook, stirring occasionally, for 1–2 minutes. Add the chard stems and cook, stirring, for another 2–3 minutes. Add the chard leaves, broth, and lemon peel. Increase the heat to high until boiling. Reduce the heat and simmer for about 10 minutes, or until the greens are wilted but still bright green.

Meanwhile, in a small bowl, whisk the egg yolks until smooth. Use a ladle to remove 1 ladleful of soup from the pot; whisk it into the egg yolks. Immediately pour the egg mixture into the soup and simmer, stirring, for another 2 minutes. Season with salt and serve hot.

BLACK AND GREEN TACOS (CHARD)

BY JAMIE DECARIA OF SAVORRA.COM

This family-friendly recipe makes tacos interesting by adding a couple of unique ingredients—mushrooms and sautéed greens—plus a spicy kick and a cooling topping of sour cream, avocado, and shredded Cheddar. Delicioso!

SERVES 4 // VEGETARIAN // MAIN DISH

INGREDIENTS

MUSHROOMS AND BEANS:

2 tablespoons olive oil

½ large onion, thinly sliced (about 1 cup)

½ pound crimini mushrooms, caps and stems thinly sliced

½ teaspoon salt, or more to taste

¼ teaspoon freshly ground black pepper

1 jalapeño, finely diced

1 (15-ounce) can black beans, drained and rinsed

1 teaspoon ground cumin

GREENS:

2 tablespoons olive oil

¼ teaspoon crushed red pepper

8 ounces mixed greens (spinach, chard, etc.), baby size or cut into 1-inch strips

¼ teaspoon salt

8 (8-inch) flour tortillas, warmed

1 large avocado, sliced

½ cup sour cream

1 cup shredded Cheddar

PROCESS

MUSHROOMS AND BEANS: In a medium pot, heat the olive oil over medium-low heat. Add the onion and sauté for 5 minutes, stirring occasionally. Stir in the mushrooms, sprinkle with salt and pepper, and continue to sauté for 5–8 minutes, or until the mushrooms and onion are soft. Stir in the jalapeño, black beans, cumin, and more salt if needed, and keep warm until the greens are finished.

GREENS: Start the greens while the mushrooms and onion are softening. Heat the olive oil over medium-low heat in a large sauté pan. Sprinkle in the crushed red pepper and heat for 1–2 minutes. Add the greens, sprinkle with salt, and sauté for about 5 minutes, stirring frequently, just until the greens wilt.

TO SERVE: Put the tortillas, mushrooms and beans, greens, avocado, sour cream, and Cheddar in separate serving dishes for individual taco assembly.

WILTED CHARD WITH DRIED CURRANTS AND NUTS
BY DANI LIND, ORIGINALLY PUBLISHED IN *EDIBLE MADISON*

Although chard tends to be a lesser-known green, it's easy to grow and great in many dishes. When shopping for chard, look for bunches that are still crisp.

SERVES 4 // VEGAN // SIDE DISH

INGREDIENTS

1 large bunch chard, stems and leaves separated

2 tablespoons butter or oil

1 tablespoon minced garlic, green garlic, or garlic scapes

3 tablespoons white wine

Salt and ground black pepper to taste

3 tablespoons dried currants

2 tablespoons toasted pine nuts or chopped walnuts

PROCESS

Slice the chard stems into ¼-inch pieces. Coarsely chop the leaves (while still wet from rinsing) and set aside. In a large skillet, heat the butter or oil over medium-high heat. When hot, add the chard stems and sauté for a couple of minutes. Add the garlic, stir a few times, and then add the wine, damp chard leaves, salt, and pepper. Stir about 2 minutes or until all the chard leaves are wilted. Add the currants and cook, stirring, for about 2 minutes more, until the liquid is evaporated. Top with nuts and serve immediately.

ESCAROLE RISOTTO (CHICORY)
BY PATRICIA MULVEY AND LAURA GILLIAM OF LOCAL THYME

With sturdy leaves and an assertive flavor, escarole is an excellent addition to risotto and other cooked dishes. In this rich winter variation, Laura and Pat add sweet golden raisins and salty olives to balance and complement the bitter greens.

SERVES 4-6 // FISH/SEAFOOD // MAIN DISH

INGREDIENTS

4–5 cups chicken or vegetable broth

2 tablespoons olive oil, divided

2 anchovies

1 clove garlic, minced

½ cup finely chopped green onions

3 cups finely shredded escarole

1 cup Arborio rice

⅓ cup dry white wine

2 tablespoons butter

¼ cup sliced black olives

¼ cup golden raisins

½ cup grated Parmesan

Salt and freshly ground black pepper to taste

PROCESS

Heat the broth to a low simmer over medium heat, then reduce the heat to keep warm. Heat 1 tablespoon of the olive oil in a saucepan over medium heat, then add the anchovies. Stir to break up the anchovies and mash into a paste. Add the garlic and green onions and cook, stirring often, until the green onions are wilted, 3–4 minutes. Add the escarole and cook until just wilted, 2–3 minutes.

Transfer the vegetable mixture to a bowl and set aside. Return the saucepan to the stovetop and heat the remaining tablespoon of olive oil. Add the rice and cook, stirring, for several minutes, until the edges of the rice become opaque. Add the wine and cook, stirring, for several minutes, until the wine is mostly absorbed.

Add 1 cup of the simmering broth and cook over moderately high heat, stirring often, until the liquid is absorbed. Continue adding broth 1 cup at a time until the rice is al dente and begins to develop a creamy texture (this usually takes about 25 minutes). Add the reserved vegetable mixture and stir well so all the vegetables are incorporated into the rice. Add the butter, olives, and raisins and stir until all ingredients are evenly distributed. Stir in the Parmesan and cook, stirring from the bottom, about 3 minutes more. Season with salt and pepper and serve immediately.

ESCAROLE SOUP (CHICORY)
BY BARBARA WRIGHT/FAIRSHARE CSA COALITION

Escarole is a popular green in Italian cooking. Its frilly leaves cook down into a restorative soup that is both slightly bitter and sweet.

SERVES 8-10 // MEAT // SIDE DISH

INGREDIENTS

1 pound sweet Italian sausage, prosciutto ends, sopressata, or pepperoni

8 cups chicken broth

6 cloves garlic, minced

3 small red bell peppers, diced

Freshly ground black pepper to taste

1 pound dry white beans, washed, soaked overnight, and drained

¼ teaspoon dried oregano

3–4 fresh basil leaves, chopped

Dash crushed red pepper

1 bay leaf (optional)

2 heads escarole, roughly chopped into 1-inch pieces (up to 4 cups)

Salt to taste

Freshly grated Pecorino Romano

PROCESS

Brown the sausage or meat in a large stockpot. Remove, cut into rounds or cubes, and set aside.

Add the broth, garlic, bell peppers, and several grinds of black pepper to the stockpot. Bring to a boil, reduce the heat to a simmer, and scrape all the browned bits from the bottom of the pot. Add the beans, oregano, basil, crushed red pepper, and bay leaf (if desired) and cook, covered, for 30 minutes. Add the meat and simmer over low heat, until the beans are tender, 30–45 minutes more. Add the escarole and cook until soft, about 5 minutes. Season with salt, discard the bay leaf, and adjust the seasonings. Serve topped with grated cheese.

ITALIAN WEDDING SOUP (CHICORY)
BY PATRICIA MULVEY AND LAURA GILLIAM OF LOCAL THYME

This classic soup of meatballs and escarole is known in Italy as "minestra maritata" because of how well the greens and meat "marry" in the soup. Some versions call for pasta, others use lots of different vegetables, but the way Pat and Laura make it is really simple and delicious. If you have homemade broth, this is a good place to use it.

SERVES 6 // MEAT // MAIN DISH

INGREDIENTS

½ cup grated onion

⅓ cup minced fresh parsley

3 large eggs, divided

1 teaspoon minced garlic

1 teaspoon salt

1 slice white bread, crusts removed, torn into bite-size pieces

½ cup plus 2 tablespoons grated Parmesan, divided

⅓ pound ground pork

⅓ pound ground beef

⅓ pound ground veal

Freshly ground black pepper to taste

12 cups chicken broth

1 head escarole, chopped

PROCESS

Mix the onion, parsley, 1 of the eggs, garlic, salt, and bread in a bowl. Using your hands, mix ½ cup of the Parmesan and the ground meats into the onion-bread mixture and season with pepper. Form the mixture into bite-size meatballs.

Bring the broth to a boil in a large pot. Add the meatballs and escarole, reduce the heat, and simmer until the escarole wilts and the meatballs are cooked through, about 8 minutes. Combine the remaining 2 eggs and 2 tablespoons of Parmesan in a small bowl. Drizzle the egg-cheese mixture into the hot soup while stirring constantly. Season with salt and pepper and serve hot.

BABY BOK CHOY SALAD WITH ROASTED CHICKEN
BY TRACY LAMPARTY

Most bok choy recipes feature the vegetable cooked, but Tracy wanted to try something a little different, so she created this fresh, crunchy salad. Be sure to make this recipe with tender and juicy baby bok choy. You can substitute other crunchy Asian greens, like hon tsai tai or tatsoi, with similar results.

SERVES 4 // POULTRY // MAIN DISH

INGREDIENTS

DRESSING:

¼ cup olive oil

2 tablespoons white vinegar

2 tablespoons plus 2 teaspoons sugar

3 tablespoons soy sauce

½ teaspoon minced garlic

Few dashes hot pepper sauce (or to taste)

SALAD:

2 boneless, skinless chicken breasts

¼ cup soy sauce

Salt, ground black pepper, garlic powder, and ground ginger (to taste)

3 heads baby bok choy, chopped

4–5 green onions (both white and green parts), sliced

¼ cup slivered almonds (toasted or raw)

3 ounces chow mein noodles

PROCESS

Whisk together all the dressing ingredients in a small bowl until combined. Let stand to meld the flavors, whisking occasionally to keep it from separating. The dressing can be made ahead of time and refrigerated; bring it to room temperature before assembling the salad.

Drizzle the chicken with soy sauce and sprinkle with salt, pepper, garlic powder, and ginger. Broil it for 10–15 minutes, or until cooked through, then let cool and slice into thin strips.

Combine the bok choy, green onions, and almonds in a salad bowl. Add the dressing and toss to combine. Serve immediately, topped with chicken slices and chow mein noodles.

SESAME SALMON FILLETS WITH BOK CHOY

BY EDITH THAYER

With a golden sesame seed crust on a bed of emerald-green bok choy, this salmon dish is as lovely as it is delicious. Serve with rice or wasabi mashed potatoes for a sophisticated supper.

SERVES 2 // FISH/SEAFOOD // MAIN DISH

INGREDIENTS

½ cup sesame seeds

½ tablespoon grated fresh ginger

1 teaspoon ground black pepper

½ teaspoon salt

1 egg

1 pound salmon fillets

1 tablespoon vegetable oil

4 cups (or more) thinly sliced baby bok choy

½ red bell pepper, seeded and diced

1 teaspoon rice vinegar

1 teaspoon soy sauce

1 teaspoon sesame oil

PROCESS

In a shallow dish, combine the sesame seeds, ginger, black pepper, and salt, stirring together until the mixture resembles wet sand. In another dish, lightly beat the egg. Dip each salmon fillet into the egg, letting the excess drip off. Gently press the fillets into the sesame mixture, turning to coat both sides (if the fillets have skin, coat only the skinless side).

In a large nonstick skillet, heat the vegetable oil over medium-high heat; cook the salmon, turning once, for 4–8 minutes, or until cooked to your preferred doneness. Transfer the cooked salmon to a plate.

Increase the heat to high. Add the bok choy, bell pepper, vinegar, soy sauce, and sesame oil to the skillet; cook, stirring often, for 1–2 minutes, or until the bok choy is wilted. Arrange the bok choy on individual plates and top with salmon.

STIR-FRIED TOFU WITH BOK CHOY

BY JAMIE BAKER OF PRIMROSE VALLEY FARM

This meatless stir-fry of bok choy and tofu may make you rethink takeout. It's colorful, flavorful, and packed with vegetables coated in a light but rich sauce. Extra-firm tofu will hold together in the pan better than regular tofu.

SERVES 4 // VEGAN // MAIN DISH

INGREDIENTS

2 tablespoons canola oil, divided

1 package extra-firm tofu, drained and cut into 1-inch cubes

1 red bell pepper, seeded and cut into thin strips

2 cloves garlic, minced

1 teaspoon ground ginger

4 green onions (white and light green parts only), chopped

1 pound bok choy, sliced crosswise

¼ cup water

2 tablespoons soy sauce

1 teaspoon Asian chile paste or hot pepper sauce

Kosher salt to taste

PROCESS

Heat 1 tablespoon of the oil over medium-high heat in a large, heavy nonstick skillet or wok and stir-fry the tofu until lightly colored. Remove from the heat and drain on paper towels.

Add the remaining oil to the pan, then add the bell pepper and stir-fry for 3 minutes (it will begin to char). Add the garlic, ginger, and green onions and stir-fry for about 15 seconds. Add the bok choy and stir-fry for about 1 minute, until the bok choy is coated with the oil and the greens have begun to wilt. Add the water and cook, stirring, until the water evaporates, 2–3 minutes (use less water if you want the bok choy to be crisper).

Once the water has evaporated, add the tofu, soy sauce, and chile paste. Stir-fry for a few minutes more, until the ingredients are well seasoned. Remove from the heat, season with salt, and serve.

GARDEN BREAKFAST SCRAMBLE (GREENS)

BY JOANNE LEHMAN AND MARTHA KAUPPI, COURTESY OF REAP

Loads of luscious vegetables transform modest scrambled eggs into an impressive breakfast feature. If you don't have summer squash and green beans, try substituting other add-ins instead.

SERVES 4-6 // VEGETARIAN // MAIN DISH

INGREDIENTS

6 eggs whisked together

2 tablespoons water

2 tablespoons olive oil

1 small onion, diced

2 small summer squash, thinly sliced

10–15 green beans, chopped

½ red bell pepper, chopped

2 Swiss chard or beet leaves and stems, chopped separately

6–8 basil leaves

2 ounces feta

PROCESS

Whisk together the eggs and water. Heat the olive oil in a large nonstick skillet over medium-high heat. Sauté the onion, squash, beans, pepper, and chard stems until lightly browned and crisp-tender (7–10 minutes). Add the chard leaves and basil and stir until wilted. Push the vegetables into a ring around the edge of the skillet; pour the egg mixture into the center of the skillet and cook until the bottom layer of the eggs is set. Crumble the feta over the eggs, then fold the vegetables into the eggs and cheese. Gently turn as needed until the eggs are cooked. Serve immediately.

GREENS QUICHE

BY HEIDI ACCOLA OF ROOTS & SHOOTS FARM

Simple and satisfying, this quiche is the perfect answer to the summertime CSA member's dilemma: what to do with all those greens? Heidi describes this recipe as flexible, forgiving, and delicious for supper on a hot summer night with iced tea and fruit salad.

SERVES 4-6 // VEGETARIAN // MAIN DISH

INGREDIENTS

CRUST:

1½ cups whole-wheat pastry flour

½ teaspoon salt

½ cup oil

3 tablespoons milk

FILLING:

1 tablespoon oil

1 onion, chopped

2–3 cloves garlic, minced

1 bunch greens of choice, chopped (about 6 cups)

6 eggs

1 cup milk

1 teaspoon salt

1 cup shredded cheese

PROCESS

CRUST: Place all the ingredients in a pie pan. Mix with a fork until well blended, then press over the bottom and up the sides of the pan. Flute the edge with your thumb and finger.

FILLING: Preheat an oven to 400°. Heat the oil in a skillet and sauté the onion and garlic until translucent, about 5 minutes. Add the greens and cook until wilted. Set aside to cool slightly.

Beat the eggs and milk in a large bowl. Mix in the salt and the greens mixture. Pour into the crust. Sprinkle the cheese on top, pushing it slightly into the egg mixture. Bake until a knife inserted into the center comes out clean, 30–40 minutes.

POLENTA WITH NUTS AND GREENS

BY ELIZABETH ABBENE

Elizabeth grew up in an Italian household where polenta was a popular item on the weekly menu. As with many grains, it works well for breakfast, lunch, or dinner. This recipe is delicious at room temperature, making it an easy choice for potlucks. Hearty greens and walnuts make it an excellent meatless main course.

SERVES 8-10 // VEGAN // MAIN DISH

INGREDIENTS

6 cups vegetable broth or water

2 teaspoons sea salt

2 cups coarsely ground yellow cornmeal

2 cups cold water

1 tablespoon olive oil

2 cups chopped green vegetables (broccoli, kale, spinach, etc.)

1 cup chopped walnuts

PROCESS

In a large pot, bring the broth to a boil and add the salt. In a blender or food processor, mix together the cornmeal and cold water. Slowly stir the blended cornmeal mixture into the boiling water, then stir in the olive oil. Reduce the heat to medium and continue stirring until the mixture begins to thicken, about 5 minutes. Add the greens and walnuts and cook, stirring frequently, for 30 minutes, or until the liquid is absorbed and the polenta begins to pull away from the sides of the pot.

Press the mixture into a lightly oiled 13 × 9-inch baking dish and let cool for 30 minutes or longer. Slice and serve plain, or serve in a pool of tomato sauce with mixed greens on the side.

SAUTÉED COLLARD GREENS
BY DELA ENDS OF SCOTCH HILL FARM

Collard greens are often flavored with bacon in the South, but they are just as delicious sautéed with olive oil for vegetarian diners. The balsamic vinegar adds a bright kick that complements the deep, earthy flavor of the greens.

SERVES 4 // VEGAN // SIDE DISH

INGREDIENTS

2 tablespoons rendered bacon fat or olive oil

3 cloves garlic, minced

1 pound collard greens, stemmed and chopped

1 cup water

1–2 tablespoons balsamic vinegar

1–2 tablespoons sugar

Salt and ground black pepper to taste

PROCESS

Heat the bacon fat or olive oil in a large sauté pan over medium heat. Add the garlic and cook until fragrant, about 1 minute (do not brown). Add the collard greens, water, and equal amounts vinegar and sugar (don't worry if the pan seems overly filled with greens; they will decrease in size as they cook). Reduce the heat and simmer, covered, for about 30 minutes. Add water as needed—don't let the greens dry out. Season with salt and pepper.

CORN AND KALE FRITTERS
BY JEANETTE PACHA

Awarded the "really yummy" seal of approval by Jeanette's picky six-year-old granddaughter, these fritters are an ingenious and delicious way to serve leafy greens to diners of all ages. Serve warm with salsa and/or sour cream.

SERVES 4-6 // VEGETARIAN // MAIN DISH

INGREDIENTS

½ cup whole-wheat flour

½ cup all-purpose flour

1 cup cornmeal

1–2 teaspoons salt (or more to taste)

2 cups corn kernels (fresh or frozen and thawed)

2 cups firmly packed finely chopped kale

2 large eggs

2 tablespoons butter, melted

2 cups milk

1 tablespoon olive oil, plus more for frying

1 cup chopped onion

PROCESS

Mix the flours, cornmeal, salt, corn, and kale in a large bowl. In a medium bowl, beat the eggs, melted butter, and milk. Pour the wet ingredients into the dry, stirring gently until just mixed, and set aside. Heat 1 tablespoon of the oil in a large skillet, add the onion, and sauté 3 minutes. Add to the batter.

Cover the bottom of a skillet with about ¼ inch of oil and heat it over medium heat. Drop ¼-cupfuls of batter into the hot oil and flatten them evenly into ½-inch-thick patties. Add more oil as needed to prevent sticking. Cook each fritter until it begins to bubble, then flip and cook 1–2 minutes more, until golden.

These fritters are also delicious with any relatively non-bitter green; just be sure to chop tough leaves very fine. They are a great use for fresh beet or turnip tops. Customize the flavor profile by adding garlic, ginger, chiles, or other aromatics to the onion sauté.

CRISPY ROASTED KALE

BY WATER HOUSE FOODS

When coated with olive oil and roasted, kale becomes translucent and crispy, with a pleasant toasted flavor. Serve roasted kale as a chip alternative; try seasoning with smoked paprika, salt, garlic salt, and pepper or your favorite spice blend to personalize your "chips."

SERVES 4-5 // VEGAN // APPETIZER

INGREDIENTS

1 bunch kale, cut into bite-size pieces

Olive oil

Salt and ground black pepper to taste

PROCESS

Preheat an oven to 400°. Place the kale in a large bowl and drizzle with olive oil. Using your hands, rub the oil into the leaves so that all the pieces are evenly coated. Sprinkle with salt and pepper, toss, and transfer to a baking sheet or roasting pan, spreading evenly in a single layer. Roast until crispy, 8–10 minutes (they will continue to crisp a bit after you remove them from the oven). The leaves will begin to brown as they are roasting, and they can easily burn, so check them often. Serve after cooling or store in an airtight container.

FRESH KALE SALAD

BY SARAH MURRAY

Kale salads have an advantage over those made of lettuce in that they only get better after they've been dressed. This one is no exception; dressing it thirty minutes before serving softens the leaves, and it stays delicious for several days. Keep it in the refrigerator for a quick meal for hot summer days, try it as a bed for grilled fish, or bring it to your next picnic or potluck.

SERVES 6-8 // VEGAN // SIDE DISH

INGREDIENTS

SALAD:

1 large bunch kale, stems removed, leaves sliced into thin ribbons (about 6 cups)

8 small or medium cloves garlic, minced

2 large oranges or 6 mandarin oranges, peeled, sectioned, and cut into bite-size pieces

1 cup chopped walnuts

½–¾ cup dried cranberries

¼ cup sesame seeds

¼ cup pine nuts

DRESSING:

Juice from ½ lime (1–2 tablespoons)

2 tablespoons rice vinegar

2 tablespoons tamari

3 tablespoons flaxseed or toasted sesame oil

PROCESS

Mix the salad ingredients in a large bowl. In a small bowl, whisk together the dressing ingredients until combined. Drizzle the dressing over the salad and toss well. For the best flavor, let stand for about 30 minutes before serving.

GREEK-STYLE KALE SALAD
BY ALISSA MOORE OF WELLSPRING CSA

Kale provides a hearty base for Alissa's version of this popular salad favorite. The sturdy leaves hold up well to the dressing, and they won't be weighed down by the olives, cucumber, and other chunky goodies.

SERVES 4-6 // VEGETARIAN // SIDE DISH

INGREDIENTS

SALAD:

1 bunch curly or Russian kale (or ½ pound baby kale), cut into bite-size pieces

½ cup chopped Kalamata olives

½ cup crumbled feta

½ small red onion, sliced

½ cucumber, sliced (optional; use when in season)

½ cup diced tomato (optional; use when in season)

DRESSING:

2 tablespoons lemon juice or vinegar of choice (red wine, balsamic, or cider recommended)

Dijon mustard to taste

Salt and ground black pepper to taste

3 tablespoons olive oil

PROCESS

This recipe may be prepared with raw or blanched kale. To blanch, bring a pot of water to a boil and add the kale. Cook for 30–60 seconds, until just tender. Rinse with cold water to stop the cooking process and drain well.

Place the raw or blanched kale and the remaining salad ingredients in a large bowl. To make the dressing, put the lemon juice or vinegar in a small bowl. Whisk in the Dijon mustard, salt, and pepper until mixed, then add the olive oil, continuing to mix until emulsified. Drizzle the dressing over the salad and toss well to coat. Serve at room temperature or chilled.

KALE SOUP WITH FARRO
BY KARIS KUCKLEBURG

Serve a loaf of crusty bread with this hearty soup for a satisfying main course. Try substituting celeriac or parsley root for celery in this recipe; the flavorful roots will add a pleasant depth to this earthy dish.

SERVES 4 // VEGAN // MAIN DISH

INGREDIENTS

2 tablespoons olive oil

1 cup chopped onion

2 cups chopped carrot

1½ cups chopped celery

2 cups chopped peeled tomatoes (fresh or canned)

5 cups vegetable broth

1½ cups farro (spelt or barley may be substituted)

3 cups chopped kale

Salt and ground black pepper to taste

PROCESS

Heat the olive oil over medium heat for 1 minute. Add the onion, carrot, and celery and sauté until softened, about 5 minutes. Add the tomatoes, broth, and farro. Bring to a boil, then reduce the heat to medium-low. Cover and simmer for 30 minutes. Stir in the kale and simmer uncovered for 5–10 minutes more. Season with salt and pepper.

DRESSING-IN-THE-BOWL SUPPER SALAD (LETTUCE)

BY DEBRA SHAPIRO/FAIRSHARE CSA COALITION

Think of this recipe as a template for a summer night's dinner. Start with your favorite grilled meats, cheeses, and nuts, then add vegetables, beans, and salad greens—and a tasty, nutritious meal is on the table without heating up the kitchen. Try using white beans, Italian canned tuna, blanched green beans, and cooked new potatoes for a delicious, Niçoise-style salad, or go Greek with chickpeas, tomatoes, and olives. Serve with bread for a no-sweat supper.

SERVES 4-6 // VEGAN // MAIN DISH

INGREDIENTS

½ medium red onion, very thinly sliced

3–4 tablespoons vinegar of choice

Generous pinch sugar

2 tablespoons mustard of choice

Salt and freshly ground black pepper to taste

½ cup canned beans (black beans, chickpeas, or kidney beans), drained and rinsed

2 cups chopped raw or lightly cooked vegetables of choice

2 tablespoons chopped parsley

1–2 cups chopped protein (cooked chicken, shrimp, tofu, ham, nuts, cheese, etc.)

1 pound salad greens, torn

4–6 tablespoons oil (olive, almond, walnut, etc.)

PROCESS

In a large bowl, stir together the onion, 3 tablespoons of vinegar, sugar, and mustard and season with salt and pepper. Add the beans and let marinate while you prepare the other vegetables.

When you're ready to eat, add the vegetables, parsley, protein, salad greens, and 4 tablespoons of oil. Mix well, taste, and adjust the vinegar, oil, salt, or pepper as necessary. Serve immediately.

FARMERS' MARKET CONFETTI SALAD WITH CHAMPAGNE-DIJON VINAIGRETTE (LETTUCE)

BY BARBARA WRIGHT/FAIRSHARE CSA COALITION

Choose a variety of brightly colored vegetables for this recipe: multicolored carrots and beets work well in the winter; try yellow squash and bell peppers in the summer. The champagne vinaigrette adds delicious brightness to nearly any combination.

SERVES 2-4 // VEGETARIAN // SIDE DISH

INGREDIENTS

½ cup olive oil

¼ cup champagne vinegar or wine vinegar

2 tablespoons coarse Dijon mustard

1 tablespoon sugar

Thinly sliced basil or other fresh herbs

Salt and ground black pepper to taste

2 cups raw vegetables of choice, very thinly sliced

¼ cup goat cheese

French bread

PROCESS

Put the oil, vinegar, mustard, sugar, and herbs into a cocktail shaker or other sealed container and shake to combine. Taste and season with salt and pepper.

Place the sliced vegetables in a large bowl. Drizzle the vinaigrette over the vegetables. Using tongs, toss the vegetables in the vinaigrette until they are thoroughly coated. Top each serving with a crumbling of goat cheese. Serve with a piece of fresh French bread to soak up all of the great taste.

HEARTY WISCONSIN SALAD WITH FAVORITE DRESSING (LETTUCE)

BY DEBRA SHAPIRO/FAIRSHARE CSA COALITION

Hard-cooked eggs, dried cranberries, garlic croutons, and goat cheese make for a salad substantial enough to play the starring role at lunch or dinner.

SERVES 4 // VEGETARIAN // MAIN DISH

INGREDIENTS

DRESSING:

1 tablespoon Dijon mustard

1 tablespoon sugar, honey, or maple syrup

2 tablespoons minced shallot, chives, or green onion; or 1 clove garlic, minced or pressed

¼ cup vinegar (half balsamic and half red wine works well)

½ cup oil of choice (or a combination)

Salt and freshly ground black pepper to taste

SALAD:

4 handfuls greens

4 radishes, thinly sliced

6 tablespoons dried cranberries

1 cup garlic croutons

4 ounces goat cheese, crumbled

4 hard-cooked eggs, peeled and cut lengthwise into quarters

4 small new potatoes, diced and steamed (optional)

PROCESS

DRESSING: Combine the mustard, sugar, shallot, and vinegar in a small bowl. Drizzle in the oil, whisking constantly, until the dressing is thick and emulsified. Alternatively, put the ingredients into a small jar with a tight lid and shake to combine. Season with salt and pepper. You will have about 6 ounces of dressing—more than you need for the salad. Store the extra in the refrigerator for future use (bring to room temperature before using).

SALAD: Toss the greens, radishes, cranberries, and croutons in the dressing. Top with goat cheese, eggs, and new potatoes (if desired).

To make your own garlic croutons: Toss 1 cup of diced bread in garlic-infused oil and salt. Toast in an oven at 375° for about 10 minutes, until golden and crisp.

For perfect hard-cooked eggs: Place the eggs in a large saucepan and cover them with cold water. Bring the water to a boil over high heat, cover, and remove from the heat. Let the eggs sit in the hot water for 13 minutes. Drain off the water and tap the eggs to crack the shells all around. Cover them with very cold water and let stand 10 minutes more.

LETTUCE WRAPS

BY DEBRA SHAPIRO/FAIRSHARE CSA COALITION

Crisp, crunchy lettuce leaves act like a tortilla or taco shell in this Asian-inspired wrap.

SERVES 4 // VEGAN // APPETIZER

INGREDIENTS

½ cup soy sauce or tamari, or to taste

1 tablespoon sesame oil

2 teaspoons sugar

1–2 teaspoons chile oil or dash crushed red pepper

1 tablespoon olive oil

6 cups chopped vegetables of choice

Romaine lettuce leaves

6 cups cooked rice

PROCESS

Make a dipping sauce by whisking together ½ cup of the soy sauce and the sesame oil, sugar, and chile oil in a small bowl until combined.

Heat the olive oil in a wok or large skillet. Stir-fry the vegetables until they are crisp-tender (cooking time will depend on the vegetables selected). If you have a mixture of firm and soft vegetables, begin with the firmest items and add the softer ones later so they aren't overcooked. Season the stir-fry with more soy sauce (if desired).

Place the lettuce leaves, rice, vegetables, and dipping sauce in separate serving dishes. To assemble, place a leaf on a plate, spoon some rice and vegetables into the center, roll up, and dip in the sauce.

RADISH AND LETTUCE SALAD DRESSED WITH ORANGES AND MINT

BY JAMIE DECARIA OF SAVORRA.COM

When you need a break from your everyday tomato and lettuce salad, or if local tomatoes are not in season, try this pretty salad instead. It brightens up the table with colorful pink and white radishes and juicy oranges popping off a green background of lettuce. And with the flavors from peppery radishes and sweet oranges and mint, you only need to add olive oil, salt, and pepper to have a very flavorful salad. Simple!

SERVES 2 // VEGAN // SIDE DISH

INGREDIENTS

1 orange, peeled

3 cups roughly torn lettuce

2 radishes, very thinly sliced

2 tablespoons fresh mint chiffonade

3 green onions (both white and green parts), chopped

3 tablespoons olive oil

Salt and ground black pepper to taste

PROCESS

Separate the orange into four quarters and thinly slice (¼-inch or thinner) each quarter. Divide the lettuce into 2 bowls and top with the orange, radishes, mint, and onions. Drizzle with the oil and sprinkle with salt and pepper.

CREAM OF NETTLE SOUP

BY SOFYA HUNDT, ORIGINALLY PUBLISHED IN *EDIBLE MADISON*

This easy yet substantial nettle-and-potato cream soup is delicious both hot and cold, and is a perfect way to utilize both the stems and leaves of the nettles. Tender early-season nettles are ideal, but nettles of any degree of maturity should work.

SERVES 4 // VEGETARIAN // SIDE DISH

INGREDIENTS

1½ cups blanched nettle leaves and stems

1 large onion, chopped

2 large or 3 medium potatoes, diced

2 cloves garlic

5 cups cold water

1 teaspoon salt, plus more to taste

1 cup milk

1½ tablespoons all-purpose flour

3 tablespoons butter, softened

Dash ground nutmeg

Ground black pepper to taste

Walnuts (optional)

PROCESS

Place the nettles, onion, potatoes, and garlic in a pot and add the water and 1 teaspoon of salt. Bring to a boil, then reduce the heat and simmer until the potatoes are tender and falling apart, 25–30 minutes. Let cool slightly and blend with an immersion blender. Stir in the milk.

In a small bowl, blend the flour and butter into a smooth paste. Stir 1 cup of the hot soup into the butter-flour mixture until incorporated, and then add the mixture to the pot. Return to a simmer for 5 minutes, stirring frequently. Remove from the heat, stir in the nutmeg, and season with salt and pepper. Serve warm or cold. Sprinkle individual portions with nuts prior to serving (if desired).

LENTIL AND NETTLE SOUP WITH SHIITAKE MUSHROOMS

BY PATRICIA MULVEY AND LAURA GILLIAM OF LOCAL THYME

Young, tender spring nettles add a bright flavor to the earthy lentils and mushrooms in this quick, hearty soup.

SERVES 6 // VEGAN // MAIN DISH

INGREDIENTS

1 tablespoon olive oil

1 small onion, minced

3 cloves garlic, minced

1 tablespoon minced fresh ginger

1 cup lentils

5 cups vegetable broth

1 bay leaf

4 ounces shiitake mushrooms, stemmed and sliced

1 bunch nettles, coarsely chopped

Lemon juice to taste

Salt and ground black pepper to taste

PROCESS

Heat the oil in a stockpot over medium heat until shimmering. Add the onion and sauté until wilted, about 6 minutes. Add the garlic and ginger and stir until fragrant, then add the lentils, broth, and bay leaf. Bring to a boil, skimming off any foam that rises to the surface. Reduce the heat to medium and simmer for about 15 minutes. Stir in the mushrooms and simmer for about 15 minutes more, until the lentils are tender. Stir in the nettles and simmer until wilted, about 5 minutes. Season with lemon juice, salt, and pepper. Discard the bay leaf before serving.

WILTED NETTLES WITH WALNUTS AND GARLIC

BY JANE ANNE MORRIS, COURTESY OF REAP

An all-purpose plant with an impressive resume, the nettle has a long history of use in medicine, textile production, and countless culinary settings. Jane advises collecting fresh nettle tops (4-5 inches of top) when nettles first come up in April and into July; once they begin flowering in late summer, the tops will be tough.

SERVES 2-4 // VEGAN // SIDE DISH

INGREDIENTS

1–2 tablespoons olive oil

1 gallon nettle tops, sliced

¼ cup chopped walnuts

1–2 cloves garlic, sliced

Sea salt and freshly ground black pepper to taste

PROCESS

Heat the olive oil in a large cast-iron skillet over medium heat. Add the nettles and cook, covered, until they are reduced to half the original volume. Add the walnuts, garlic, salt, and pepper and cook for 10–15 minutes, stirring occasionally. Serve immediately.

FLAMIN' HOT SPINACH

BY ANN HARSTE

Our tester loved this recipe, describing it as richly green and aromatic. Ann recommends serving it over coconut jasmine rice.

SERVES 4 // VEGETARIAN // SIDE DISH

INGREDIENTS

2 tablespoons olive oil

1 small onion, diced

2–3 cloves garlic, minced

2 jalapeños, seeded and diced

Salt and ground black pepper to taste

1 pound spinach

½ cup low-sodium chicken or vegetable broth

¼ cup sour cream

PROCESS

Heat the olive oil in a large sauté pan over medium-high heat. Add the onion, garlic, jalapeños, and a generous pinch of salt and pepper. Reduce the heat to medium and cook, stirring occasionally, until the onion is translucent, 5–10 minutes. Stir in the spinach, add the broth, and cover. Simmer for 10–15 minutes, or until the spinach is very tender. Remove from the heat, stir in the sour cream, and adjust the seasonings.

HEARTY TOMATO SOUP WITH SPINACH
BY ANNETTE GERLECKI

A bumper crop of spinach inspired this hearty pasta soup. Soups are an easy and satisfying way to enjoy farm-fresh produce, and they keep well. Just be sure to save any leftover pasta separately to prevent it from absorbing too much liquid.

SERVES 6-8 // VEGETARIAN // SIDE DISH

INGREDIENTS

2–3 tablespoons olive oil

1 large white onion, coarsely chopped

1–2 cloves garlic, thinly sliced

1 teaspoon dried oregano

4 cups vegetable broth

3 cups chopped roasted tomatoes or 1 (28-ounce) can diced tomatoes

1 bunch spinach, stems removed, chopped (about 4 cups)

Salt to taste

1–2 cups orecchiette pasta, cooked according to package directions

Grated Parmesan

Freshly ground black pepper to taste

PROCESS

Heat the olive oil in a stockpot. Add the onions and garlic and sauté for 3–5 minutes, or until the onion begins to turn translucent. Add the oregano, broth, and tomatoes and bring to a boil. Reduce the heat, add the spinach, and simmer for 10 minutes. Season with salt. If a smooth soup is desired, puree with an immersion blender or in a food processor.

To serve, ladle the soup over the pasta in individual bowls. Top with grated Parmesan and freshly ground pepper.

ITALIAN QUINOA WITH TOMATO, SPINACH, AND SHRIMP
BY KRISTI SEAVERSON

Word is out that quinoa is good for you, but many are left wondering what to do with it. Kristi threw her favorite ingredients together, and the result was this easy, tasty dish. Use this recipe as written, or treat it as a template for your own innovation. You can use heartier greens in place of the spinach; just cook them along with the quinoa. Try sun-dried tomatoes in the winter, or play with your own favorite spice blends. Soon you'll be wondering what can't *you do with quinoa.*

SERVES 4 // FISH/SEAFOOD // MAIN DISH

INGREDIENTS

1 cup water

1 cup chicken or vegetable broth

1 cup quinoa

4 red tomatoes, diced

3 handfuls spinach, chopped or shredded

1 tablespoon Italian seasoning

1 cup cooked shrimp

¼ cup grated Parmesan

Salt and ground black pepper to taste

PROCESS

Boil the water and broth in a medium pot. Add the quinoa, reduce the heat, and simmer, covered, for 10–15 minutes, or until the quinoa is tender. Remove from the heat and let stand for 10 minutes to allow any remaining liquid to be absorbed. Fluff the quinoa with a fork and add the tomatoes, spinach, Italian seasoning, and shrimp. Stir until the spinach is wilted. Spoon into individual serving bowls and top with Parmesan, salt, and pepper.

MEAT AND VEGGIE BALLS (SPINACH)

BY ERIN WILICHOWSKI

These meatballs are a versatile and delicious way to use whatever is fresh from the market or in your CSA box. The veggies make the meatballs moist and delicious. No fresh basil? No problem. Try sage, thyme, oregano, or marjoram. Serve with a side of garlic bread, a green salad, and your favorite wine.

SERVES 4–6 // MEAT OR POULTRY // MAIN DISH

INGREDIENTS

2 slices bread, toasted and diced into ¼-inch cubes

Milk to cover the bread

1 pound ground chicken or beef

⅓ cup grated zucchini

¼ cup grated carrot

3 tablespoons grated Parmesan

1 large egg, lightly beaten

½ cup finely chopped spinach

1 tablespoon minced fresh basil

2 cloves garlic, minced

1 teaspoon salt

1 teaspoon ground black pepper

2 tablespoons olive oil

PROCESS

Place the bread in a large bowl and cover it with milk. Add the meat and the next 9 ingredients (zucchini through pepper). Mix until thoroughly combined. Shape the mixture into 24 meatballs (about 1 rounded tablespoon per meatball).

Heat the oil in a large heavy skillet over medium heat. Sauté the meatballs until brown and cooked through, turning often, about 15 minutes. To serve, simmer the meatballs in your favorite sauce until heated through and serve over pasta; or layer them on toasted rolls and top with tomato sauce and a sprinkling of Parmesan.

SPINACH LASAGNA

BY EDITH THAYER

This recipe makes quick work of traditional lasagna with raw spinach and no-boil noodles. It is even better on the second day, when the flavors have had a chance to meld, and it freezes well. Kale, chard, or any non-bitter green can be used in place of spinach; just reduce the amount of sturdy greens to 2–3 cups, or precook them slightly.

SERVES 8 // MEAT // MAIN DISH

INGREDIENTS

1 pound bulk Italian sausage, crumbled

½ cup finely chopped onion

1 quart homemade tomato sauce or 1 (32-ounce) jar pasta sauce

8 ounces shredded mozzarella (2 cups)

4 cups coarsely chopped fresh spinach

1 cup ricotta

2 eggs, slightly beaten

1–4 cloves garlic, minced; or ¼ teaspoon garlic powder

8 ounces lasagna noodles

⅓ cup water

½ cup grated Parmesan

PROCESS

Preheat an oven to 350°. In a large skillet or stockpot, brown the sausage and onion over medium heat; drain if necessary. Stir in the tomato sauce and simmer for 10 minutes (to heat through), stirring occasionally.

In a medium bowl, combine the mozzarella, spinach, ricotta, eggs, and garlic and stir until well blended.

Cover the bottom of a 13 × 9-inch baking dish with about ½ cup of the meat sauce, then layer half of the uncooked noodles, half of the remaining meat sauce, all of the spinach mixture, the remaining noodles, and the remaining meat sauce. Pour the water over the lasagna. Cover the dish tightly with aluminum foil and bake, covered, for 45 minutes. Remove the foil from the lasagna and sprinkle with Parmesan. Bake uncovered for an additional 10–15 minutes, or until hot and bubbly and the noodles are tender. Let stand for 10 minutes before serving.

ROAST BEEF SANDWICHES WITH SWEET AND SOUR ONIONS AND WATERCRESS

BY PATRICIA MULVEY AND LAURA GILLIAM OF LOCAL THYME

The onions in this recipe are quick-pickled in about an hour and are a delicious accent to the roasted meat. Crusty bread, peppery watercress, and pungent cheese make an everyday roast beef sandwich taste gourmet.

SERVES 4 // MEAT // MAIN DISH

INGREDIENTS

2 cups julienned red onion

2 tablespoons red wine vinegar

1 teaspoon sugar

Pinch salt

4 whole-grain rolls

2 cups watercress (leaves and upper stems)

½ cup crumbled blue cheese

8 ounces roast beef

PROCESS

Place the onion in a medium bowl. Add the vinegar, sugar, and salt and stir well. Allow the mixture to marinate for about 1 hour. Divide the rolls to create tops and bottoms for 4 sandwiches. Place each bottom half on an individual serving plate and layer one fourth of the onion, watercress, blue cheese, and roast beef onto each roll. Top each sandwich with a roll top and serve.

WATERCRESS AND GREEN ONION DEVILED EGGS

BY PATRICIA MULVEY AND LAURA GILLIAM OF LOCAL THYME

Watercress and green onions add a twist of spring to classic deviled eggs. The mustardy bite of the watercress makes it a natural partner for eggs. Plus, it looks beautiful on the plate.

SERVES 16 // VEGETARIAN // APPETIZER

INGREDIENTS

8 hard-cooked eggs, peeled

1 tablespoon olive oil

1 cup lightly packed watercress leaves, plus a few more for garnish

4 green onions, finely chopped

⅓ cup mayonnaise

2 teaspoons Dijon mustard

Salt to taste

Dash cayenne

PROCESS

Cut the eggs in halve lengthwise, separate the yolks from the whites, and set both parts aside. Heat the oil in a medium skillet over medium heat. Add 1 cup of the watercress leaves and green onions. Cook, stirring, until the vegetables are very tender, 3–4 minutes. Set aside to cool.

In a food processor, combine the egg yolks, watercress-green onion mixture, mayonnaise, mustard, salt, and cayenne. Pulse until very smooth, about 1 minute, stopping to scrape the sides of the bowl once or twice. Spoon the yolk mixture into the egg white halves, place them on a platter, and surround them with the reserved watercress leaves.

WATERCRESS, ONION, AND GOAT CHEESE TART

BY MACON LUHNING, ORIGINALLY PUBLISHED IN *EDIBLE MADISON*

Watercress is one of the oldest green foods known to humans. Its peppery pungency is refreshing and lively in salads, sandwiches, pesto, and dips, or as a garnish.

SERVES 10 // VEGETARIAN // MAIN DISH

INGREDIENTS

2 (8-ounce) packages cream cheese, softened

10 ounces pastry flour

¼ cup olive oil (for oiling the pan)

3 eggs, beaten

½ cup whipping cream

1 teaspoon ground black pepper

2 cups watercress, lower stems removed

2 large yellow onions, sliced

¾ cup fresh goat cheese

PROCESS

Using the paddle attachment on an electric mixer, beat the cream cheese on low speed until creamy. Add the pastry flour and mix on low speed until the dough comes together and starts to pull away from the sides of the bowl. Do not over-mix. Remove the dough from the mixing bowl and form into a flattened disk. Wrap the dough in plastic wrap and refrigerate for at least 2 hours.

Preheat an oven to 375°. Roll out the dough until it is ⅛ inch thick, dusting with flour as needed. Cut an 11-inch circle out of the rolled dough. Brush the sides and bottom of a 9½-inch tart pan with the oil. Line the tart pan with the dough, pressing it up the sides of the pan. Be sure not to leave any slack in the dough. Prick the surface of the dough with a fork. Keep it in the refrigerator until ready to bake.

PHOTO BY JIM KLOUSIA © 2012
FOR *EDIBLE MADISON*

In a large bowl, mix the eggs, cream, and black pepper together. Add the watercress and onions and mix. Fill the tart shell with the egg mixture and place the goat cheese evenly around the tart in about 12 dollops. Bake the tart for 30 minutes. Using a small knife, release the tart from the edges of the pan and unmold the tart by removing the pan bottom. Serve immediately.

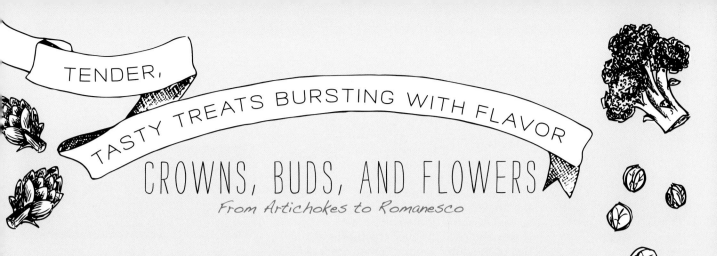

CROWNS, BUDS, AND FLOWERS
From Artichokes to Romanesco

Cauliflowers are flowers, or more precisely, members of the mustard family (Brassicaceae) grown for their flowery crowns. Broccoli and artichokes are also flowers eaten as vegetables. If left on the plant to bloom, artichokes open into brilliant purple, spiky blooms befitting their membership in the thistle genus (Cynara). Broccoli, cauliflower, and their variations have crowns made of flower tissue that is underdeveloped rather than unopened. This tissue, called curd, lacks the fiber of stems or leaves and is thus exceptionally tender.

> *Cauliflower is nothing but cabbage with a college education.*
>
> —MARK TWAIN

Brussels sprouts are not flowers, but edible buds. They have been cultivated since the thirteenth century in (not surprisingly) Belgium, and grown in the United States since the eighteenth century. Despite this long agricultural history, do not expect to see heirloom varieties of brussels sprouts in today's markets; historical cultivars have an excessively bitter flavor that is unpalatable to many people. Plant breeders in the last few decades have developed sprouts that are much tastier than their predecessors, so those who last sampled them in the 1960s or '70s (and vowed never to eat them again) may be pleasantly surprised by the brussels sprouts of today.

Selection. Despite their hearty appearance, these vegetables quickly begin to decline after harvest. Fresh specimens will have tightly closed floral tissue and feel heavy for their size. Additionally:

◆ Brussels sprouts still on the stem may be fresher than those that have been removed. They should be firm when lightly squeezed, rather than airy.

◆ Broccoli and cauliflower should be pale at the cut ends. They will begin to decline before they look old. Avoid any heads that give off a stale-cabbage smell. Bypass those with wilted leaves, if the leaves are still attached.

◆ Artichokes should have stems that are proportional to the size of the blossom. If the stems seem skinny, skip them, as it's likely that the plants did not get enough water while growing. In the fall, artichokes sometimes have brown petal tips from frost damage, but this minor flaw does not affect quality.

Storage. Store all vegetables in this category unwashed and loosely wrapped, refrigerated. Condensation causes discoloration on cauliflower; to keep it dry, store it wrapped in barely damp paper towels and then perforated plastic, stem end up. Avoid long storage times for all.

Preparation. Artichokes can be served pared down to their hearts or bases, or halved, trimmed, and stuffed with the leaves retained. All preparations will need to have the choke removed, either before or after cooking. Artichoke flesh darkens quickly after cutting; to slow this process, immediately place cut pieces in a bowl filled with water and a little lemon juice or vinegar, keeping them submerged as you work. Acid can also be added to cooking water, but artichokes will naturally turn a uniform gray-green after cooking, despite pretreatment.

Brussels sprouts can be cooked whole, cut in half, sliced, or prepared for quick cooking by peeling away the leaves from the base. Cauliflower, broccoli, and related vegetables are usually cut into florets, but they can also be steamed or baked whole. Long broccolini stems are typically retained and eaten along with the flower. Regular broccoli stems are also edible and delicious; peel and slice them for a stir-fry, or shred them for slaw.

> If you suspect that your organic cauliflower (or broccoflower or Romanesco) is harboring insects, soak it for at least half an hour in water with lemon juice or vinegar and salt added.

ARTICHOKE

Most of the work in cooking artichokes is in their preparation; larger artichokes need to have the prickly inner choke removed, as well as some of the spiky inner leaves and perhaps even the thorns at the tips of the outer "petals." Small artichokes do not have an inner choke, but they still require some trimming. Artichokes are most often boiled and served with rich sauces, but they are delicious cooked in almost any way, or sliced thin and served raw.

> Artichokes contain a compound that makes other foods taste sweeter. This can make them difficult to pair with wine, so save the good stuff for a different dish.

BROCCOFLOWER

While its name suggests a cross between broccoli and cauliflower, broccoflower is actually a variety of green cauliflower. It is very similar in flavor to its white relative, sweet and mild when fresh, more strongly flavored and cabbagelike as it ages. It can be served raw or cooked. Substitute broccoflower for cauliflower in "Cauliflower Salad" (page 204) or "Cabbage Soup" (page 170).

BROCCOLI

Broccoli is a popular vegetable for its mild, slightly sweet crunch and its versatility. It can be served raw or cooked in nearly any way. Stems can be peeled, sliced, and used in addition to florets. To retain nutrients and preserve the attractive, bright green color, avoid overcooking.

BROCCOLINI

Also called baby broccoli or Asparation (a trademarked name invented by marketers, as is broccolini), broccolini is a cross between broccoli and Chinese broccoli. It has small florets and long, slender stems. With a subtly sweet flavor and a slight peppery kick, it is good both raw and cooked. Stalks do not need to be peeled, but the dry ends should be trimmed. Use broccolini interchangeably with broccoli in "Broccoli and Shrimp Chowder" (page 199) or asparagus in "Asparagus Cashew Pilaf" (page 55).

BRUSSELS SPROUT

Cute little brussels sprouts sometimes get a bad rap, but they are gaining popularity as more cooks discover that, when correctly prepared, they are deliciously sweet and nutty. They must be fresh for optimal flavor; look for dense, tightly closed buds that feel firm when lightly squeezed. Unless they are yellowed, color does not affect quality. Keep a close eye on brussels sprouts as they cook, and check them often. They should be cooked until just tender; overcooking produces a mushy texture and an unappetizing smell.

> Think oranges have all the vitamin C? It turns out that brussels sprouts are vitamin C powerhouses. A half cup of sprouts contains 80% of your recommended daily intake of vitamin C. They are also chock full of vitamin A, folic acid, and dietary fiber. Rumor has it that Captain Cook made his crew eat brussels sprouts to combat scurvy on his long ocean voyages.

CAULIFLOWER

White, gold, and purple.   Fresh cauliflower is tender, mild, and slightly sweet. As it gets older, it develops a stronger, cabbagelike flavor, although it won't look much different. If possible, taste cauliflower before purchasing to assure that it is fresh. Purple and gold varieties may be slightly more strongly flavored than white. Like many purple vegetables, purple cauliflower loses color when cooked, but microwaving with a little water will preserve much of the pigment. Gold varieties are fun for gratins, as they are naturally cheese colored. Cauliflower can be served raw, or cooked almost any way. It can be seasoned simply or paired with assertive flavors.

Miniature.   Recently, miniature cauliflowers have made their way to markets. These dainty vegetables can be white, purple, gold, or green, as they mirror the colors and proportions of their full-size counterparts. They are the same plants as regular cauliflower, or even Romanesco, just grown closely together and harvested small. Because such growing conditions can be stressful for the plants, the flavor of these miniatures is sometimes quite strong. Taste them before buying, if possible. Serve them with other baby vegetables for a charming presentation.

ROMANESCO

Romanesco, or Roman broccoli, is a type of green cauliflower, although some vegetable classifiers believe that there is enough overlap between broccoli and cauliflower that it can fit in either category. It is a beautiful vegetable, bright yellow green with florets that grow in mesmerizing fractal spires. Its flavor is similar to that of cauliflower, with a delicate nuttiness. It can be used in place of cauliflower or broccoli, but it really shines in recipes that keep florets or even whole heads intact to show off its beautiful forms. Use Romanesco in "Lemony Roasted Veggies" (page 204) or "Quinoa and Rotating Vegetables Salad" (page 205).

CROWNS, BUDS, AND FLOWERS
Storage and Usage Guide

VEGETABLE	STORAGE AND PRESERVATION				USAGE SUGGESTIONS						
	IDEAL CONDITIONS	PICKLE	FREEZE	DEHYDRATE	RAW	STEAM	BRAISE	BOIL	GRILL	ROAST	SAUTÉ
ARTICHOKE	loosely wrapped, refrigerated	•	•	•	•	•	•	•	•	•	•
BROCCOFLOWER	loosely wrapped, refrigerated	•	•	•	•	•		•	•	•	•
BROCCOLI	loosely wrapped, refrigerated	•	•	•	•	•	•	•	•	•	•
BROCCOLINI	loosely wrapped, refrigerated		•	•	•	•	•	•	•	•	•
BRUSSELS SPROUT	loosely wrapped, refrigerated	•	•	•	•	•	•	•	•	•	•
CAULIFLOWER	wrapped in damp paper towel, then perforated plastic, refrigerated	•	•	•	•	•					
ROMANESCO	wrapped in damp paper towel, then perforated plastic, refrigerated	•	•	•	•	•		•	•	•	•

MASTER RECIPE: FOUR-WAY ROASTED VEGETABLES

Roasting is a convenient cooking method appropriate for almost any type of vegetable. It's also delicious, as it caramelizes vegetables' natural sugars, making them taste rich and sweet. Roasting is done at a relatively high temperature, with 425° being ideal for many vegetables. Vegetables are finished roasting when they are tender and starting to brown a bit around the edges.

THE BASICS

Vegetable(s): any combination, cut into uniform pieces

Oil

Flavorings and seasonings: vinegar, honey, citrus, garlic, spices, hearty herbs, salt and pepper

Add-ins and garnishes: dressing, cheese, sauce, cooked meat, delicate herbs, toasted nuts (optional)

PROCESS

Preheat an oven. Toss the **vegetable(s)** with **oil** and **flavorings and seasonings**, stirring to coat evenly. Spread the vegetables in a single layer in a large roasting pan (make sure the pan has sides to prevent juices from dripping into the oven). Roast the vegetables until they are tender and browned, stirring them around in the pan partway through the roasting time. Remove the vegetables from the oven and toss with **add-ins** such as dressing, sauce, herbs, or cheese, or **garnish** as desired.

VARIATIONS

BALSAMIC ROASTED CAULIFLOWER WITH PARMESAN

By Patricia Mulvey and Laura Gilliam

SERVES 4

ROAST AT 425°
FOR 25 MINUTES:

1 head cauliflower, cut into 1-inch florets

2 tablespoons olive oil

2 tablespoons balsamic vinegar

2 cloves garlic, minced

1 teaspoon dried oregano

Salt and ground black pepper to taste

ADD AS GARNISH:

⅓ cup grated Parmesan

ROASTED BRUSSELS SPROUTS WITH PANCETTA

By Patricia Mulvey and Laura Gilliam

SERVES 4

ROAST AT 425°
FOR 25 MINUTES:

1 pound brussels sprouts, trimmed and halved

2 tablespoons olive oil

Salt and ground black pepper to taste

ADD AS GARNISH:

4 ounces cooked, chopped pancetta

BROCCOLI ROASTED WITH GARLIC AND CHILI

By Patricia Mulvey and Laura Gilliam

SERVES 4

ROAST AT 425°
FOR 25 MINUTES:

1 head broccoli, cut into 1-inch florets

3 tablespoons olive oil

2 cloves garlic, minced

1½ tablespoons chili powder

Salt and ground black pepper to taste

OVEN-ROASTED CAULIFLOWER, BROCCOLI, RED PEPPER, AND ONION

By Samantha Haddow

SERVES 4

ROAST AT 450°
FOR 30–40 MINUTES:

1 head cauliflower, cut into florets

2 heads broccoli, cut into florets

1 red bell pepper, sliced

1 onion, sliced

2 tablespoons olive oil

¼ cup orange juice

1 teaspoon dried oregano

1 teaspoon ground cumin

Salt and ground black pepper to taste

IDEA STARTERS

Red potatoes, olive oil, garlic, rosemary

Romanesco, peanut oil, curry powder, crushed red pepper

Asparagus, olive oil; garnish: vinaigrette, mint

Endive, sunflower oil, honey, thyme

Broccolini, olive oil, lemon, anchovy, crushed red pepper

Delicata squash, apple, pumpkin seed oil, maple syrup, sage, thyme

Cauliflower, peanut oil, curry powder, fennel seed, cayenne

Rutabaga, olive oil, apple cider reduction; garnish: fresh parsley

SERVING SUGGESTIONS

◆ Puree with broth to create a flavorful soup.

◆ Puree or finely chop to make a dip.

◆ Puree with nuts, cheese, and oil for an inventive pesto.

◆ Toss with pasta or grains.

◆ Use as a pizza topping.

◆ Pile onto crusty bread along with herbed goat cheese and cured meat for a tasty sandwich.

LEMON-BRAISED ARTICHOKES

BY PATRICIA MULVEY AND LAURA GILLIAM OF LOCAL THYME

Preparing artichokes can intimidate even the most seasoned chef, and it's no wonder—these thistle relatives protect their delicate interiors with an arsenal of deterrents, including prickly thorns; tough, bitter outer leaves; and a shield of fuzzy bristles over their hearts. But don't be discouraged! These artichokes lend themselves to dozens of uses: as an appetizer, in pasta, on a salad, or with fish or meat.

SERVES 4 // VEGAN // SIDE DISH

INGREDIENTS

1 lemon

2 artichokes, cleaned and trimmed

1 teaspoon dried thyme

2 cloves garlic, halved

Salt and ground black pepper to taste

¼ cup olive oil

2 cups chicken or vegetable broth

PROCESS

Preheat an oven to 425°. Cut the lemon into thin slices and lay in the bottom of a 13 × 9-inch baking dish. Sprinkle the thyme over the lemon slices. Place one of the garlic clove halves in the center of each artichoke half, and lay the artichoke halves, cut side down, on top of the lemon slices. Sprinkle with salt and pepper, drizzle with olive oil, and pour the broth on top. Cover the baking dish tightly with aluminum foil and bake until the artichokes are very tender, about 1 hour. Serve hot, cold, or at room temperature.

> To clean and trim artichokes: Cut a lemon in half and squeeze the juice into a big bowl of water. Trim the sharp thorns off the tips of the artichoke leaves and chop off one inch from the bud end of each artichoke. Rub any cut surfaces with one of the juiced lemon halves to prevent the artichoke from browning. Trim and discard any tough outer leaves. Cut the artichokes in half lengthwise, then scoop out the purple-tipped leaves and the fuzzy choke with a spoon. Place each artichoke half into the lemon water as you finish cleaning and trimming it.

STEAMED ARTICHOKES WITH DIPPING SAUCE

BY PATRICIA MULVEY AND LAURA GILLIAM OF LOCAL THYME

Steamed artichoke leaves served with a tasty dipping sauce are a simple and versatile addition to any meal. You can serve them hot or cold and can adapt the dipping sauce to suit your palate or a particular occasion.

SERVES 4–8 // VEGAN // SIDE DISH

INGREDIENTS

4 artichokes, cleaned and trimmed

Dipping sauce of choice

PROCESS

Bring a large pot of water to a boil over medium-high heat. Place the artichoke halves in a steamer basket and set them over the boiling water. Cover and steam the artichokes until they are tender, about 45 minutes. (Check periodically to make sure that the water doesn't boil away completely; if necessary, add more water to the pot.)

Serve hot with plain melted butter; butter infused with garlic, lemon, and herbs; or your favorite vinaigrette. Serve cold with mayonnaise or flavored aioli (see the master recipe for "Blender Mayonnaise" on page 231 for suggestions).

ROSEMARY-SCENTED BABY ARTICHOKES EN PAPILLOTE

BY PATRICIA MULVEY AND LAURA GILLIAM OF LOCAL THYME

If you find baby artichokes at your market, scoop them up. They possess all the delicious qualities of fully developed artichokes but have not yet grown the furry choke in the center of their flower, which makes for great eating without the usual effort. Cooking them en papillote *(i.e., folded in parchment-paper packets) makes them extra moist and tender.*

SERVES 4 // VEGAN // SIDE DISH

INGREDIENTS

Juice from 2 lemons, divided

8 baby artichokes

4 cloves garlic, thinly sliced

½ cup white wine

4 sprigs fresh rosemary

Salt and ground black pepper to taste

PROCESS

Preheat an oven to 350°. Fill a large bowl with water and add half of the lemon juice. Trim the sharp tips from the artichoke leaves and peel the stems. Cut each artichoke in half, placing the halves in the acidulated water while you trim the remaining artichokes.

Lay out 4 sheets of parchment paper or aluminum foil. Place 4 artichoke halves on each sheet, topping them with equal amounts of the remaining lemon juice, garlic, wine, and rosemary (1 sprig per sheet). Sprinkle the artichokes with salt and pepper. Carefully seal the sheets into neat packets by rolling and tucking the edges of the paper or foil. Place the packets on a baking sheet and bake for about 30 minutes, or until tender. Remove the sheet from the oven and open the packets carefully, as steam will escape and could burn you. Serve hot.

BROCCOLI AND SHRIMP CHOWDER

BY EDITH THAYER

Here's a creamy chowder that combines shrimp with lots of healthy broccoli—tasty and filling for cool days.

SERVES 6 // FISH/SEAFOOD // MAIN DISH

INGREDIENTS

1 medium potato, diced

1 medium sweet potato, diced

4 cups chopped broccoli (florets and stems)

1 medium onion, diced

3 cups chicken broth

1 sprig fresh thyme, 1 bay leaf, and a few sprigs parsley, tied together with kitchen twine

½ pound bay shrimp, peeled

1 cup milk

½–1 cup sour cream

Salt and ground black pepper to taste

PROCESS

Combine the potato, sweet potato, broccoli, onion, broth, and bundled herbs in a medium-size stockpot. Bring to a boil, partially cover, and cook until the vegetables are tender, about 15 minutes. Remove the herbs and puree the soup in the pot using an immersion blender, leaving a few chunks. Stir in the shrimp, milk, and sour cream; simmer until the liquid is hot and the shrimp is cooked, about 3 minutes (do not allow to boil). Season with salt and pepper.

GRILLED ANTIPASTO (BROCCOLI)

BY BARBARA ESTABROOK, COURTESY OF REAP

Italian antipasto serves the same function as hors d'oeuvres or appetizers, preparing the palate for the meal to come. Colorful and gorgeous, they typically consist of meats, cheeses, olives, and pickled vegetables. In this version the vegetables are grilled rather than pickled, and the ingredients are tossed together and served as a chunky salad.

SERVES 6 // MEAT // SIDE DISH

INGREDIENTS

1 medium green bell pepper, cut into strips

1 medium red bell pepper, cut into strips

½ medium sweet onion, thinly sliced

1 cup cauliflower florets

1 cup broccoli florets

5 white mushrooms, sliced

1 small zucchini, cut in half lengthwise and then into 3-inch strips

2 tablespoons olive oil

1 tablespoon chopped fresh oregano

3 tablespoons chopped fresh basil

4 ounces prosciutto, cut into ½-inch strips

Looseleaf lettuce

10 small cherry tomatoes

10 small ripe olives

4 ounces feta, crumbled

2 tablespoons Italian dressing

PROCESS

Heat a charcoal grill to medium-hot. In a large bowl, combine the peppers, onion, cauliflower, broccoli, mushrooms, and zucchini. Drizzle with oil, toss to coat, and transfer to a nonstick grilling tray. Place the tray on the grill rack and cook, stirring and tossing the vegetables, for 5 minutes. Add the oregano, basil, and prosciutto. Continue to stir and toss until the vegetables are crisp-tender, 2–3 minutes. Remove from the grill and spoon onto a lettuce-lined serving plate. In a small bowl, lightly toss the tomatoes, olives, and cheese with the dressing. Spoon evenly over the vegetables and serve.

HOT AND SOUR EGGPLANT, CABBAGE, AND BROCCOLI STIR-FRY
BY DEBRA SHAPIRO/FAIRSHARE CSA COALITION

The sweet and sour combination of sugar and vinegar is a hallmark of Chinese cuisine. This recipe adds chile oil to introduce a spicy element into the mix. Serve with hot brown rice and/or lettuce leaves for wrapping.

SERVES 4-6 // VEGAN // MAIN DISH

INGREDIENTS

2 Chinese or Japanese eggplants, diced

2 teaspoons coarse salt

3 tablespoons soy sauce

2 tablespoons red wine vinegar

2 tablespoons sugar

2 teaspoons cornstarch

1 teaspoon chile oil, or to taste

¼ cup vegetable oil

2 cups thinly sliced cabbage

½ cup chopped broccoli (florets and stems)

PROCESS

Place the eggplant cubes in a colander, sprinkle with the salt, and let stand for 30 minutes. Rinse well and drain. In a small bowl, stir together the soy sauce, vinegar, sugar, cornstarch, and chile oil. Set the sauce aside.

Heat the vegetable oil in a large skillet or wok over medium-high heat. Fry the eggplant until it is tender and beginning to brown, 5–10 minutes. Add the cabbage and broccoli. Pour in the sauce; cook and stir until the sauce is thick and the vegetables are evenly coated. Serve immediately.

BRUSSELS SPROUTS BRAISED IN APPLE CIDER
BY PATRICIA MULVEY AND LAURA GILLIAM OF LOCAL THYME

A sweet-tart glaze of apple cider and balsamic vinegar turns brussels sprouts into a succulent treat.

SERVES 4 // VEGETARIAN // SIDE DISH

INGREDIENTS

2 tablespoons olive oil

2 tablespoons butter

1 onion, chopped

1 pound brussels sprouts, halved

1 cinnamon stick

1½ cups apple cider

2 tablespoons balsamic vinegar

PROCESS

Heat a large, heavy skillet over high heat and warm the oil and butter until the foaming subsides. Add the onion and sauté for about 4 minutes. Add the brussels sprouts and sauté for another 4 minutes. Add the cinnamon stick and apple cider, bring to a boil, cover, reduce the heat, and simmer for about 10 minutes. Remove the cinnamon stick and discard. Remove the vegetables with a slotted spoon and set aside. Continue to cook the liquid until it is reduced by half. Add the vinegar and cook until it thickens into a glaze. Pour the glaze over the vegetables, toss to coat, and serve.

BRUSSELS SPROUTS IN PECAN BROWN BUTTER
BY PATRICIA MULVEY AND LAURA GILLIAM OF LOCAL THYME

Brown butter makes everything better. Here, it joins forces with sweet toasted pecans to heighten the nutty flavor of brussels sprouts and balance their bitterness.

SERVES 4 // VEGETARIAN // SIDE DISH

INGREDIENTS

1 pound brussels sprouts

Salt for cooking water

3 tablespoons unsalted butter

4 ounces pecans, chopped

Salt and ground black pepper to taste

PROCESS

Trim the brussels sprouts and cut an X in the bottom of each one with a paring knife. Boil the sprouts in salted water until tender, about 8 minutes, then drain. Melt the butter in a sauté pan over medium heat and gently cook until it begins to turn light brown. Add the pecans and toss to coat them with butter, cooking for a few minutes until lightly browned and fragrant. Add the brussels sprouts and cook, stirring, until warmed through. Season with salt and pepper.

FALL HARVEST GRATIN (BRUSSELS SPROUT)
BY ERICA KRUG

This recipe is delicious exactly as written, or with other cool-weather vegetables (like parsnips, turnips, or fennel) swapped for some or all of the vegetables. You should have 6–8 cups total, including the apple. Serve with a simple green salad.

SERVES 2-4 // VEGETARIAN // SIDE DISH

INGREDIENTS

2 tablespoons olive oil

1 clove garlic, minced

1 leek, roughly chopped

1 medium sweet potato, peeled and diced into 1-inch cubes

1 medium beet, peeled and diced into 1-inch cubes

2 handfuls brussels sprouts (about 10), halved

3 red potatoes, diced into 1-inch cubes

1 slice whole-grain bread (to yield ½ cup crumbs)

1 Pink Lady apple, cored and diced into 1-inch cubes

Freshly ground sea salt and black pepper to taste

⅔ cup freshly grated sharp white Cheddar

Chopped fresh flat-leaf parsiey (optional)

PROCESS

Preheat an oven to 375°. Warm the olive oil and garlic in an ovenproof Dutch oven over medium-high heat. Add the leek, sweet potato, beet, brussels sprouts, and potatoes and toss to coat. Cook over medium-high heat for 12–15 minutes, shaking the pan a couple of times. The vegetables should start to brown. Meanwhile, place the whole-grain bread in a blender and pulse into fine crumbs.

When the vegetables are finished cooking, remove the Dutch oven from the heat and stir in the apple. Season with freshly ground salt and pepper. Sprinkle with the breadcrumbs and the freshly grated cheese. Place the Dutch oven, uncovered, in the oven. Bake for 35–40 minutes, or until the crumbs and cheese are starting to brown. Garnish with chopped flat-leaf parsley (if desired).

HOLIDAY BRAISED BRUSSELS SPROUTS

BY PETER GENTRY

Featuring tender small sprouts, perfectly cooked and accented by shallots and a bit of cream, this dish will convert anyone who claims to hate brussels sprouts. Peter likes these served with hearty holiday fare, like roast beef tenderloin or turkey, but our tester liked them so much she plans to add the recipe to her winter weekday repertoire.

SERVES 4 // VEGETARIAN // SIDE DISH

INGREDIENTS

1 pound small brussels sprouts

1 tablespoon butter

2 medium shallots or 1 small mild onion, minced

¼ cup chicken or vegetable broth

¼ cup whipping cream

Salt to taste

1 tablespoon Dijon mustard

Freshly ground black pepper to taste

1 tablespoon chopped fresh parsley (optional)

PROCESS

Trim the stem end of each brussels sprout and remove the loose leaves so you have small, tight sprouts. Melt the butter in a large sauté pan. Sauté the shallots over medium heat until soft, 3–4 minutes. Add the brussels sprouts, broth, cream, and salt. Cover and simmer until the sprouts are tender, about 10 minutes. Stir in the mustard, pepper, and parsley (if desired). Serve hot.

ROASTED BRUSSELS SPROUTS WITH SHALLOTS

BY PATRICIA MULVEY AND LAURA GILLIAM OF LOCAL THYME

Most people who dislike brussels sprouts have never eaten them roasted. Time spent in the oven creates pleasantly charred, crisp-tender leaves that are balanced by the natural sweetness of shallots.

SERVES 4 // VEGAN // SIDE DISH

INGREDIENTS

2 cups brussels sprouts

2 shallots, julienned

2 tablespoons canola oil

Salt and ground black pepper to taste

PROCESS

Preheat an oven to 400°. Toss the brussels sprouts with the shallots, oil, salt, and pepper. Spread in a single layer in a roasting pan and roast until the sprouts are speckled brown and tender, 20–25 minutes, shaking the pan halfway through the cooking time.

CAULIFLOWER SALAD

BY RACHEL ARMSTRONG, COURTESY OF REAP

Cauliflower provides the backdrop for a fiesta of flavors and colors in this lively salad.

SERVES 6 // VEGAN // SIDE DISH

INGREDIENTS

SALAD:

1 small head cauliflower

½ red onion, finely chopped

1 stalk celery, finely chopped

1 large green bell pepper, finely chopped

1 large cucumber, finely chopped

12 green olives, sliced

¼ cup chopped fresh flat-leaf parsley

DRESSING:

2 tablespoons fresh lemon juice

1 tablespoon stone-ground mustard

⅓ cup olive oil

1 clove garlic, smashed

Salt and ground black pepper to taste

PROCESS

Place the head of cauliflower on a cutting board, stem side up. Beginning at the edge, thinly slice the cauliflower, shaving off cauliflower crumbs until you reach the center core. Rotate the cauliflower and continue slicing all the way around. Then turn the core on its side and thinly slice from the top until only the center core remains. Discard the core. Toss the chopped cauliflower with the onion, celery, green pepper, cucumber, olives, and parsley.

Blend the dressing ingredients together in a small jar, shaking to mix well. Pour over the salad and mix together. Let the salad marinate in the refrigerator for about 1 hour before serving.

LEMONY ROASTED VEGGIES (CAULIFLOWER)

BY ANNA VANDERPOEL OF TROY COMMUNITY FARM

This delicious variation on roasted vegetables fills the kitchen with a sunny citrus fragrance. Lemon adds a bright flavor, and its natural sugars help caramelize the vegetables.

SERVES 6-8 // VEGETARIAN // SIDE DISH

INGREDIENTS

3 tablespoons olive oil

Juice from 3 lemons (include some grated peel for a more intense lemon flavor)

2 teaspoons ground cumin

2 teaspoons ground coriander

½ teaspoon ground black pepper

½ teaspoon cayenne

3 cloves garlic, minced

1 pound cauliflower florets, chopped

1 red onion, cut into thin strips

1 large fennel bulb, cut into thin strips

2 carrots, diced into ½-inch cubes

1 pound butternut squash, peeled and diced into ½-inch cubes

6 ounces feta, crumbled

PROCESS

Preheat an oven to 425°. In a small bowl, combine the oil, lemon juice (and peel, if desired), cumin, coriander, black pepper, cayenne, and garlic. Set aside.

Combine the cauliflower, onion, fennel, carrot, and squash in a 13 × 9-inch baking dish (or two dishes if necessary; the vegetables should be in a single layer). Drizzle the oil mixture over the vegetables and toss to coat. Cover and roast for 20 minutes. Remove the dish from the oven, uncover, and toss the vegetables carefully. Roast uncovered for 15 minutes more. Remove the dish from the oven again and top the vegetables with crumbled feta. Roast uncovered for 10 minutes more, or until the feta and vegetables are lightly browned.

QUINOA AND ROTATING VEGETABLES SALAD (CAULIFLOWER)
BY CLAIRE STRADER OF TROY COMMUNITY FARM

Versatile and tasty, this salad is a go-to for Claire. She serves it in all seasons, alone or on a bed of salad greens. It is excellent cold or at room temperature, perfect for picnics and potlucks.

SERVES 4-6 // VEGAN // SIDE DISH

INGREDIENTS

1 cup quinoa

1¾ cups water, plus more for soaking

2–4 tablespoons packed chopped fresh parsley

¼ cup finely chopped green onions

Juice from 1–2 lemons

½ cup olive oil

½–1 teaspoon ground cumin

½ teaspoon salt

ROTATING VEGETABLES (CHOOSE AT LEAST 2):

½ cup diced carrots

½ cup diced celery or celeriac

½ cup diced tomatoes

½ cup diced red or green bell peppers

½ cup chopped cauliflower

½ cup diced cucumber

½ cup diced summer squash

½ cup chopped dragon tongue beans (bite-size pieces)

½ cup shelled peas

PROCESS

Cover the quinoa with water and soak for 15 minutes. Pour the soaked quinoa into a fine-mesh strainer and rinse under running water for 1–2 minutes. Put the quinoa and 1¾ cups of water into a saucepan, cover, and bring to a boil. Reduce the heat and simmer for 15 minutes. Remove the lid and fluff the cooked quinoa with a fork.

Combine the quinoa with the remaining "required" ingredients (parsley through salt) and your choice of at least 2 "rotating" vegetables. Let stand for 20 minutes before serving to allow the flavors to blend.

VEGGIE FRIED RICE (CAULIFLOWER)
BY LESLIE ELKINS

Leslie learned to make fried rice in college from a Filipina roommate. Over the years, she has altered her method to suit her own tastes and the ingredients she has on hand. She uses this recipe as a template, with whatever vegetables are in season (about 3 cups total). If kohlrabi isn't available, use cashews or peanuts for a crunchy topping.

SERVES 4 // VEGAN // MAIN DISH

INGREDIENTS

3 tablespoons olive oil, divided

3 eggs, lightly beaten (optional)

4 cloves garlic, minced

1 chile pepper, minced

2 tablespoons grated fresh ginger

1 cup diced zucchini

2 carrots, sliced into half-moons

½ cup sliced cabbage

½ cup cauliflower florets

⅓ cup sliced mushrooms

¼ cup soy sauce

1½ tablespoons oyster or fish sauce (optional)

1 tablespoon Dijon mustard

1 tablespoon rice vinegar or other light vinegar

3 cups cooked white or brown rice*

1 cup cooked shrimp, chicken, tofu, or other protein (optional)

3 green onions, sliced

¼ cup julienned kohlrabi

*If you start cooking the rice just before you begin chopping the vegetables, they will both be finished at about the same time. You may also cook the rice the day before or earlier in the day.

PROCESS

Heat a wok or large skillet over high heat. Add 1 tablespoon of the olive oil. Pour in the eggs (if desired) and scramble into small pieces. Remove from the pan. Add the remaining 2 tablespoons of olive oil to the skillet (still on high heat). Add the garlic, chile, ginger, zucchini, carrots, cabbage, cauliflower, mushrooms, soy sauce, fish sauce (if desired), mustard, and vinegar and cook for 4–5 minutes, stirring frequently. Add the cooked rice. Cook for another 5–7 minutes, stirring less frequently. Mix in the eggs and cooked protein and heat through, about 2 minutes. Remove from the heat and top with sliced green onions and kohlrabi.

AROMATIC ACCENTS
From Chile Peppers to Shallots

Onions, herbs, chiles, ginger, and garlic are ingredients that create the flavor profiles of dishes. Try to imagine Italian cuisine without garlic and basil, or Mexican fare without white onion, chiles, and cilantro. Without these accents, the fundamental qualities of most savory recipes (and even some sweet ones) would be lost.

When we think of aromatics, we usually think of the Allium genus, which includes onions, garlic, and leeks. These plants produce defensive chemicals that we humans find delectable. Our attraction to alliums seems to have developed early in our history: onions have likely been cultivated for over 5,000 years. For ancient Egyptians, their circular shape and the rings of their cut halves represented eternal life. Garlic is mentioned in both the Bible and the Talmud, and the ancient Greeks and Romans valued its medicinal properties. The culinary legacy of alliums lives on today, as both cooked and raw, they form the essential flavor bases for most of the world's cuisines.

> *I am thinking of the onion again…a modest, self-effacing vegetable, questioning, introspective, peeling itself away, or merely radiating halos like ripples.*
> —ERICA JONG,
> *Fruits and Vegetables*

Also enjoyed worldwide are chiles, another aromatic (technically a fruit) with defensive chemicals that attract thrill-seeking humans. Hot peppers produce capsaicin, a potent irritant, in their seed-bearing inner membranes. The more of this chemical present in the membrane, the hotter the chile. The amount of capsaicin depends on the type of chile and its growing conditions, and it's measured by units on the Scoville scale, named for the pharmacist who developed it in 1912. A Scoville measure of zero to 5,000 is mild, and anything over 50,000 is very hot.

Capsaicin levels continue to increase in chiles from pollination to ripening, after which they begin to decline. Therefore, chiles are at their hottest when they've just begun to change color, usually from green to red.

Ginger and herbs add fresh, bright notes to foods, and they are often used in combination with chiles. Sweetly hot ginger is essential in Asian cuisines from Mumbai to Tokyo, and piles of fresh cilantro and mint complete many Southeast Asian dishes. Heat is not typically an element in traditional Western cooking, but fresh herbs are a staple. In classic French cooking, bay leaves, thyme, and parsley flavor the broths, soups, and sauces that the cuisine is built upon, and many dishes are dusted with fines herbes.

Psst! Wanna know a secret? Culinary students use a sound-based mnemonic to remember the French fines herbes combination. Parsley, chervil, chives, tarragon: PSST.

Selection. Choose firm, glossy chiles without wrinkled skin or soft spots. Onions, garlic, and shallots should be plump, firm, and dry, with papery skins intact. Check ginger for soft spots or shriveled areas, and mold. Green onions, green garlic, garlic chives, leeks, and ramps should have unwilted greens. Scapes get more fibrous (and curlier) as they grow, so avoid them if they have more than one loop. Herbs should be perky and lush.

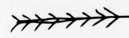

Storage. Store onions, garlic, and shallots in a cool, dry, well-ventilated environment. Chiles, green onions and garlic, leeks, ramps, and ginger should be well wrapped and stored in a crisper drawer. Be aware that the smell of green garlic, scapes, and ramps may be quite strong, so you may want to store them in airtight containers. Garlic chives and herbs should be loosened from bundles, wrapped in a barely damp paper towel and then loose plastic, and refrigerated. Alternatively, snip the ends of herbs and place them in a sturdy container with water at the bottom. Cover the exposed greens loosely with a plastic bag and store them in the refrigerator.

Basil leaves are very susceptible to chilling injury. Snip the ends of these and store them upright in a container of water at room temperature.

Preparation. Wear gloves when chopping chiles, and wash cutting boards and knives thoroughly in hot, soapy water after use, as the stinging capsaicin can be persistent. To reduce the heat of chiles, remove the white inner tissue and seeds before chopping. Garlic and shallot cloves should be peeled before use, or roasted with skins intact and peeled or squeezed after cooking. Ginger should be sliced into thin rounds (to cut through tough fibers) and then chopped. If herb stems are tender, they can be included in chopped preparations; otherwise, separate the stems from the leaves and discard. Chopped herbs can be frozen with a little water in ice cube trays for ease of use through winter.

To make chopping onions a less teary job, soak them in ice water for at least half an hour before cutting. This step does not eliminate the sulfurous gas that irritates the eyes, but it slows its dissipation. It also hydrates the papery skin, making onions easier to peel.

ONION

Yellow, white, and red.   Yellow, white, and red onions, called storage onions by growers and marketers, last several for months in a cool, dry, well-ventilated environment. Yellow onions, sometimes called brown onions for their papery skin, are versatile and flavorful, and they caramelize beautifully. White onions are a little moister than yellow onions and do not last as long in storage, but they are otherwise comparable to yellow onions. Red onions are best eaten raw or cooked briefly, as they lose color when thoroughly cooked.

Sweet.   Often named after their original growing regions, like Walla Walla, Maui, and Vidalia, sweet onions are more correctly called mild onions. They do not have more sugar than storage onions; rather, they have less heat, so their sweetness becomes more apparent. They are at their best when used raw or lightly cooked. They do not store as well as storage onions, so keep them in a cool, dry place with good circulation, and use them within a couple of weeks. They can be refrigerated for several months, but they will lose some of their fresh flavor.

Green.   Tender green onions also go by the name scallion, and the two terms are interchangeable in recipes. Green onions are picked before they have had a chance to form a bulb at the base, and their flavor is milder and fresher than mature bulb onions. Whether to use the white or green part is a matter of preference. Most Western cooks use the tenderer white and pale green parts, while Asian cookery usually calls for the green.

Spring.   These onions are somewhere between green onions and mature onions in development: onions grown long enough to form a small bulb at the base, but with fresh green tops still intact. The bulbs are usually white, but they can be yellow or red. They have the freshness of green onions but more of the pungency and heat of mature onions. Use spring onions in place of either green or mature onions in recipes, slice them raw for salads, or trim, cut in half, and grill.

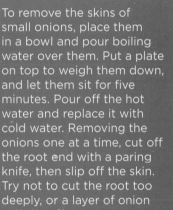

To remove the skins of small onions, place them in a bowl and pour boiling water over them. Put a plate on top to weigh them down, and let them sit for five minutes. Pour off the hot water and replace it with cold water. Removing the onions one at a time, cut off the root end with a paring knife, then slip off the skin. Try not to cut the root too deeply, or a layer of onion will slip off, too.

Small.   Whether pearl onions, boilers, picklers, or creamers, small onions are the same species as their large counterparts, just grown closely together and harvested small. Except for cipolline, which are flattened small onions of Italian origin, the names pearl, pickler, etc., describe the relative size of the onion, rather than specific varieties. Small onions are great for roasting (remove the skins after cooking), in stews, or as side dishes.

RAMP

Ramps, or ramson, are wild leeks. They are lovely members of the Allium genus, with graceful, broad green leaves, purple stems, and slim, white, bulbous bases. Although they are very pretty, the fact that they are leeks is undeniable, for they have quite a strong odor. When cooked, they turn sweet and mild. Use them in place of spring onions or leeks (but shorten the cooking time).

SHALLOT

Few French sauces would be complete without shallots. They are used both raw and cooked—in vinaigrettes, with red wine in bordelaise sauce, in buttery béarnaise sauce, and fragile beurre blanc. In Southeast Asian cuisine they play a vital role, too, as a seasoning for pastes, as crispy fried garnishes, and raw in salads. They are mild, savory members of the Allium genus worthy of being pantry staples. Use shallots interchangeably with onions, or cook them as you would small onions, roasted or glazed and served as a side dish.

AROMATIC ACCENTS
Storage and Usage Guide

VEGETABLE	STORAGE AND PRESERVATION				USAGE SUGGESTIONS			
	IDEAL CONDITIONS	PICKLE	FREEZE	DEHYDRATE	RAW	CARAMELIZE	ROAST	SAUTÉ
CHILE PEPPER	wrapped, refrigerated	•	•	•	•		•	•
GARLIC								
common, elephant, rocambole	cool and dry	•	•	•	•		•	•
green, scape	wrapped, refrigerated	•	•	•	•			•
garlic chive	wrapped, refrigerated		•	•	•			•
GINGER	wrapped, refrigerated	•	•	•				•
HERBS	wrapped, refrigerated		•	•	•			•
LEEK	wrapped, refrigerated	•		•			•	•
ONION								
yellow, white, red	cool and dry	•	•	•	•	•	•	•
sweet	refrigerated	•	•	•	•	•	•	•
green	wrapped, refrigerated	•	•	•	•			•
spring	wrapped, refrigerated	•			•			•
small	cool and dry	•	•	•		•	•	•
RAMP	wrapped, refrigerated	•						•
SHALLOT	cool and dry	•	•	•	•	•	•	•

MASTER RECIPE: FOUR-WAY PESTO

Pesto is a versatile and quick way to add a flavorful punch to a range of dishes. It also freezes well, so you can easily enjoy the fresh flavors of summer year-round. Traditionally, pesto is made with a mortar and pestle, but it can also be made in a food processor or blender. Our proportions are merely suggestions—let your preferences, ingredients, and intended use guide you.

THE BASICS

Fresh herbs or leafy greens

Nuts or seeds

Cheese

Aromatics and seasonings: chopped garlic or onions, acid (lemon, vinegar), salt and pepper

Oil

PROCESS

Chop or crush the **herbs** in a blender, food processor, or mortar and pestle. Add the **nuts**, **cheese**, and **aromatics and seasonings**. Puree or grind until smooth. Drizzle in the **oil** until the pesto reaches the desired consistency. Taste and adjust the seasonings as desired.

VARIATIONS

SIMPLE PESTO

By Peter Gentry

SERVES 6

2 cups basil leaves, loosely packed

1 cup toasted nuts (walnuts, hickory nuts, or pecans)

1½–2 cups grated Parmesan

3 large cloves garlic (or more to taste)

Salt and ground black pepper to taste

½–1 cup olive oil

CILANTRO AND GARLIC SCAPE PESTO

By Dani Lind

SERVES 2–4

6–8 garlic scapes, cut into 1-inch pieces (about 1 cup)

1 bunch cilantro, coarsely chopped (leaves and stems)

½ cup pumpkin or sunflower seeds, toasted and cooled

½ teaspoon salt

⅓ cup oil (sunflower, olive, etc.)

ARUGULA PESTO

By Barbara Wright/ FairShare CSA Coalition

SERVES 4–6

2 cups packed arugula leaves, stems removed

½ cup walnuts

½ cup freshly grated Parmesan

6 cloves garlic, roasted

½ clove garlic, peeled and minced

½ teaspoon salt

½ cup extra-virgin olive oil

PARSLEY AND WALNUT PESTO

By Beth Fortune

SERVES 6

2 cups packed parsley leaves

½ cup toasted walnuts

1 tablespoon lemon juice

Salt and ground black pepper to taste

⅓ cup olive oil

IDEA STARTERS

Young mustard greens, walnuts, Parmesan, garlic, olive oil

Parsley, mint, pine nuts, Cotija, shallot, grape seed oil

Lemon verbena, pecans, ricotta salata, sweet onion, grated lemon peel, grape seed oil

Mizuna, walnuts, aged Gouda, green onion, nut oil

Cilantro, pumpkin seeds, Cotija, red onion, lime juice, toasted pumpkin seed oil

Tarragon, parsley, almonds, Pecorino Romano, garlic, olive oil

Ramp greens, toasted pumpkin seeds, Parmesan, lemon juice, olive oil

Radish greens, turnip greens, sunflower seeds, Gruyère, garlic, olive oil

SERVING SUGGESTIONS

- ◆ Use plain or mixed with mayonnaise or cream cheese as a sandwich spread.
- ◆ Toss with roasted vegetables.
- ◆ Mix into vinaigrette for a salad dressing.
- ◆ Use as pizza sauce, with or in place of cheese.
- ◆ Mix with Greek-style yogurt or sour cream for a dip.
- ◆ Drizzle over sliced tomatoes and mozzarella.
- ◆ Mix into mashed potatoes.
- ◆ Make a red, white, and green layered dip with cream cheese and chopped oil-packed sun-dried tomatoes.

CHEESE-STUFFED CHILE PEPPER "STOCKINGS"

BY MARTIN, JURE, AND JOSEPH ERLIC, COURTESY OF REAP

When the Erlics were young, they created these stuffed chile peppers to imitate Christmas stockings filled with goodies. Try stuffing them with other "goodies" for variety.

SERVES 4 // VEGETARIAN // SNACK

INGREDIENTS

4 yellow or red banana peppers

1 cup diced Cheddar

PROCESS

Cut the tops off the peppers and cut out the core and seeds. Fill each pepper with ¼ cup of the cheese. You can eat them cold or bake them in the oven at 300° for 5–10 minutes.

CORNBREAD WITH JALAPEÑO AND CHEDDAR (CHILE)

BY PATRICIA MULVEY AND LAURA GILLIAM OF LOCAL THYME

A perfect side dish for a bowl of chili, this cornbread is extra moist from the addition of creamed corn.

SERVES 8 // VEGETARIAN // SIDE DISH

INGREDIENTS

1 cup cornmeal

1 cup all-purpose flour

1 teaspoon salt

½ teaspoon baking soda

1 teaspoon baking powder

2 cups creamed corn

1 cup buttermilk

¼ cup honey

3 tablespoons butter, melted

1 egg

2–3 jalapeños, minced

½ cup grated Cheddar

PROCESS

Preheat an oven to 400°. Butter an 8 × 8-inch baking dish. Combine the dry ingredients (cornmeal through baking powder) in a medium bowl. Combine the wet ingredients (creamed corn through egg) in a large bowl. Mix the dry ingredients into the wet until just combined, then fold in the jalapeños and cheese. Bake for 30–35 minutes, or until the top is golden brown and a knife inserted in the center comes out clean.

JALAPEÑO JELLY (CHILE)

BY PATRICIA MULVEY AND LAURA GILLIAM OF LOCAL THYME

A dab of this spicy jelly will instantly transform an otherwise bland dish. It's especially delicious spread on crackers over mild, creamy goat cheese.

YIELDS 2½ PINTS // VEGAN // CONDIMENT

INGREDIENTS

¾ pound jalapeños (seeded or not, as desired)

2 cups cider vinegar, divided

6 cups sugar

2 pouches liquid pectin

PROCESS

Puree the jalapeños in a food processor with 1 cup of the vinegar. Pour the mixture into a medium saucepan and add the remaining vinegar and the sugar. Boil for about 10 minutes, add the pectin, and boil for 1 minute longer. Skim off any foam that rises to the surface.

Ladle the jelly into 5 sterilized half-pint canning jars, leaving ¼-inch of space at the top. Seal the lids and process in a boiling water bath for 10 minutes. Check the seals. If they are not tightly closed, remove the lid, check for nicks or food particles on the rim, and make sure there is not too much headspace (these are problems that will prevent proper sealing), and then reprocess the jar with a new lid. When the lids are sealed, store at room temperature until opened.

JALAPEÑO POPPER CHICKEN SKILLET (CHILE)

BY ASHLEY RAMAKER

Inspired by the popular appetizer, this chicken dish features the same richness and heat as cheese-stuffed poppers. Serve as a main dish over rice or pasta as Ashley does, or chop the chicken before cooking and serve with tortillas.

SERVES 2 // POULTRY // MAIN DISH

INGREDIENTS

1 onion, diced

1 large jalapeño, sliced thin

1 tablespoon olive oil

2 boneless, skinless chicken breasts (about 6 ounces each)

⅛ teaspoon salt

⅛ teaspoon ground black pepper

White wine (optional)

1 small tomato, seeded and diced

1 teaspoon ground cumin

½ cup chicken broth

2 ounces cream cheese

2 tablespoons sour cream

PROCESS

In a large skillet with a fitted lid, sauté the onion and jalapeño in the olive oil over medium-high heat. While the vegetables are cooking, season the chicken with salt and pepper. When the vegetables start to become tender (about 6 minutes), add a splash of wine (if desired) and the tomato, cumin, and broth. Bring to a boil and immediately reduce the heat to medium. Add the chicken and simmer, covered, for about 20 minutes, or until the chicken is cooked through. Remove from the heat and stir in the cream cheese and sour cream.

ANGEL HAIR PASTA WITH GARLIC BUTTER, FRESH TOMATOES, AND BASIL (HERBS)

BY KARI SPELTZ

To create this simple pasta dish, Kari combined "deconstructed pesto" (basil, Parmesan, and pine nuts) with fresh, local tomatoes to make it taste like summer. She and her husband eat some variation of this dish at least once a week during tomato season.

SERVES 2 // VEGETARIAN // MAIN DISH

INGREDIENTS

6 ounces angel hair pasta

2 tablespoons butter

2–3 tablespoons olive oil

2 large cloves garlic, minced

Dash salt (optional)

4–6 medium red tomatoes, roughly chopped

½ cup thinly sliced basil leaves, divided

Shaved Parmesan

¼ cup pine nuts, toasted

PROCESS

Cook the pasta according to the package directions, then drain and set aside. In the same pot, heat the butter and olive oil over medium heat. When the butter is melted, add the garlic and a dash of salt (if desired) and sauté for 2–4 minutes, until soft but not browned. Turn off the heat, add the pasta to the pot, and mix well. Add the tomatoes and most of the basil, mixing well. Serve topped with shaved Parmesan, the rest of the basil, and the toasted pine nuts.

LEMON BALM CHICKEN BREAST (HERBS)

BY CHRISTINE STONE, COURTESY OF REAP

Lemon balm and lemon peel join forces in a luscious marinade that will create, as Christine says, "the juiciest chicken ever!" This dish requires a bit of time for marinating and cooking, but the active preparation takes just minutes.

SERVES 6 // POULTRY // MAIN DISH

INGREDIENTS

6 tablespoons Worcestershire sauce

3 tablespoons extra-virgin olive oil

2 tablespoons honey

3 large cloves garlic, pressed

Grated peel from 1 large lemon

12 lemon balm leaves

6 chicken breasts

PROCESS

In a large zipper-lock bag, combine all ingredients except the chicken breasts and mix well. Add the chicken breasts and toss well to thoroughly coat the chicken with the seasonings. Marinate in the refrigerator for 1–4 hours.

Preheat an oven to 400°. Remove the chicken breasts from the marinade and place them in a single layer on a rimmed baking sheet or large baking dish. Bake for 45–60 minutes, or until the juices run clear. Remove and let the chicken rest for at least 5 minutes to reabsorb the juices before serving.

SUMMER TABBOULEH SALAD (HERBS)
BY TERI GEHIN

Frequently a dish in a meze spread, tabbouleh is the most popular salad in the Middle East. Teri's delicious version is enlivened with pesto and meaty Kalamata olives. Try it with the traditional cracked wheat, or, for a higher-protein version, substitute cooked quinoa for the bulgur.

SERVES 8 // VEGETARIAN // SIDE DISH

INGREDIENTS

2 cups boiling water

2 cups bulgur wheat

¼ cup olive oil

6 ounces pesto

Juice from 1 lemon

1 cup crumbled feta

2 cups grape tomatoes

1 green bell pepper, seeded and diced

1 bunch green onions, finely chopped

1 cucumber, sliced lengthwise, seeded and diced

1 cup finely chopped fresh parsley

1 (15-ounce) can chickpeas, drained

1 cup sliced Kalamata olives

Freshly ground black pepper to taste

Fleur de sel or kosher salt to taste

PROCESS

In a large heatproof bowl, pour the boiling water over the bulgur and let stand for 30 minutes. Drizzle the olive oil, pesto, and lemon juice over the prepared bulgur. Add the remaining ingredients and toss to combine.

YOGURT CHEESE WITH FRESH HERBS
BY DANIELLE PACHA

Cool, creamy yogurt cheese is simple to prepare and delicious with the addition of fresh herbs, vegetables, fruits, or honey. Try it with dill and cucumber as part of a meze platter, or with honey and grated lemon peel for a sweet spread.

SERVES 8 // VEGETARIAN // APPETIZER

INGREDIENTS

4 cups regular or low-fat yogurt, without pectin or other thickeners (Greek-style yogurt works well)

Salt and ground black pepper to taste

¼ cup chopped herbs of choice

PROCESS

Line a strainer with cheesecloth or torn coffee filters, completely covering the bottom and sides. In a medium bowl, combine the yogurt with about 1 teaspoon of salt and a few grinds of pepper, stirring well. Pour the yogurt into the lined strainer. Set the strainer over a larger bowl, leaving space at the bottom for the liquid to drain from the yogurt. Cover and refrigerate overnight, or until the consistency is similar to cream cheese (Greek-style yogurt will take less time).

When the yogurt has reached the desired consistency, remove it from the refrigerator, discard the drained liquid, and transfer the yogurt cheese to a sealable storage container. Stir in the chopped herbs and adjust the seasonings. Store in the refrigerator.

SAFFRON RICE WITH FRIZZLED LEEK

BY PATRICIA MULVEY AND LAURA GILLIAM OF LOCAL THYME

Bright yellow with dark green and brown flecks, this pretty side dish goes especially well with seafood entrées.

SERVES 4 // VEGETARIAN // SIDE DISH

INGREDIENTS

1 tablespoon canola oil

1 tablespoon butter

1 leek (white and light green parts only), halved lengthwise and cut into slices

1 cup white rice

Generous pinch saffron

2 cups chicken or vegetable broth

Salt and ground black pepper to taste

PROCESS

Heat the oil and butter in a medium pot with a tight-fitting lid. Add the leek and cook over high heat until browned and crisp. Stir in the rice, saffron, broth, salt, and pepper. Bring to a boil, cover, reduce the heat to medium low, and cook until the rice is tender, 15–20 minutes. Fluff the rice with a fork and serve hot.

HEARTWARMING CHEESE AND ONION SOUP

BY MARIANNE O'RIORDAN, COURTESY OF REAP

Some cheeses become gooey or stringy when heated, but grated Cheddar melts beautifully when stirred into warm broth. Marianne recommends eating this soup in front of a roaring fire.

SERVES 4 // VEGETARIAN // MAIN DISH

INGREDIENTS

2 tablespoons salted butter

4 spring onions, thinly sliced

2 tablespoons all-purpose flour

3 cups milk

1½ cups chicken or vegetable broth

Salt and freshly ground black pepper to taste

4 ounces Cheddar or other semi-hard cheese, grated

2 tablespoons chopped fresh parsley

PROCESS

Melt the butter in a pot and sauté the onions, without browning, about 5 minutes. Add the flour and cook for 3 minutes. Gradually beat in the milk, broth, salt, and pepper. Heat, stirring constantly, until the soup comes to a boil and thickens slightly. Reduce the heat and stir for 3 minutes. Remove from the heat and stir in the cheese. Pour into warmed soup bowls and garnish with parsley and freshly ground pepper.

ROASTED ONION SANDWICHES
BY MOLLY TULL, COURTESY OF REAP

Molly's grandmother ate onion sandwiches during the Depression, and Molly loved the idea of golden grilled onions served on toast. Here she's dressed up her grandmother's recipe with spicy mustard and horseradish and a slice of creamy cheese.

SERVES 4 // VEGETARIAN // MAIN DISH

INGREDIENTS

1 large onion, cut into 4 large slices

2 tablespoons butter, melted

1 loaf crusty bread, cut into 8 slices

4 slices Muenster

1–2 tablespoons prepared horseradish

1–2 tablespoons stone-ground mustard

PROCESS

Preheat an oven to 425°. Brush the onion slices with butter and put them in a baking dish. Roast for 20–30 minutes, or until well browned, turning at least once. To assemble each sandwich, lay a roasted onion slice on a slice of bread and top with cheese. Spread a little horseradish and a little mustard on another slice of bread and place on top.

RUSTIC RAMP TART
BY ANN HARSTE

Puff pastry is a dream come true for time-pressed cooks. Buttery, flaky, and delicious, puff pastry makes impressive and easy meals both sweet and savory. The pungent, garlicky ramps really shine when paired with earthy pancetta and creamy cheese in this tart.

SERVES 8 // MEAT // MAIN DISH

INGREDIENTS

1 large (about 15 × 10-inch) sheet puff pastry (if necessary, pinch 2 smaller sheets together)

2 tablespoons olive oil

4 slices pancetta (or more), cut into ½-inch strips

1 bunch ramps, thinly sliced (leeks may be substituted)

1 clove garlic, minced

1 cup fresh herbed goat cheese

1 cup whole-milk ricotta

⅓ cup freshly grated Parmesan

Salt (optional)

Ground black pepper to taste

PROCESS

Preheat an oven to 425°. Line a baking sheet with parchment paper or a silicone liner and lay the puff pastry on top. Set aside.

Heat the olive oil in a skillet over medium-high heat. Add the pancetta, ramps, and garlic and sauté for about 5 minutes. In a mixing bowl, stir together the cheeses. Add the contents of the skillet and mix everything together, adding salt if necessary.

Spread the cheese mixture onto the puff pastry, leaving a 1-inch margin around the edge. Grind black pepper over the surface of the tart. Fold the 1-inch edge over onto itself, so you now have a ½-inch border. Bake the tart for 20–25 minutes, until it is golden brown. Let stand for at least 5 minutes before slicing. Serve warm or at room temperature.

BACON AND RAMP SKILLET CORNBREAD
BY BJORN BERGMAN, ORIGINALLY PUBLISHED IN *EDIBLE MADISON*

Nothing beats a piping-hot slice of cornbread after a day of ramp hunting. Serve warm slathered in local butter and honey.

SERVES 8 // MEAT // SIDE DISH

INGREDIENTS

1½ cups yellow cornmeal

½ cup whole-wheat flour

2 teaspoons baking powder

½ teaspoon salt

1 egg

1 cup milk

1 tablespoon maple syrup

3 slices uncooked bacon

6–8 ramps, roots removed

2 tablespoons unsalted butter, melted

PROCESS

Preheat an oven to 450°. In small bowl, mix together the cornmeal, whole-wheat flour, baking powder, and salt. In a large bowl, whisk together the egg, milk, and maple syrup. Mix the dry ingredients into the wet ingredients. Set the batter aside.

Over medium-high heat, fry the bacon in an 8-inch cast-iron skillet. When the bacon is crisp, transfer it to a paper towel to drain, reserving the fat in the skillet. Crumble the bacon when cooled.

Separate the ramp bulbs and stems from the leaves. Mince the bulbs and stems. Chop the leaves into ¼-inch pieces. Sauté the minced bulbs and stems in the reserved bacon fat for 1 minute. Add the sautéed ramps, bacon fat, chopped ramp leaves, crumbled bacon, and melted butter to the cornbread batter and mix well. Pour the batter into the same hot 8-inch skillet that the bacon and ramps were fried in. Place the skillet on the center rack of the oven and bake for 15–25 minutes, or until a knife inserted into the center of the cornbread comes out clean. Cool for 10 minutes before cutting.

PHOTO BY BJORN BERGMAN
FOR *EDIBLE MADISON*

GALETTE WITH WILD MUSHROOMS AND RAMPS

BY DANI LIND, ORIGINALLY PUBLISHED IN *EDIBLE MADISON*

This recipe is easily doubled to make two galettes (they freeze beautifully before baking) or one big galette. The filling can be made without the dough and used to top pizza, polenta, or pasta.

SERVES 6 // VEGETARIAN // MAIN DISH

INGREDIENTS

CRUST:

½ pound all-purpose flour (about 1¾ cups)

½ teaspoon salt

½ teaspoon sugar

½ cup unsalted butter, chilled, cut into 1-inch pieces

4–5 tablespoons ice water

FILLING:

1 tablespoon butter

1 bunch ramps, bulbs and stems coarsely chopped and leaves reserved

½ pound mixed mushrooms (morels, shiitakes, oysters, criminis, etc.), coarsely chopped (about 3 cups)

3 tablespoons white wine

2 teaspoons chopped fresh rosemary or thyme

Salt and ground black pepper to taste

⅓ cup crumbled goat cheese

⅓ cup black walnuts, hickory nuts, or walnuts (optional)

1 egg, beaten

PROCESS

CRUST: In a food processor, mix the flour, salt, and sugar. Pulse the chunks of cold butter into the flour mixture until they're the size of peas. Pulse in the ice water 1 tablespoon at a time until the dough just clumps together when you pick up a piece. If it crumbles, add a bit more ice water. Shape the dough firmly into a disk, wrap it tightly with plastic wrap, and refrigerate it while you make the filling.

FILLING: In a medium cast-iron or other heavy-bottomed sauté pan, melt the butter over medium heat and add the ramp bulbs and stems. Sauté until the ramps start to caramelize, 8–10 minutes. Add the mushrooms, stir once, and let them sweat for a few minutes, stirring once or twice. Add the wine, herbs, salt, and pepper. Sauté for a few minutes more, until the wine is evaporated. Coarsely chop the ramp leaves and stir into the mushroom mixture. Remove from the heat and let cool.

Preheat an oven to 350°. Butter a baking sheet (or line it with parchment paper). On a lightly floured surface, roll the dough out into a 12-inch circle. Place the circle on the baking sheet. Spoon the cooled filling evenly in the center, leaving about 3 inches of dough around the outside of the circle. Tuck chunks of goat cheese into the filling and top with nuts (if desired).

Carefully fold the edge of the dough up and over the filling, going around the circle and pinching the dough together on top of the filling as you go. There should be a 6-inch circle of visible filling in the center of the galette. Brush the top with the beaten egg. Bake for about 30 minutes, or until the crust is golden and starting to brown on the edges.

LIME, CILANTRO, AND SHALLOT SAUCE
BY PATRICIA MULVEY AND LAURA GILLIAM OF LOCAL THYME

Pat and Laura compare this sauce to chimichurri, a South American vinegar-and-herb-based condiment served with grilled meats. This Asian-inspired version is great spread on grilled fish, poultry, meat, and tofu, or poured over rice.

SERVES 4 // VEGAN // CONDIMENT

INGREDIENTS

¼ cup lime juice

3 tablespoons soy sauce

3 tablespoons chopped fresh cilantro

2 tablespoons grated fresh ginger

2 tablespoons minced shallot

3 tablespoons canola oil

1 tablespoon toasted sesame oil

1 tablespoon water, or more to taste

PROCESS

Mix together the lime juice, soy sauce, cilantro, ginger, shallot, and oils in a bowl. Taste and adjust the flavor, adding water if necessary to make it less salty.

SHALLOT HERB BUTTER
BY PATRICIA MULVEY AND LAURA GILLIAM OF LOCAL THYME

This easy compound butter is delicious on fresh corn and grilled foods; you can substitute lots of different herbs for the thyme, depending on your taste and what you have on hand. Compound butter freezes well, too, so it's a great vehicle for preserving fresh herbs for use through the winter.

SERVES 8 // VEGETARIAN // CONDIMENT

INGREDIENTS

½ cup plus 1 tablespoon unsalted butter, softened, divided

1 shallot, peeled and finely minced

1 tablespoon finely chopped fresh thyme

Salt to taste

PROCESS

In a small skillet, melt 1 tablespoon of the butter over medium heat. Add the shallot and sauté until fragrant and just beginning to soften, about 5 minutes. Transfer the shallot to a bowl and allow to cool to room temperature. When cool, add the thyme, the remaining butter, and a pinch of salt. Mix well, pack into a ramekin or other small container, and chill until ready to use. Alternatively, roll the butter mixture into a log shape using wax or parchment paper, wrap in aluminum foil, and freeze. You can remove the roll of butter and slice off rounds from the log as needed.

VINEGAR-GLAZED SHALLOTS

BY PATRICIA MULVEY AND LAURA GILLIAM OF LOCAL THYME

This beautifully caramelized shallot dish delicately balances sweet and sour notes. It is lovely tossed with steamed green vegetables or scattered on pureed soups as a garnish.

SERVES 6 // VEGETARIAN // SIDE DISH

INGREDIENTS

6 tablespoons butter

2 pounds shallots, peeled and sliced

3 tablespoons sugar

Salt and ground black pepper to taste

3 tablespoons red wine vinegar

PROCESS

Melt the butter in a large skillet. Add the shallots, sugar, salt, and pepper and sauté over medium heat until the shallots begin to brown, 10–12 minutes. Stir in the vinegar, cover, and braise until the shallots are very tender and glazed, 15–20 minutes.

EXTRAS

From Eggs to Preserves

Fruits and vegetables aren't the only things that come from farms. Many growers offer specialty products, such as meat, cheese, mushrooms, flowers, honey, or preserves, in addition to their regular crops. These products are usually considered optional "extras" for CSA members, who may add them to their regular deliveries by request. To find out more about the specialty products available in your area, visit a farmers' market to meet the producers in person. Talking with local artisans—and sampling their wares!—is a good way to discover whether you prefer buckwheat or alfalfa honey, when morels are in season, and who makes preserves perfectly sweetened to your palate.

With growing concerns about food safety and the welfare of food animals, many consumers are increasingly interested in where their animal products come from. Rather than relying on the claims of commercial labels, which can be confusing, many prefer to learn about the products they buy through face-to-face conversations with farmers, or even by visiting the farms in person. Animal products from small farms are sometimes more expensive than commercial meat, poultry, and dairy products because they require more labor, acreage, and expensive feed to produce. However, many find the cost well worth the quality and peace of mind these products offer, and they offset the expense by consuming fewer animal products overall.

Selection.   Shop around for specialty products, since different sellers will have their own specialties and some may be more local than others. To ensure that food is safe, find out what regulations vendors at your favorite farmers' markets must meet, and check how often they are inspected for compliance.

◆ **Mushrooms.**   Avoid mushrooms that seem wet, dried out, or excessively dirty (these may be severely damaged by the effort it takes to clean them). If mushrooms are foraged, ask what efforts the seller is using to ensure that they are edible.

◆ **Flowers.**   To confirm that flowers meant to decorate cakes or platters are food safe, buy them from organic farms and inspect them carefully for insects. For flowers used for display, find out how long they usually last and how best to handle them once they're home.

◆ **Honey, maple syrup, and preserves.**   Ask about the flavor profiles of different varieties and sample to find your favorites.

◆ **Meat, poultry, dairy products, and eggs.**   Ask around to find farms that have good reputations in the community, and chat with their representatives to determine their core values. Ask about the details of production and request to visit the farm if possible. A farmer with clean, humane facilities should not be opposed to customers dropping by.

> *"Well," said Pooh, "what I like best?" and then he had to stop and think. Because although Eating Honey was a very good thing to do, there was a moment just before you began to eat it which was better than when you were, but he didn't know what it was called.*
>
> —A. A. MILNE,
> *The House at Pooh Corner*

For a comprehensive guide to commercial meat and poultry labels, see the free download "Food Labeling for Dummies" from Animal Welfare Approved, www.animalwelfareapproved.org/consumers/food-labels.

Storage. Each product in this category has particular storage requirements:

◆ Mushrooms should be kept dry and stored in the refrigerator for no more than a few days. They can be dehydrated if they need to be kept longer, and shiitake caps even freeze well.

◆ Eggs should be kept cold and used as soon as possible.

◆ Meat and poultry sold frozen can remain frozen until use (thaw in the refrigerator before using). Ask about specific handling and storage times of refrigerated meat; if it will not be used within the specified window, it should be frozen.

◆ Honey never spoils, due to its low moisture content and acidic pH. It should be kept at room temperature to minimize crystallization.

◆ Maple syrup and preserves can be stored at room temperature while sealed, but they should be refrigerated after opening.

Preparation. Avoid washing mushrooms, if possible; wipe them clean with a paper towel instead. Eggs, poultry, and meat can be rinsed and patted dry before cooking. Meats will sear better and cook more evenly if they are allowed to warm slightly at room temperature, rather than going straight from the refrigerator to the pan or grill.

ABOUT THE EXTRAS

EGGS

Farm-fresh eggs may not look as uniformly perfect as commercial eggs, but they make up for it in flavor. Ideally, eggs should be from hens that are pastured; that is, allowed to scratch and roam outside. (Pastured hens can include those that are labeled "vegetarian fed," as this term refers only to their supplemental feed and not to the insects they eat while foraging.) Pastured hens produce eggs with yolks that are dark yellow to orange, depending on what they've been eating. Shell color depends on the type of chicken and is not an indicator of quality or flavor. Do not wash eggs until right before use; shells have a natural bloom that protects them from bacteria.

The standard egg size for recipes is "large," which means 2 ounces by weight (extra-large is 2¼ ounces). Be sure to use large eggs for delicate baked goods, especially if they are egg-based or if you are baking in large quantities. A dozen extra-large eggs equals 13½ large eggs by weight, a difference that could affect the success of a recipe.

FLOWERS

Most often, flowers are used for décor, but a few varieties are edible. Some, like roses, are best for garnishes, either whole on cakes or as candied petals. Others, like nasturtiums and marigolds, add a pleasant, peppery flavor to dishes. Still others, like peonies, clover, and gardenias, make excellent tea; and sweet flowers like pansies and violets are charming in fresh salads. Any flower that will be eaten or used as a garnish should be absolutely free of pesticides and any other harmful residues. Be sure to confirm with the seller that flowers are food safe.

HONEY

Local beekeepers sell honey in a range of colors, flavors, and textures, depending on the time of year and the types of flora the bees have visited. They may also offer honey sticks, bee pollen, royal jelly, and beeswax candles in addition to liquid honey. Fresh, local honey may crystallize more easily than mass-market products; this is because commercial honey is often heated and strained to slow crystal formation. Some believe that this refinement process removes nutrients, making commercial honey less healthy than raw honey. Crystallization occurs fastest at refrigerator temperatures; warm and freezing temperatures both slow the formation of crystals. Crystallization does not affect the quality of honey, but it can make it difficult to use in cooking. To return crystallized honey to a liquid state, place the honey jar in a container full of hot water (but do not overheat it), letting it sit until the crystals dissolve.

MAPLE SYRUP

In the spring, sugar maple trees are tapped for their sap, which is then boiled and filtered to make maple syrup. Like wine, maple syrup can have subtle variations in flavor depending on the trees, growing region, season, and processing technique. Maple syrup is graded according to color; in the United States there are five grades, the palest syrup being Grade A Light Amber, and the darkest Grade B (Canada has a slightly different scale). Maple syrup is delicious drizzled on pancakes, French toast, ice cream, and hot cereals; in dressings, sauces, and frosting; and as candy.

MEAT AND POULTRY

Not only are local farms a good resource for meat that is raised humanely, they may also be a good source for specialties that are often too costly or time consuming to produce commercially. A few to look for are:

Grass-fed beef.   Many prefer beef that is 100% grass fed, as opposed to "finished with grain"; that is, fed grain before slaughter. Grass is the natural diet of cows, and animals fed only grass are healthier. As a result, the meat from these animals has a more balanced ratio of omega-3 and omega-6 fatty acids, which is healthier for humans. Note that grass-fed beef is leaner than commercial grain-fed beef, so it may need to be cooked less or at lower temperatures, lest it become dry.

Dry-aged beef.   In the United States, all beef is aged. This is a process during which natural enzymes begin breaking down the meat after butchering, resulting in beef that is flavorful and tender. Most commercially sold meat is wet-aged, meaning it is wrapped in plastic and refrigerated. Often much of the "aging" takes place during transportation. Dry-aged beef is hung in a special temperature- and humidity-controlled room for fifteen to twenty-eight days. This process results in flavorful, finely textured beef. It is an expensive process that is usually reserved for steak houses and upscale butcher shops. Chefs prefer this beef for superior flavor and texture, so it is best saved for cuts that will showcase these characteristics, like steaks or rib roasts.

Heritage breeds.   Like heirloom fruits and vegetables, heritage animal breeds are those that have fallen out of favor commercially but may have desirable characteristics. Often they are well suited to their local environment, making for healthier herds and flocks. They often grow more slowly than commercial breeds and therefore do not suffer the health problems of animals rushed to full growth. Heritage breeds are most often found among pigs and turkeys.

Air-chilled chicken.   After slaughter, chicken must be cooled immediately to reduce the growth of bacteria. Most commercially processed (even organically certified) chicken is immersed in an ice-water bath with chlorine added to reduce pathogens. Chicken processed this way retains some water, which can dilute flavor and create an undesirable texture. Air-chilled chicken is cooled entirely with cold air, or with a combination of icy mist and air, leaving the texture and flavor unaltered.

MUSHROOMS

Crimini and portobello.   A mushroom with many names, the crimini is also called baby bella, golden Italian, Roman, or brown, and it is, in fact, the same mushroom as portobello (a.k.a portobella), just younger. Criminis are also the same as white mushrooms, but a different strain. Criminis are a little denser in texture and deeper in flavor than white mushrooms, but they can be used interchangeably with them. Portobellos are excellent meat stand-ins, and they are often marinated, grilled, and used in sandwiches. Both criminis and portobellos should be firm and plump, with no shriveling or sliminess. To determine freshness in portobellos, look under the cap at the gills. They should be dry and distinct, not damp or dented, and should range in color from taupe to chocolate brown rather than black, as gills darken with age. The gills will darken the mushroom and anything else they are cooked with, so some chefs prefer to scrape them out with a spoon before using.

Morel.   Earthy, nutty, and even slightly smoky, the flavor of morel mushrooms is a cause for celebration when they emerge in the spring. Their unique, deeply whorled caps are perfect for absorbing flavorful sauces, and their hollow interiors are popular for stuffing. Spread foraged morels on a white towel to check carefully for insects, as just a few hitchhikers can devour the mushrooms overnight. Morels should be thoroughly cleaned and must be thoroughly cooked. They are excellent sliced or halved and cooked in liquid along with other vegetables or meats.

Always bring an experienced forager along when hunting for mushrooms. Some edible and toxic varieties look similar, and an expert will be able to determine what is safe.

Oyster.   Cultivated oyster mushrooms come in a variety of colors, including yellow, pink, blue, and black, but white is the most common. These grow in clusters of white stems and rounded, cream- to taupe-colored caps. They are tender and mild and should be cooked. To prepare them, break the stems away from the caps. Searing sometimes makes oyster mushrooms bitter; instead, roast or sauté them with a little liquid, such as broth, water, or oil. Yellow and pink varieties are rare, but if found, they should be purchased only if absolutely fresh, and then used the same day, as they have a very short shelf life.

Shiitake.   Intensely savory and robust, shiitake mushrooms are becoming more and more popular in the United States. Selection is the key to success; look for small shiitakes with solid, thick caps, preferably domed and dotted with a whitish bloom. Look for curled-under cap edges; mushrooms that have opened fully are in decline. The stems are not edible, so pull or cut them off and save them for broth or compost. Shiitakes are drier than other mushrooms, so cook them with a little liquid or with other, moister mushrooms to avoid scorching. They are excellent dehydrated, and they can be powdered for a savory addition to soups and vegetarian dishes.

White.   Also called button or white button mushrooms, and champignons in the restaurant trade, ubiquitous white mushrooms are agreeable to many palates. They can be eaten raw or cooked. Look for white mushrooms that are clean and free from dents. Check the stems and undersides to determine freshness—darkening stems and exposed gills are signs of aging.

PRESERVES

Homemade preserves are an excellent way to enjoy seasonal fruit all year. Not just spreads for toast, they can be used in sauces for meats, as ice cream or yogurt toppings, or as pastry fillings. To find your preferred preserve makers, start with those who grow the fruit. Sample and ask questions until you find your favorites.

EXTRAS

Storage Guide

PRODUCT	STORAGE AND PRESERVATION		
	IDEAL CONDITIONS	FREEZE	DEHYDRATE
EGGS	refrigerated	•	
FLOWERS	fresh water, room temperature or refrigerated		•
HONEY	room temperature	•	
MAPLE SYRUP	room temperature until opened, then refrigerated		
MEAT AND POULTRY	refrigerated	•	•
MUSHROOMS	loosely wrapped, refrigerated	•	•
PRESERVES	room temperature until opened, then refrigerated		

MASTER RECIPE: FOUR-WAY BLENDER MAYONNAISE

Commercially produced mayonnaise is fine for sandwiches and when used in small amounts for a recipe. But when mayonnaise takes center stage—say, in a potato salad or as a topping for roasted asparagus or grilled fish—using mayonnaise made from scratch makes the difference between "meh" and "wow!" Homemade mayonnaise is very easy to prepare. It doesn't last long, though, so make small batches, flavoring each one as desired for a particular meal or use.

THE BASICS

Whole egg

Acid: lemon juice or vinegar

Flavorings and seasonings: mustard, salt, pepper, paprika, sugar, hot pepper sauce (optional)

Neutral oil such as grape seed or canola

Add-ins: mashed garlic, chopped herbs, minced roasted vegetables

PROCESS

Make sure that all ingredients are at room temperature. Place the **egg**, **acid**, and **flavorings and seasonings** (if desired) in a blender and pulse to combine. With the motor running, add the **oil** in a very slow drizzle (pour the oil through the feed chute in the lid or lift just the corner of the lid to avoid splatter). Continue blending until the oil is incorporated. Pour into a glass container and stir in any **add-ins**. Use immediately, or store in the refrigerator for up to 3 days.

VARIATIONS

By Patricia Mulvey and Laura Gilliam

BASIC MAYONNAISE   (Yields about 1 cup)

1 whole egg

1½ teaspoons lemon juice

1 teaspoon white wine vinegar

¼ teaspoon Dijon mustard

¼ teaspoon salt

¾ cup neutral oil

To make chipotle mayonnaise:

Stir in 1 tablespoon pureed chipotle in adobo sauce

To make tarragon mayonnaise:

Stir in 1 tablespoon chopped fresh tarragon

To make aioli (garlic mayonnaise):

Stir in 2 cloves garlic mashed to a paste with ¼ teaspoon salt

To make red pepper mayonnaise:

Stir in 3–4 tablespoons chopped roasted red bell pepper

IDEA STARTERS

Substitute lime juice for lemon; stir in ½ teaspoon grated lime peel and 1 tablespoon chopped fresh cilantro (great for fish tacos)

Stir in 1 teaspoon wasabi powder (great with Japanese-inspired dishes)

Stir in 1 tablespoon chopped fresh mild herbs (e.g., basil, parsley, chives) (great with grilled summer vegetables)

Stir in 1 tablespoon chopped fresh strong herbs (e.g., marjoram, rosemary, oregano) (great with grilled or roasted root vegetables)

Stir in chopped dill pickles, capers, cayenne, garlic, and lemon juice (for remoulade)

Stir in chopped sweet pickles, onion, and lemon juice (for tartar sauce)

SERVING SUGGESTIONS

◆ Use as a dip for steamed, grilled, or roasted vegetables or for French fries.

◆ Roll into sushi rolls.

◆ Mix with cubed cooked poultry, fish, or tofu; chopped herbs; sliced apples or grapes; dried fruit; nuts; and green onions for a hearty, Waldorf-inspired salad.

◆ Stir into potato salad, pasta salad, or slaw.

◆ Use as a base for homemade dressings.

EGG DROP SOUP WITH GARLIC MUSTARD

BY CYNTHIA JASPER, COURTESY OF REAP

An invasive pest in the forest, garlic mustard is the soul of this simple soup.

SERVES 2 // VEGETARIAN // SIDE DISH

INGREDIENTS

2 cups beef or vegetable broth

20 fresh or dried garlic mustard leaves, chopped

2 large eggs

PROCESS

Bring the beef broth to a rolling boil in a pot. Add the garlic mustard leaves to the broth and gently stir. Crack the eggs into a small bowl and gently stir to break the yolks. Add the stirred eggs to the boiling broth and stir twice. Reduce the heat and simmer for 1 minute, or until the eggs are cooked.

ITALIAN PEPPER AND EGG SANDWICHES

BY EDITH THAYER

A popular dish in Italian-American households on meatless Lenten Fridays, pepper and egg sandwiches are particularly good with farm-fresh eggs. They are delicious and filling for any meal, any time of the year.

SERVES 4 // VEGETARIAN // MAIN DISH

INGREDIENTS

1–2 tablespoons olive oil

1 clove garlic, finely minced

½ teaspoon crushed red pepper

1 medium onion, thinly sliced

1 large green bell pepper, thinly sliced

4 eggs, beaten

Salt and freshly ground black pepper to taste

1 loaf Italian bread

PROCESS

Heat a skillet over medium heat and add enough olive oil to cover the bottom. Add the garlic and crushed red pepper and sauté for 1–2 minutes. Add the onion and bell pepper and cook until they have softened, about 5 minutes.

Increase the heat to medium-high and add the beaten eggs. Stir to combine with the onion and bell pepper and season with salt and pepper. Cook, stirring occasionally, until the eggs are set, 7–10 minutes.

Slice the bread crosswise into 4 sections, then slice each section in half, without cutting all the way through. When the eggs are done, gently slide a portion of them between the 2 halves of each section to make 4 sandwiches.

SPANISH TORTILLA WITH KALE (EGGS)

BY PATRICIA MULVEY AND LAURA GILLIAM OF LOCAL THYME

Pat and Laura love the classic version of this ubiquitous Spanish tapa, but they wanted a healthier, easier rendition for everyday meals. This recipe is a favorite among their clients, and when Pat serves it at home her kids say, "Yay! We love this!" You can gussy it up for a party with a dollop of aioli flavored with smoked paprika.

SERVES 8 // VEGETARIAN // MAIN DISH

INGREDIENTS

1 teaspoon salt, divided (plus more for the cooking water)

1 bunch kale, stems removed and roughly chopped

1 pound potatoes, cut into ¼-inch slices

2 tablespoons olive oil

1 onion, thinly sliced

2 cloves garlic, finely minced

7 eggs, lightly beaten

PROCESS

Preheat an oven to 375°. Bring a pot of water to a boil and add some salt. Add the kale and cook until wilted, 3–5 minutes. Leaving the boiling water on the stove, remove the kale to a colander with a slotted spoon, and cool by running cold water over it. Meanwhile, put the potatoes into the boiling salted water and parboil until just tender, about 5 minutes. While the potatoes cook, squeeze the excess moisture from the kale and transfer it to a small bowl. Drain the potatoes in the colander.

Heat a 9-inch ovenproof nonstick skillet over medium-high heat. Add the oil and heat until shimmering. Add the onions and garlic and sauté until softened, about 2 minutes. Add the kale, potatoes, and ½ teaspoon of the salt, stirring until they are well mingled. Stir the remaining ½ teaspoon of salt into the beaten eggs. Pour the egg mixture over the vegetables in the skillet and tip the pan a bit to distribute the eggs evenly.

Place the skillet in the oven and bake for about 10 minutes, or until the eggs are fully set. To test, shake the pan gently; if you see any liquid movement in the eggs, return the skillet to the oven and check at 2-minute intervals until the eggs are set. Remove the skillet from the oven, place a large plate on top of the skillet, and carefully invert it so the eggs flip out onto the plate. Serve hot, at room temperature, or cold.

CANDIED FLOWERS

BY PATRICIA MULVEY AND LAURA GILLIAM OF LOCAL THYME

A special cake can be made even more beautiful with the addition of delicate blossoms preserved with a crystalline layer of sparkling sugar. Candying flowers preserves them longer and gives them a delightful crunch and sweetness. The best edible flowers to use are those that have surfaces that can be easily "painted" with egg white and sugar, like rose petals, pansies, and single florets of lilacs, Johnny-jump-ups, or apple blossoms. Use small simple flowers, and choose colorful shades, as the encrusted sugar will mute bright shades to delicate pastel hues.

YIELDS 1 DOZEN FLOWERS // VEGETARIAN // CONDIMENT

INGREDIENTS

1 egg white

Few drops water

1 dozen fresh edible flowers (plus a few extras for practice), rinsed and air-dried

1 cup superfine sugar

PROCESS

Beat the egg white in a small bowl just until it begins to get frothy, then whisk in a few drops of water. Hold a flower firmly by the stem. Using a clean fine paintbrush, brush the egg white onto all surfaces of the flower. Gently hold the flower over a dish and sprinkle it with a thin coating of sugar. Shake off the excess sugar and place the flower on waxed paper. Repeat these steps to candy all the flowers. Allow the candied flowers to air-dry for 12–36 hours. Once preserved in this way, the flowers will be edible and delicious for at least a week. For longer storage, keep them in a sealed container with a desiccant packet (found in craft stores).

HONEY CHIPOTLE GLAZED TROUT

BY PATRICIA MULVEY AND LAURA GILLIAM OF LOCAL THYME

The combination of honey and chipotle chile in this simple glaze magically transforms grilled fish or meat into a specialty food. The beauty of this "recipe" is that you can adjust it to your taste with great ease. If you like it sweeter, add more honey; if you like it spicier, add more chipotle.

SERVES 4 // FISH/SEAFOOD // MAIN DISH

INGREDIENTS

½ cup honey

2 tablespoons pureed chipotle in adobo sauce (from a 7-ounce can)

4 trout fillets

PROCESS

Heat a grill to medium-hot. Combine the honey and chipotle in a small bowl, mixing well. Brush the glaze onto both sides of each fish fillet. Place the fish in a fish-grilling basket and set the basket on the grill. Grill the fish until cooked through, turning once (about 6 minutes per side).

PHOTO BY JIM KLOUSIA © 2012
FOR *EDIBLE MADISON*

HONEY AND CARDAMOM FLAN

BY MACON LUHNING, ORIGINALLY PUBLISHED IN *EDIBLE MADISON*

Light, subtle, and singing with honey and cardamom tones, this flan is the perfect summertime treat. Flan needs to chill for at least five hours before unmolding, so make it the day before you plan to serve it.

SERVES 6 // VEGETARIAN // DESSERT

INGREDIENTS

4 eggs

2 egg yolks

½ cup plus 6 tablespoons honey, divided

3 cups half-and-half

1 vanilla bean, split in half and pulp scraped out

⅛ teaspoon ground cardamom

⅛ teaspoon salt

PROCESS

Preheat an oven to 325°. In a bowl, whisk together the eggs, egg yolks, and ½ cup of the honey and set aside. In a medium saucepan, whisk together the half-and-half, vanilla bean (seeds and pulp), cardamom, and salt. Heat over medium-high heat until the cream mixture starts to steam. While the cream mixture is heating, add 1 tablespoon of the remaining honey to each of 6 (7-ounce) ramekins. Place the ramekins in a baking dish, leaving space between them.

Slowly, and a little at a time, whisk the warm cream mixture into the egg mixture. Evenly distribute the cream and egg mixture among the 6 ramekins. Fill the baking dish with hot tap water until the ramekins are ¾ submerged and place it in the oven. Bake for 40–50 minutes, or until the custard is set. Cool completely, then cover and refrigerate for at least 5 hours. To unmold the flan, dip each ramekin in hot water for a few seconds, then carefully slide a knife around the edge of the flan and turn over onto a plate. Tapping or shaking the ramekin may be necessary.

HONEY APPLE CAKE

BY JAMIE BAKER OF PRIMROSE VALLEY FARM

Apples and honey are traditional foods for Rosh Hashanah, the Jewish New Year. Together, these two ingredients make for a super-moist cake that smells divine and tastes even better.

SERVES 6–8 // VEGETARIAN // DESSERT

INGREDIENTS

⅓ cup honey

Juice from 1 lemon

3 apples, peeled, cored, and cut into eighths

¾ cup sugar

6 tablespoons butter or margarine, softened

¼ cup packed dark brown sugar

1 teaspoon vanilla extract

½ teaspoon almond extract

2 large eggs

1 cup all-purpose flour

1 teaspoon baking powder

¼ teaspoon salt

PROCESS

Preheat an oven to 350°. Spray the bottom and sides of a 9-inch springform pan with nonstick cooking spray. Combine the honey and lemon juice in a large nonstick pot and bring to a simmer over medium heat. Add the apples, stirring occasionally to coat them with honey. Cook the apples until they are quite tender and have absorbed most of the honey mixture, about 15 minutes. Remove from the heat and set aside while making the cake. The apples will continue to absorb the honey as they sit.

In a mixing bowl, combine the sugar, butter or margarine, brown sugar, and vanilla and almond extracts. Beat with an electric mixer on medium speed until well blended, about 1 minute. Add the eggs and beat to incorporate.

In a separate bowl, whisk together the flour, baking powder, and salt. Add the flour mixture to the sugar-egg mixture a little at a time, scraping the sides of the bowl with each addition. Beat on low until blended.

Pour the batter into the prepared springform pan and press to spread evenly over the bottom (it will seem like it hardly covers it). By this time, the apples should have absorbed almost all, if not all, the honey liquid. Arrange the apples on top of the batter and drizzle any remaining liquid over the apples. Bake for 1 hour. Cool completely. Release the sides of the springform pan and, using a spatula, lift the cake off the base and onto a serving plate.

MAPLE NUT GRANOLA

BY DANI LIND, ORIGINALLY PUBLISHED IN *EDIBLE MADISON*

Save money and have fun shopping in your grocer's bulk section for this delicious granola recipe's ingredients. Be sure to pick up a Wisconsin-produced maple syrup while you're at it.

SERVES 12 // VEGAN // MAIN DISH

INGREDIENTS

4 cups regular rolled oats

1 cup oat flour (to make your own, grind oats in a spice grinder or blender)

½ teaspoon salt

1 cup raw nuts (almonds, walnuts, cashews, etc.)

¼ cup raw pumpkin or sunflower seeds

¼ cup flaked coconut

⅔ cup maple syrup

⅓ cup oil

1 teaspoon ground cinnamon

½ teaspoon ground allspice

1 teaspoon freshly grated orange peel (optional)

⅔ cup dried fruit (raisins, chopped dates, figs, cranberries, etc.)

PROCESS

Preheat an oven to 275°. Oil 2 rimmed baking sheets. In a large bowl, mix the oats, oat flour, salt, nuts, seeds, and coconut. In a small saucepan, mix together the maple syrup, oil, cinnamon, allspice, and orange peel (if desired) and bring to a boil. Immediately remove from the heat, drizzle over the oat mixture, and thoroughly mix with a wooden spoon or your hands.

With your hands, pick up clumps of granola and spread over the oiled baking sheets in a single layer, breaking up any large clumps. Bake for 35 minutes, stirring a couple of times and rotating the pan to ensure even baking. Add the dried fruit and bake for another 5–10 minutes, or until golden brown. Cool completely and store in an airtight container.

TWICE MAPLE CHEESECAKE

BY HEATHER WORKMAN

From mid-February to mid-April, Heather's grandfather could be found at Wehr Nature Center in Hales Corners, Wisconsin, tapping the sugar maples, collecting and transporting the sap to the sugar house, and then drawing the syrup to be filtered, graded, and bottled. She often went to watch him work, fascinated and charmed—groomed to be a maple addict. She created this doubly maple cheesecake in honor of him.

SERVES 6-8 // VEGETARIAN // DESSERT

INGREDIENTS

BASE:

4–6 graham crackers

¼ cup walnuts, toasted and skins rubbed off

1 tablespoon butter, melted

½ tablespoon maple syrup (preferably Grade B)

FILLING:

1 (8-ounce) package cream cheese, softened

3 tablespoons sugar

2 teaspoons cornstarch

½ cup maple syrup (preferably Grade B), plus more for drizzling on top

1 egg

½ teaspoon lemon juice

Dash ground cinnamon

1 egg white, at room temperature

Maple leaf-shaped candy or glazed walnuts (optional)

PROCESS

Preheat an oven to 350°. Place the graham crackers and walnuts in a food processor and pulse into fine crumbs. Add the butter and syrup and pulse until the mixture comes together. Pour into an ungreased 7-inch springform pan and, with damp hands, press to cover the entire bottom. If there is a bit extra, create a rim around the edge. Bake until the edges are golden brown, 8–12 minutes. (Note: If you use a larger pan, the baking time will be less.) Remove from the oven and reduce the oven temperature to 325°. Set the base aside to cool.

In a stand mixer fitted with the paddle attachment, beat the cream cheese, sugar, cornstarch, and maple syrup until smooth. Add the whole egg, lemon juice, and cinnamon and beat again until incorporated.

In a separate bowl, whisk the egg white until stiff peaks form. With a rubber spatula, gently fold the egg white into the filling mixture (do not over-mix). Pour over the cooled base. Place the springform pan onto a baking sheet and bake on the center rack of the oven for 45–60 minutes. The outside should be set, and the inside mostly set with only a slight wobble. If the cheesecake needs additional baking time, continue baking for another 10–20 minutes, checking for doneness every 5 minutes. Let cool completely.

If serving immediately: Run a knife along the outside of the cheesecake, then release the sides of the springform pan. Place the cheesecake onto a serving plate without removing the bottom of the pan. Drizzle a bit of maple syrup over the top and use a pastry brush or clean fingers to spread it evenly, creating a nice glaze. Garnish each slice with a single maple leaf-shaped candy or a glazed walnut half (if desired).

If serving at a later time: Leave the cheesecake in the pan, cover loosely with plastic wrap, and chill. To serve, follow the same directions as above.

BAKED STUFFED MOREL MUSHROOMS

BY KAREN PAULUS, COURTESY OF REAP

This dish benefits from morel anatomy. The conical shape and plentiful pockets in their caps make them ideal for stuffing and for soaking up pan juices.

SERVES 10 // VEGETARIAN // SIDE DISH

INGREDIENTS

3 dozen large morels, rinsed in salted water

2 tablespoons butter

1 tablespoon chopped shallots

Salt to taste

Freshly ground black pepper to taste

1 tablespoon chopped fresh parsley

2 cloves garlic, crushed

3 tablespoons breadcrumbs

Grated Asiago or Parmesan

PROCESS

Preheat an oven to 350° and butter a 13 × 9-inch baking dish. Remove the stems from the morels and finely chop them. Cut the large caps in half and set aside. Melt the butter in a small skillet, add the shallots, chopped stems, and salt, and cook until the moisture evaporates. Add a little freshly ground pepper and the parsley, garlic, and breadcrumbs and mix well. Arrange the morel caps in the baking dish and stuff with the shallot-mushroom stem mixture. Top with grated cheese and bake for 20 minutes.

GARLICKY CRIMINI MUSHROOMS WITH LEEKS ON PASTA

BY KARI SPELTZ

Earthy, savory crimini mushrooms are delicious in combination with meltingly sweet leeks in this quick pasta dish. If crimini mushrooms aren't available, substitute an equally flavorful variety, like morel or shiitake, or use a mixture of various mushrooms.

SERVES 2 // VEGETARIAN // MAIN DISH

INGREDIENTS

5 ounces linguini

2 tablespoons butter

3 tablespoons extra-virgin olive oil, divided

1 large leek (white and light green parts only), sliced crosswise

8 ounces crimini mushrooms, sliced

2 large cloves garlic, minced (about 2 tablespoons)

Salt to taste

3 tablespoons grated Parmesan

PROCESS

Cook the pasta according to the package directions. Drain, reserving ½ cup of the water for later use, and set aside.

Meanwhile, melt the butter in a large sauté pan over medium heat. Add 2 tablespoons of the olive oil. Add the leek and sauté for 5–10 minutes, or until slightly softened, separating the individual rings of the slices. Add the mushrooms, garlic, and the remaining tablespoon of olive oil and season with salt. Cook until the mushrooms and garlic are softened, 3–5 minutes, stirring occasionally.

When the vegetable mixture is done, add the reserved pasta water and increase the heat to medium-high. Sprinkle the Parmesan into the vegetable mixture, stir well, then add the cooked pasta. Continue stirring until all the liquid is absorbed.

MARINATED PORTOBELLO MUSHROOM BURGERS WITH SWISS CHEESE

BY HEATHER WORKMAN

A little extra prep time elevates these burgers to knockout status. Our tester said this recipe is one of her new favorites; she suggested serving with sweet potato fries. Heather suggests serving with a cold beer, and we couldn't agree more. These burgers are great for a lazy summer day or a lively cookout.

SERVES 4 // MEAT // MAIN DISH

INGREDIENTS

½ cup balsamic vinegar

½ cup dry red wine

½–¾ cup olive oil

4 medium to large portobello mushrooms, stems removed

1½–1⅔ pound 90% lean ground beef, chilled

1 tablespoon Worcestershire sauce

1 teaspoon prepared horseradish

1 teaspoon minced fresh rosemary, or more to taste

¼ teaspoon salt

¼ teaspoon freshly ground black pepper

4 thin slices Swiss cheese

4 onion rolls, sliced into top and bottom halves

PROCESS

In a shallow baking dish, whisk together the vinegar, wine, and olive oil. Add the portobellos and turn several times to coat thoroughly in oil. Allow them to marinate at room temperature for about 1 hour, turning occasionally.

In a medium bowl, mix together the beef, Worcestershire sauce, horseradish, rosemary, salt, and pepper. Form into 4 patties and set on a plate; chill in the refrigerator for 30–60 minutes. (Patties may be frozen for later use at this point.)

Heat a stovetop (or outdoor) grill to medium-hot. Lightly spray the grates with cooking spray, or rub with a paper towel dipped in oil. Lay the beef patties and mushrooms on the grill.

For the patties: Grill for 4 minutes per side for medium doneness or 5 minutes per side for medium well. Top with the cheese during the last 2 minutes of cooking and cover with a grilling lid.

For the portobellos: Grill for 5 minutes per side, or until tender and browned. If the portobellos are quite large, grill for about 1 minute more.

While the patties and mushrooms are grilling, toast the roll halves under a broiler for about 2 minutes, or until golden brown. Layer the patties and mushrooms between the roll halves and serve.

HIRAM VALLIER'S LAC DU FLAMBEAU WILD RICE WITH MUSHROOMS

BY MARY PRYZINA, COURTESY OF REAP

With a cooking time of 45–60 minutes, wild rice can be daunting for busy cooks. This recipe uses overnight soaking to cut down the cooking time, making meal-day preparation quick and easy.

SERVES 4 // VEGETARIAN // SIDE DISH

INGREDIENTS

1 cup wild rice

1 teaspoon salt

8 ounces mushrooms, sliced

1 tablespoon butter

PROCESS

Place the rice in a strainer and rinse until the water runs clear, then rinse briefly with hot water. Transfer the rice to a heatproof bowl, cover with hot water, and let it soak overnight. In the morning, drain and rinse the rice again. Transfer the rice to a pan and cover with hot water. Add the salt and boil over medium heat for 15–20 minutes. Drain and set aside. Sauté the mushrooms in the butter and fold into the rice just before serving.

MENUS, TIPS, AND OTHER RESOURCES

THEME MENUS

MOTHERS' DAY BRUNCH
SERVES 6–8

Rhubarb Bread (page 154)

Oat Scones with Dried Fruit and Lavender (page 142)

Rustic Ramp Tart (page 219)

Farmers' Market Confetti Salad with Champagne-Dijon Vinaigrette (double) (page 183)

Vanilla yogurt (purchased) topped with Maple Nut Granola (page 237)

BEVERAGE SUGGESTIONS. Rhubarb Shrub (page 156); Cava; Belgian Wheat

STARRY SPRING NIGHT DINNER PARTY
SERVES 4–6

Creamy Radish Greens Soup (page 13)

Grilled Shrimp, Fennel, and White Bean Salad (double) (page 58)

Fish Tacos (page 40)

Asparagus Cashew Pilaf (page 55)

Angel food cake (purchased) with Strawberry Rhubarb Ginger Compote* (page 129) and whipped cream

*If fresh strawberries are not available, use frozen.

BEVERAGE SUGGESTIONS. Vinho Verde; Maibock

JUNE GRADUATION BASH
SERVES 4

Baby Beets with Beet Greens (double) (page 16)

Strawberry Arugula Salad (page 170)

Baby Bok Choy Salad with Roasted Chicken (page 176)

Kohlrabi, Snap Pea, and Turnip Lettuce Wraps with Choice of Meat (page 47)

Radish, Turnip, and Smoked Trout Salad with Wasabi Vinaigrette (page 41)

Blackberry Raspberry Pie (page 137)

BEVERAGE SUGGESTIONS. Sauvignon blanc; Hefeweizen

SUMMER BACKYARD PARTY
SERVES 8

Best Gazpacho Ever (page 89)

Marinated Portobello Mushroom Burgers with Swiss Cheese (double) (page 240)

Zucchini Carpaccio (quadruple) (page 106)

Elote (cut cobs in half to serve 8–12) (page 76)

Summer Melon Dessert (page 145)

BEVERAGE SUGGESTIONS. Chardonnay; Pilsner

MEZE PLATTER
SERVES 6-8

Yogurt Cheese with Herbs (page 217)

Hummus with a Twist (page 69)

Summer Tabbouleh Salad (page 217)

Yoğurtlu Havuç Salatasi (Carrot Salad with Yogurt) (double) (page 26)

Mouhamara (Roasted Red Bell Pepper and Walnut Spread) (page 94)

Fried Stuffed Summer Squash Blossoms (double) (page 103)

Pita bread and mixed olives (purchased)

BEVERAGE SUGGESTIONS.   Liqueur; Petite Syrah; Lager

LABOR DAY BARBECUE
SERVES 8

Watercress and Green Onion Deviled Eggs (page 191)

Apple Radish Salad (double) (page 39)

Carrot Slaw (double) (page 24)

Mediterranean Potato Salad with Kohlrabi (page 32)

Fennel and Feta Burgers (increase by about one third to make 8) (page 58) topped with Heirloom Spiced Tomato Preserves (page 114)

Watercress, Onion, and Goat Cheese Tart (page 192)

Concord Grape Streusel Pie (page 144)

BEVERAGE SUGGESTIONS.   Riesling; Pale Ale

HOMECOMING FOOTBALL TAILGATE
SERVES 6-8

Tomatillo Salsa Verde (page 109) with tortilla chips (purchased)

Unky Dave's Potato Salad (page 39)

Miss Cheriezee's Faboo Slaw (page 167)

Roast Beef Sandwiches with Sweet and Sour Onions and Watercress (page 191)

Roasted Onion Sandwiches (page 219)

Triple T Chili (page 109)

Cornbread with Jalapeño and Cheddar (page 214)

Twice Maple Cheesecake (page 238)

BEVERAGE SUGGESTIONS.   Zinfandel; Oktoberfest

COCKTAIL PARTY NIBBLES
SERVES 6-8

Sweet Curry Winter Squash Fritters (page 121)

Crispy Roasted Kale (double) (page 181)

Lettuce Wraps (double) (page 185)

Nepali Potato-Filled Flatbread with Spicy Tomato Chutney (double, cut into wedges) (page 37)

Honey Apple Cake (page 236)

BEVERAGE SUGGESTIONS.   Cocktails of choice (page 249)

VEGETARIAN THANKSGIVING FEAST
SERVES 6-8

Autumn Harvest Soup (double) (page 35)

Fall Pumpkin Pasta with Apples and Sage (page 131)

Holiday Braised Brussels Sprouts (double) (page 203)

Amaretto Sweet Potatoes (page 45)

Cheesy Celeriac and Potato Mash (page 28)

Saffron Rice with Frizzled Leek (page 218)

Apple Cranberry Crisp Pie (page 136)

BEVERAGE SUGGESTIONS. Beaujolais nouveaux or Pinot grigio; Amber or Nut Brown Ale

WARMING WINTER SUPPER
SERVES 6-8

Rutabaga Bisque (page 43)

Goat Cheese, Sweet Onion, Apple, and Brandy Stuffed Chicken (double) (page 131)

Hiram Vallier's Lac du Flambeau Wild Rice with Mushrooms (page 241)

Lemony Roasted Veggies (page 204)

Apple and Pear Pie with Maple Syrup and Toasted Walnuts (page 150)

BEVERAGE SUGGESTIONS. Pinot noir; Samichlaus

WINTER SOLSTICE CELEBRATION
SERVES 6

Curried Parsnip Soup (page 34)

Beet, Orange, and Blue Cheese Salad* (increase by one half) (page 18)

Polenta with Nuts and Greens (you'll have leftovers) (page 179)

Honey Chipotle Glazed Trout (increase by one half) (page 234)

Ginger Cranberry Stuffed Winter Squash (triple) (page 117)

Honey and Cardamom Flan (page 235)

Hazelnut biscotti (purchased)

*Substitute dry herbs (3 teaspoons total) if fresh are not available.

BEVERAGE SUGGESTIONS. Malbec or Champagne; Winter or Christmas Ale; Eggnog

COCKTAILS

Delicious meals aren't the only way to enjoy seasonal produce. Why not use your local bounty to whip up an inventive potation? Fruits, herbs, and many vegetables are excellent cocktail enhancers, adding sweet, savory, and even spicy notes to your favorite beverages. Fresh produce and spirits are consummate companions in the right hands, and Wisconsin is fortunate to have four sets of those hands in Madison-area mixologists Grant Hurless (Forequarter and Merchant), Hastings Cameron and Mark Bystrom (Underground Food Collective), and John Kinder (Death's Door Spirits). Let their recipes guide you in muddling, mashing, and mixing up liquid treats. Here's to farm-fresh food—and drinks!

APRY SKI
BY JOHN KINDER

INGREDIENTS

1 apricot, halved and pitted

1 ounce pineapple juice

1 ounce lemon juice

2 ounces Death's Door gin

Sage leaf, for garnish

> To "slap" a leaf for garnish: Place the leaf in the palm of your hand and tap it a few times with the other hand, as if clapping, to release the oils.

PROCESS

Muddle the apricot, pineapple juice, and lemon juice in a cocktail shaker. Add the Death's Door gin and some ice and sharply shake. Strain into a martini glass and garnish with a slapped sage leaf.

> To "muddle" is to crush ingredients to release their flavors into a drink. The technique is similar to using a mortar and pestle to crush herbs for cooking.

BASIL FAWLTY
BY JOHN KINDER

INGREDIENTS

1–2 basil leaves

1½ ounces Death's Door vodka

½ ounce elderflower liqueur

½ ounce Yellow Chartreuse

1 ounce dry vermouth

1 twist lemon peel, for garnish

PROCESS

Sharply shake all ingredients (except the lemon twist) with some ice in a cocktail shaker. Strain into a chilled martini glass and garnish with a twist of lemon peel.

> To make perfect lemon twists: Cut both ends off a lemon and set it upright on a cutting board. Insert a small knife or other sharp utensil into the white pith and slowly work your way around the fruit to separate the peel from the flesh (it helps to work from both ends). Once the peel is completely separated, make one lengthwise cut through the peel, then turn the lemon on its side and slice into rings. Pull the separated flesh out of each ring and twist the rings into spirals.

CARROT AND THE STICK
BY JOHN KINDER

INGREDIENTS

1½ ounces Death's Door gin

2 ounces carrot juice

½ ounce honey syrup (1:1 honey and water)

¾ ounce grapefruit juice

Freshly grated cinnamon stick, for garnish

PROCESS

Sharply shake all ingredients (except the cinnamon) with some ice in a cocktail shaker. Strain into a chilled martini glass and grate cinnamon over the top.

Honey Syrup: Combine honey and water (see recipes for specific ratios) in a saucepan. Stir over medium heat until incorporated. Store in the refrigerator.

CHUPAROSA
BY GRANT HURLESS

INGREDIENTS

¾ ounce lime juice

½ ounce honey syrup (3:1 honey and water)

5 blackcap raspberries

¼ ounce Hum Botanical Spirit

1½ ounces Death's Door vodka

1 sprig thyme, for garnish

PROCESS

Muddle the lime juice, honey syrup, and raspberries in a cocktail shaker. Add the Hum Botanical Spirit, Death's Door vodka, and some ice and sharply shake. Strain into an ice-filled old-fashioned glass and garnish with a sprig of thyme.

CUCUMBER MARTINI
BY JOHN KINDER

INGREDIENTS

5–7 cucumber slices

1 ounce apple juice

½ ounce simple syrup

½ ounce lime juice

2 ounces Death's Door vodka

1 strip cucumber, for garnish

PROCESS

Muddle the cucumber, apple juice, simple syrup, and lime juice in a cocktail shaker. Add the Death's Door vodka and some ice and sharply shake. Strain into a chilled martini glass and garnish with a cucumber strip.

Simple Syrup: Combine 1 part water and 1 part sugar in a saucepan. Stir over medium heat until incorporated. Store in the refrigerator.

EVE'S APPLE
BY GRANT HURLESS

INGREDIENTS

1 egg white

¾ ounce lemon juice

¼ ounce maple syrup

½ ounce Koval Ginger Cordial

1½ ounces Germain-Robin Craft-Method Brandy

1½ ounces ÆppleTreow Appely Doux

4 drops Bittercube Jamaican #1 bitters

PROCESS

Combine the first 5 ingredients (egg white through brandy) in a cocktail shaker. Dry shake (without ice) for 40 seconds; add ice and wet shake for 12 seconds. Strain into an ice-filled old-fashioned glass. Add the Appely Doux and drop the bitters over the top.

HAIR OF THE CAT
BY HASTINGS CAMERON

INGREDIENTS

2 barspoons coriander syrup

5 dashes Bitter Truth Celery bitters

½ ounce bianco vermouth

1¾ ounces North Shore Gin No. 6

2 fat sprigs lovage (1 for mixing, 1 for garnish)

1 (2-inch) piece lemon peel

PROCESS

Combine the first 4 ingredients (coriander syrup through gin) and 1 sprig of the lovage in a mixing glass and stir with ice for 15 seconds. Strain into a martini glass. Slap the second sprig of lovage and drop it into the glass. Squeeze the lemon peel to express the oil onto the surface of the drink.

Coriander Syrup: Toast 1 cup of coriander seeds in a skillet until the seeds sizzle, pop, and hiss. Add to a saucepan with 25 ounces water and 25 ounces sugar. Heat to a rolling boil, then cool and strain. Store in the refrigerator.

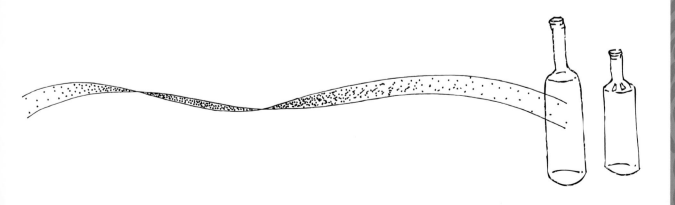

KHAO PAD SMASH
BY JOHN KINDER

INGREDIENTS

½ ounce fresh lime juice

3–4 lime wedges (from ½ lime)

¾–1 ounce simple syrup

2 small sprigs cilantro

2 (1- to 2-inch) pieces garlic scape or whites from green onions

2 ounces Death's Door white whisky

PROCESS

Muddle the lime juice, lime wedges, simple syrup, cilantro, and garlic scapes in an old-fashioned glass. Add the Death's Door white whisky and ice to fill. Empty the contents of the glass into a cocktail shaker and sharply shake. Pour everything (used ice included) back into the old-fashioned glass and enjoy with your favorite fried rice.

MELONCHOLY AND THE GINFINITE SADNESS
BY GRANT HURLESS

INGREDIENTS

1 (2-inch) slice fresh cantaloupe

¾ ounce lemon juice

½ ounce honey syrup (3:1 honey and water)

½ ounce Domaine de Canton ginger liqueur

1½ ounce Death's Door gin

Sparkling water, for topping

1 twist orange peel, for garnish

PROCESS

Muddle the cantaloupe and lemon juice in a cocktail shaker. Add the honey syrup, Domaine de Canton, Death's Door gin, and some ice and sharply shake. Strain into an ice-filled Collins glass. Top with sparkling water, gently stir, and garnish with a twist of orange peel.

PRESERVATION SOCIETY
BY JOHN KINDER

INGREDIENTS

1 tablespoon seasonal fruit preserves

½ ounce lemon juice

1½ ounces Death's Door vodka

Sparkling water, for topping

Seasonal fruit and 1 mint sprig, for garnish

PROCESS

Place the preserves and lemon juice in the bottom of a cocktail shaker. Stir to combine and loosen the preserves. Add the Death's Door vodka and some ice and sharply shake. Strain into an ice-filled highball glass. Top with sparkling water and garnish with seasonal fruit and a mint sprig.

PRINCESS AND THE PEA

BY JOHN KINDER

INGREDIENTS

1½ ounces Death's Door white whisky (optional: infused with high-quality bacon)

2 ounces sugar snap pea juice*

½ ounce simple syrup

¼ ounce lemon juice

1 twist lemon peel, for garnish

*Run some peas through a juicer or process in a blender and then strain the liquid through a coffee filter. Reserve the pulp for "Sugar Snap Sour" on page 254.

PROCESS

Sharply shake all ingredients (except the lemon twist) with some ice in a cocktail shaker. Strain into a chilled martini glass and garnish with a twist of lemon peel.

PURPLE RAIN PUNCH

BY HASTINGS CAMERON

(fills one punch bowl)

INGREDIENTS

1 bottle Death's Door vodka

17 ounces beet juice*

9 ounces fresh lemon juice

9 ounces honey syrup (3:1 honey and water)

12 dashes Angostura bitters

12 pinches salt

24 ounces cold water

Thyme sprigs and thinly sliced golden beets, for garnish

*Run some beets through a juicer or process in a blender and then strain the liquid through a coffee filter.

PROCESS

Combine all ingredients (except the garnishes) in a large punch bowl and stir to combine. If serving at once for a crowd, add the garnishes and about 4 cups of ice to chill and serve immediately. If serving over a number of hours, leave the punch un-iced and ladle into individually garnished, icefilled glasses as needed.

RHUBARB LIQUEUR

BY HASTINGS CAMERON AND MARK BYSTROM

INGREDIENTS

17 ounces (500 ml) vodka

8½ ounces (250 ml) Sauvignon blanc or other dry white wine

1 pound rhubarb, finely chopped

Grated peel from 1 orange

6 artichoke leaves

¾ cup sugar

2 cloves

½ star anise

PROCESS

Combine all ingredients in a glass jar or other nonreactive container with a lid; allow to macerate at room temperature for 2 weeks. Strain the liquid into another container (discard the solids).

STRAWBERRY-BALSAMIC-BASIL MARTINI

BY JOHN KINDER

INGREDIENTS

3–5 fresh strawberries

1–2 basil leaves

1 teaspoon balsamic vinegar

1 teaspoon sugar

1 lemon wedge

2 ounces Death's Door vodka

1 strawberry and 1 basil leaf, for garnish

PROCESS

Muddle the strawberries, basil, balsamic vinegar, sugar, and lemon in a cocktail shaker. Add the Death's Door vodka and some ice and sharply shake. Strain into a chilled martini glass. Make a small incision in the top of the strawberry and insert the basil leaf into the slit; place in the glass as a garnish.

SUGAR SNAP SOUR

BY JOHN KINDER

INGREDIENTS

2 ounces Death's Door white whisky

1 ounce sugar snap syrup

1 ounce lemon juice

Pea tendrils, for garnish

> Sugar Snap Syrup: Combine equal parts sugar and water with reserved pulp from "Princess and the Pea" (page 253) in a saucepan. Stir over medium heat until incorporated. Strain and store in the refrigerator.

PROCESS

Sharply shake all ingredients (except the pea tendrils) with some ice in a cocktail shaker. Strain into an ice-filled Collins glass and garnish with pea tendrils.

SUMMER GRAPE MARTINI

BY JOHN KINDER

INGREDIENTS

5–7 Concord grapes

½ ounce agave nectar

1 ounce dry white wine

2 ounces Death's Door vodka

Concord grapes, for garnish

PROCESS

Muddle the grapes, agave nectar, and white wine in a cocktail shaker. Add the Death's Door vodka and some ice and sharply shake. Strain into a chilled martini glass and garnish with grapes.

SUNGOLDS

BY HASTINGS CAMERON

INGREDIENTS

4 Sungold cherry tomatoes

1–2 thinly sliced jalapeño rings

3 teaspoons honey syrup (3:1 honey and water)

¾ ounce fresh lemon juice

2 ounces Death's Door gin

1 sprig cilantro, for garnish

PROCESS

Muddle the Sungolds, jalapeño, and honey syrup in a cocktail shaker. Add the lemon juice, Death's Door gin, and some ice and sharply shake. Double-strain into an ice-filled old-fashioned glass and garnish with a sprig of cilantro.

TIPSY CUCUMBER

BY GRANT HURLESS

INGREDIENTS

1 (2-inch) piece cucumber, cut into quarters

Pinch salt

¾ ounce lime juice

2 sprigs dill

½ ounce honey syrup (3:1 honey and water)

¾ ounce St. Germain elderflower liqueur

1½ ounces North Shore aquavit

⅛ ounce pickle juice

Sparkling water, for topping

PROCESS

Muddle the cucumber, salt, lime juice, and dill in a cocktail shaker. Add the next 4 ingredients (honey syrup through pickle juice) and some ice and sharply shake. Strain into an ice-filled Collins glass and top with sparkling water.

TOM AND CHERRY

BY JOHN KINDER

INGREDIENTS

3 fresh cherries

¾ ounce honey syrup (1:1 honey and water)

¾ ounce lemon juice

1½ ounces Death's Door gin

Root beer, for topping

1 skewered cherry, for garnish

PROCESS

Muddle the cherries, honey syrup, and lemon juice in a cocktail shaker. Add the Death's Door gin and some ice and sharply shake. Strain into an ice-filled highball glass and top with root beer. Gently stir and garnish with a skewered cherry.

WATERMELON NEGRONI

BY JOHN KINDER

INGREDIENTS

1 ounce Death's Door gin

1 ounce sweet vermouth

1 ounce Campari

2 ounces fresh watermelon juice

1 mint leaf, for garnish

PROCESS

Sharply shake all ingredients (except the mint) with some ice in a cocktail shaker. Strain into a martini glass and garnish with a mint leaf.

WATERMELON PORT MARTINI

BY JOHN KINDER

INGREDIENTS

3 medium-size watermelon pieces

3–5 mint leaves

1 teaspoon sugar

1½ ounces Death's Door vodka

1½ ounces white port

1 twist lemon peel, for garnish

PROCESS

Muddle the watermelon, mint, and sugar in a cocktail shaker. Add the Death's Door vodka, white port, and some ice and sharply shake. Strain into a chilled martini glass and garnish with a twist of lemon peel.

FOOD HANDLING TIPS AND TERMINOLOGY

FOOD SAFETY

Foodborne illness is a serious threat, but every cook can avoid the pitfalls that lead to contamination by following a few simple food-safety practices.

◆ Begin the cooking process by washing your hands, and wash them often while you cook.

◆ Keep counters clean, and change and wash kitchen towels frequently. Wash sponges in a dishwasher (be sure to rinse out the excess soap before using them again), or microwave them for a minute, at least once a week (daily is an even safer option); replace them as soon as they look dirty or develop any odors.

◆ Wash fruits and vegetables before cutting, even if they have thick peels. Cutting fruit with rinds, like melons, without washing them first will drag any surface bacteria inside the fruit, contaminating the flesh.

◆ To prevent cross-contamination, wash hands, cutting boards, knives, and any other tools used to prepare meat, poultry, or eggs before using them to prepare other ingredients.

◆ Never put cooked and raw meat on the same plate (as when carrying items to and from an outdoor grill). Never put vegetables on a plate with raw meat unless they are all going to be cooked together.

◆ Make sure your refrigerator is set to about 35° (40° is too high) and your freezer is set to 0°.

◆ Avoid storing most prepared foods (e.g., most finished recipes or cut fruits and vegetables) for long periods at temperatures between 40° and 140°—the "danger zone" range in which a number of pathogens will grow quickly in both raw and cooked food. Food temperature should never fall within the danger zone for more than four consecutive hours; if food has been in this zone for two hours and you wish to preserve it, refrigerate or reheat it without delay. If you are uncertain of how long food has been sitting at danger zone temperatures, or if you know it has been more than four hours, discard it. Additionally:

   • Thaw frozen meats in the refrigerator instead of at room temperature.

   • Make sure older models of slow cookers heat foods above 140°.

◆ Cool large pots of broth, soup, or stew before putting them in the refrigerator. Otherwise, they will raise the temperature inside the appliance into the danger zone, keeping it there for too long before it can return to its programmed temperature setting. A large pot of food removed from the heat and left to cool on its own may not cool down quickly enough. To be safe, shorten the cooling time in one of two ways:

   • Fill a sink with ice and water. Place a second pot or other large container into the ice-water bath and transfer the food into it (avoid putting the hot pot into the ice water, as the rapid temperature change can harm your cookware). Make sure the ice water level is low enough that it does not spill into the food. Stir frequently so the food cools evenly. When cool, remove the pot from the ice water, cover, and refrigerate.

   • Transfer the food from the large pot into separate, smaller containers. Leave the containers uncovered or cover them loosely. Cool for no more than one hour before covering tightly and refrigerating.

FOOD STORAGE

When compared with industrial produce, locally grown fruits and vegetables last longer after purchase, since they haven't spent precious time sitting in stores or at distribution centers. But even so, they don't last forever. Fortunately, proper storage can help maximize the shelf life of most foods; in particular, protecting them with wrappers and selecting ideal storage locations will go a long way toward ensuring that produce and other farm products stay fresh until their turn comes to shine in a recipe.

Wrappers

Most produce is best loosely wrapped. There are several materials that will provide sufficient protection, but each has its pros and cons:

◆ Plastic is great for keeping food fresh, but it can trap too much moisture and carbon dioxide, so do not close the bags tightly if using them to protect fresh produce. Perforated plastic bags are preferable for fruits and vegetables, because they allow the produce to breathe while still preventing dehydration. Plastic bags can be recycled, and many grocery stores have installed plastic bag receptacles in an effort to increase recycling participation. Despite these efforts, the majority of bags still end up in landfills, and the use of plastic bags is therefore discouraged, and even banned in some areas.

◆ Paper bags can be used to hasten the ripening of some fruits (see "Sweet Fruits" on page 123 for details), because at room temperature they effectively trap gases without trapping moisture. In the refrigerator, paper bags absorb moisture, so they're best for produce that must stay dry, like mushrooms. When using paper bags to store succulent produce, monitor the contents frequently so they do not become desiccated.

◆ Washable, reusable cloth bags are a good choice for those who wish to reduce their use of disposable materials. A number of retailers sell prefabricated bags, made of recycled polyester or natural materials, in different sizes and weights. Check natural foods grocers, online retailers, and craft markets for options. These bags are not just for storage—they are also good substitutes for the plastic grocery store bags that have long been used to transport groceries home from the market. Some bags have their tare weight printed on the label, so the cashier can deduct the weight of the bag from bulk purchases. Not all cloth bags are suitable for all produce; use tightly woven muslin or cotton bags for leafy greens and other produce that is likely to wilt (the produce can be dampened first to delay dehydration), and loose mesh for produce that needs to breathe, like apples.

> For a fun project, have kids decorate reusable non-mesh cloth bags with paint or markers suitable for fabric (available at craft stores), drawing color-coded pictures of what should go in each bag (leafy greens, root vegetables, fruits, etc.). Heat-set the designs (following the manufacturer's directions) to make them wash resistant.

◆ Baskets and other containers are also good non-disposable food-storage products. Breathable baskets are best for delicate items like pea pods. Glass or plastic containers can also be used, but they should not be sealed when storing fresh produce. Instead, drape them with dishcloths or other loose coverings to allow some air circulation. Avoid using containers that are so deep that the bottom layers of food become compacted, as the buried items will spoil quickly.

Storage Location

As mentioned in "Sweet Fruits" above, some fruits, called climacteric, continue to ripen after harvest. Once they begin to ripen, they naturally produce ethylene gas, consume oxygen, and produce carbon dioxide two to five times faster than they did before ripening began. This natural process can trigger other climacteric fruits stored nearby to ripen faster, and it can hasten the spoilage of some non-climacteric produce. To preserve the life of your produce, separate fruits and vegetables according to the guide below.

CLIMACTERIC FRUIT STORAGE RECOMMENDATIONS	
STORE THESE CLIMACTERIC FRUITS	AWAY FROM THESE VEGETABLES AND FRUITS
APPLE	BROCCOLI
APRICOT	BRUSSELS SPROUT
AVOCADO	CABBAGE
BANANA	CARROT
CANTALOUPE	CAULIFLOWER
FIG	CUCUMBER
HONEYDEW	EGGPLANT
MANGO	LEAFY GREENS, INCLUDING LETTUCE
PEACH/NECTARINE	PARSLEY
PEAR	SUMMER SQUASH
PLUM	SWEET POTATO
PLUOT	WATERMELON

COOKING GLOSSARY

Bake. To cook food by surrounding it with hot air in an oven. For this book, we use the term "bake" for foods cooked at moderate temperatures, around 350°, and for foods cooked whole or nearly whole, like potatoes or winter squash. The difference between baking and roasting is largely an issue of semantics. We say "roast" for foods cooked at higher temperatures, usually around 425°, and for large cuts of meat or whole chickens. For successful baking:

◆ Ensure that the oven temperature is correct. An accurate temperature reading is especially important for baking delicate doughs and pastries. The best way to monitor oven temperature is to check it with an oven thermometer.

◆ Check for doneness slightly before the end of the suggested cooking time when baking in dark metal pans, as they will brown foods more quickly than light-colored pans.

◆ Reduce the oven temperature by about 25° if using glass or ceramic baking dishes, as they hold heat better than metal. Check the food slightly before the end of the suggested cooking time to prevent overbaking.

◆ Reduce the heat by 25° if using a convection oven, as it will distribute heat more efficiently than a conventional oven.

Blanch. To cook food in rapidly boiling water, usually just until it is crisp-tender but still vibrantly colored. After blanching, the food is moved to an ice-water bath to immediately halt the cooking process. This procedure is ideal for preparing vegetables that are to be served crisp-tender, such as green beans in a salad. It is also a common first step in food preservation, as it reduces enzymes that degrade flavor and color in some dehydrated or frozen foods.

> The term "blanch" is also used in horticulture. It means to cover all or part of a plant while it is growing to prevent pigment from developing, so that the plant stays white or pale. Growers usually cover the plants with soil, paper, or the plant's own leaves.

Foods can also be blanched in oil, chilled, and then deep-fried a second time, as are potatoes for commercial French fries. For successful blanching:

◆ Add salt to the cooking and cooling water to season vegetables. (Never salt food surfaces before deep-frying; see "deep-fry" below.)

◆ Remove vegetables from the ice-water bath as soon as they are cool to prevent them from becoming waterlogged.

◆ Blanch vegetables like asparagus, green beans, and artichokes before sautéing or grilling them to ensure that they will be cooked through without becoming dehydrated. Blanching can be done hours in advance of the final cooking stage, as long as the blanched vegetables are stored in the refrigerator.

Boil. To cook food in water that is rapidly bubbling, 212° at sea level. It is good for dry ingredients like starches and dried beans, and it works well for some vegetables. Some thickeners, like cornstarch, must be brought to a boil to properly hydrate them, while others, like potato starch, should not be boiled. Follow the recipe or package instructions when using these thickeners. For successful boiling:

◆ Start root vegetables in cold water, and bring them to a boil with the cooking water to avoid overcooking vegetable exteriors. Otherwise, boil the water first, and then add vegetables and starches.

◆ Use a large pot and plenty of water, so that the water may come back to a boil as quickly as possible after the food is added.

◆ Add salt to the cooking water to season starches and vegetables.

◆ Drain foods immediately after cooking to prevent overcooking.

◆ For foods that will be heated with other ingredients later, such as pasta that will be added to sauce, stop the boiling process when the food is slightly undercooked.

Braise. To cook foods slowly in a flavorful liquid. Entrées like pot roasts, curries, and meatballs cooked in sauce are considered braises. Braising can be done on a stovetop or in an oven, as long as the temperature is kept low and the liquid does not boil. Braising is generally used for meats, especially those that require lengthy, gentle cooking to become tender. For successful braising:

◆ Use a large, heavy pan with a tight-fitting lid. Dutch ovens are ideal.

◆ Brown foods before adding the liquid to add depth of flavor to the finished dish.

◆ Bring the cooking liquid to a boil, then cover the pot and reduce the heat to a simmer.

◆ Add vegetables to the pot later than meats, as they usually require less cooking.

◆ Check the pot occasionally and stir to make sure there is enough cooking liquid. Add water if necessary and adjust the heat if the liquid is too hot (bubbling rapidly) or too cold (lying still).

◆ Before reheating refrigerated braises, remove any fat from the surface.

◆ To reduce the cooking liquid into a sauce, first remove the food and cover it to keep it warm. Strain any solids from the liquid and bring it to a boil. Cook until the liquid is thickened. Taste, adjust the seasoning, and, if desired, stir in a tablespoon or so of cold butter (butter adds richness and creates a smooth texture). Before serving, re-moisten the cooked food in the sauce.

Caramelize. To cook food until it becomes golden brown. Sugar turns to liquid caramel at 320°, and the sugars within other foods undergo the same process when heated above 300°.

Chiffonade. To cut herbs or leafy greens into thin, delicate ribbons. To do this easily, roll leaves into a cigarlike shape and slice crosswise with a sharp knife or scissors.

Deep-fry. To cook food by submerging it in hot oil (usually around 350°). Deep-fried food is usually crisp and browned on the outside, and moist and cooked through on the inside. Good oil and correct temperature are essential for deep-frying success. Use a neutral-flavored oil with a high smoke point and check the temperature with a thermometer. Also:

> The "smoke point" is the temperature at which fats begin to smoke and develop unpleasant flavors. High-temperature cooking requires the use of fats with a high smoke point, such as grape seed oil or various refined oils, for best results. To cook at high temperatures with heat-sensitive fats, like butter or olive oil, mix them with a high-smoke-point oil to reduce the risk of burning them.

◆ Cut food to a uniform size for even cooking.

◆ Do not salt the outer surfaces of food before frying, as salt breaks down the cooking oil.

◆ Do not add too much food at a time, as this will lower the temperature of the oil and result in food that is soggy and undercooked.

◆ Turn food gently with tongs to cook all sides evenly.

◆ Briefly drain deep-fried food on paper towels to absorb excess oil, then move it to a nonabsorbent surface, such as a cookie sheet (food left on paper towels will become soggy).

◆ Keep an eye on the temperature of the cooking oil, and turn off the heat immediately if it begins to smoke.

Dice. To cut into roughly square pieces of even size. The pieces may be large or small, but they should all be the same size for uniform cooking.

Emulsify. To combine two disparate liquids (like oil and vinegar) by whisking or blending, and stabilizing the mixture with a binder like egg or mustard. Hollandaise, mayonnaise, and thickened vinaigrettes are examples of emulsions.

Grill. To cook food on a metal rack over a direct heat source, either gas flames or charcoal. It can be done indoors on a specialty grill pan with adequate ventilation. Grilling is best for foods with short cooking times, like tender meats and vegetables. Some ingredients that need more cooking, like artichokes, can be blanched or steamed first and finished on the grill. For successful grilling:

◆ Preheat the grill, and wipe the grate with a little cooking oil just before adding the food (a paper towel held with tongs, or a long-handled non-plastic brush works well for this).

◆ Pat food dry before setting it on the grill to get a good sear.

◆ Do not use force to remove food from the grill; instead, wait until it releases naturally. If food is stuck to the grate, it probably hasn't finished searing.

Julienne. To cut food into long, thin pieces. Traditionally "julienne" referred to strips of matchstick size (1 ½ × ⅛ × ⅛-inch), but today the measurement is less precise. Specialty tools, like mandolines, can quickly cut ingredients into julienne strips, as can sharp knives.

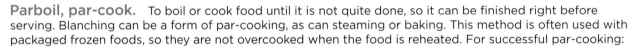

Mince. To cut food into small pieces, usually ⅛ inch or less.

Parboil, par-cook. To boil or cook food until it is not quite done, so it can be finished right before serving. Blanching can be a form of par-cooking, as can steaming or baking. This method is often used with packaged frozen foods, so they are not overcooked when the food is reheated. For successful par-cooking:

◆ Cool and refrigerate par-cooked foods immediately to prevent the growth of harmful bacteria.

◆ Avoid par-cooking meats, or undercooking any foods in the microwave, unless you intend to finish cooking them immediately.

Poach. To cook food in liquid that is hot but not boiling, around 160°, when the surface of the liquid is slightly shimmering. Poaching is best for delicate foods like eggs or fish that would fall apart with the agitation of boiling water. For successful poaching:

◆ Add a splash of vinegar (about a tablespoon) to the water when poaching eggs. The acid helps the whites coagulate more quickly so the egg keeps its shape.

◆ When poaching fish or meats, add herbs, spices, and aromatics to the water to add flavor.

◆ Place a rack in the bottom of the pan when poaching large, delicate foods like fish fillets. The raised structure prevents food from sticking to the pan and helps lift it out of the poaching liquid when finished.

Roast. To cook food in an oven, usually at a temperature above 400°, until it develops a golden brown crust on the outside and is cooked through on the inside. Since roasting temperatures are high, food is usually coated or drizzled with a fat, like olive oil, to protect it from becoming too dry. The oil also distributes heat on the surface of the food more evenly, which aids in browning. It is important to avoid crowding the roasting pan, since air must circulate around the food to cook it evenly. Ingredients that are too crowded will steam rather than roast, and therefore will not develop a crust.

Sauté. To cook food quickly in a small amount of fat. The term *sauté* comes from the French word "to jump," which likely describes the action of the food as it is flipped in a sauté pan. It is usually desirable for sautéed foods to develop some browning, or caramelization, to enhance flavor. For successful sautéing:

◆ Heat the pan first, then add oil or butter. When the oil shimmers or the butter bubbles, drop the food into the pan. The food should sizzle when it touches the oil.

◆ Do not overheat the oil. If it begins to smoke, remove the pan from the heat, wipe it out with a paper towel, and start with fresh oil.

◆ Do not crowd the pan. Food that is too close together will cool the pan down too much and will steam rather than brown.

◆ Make sure food is dry before adding it to the pan. Otherwise, it will not brown.

Sear. To cook food quickly in a hot pan in order to brown the surface. Searing is used to add flavor and texture to foods that will be served raw inside, such as tuna steaks, or for foods that will finish cooking a different way, such as braises. It is important to use a hot pan and make sure the surface of the food is dry before searing so it will brown before the inside cooks.

Simmer. To heat liquid to a temperature that is somewhere between a poach and a boil. The surface of the liquid should move and bubble occasionally. Simmering, rather than boiling, is often used for soups, stews, and braises because it gives flavors time to meld and soften without overcooking ingredients or evaporating too much liquid.

Steam. To cook food with steam rather than liquid. Foods that are steamed are placed on a rack over boiling water in a covered pan. Steaming can be done using a pot with an inserted rack or a steamer basket, in a wok with a bamboo steamer, or in a specialized appliance. Since steaming does not add flavor through oils or caramelization, reserve it for fresh, best-of-the-season produce and foods with plenty of flavor of their own. For successful steaming:

◆ Add aromatics like ginger or spices to cooking water to boost flavor.

◆ Make sure your pan has a tight-fitting lid to keep the steam inside. Alternatively, use a skillet or a baking sheet to cover the pot.

◆ Always open the lid away from you—steam is very hot!

◆ Avoid overcooking. Steamed vegetables should be brightly colored and crisp-tender.

◆ When steaming moist items like fish, place them on a lettuce leaf to absorb drips, then discard the leaf before serving.

Stir-fry. To cook food in a small amount of fat at a high temperature. Stir-frying is very similar to sautéing, although it is usually done in a wok or stir-fry pan. Generally, cooking temperatures are higher for stir-fries than sautés, so be sure to use an oil with a high smoke point and prepare all ingredients before you begin to cook. For successful stir-frying:

◆ Cut foods to uniform sizes so they cook evenly.

◆ Cook food in stages, keeping similar ingredients together and mixing them all together with the sauce at the end of cooking. An alternative method is to cut ingredients differently so they can cook at the same time; for example, cutting dense carrots into thin coins that will cook at the same rate as thicker zucchini slices. This method is difficult to execute perfectly, however, and trying to cook everything at once often crowds the pan and prevents food from browning.

◆ Cook garlic and ginger separately from ingredients cut into larger pieces, and stir them continuously while cooking. Otherwise, since they are usually cut very small, they will burn easily.

Sweat. To cook food over low heat, usually with a little fat, until it is softened but not browned. Sweating is usually used to describe cooking aromatics.

PANTRY BASICS

A well-stocked pantry makes meal planning and prep easy and efficient. The following list will help keep your pantry equipped to whip up the recipes in this book, and to tackle most cooking projects, at a moment's notice. We've divided the ingredients into two categories to streamline pantry organization: "Essentials" are used in numerous recipes and are good to have on hand at all times; and "Specialties" have more limited uses and/or shelf lives and should be purchased as needed.

FLOURS

ESSENTIALS	SPECIALTIES
All-purpose	Bread
Cornmeal	Chickpea
Whole-wheat	Flaxseed meal
	Nut
	Oat
	Pastry
	Rice
	Semolina

Wheat flours are sold for different purposes based on the amount of gluten protein they contain. Gluten gives structure, strength, and texture to baked goods. All-purpose flour (11%–12% protein) is usually strong enough for bread making but also tender enough for piecrust. Pastry flour (8%–9% protein) is ideal for piecrusts and biscuits. Bread flour (12%–13% protein) lends body to breads and pizza dough. Whole-wheat flour (about 13% protein) is ground from the entire wheat kernel, leaving the nutritious bran, germ, and endosperm intact; it is high in protein, but since some of the protein is from parts of the grain that do not form gluten, it does not rise as well when baked into bread (instead, it makes dense and flavorful loaves).

BAKING STAPLES

ESSENTIALS		SPECIALTIES	
Breadcrumbs (or make fresh as needed)	Brown sugar	Agave nectar	Molasses
	White sugar	Coconut milk	Powdered sugar
Baking powder		Cornstarch	Superfine sugar
Baking soda		Cream of tartar	

NUTS AND SEEDS

ESSENTIALS

Almonds

Peanuts

Sesame seeds

Walnuts

SPECIALTIES

Cashews

Hazelnuts

Hickory nuts

Pecans

Pine nuts

Pistachios

Poppy seeds

Pumpkin seeds

Sunflower seeds

It's easy to toast nuts on a stovetop, in an oven, or even in a microwave. We like this simple stovetop method best: Spread the nuts in a single layer in a skillet and heat over medium-high heat. Shake the nuts around in the skillet or stir them with a spatula frequently to toast evenly. Continue toasting for 5–7 minutes, or until the nuts are fragrant and beginning to brown. Remove from the heat immediately to avoid burning.

DRIED SHELL BEANS

ESSENTIALS

Black

Cannellini

Chickpea

Kidney

Lentil

SPECIALTIES

Black-eyed pea

Fava

Great Northern

Mung

Navy

Pinto

Soy

Lentils come in a variety of colors, including red, green, yellow, brown, and black. Brown lentils have a mild flavor and hold their shape well after cooking. Red lentils are sweet and nutty; they cook fastener than other lentils and become very soft, so they are best in soups and purees. Green lentils have a rich flavor and remain quite firm after cooking; they are excellent in salads.

GRAINS

ESSENTIALS	SPECIALTIES
Brown rice	Arborio rice
Oats	Barley
Polenta	Basmati rice
Quinoa	Bulgur
White rice	Farro
	Jasmine rice
	Wheat berries
	Wild rice

PASTAS

ESSENTIALS	SPECIALTIES
Angel hair	Cavatappi
Couscous	Cavatelli
Fettuccine	Lasagna
Macaroni	Linguini
Spaghetti	Mostaccioli
	Orecchiette
	Orzo
	Penne

OILS

ESSENTIALS	SPECIALTIES
Canola/rapeseed	Avocado
Extra-virgin olive	Flax seed
Olive	Grape seed
Sesame	Peanut
	Safflower
	Sunflower
	Truffle
	Vegetable

Different oils serve different purposes, so it's best to keep several types on hand: Oils with high smoke points (e.g., avocado oil, grape seed oil, or various refined oils) are best for high-temperature cooking (such as stir-frying). Neutral oils (e.g., canola and vegetable oil) are ideal for baking. Strongly flavored oils (e.g., nut, seed, and truffle oil) are excellent in salad dressings and as flavor accents.

VINEGARS AND COOKING WINES

ESSENTIALS

Balsamic vinegar

Cider vinegar

White vinegar

SPECIALTIES

Mirin (Japanese rice wine)

Red wine vinegar

Rice vinegar

Sherry/Madeira

White wine vinegar

There are many varieties of soy sauce, an Asian condiment made from fermented grain and soy beans. Shoyu is the generic Japanese name for soy sauce; most types contain wheat and tend to be sweeter than Chinese soy sauce. Tamari, a specific variety of Japanese soy sauce, contains little or no wheat and is thicker, richer, and less salty than regular soy sauce.

CONDIMENTS

ESSENTIALS

Dijon mustard

Hot pepper sauce

Ketchup

Mayonnaise

Soy sauce/shoyu/tamari

Yellow mustard

SPECIALTIES

Fish/oyster sauce

Harissa (Tunisian hot chile sauce)

Hoisin sauce

Horseradish/wasabi

Miso

Sriracha sauce (Thai hot sauce)

Teriyaki sauce

Worcestershire sauce

OTHER STAPLES

ESSENTIALS

Broth

Honey

Peanut butter

SPECIALTIES

Anchovies (in olive oil)

Capers

Nori (edible seaweed)

Olives (green, black, Kalamata)

Panko (Japanese-style breadcrumbs)

Tahini

Tomato paste (preferably in a tube, not a can)

Wheat germ

To make homemade broth, try this recipe by Liz Boyle: Keep a clean half-gallon milk box in the freezer with the top cut off. Put clean carrot or potato peels, the dark-green parts of green onions or leeks, onion tops and bottoms, spinach stems, carrot greens, etc. into the box whenever you have them left over from a meal. (Avoid cruciferous vegetables like broccoli, cabbage, and cauliflower.) When the box is full, dump the contents into a large stockpot with a fresh or frozen chicken back (optional). Add cold water to cover and bring to a boil. Skim off the foam. Keep the broth on a low simmer for 30–60 minutes. Strain the broth and allow it to come to room temperature. Put 2-cup portions in labeled quart-size freezer bags and freeze for later use. Note that this is unsalted broth, so you might have to add more salt than usual to recipes when you use it.

SPICES AND FLAVORINGS

ESSENTIALS

Bay leaf

Black pepper

Cayenne

Chili powder

Cinnamon

Coriander

Cumin

Curry powder

Crushed red pepper

Oregano

Paprika

Salt

Thyme

Vanilla extract

White pepper

SPECIALTIES

Allspice

Almond extract

Cardamom

Celery seed

Cloves

Curry pastes (Indian, Thai)

Garlic powder

Marjoram

Mustard seeds

Nutmeg

Nutritional yeast

Rosemary

Saffron

Sage

Tarragon

Turmeric

Vanilla bean

CHEESES

ESSENTIALS

Blue

Cheddar

Cream cheese/
Neufchâtel

Feta

Goat

Mozzarella

Parmesan

SPECIALTIES

Asiago

Colby

Cotija

Emmentaler

Fontina

Gouda

Jarlsberg

Monterey Jack

Muenster

Pecorino
Romano

Pepper jack

Ricotta

Swiss

REFRIGERATOR

ESSENTIALS

Butter

Eggs

Lemons

Limes

Milk

SPECIALTIES

Buttermilk

Crème fraîche

Ghee
(clarified butter)

Half-and-half

Sour cream

Tofu

Yogurt

Whipping cream

Butter can be salted or unsalted. Salted butter will enhance the flavor of finished dishes and is best used as a condiment (such as spread on toast, waffles, or mixed into steamed vegetables). For recipes (especially baked goods and desserts), it is preferable to use unsalted butter, unless the recipe specifically calls for salted butter; if you must use salted butter in a recipe, reduce the amount of additional salt by $\frac{1}{4}$ teaspoon per $\frac{1}{2}$ cup (1 stick) of butter.

BOOKS WE LOVE AND USE

Allen, Darina. *Forgotten Skills of Cooking: The Time-Honored Ways Are the Best—Over 700 Recipes Show You Why.* [London]: Kyle, 2009.

Bell, Mary. *Mary Bell's Complete Dehydrator Cookbook.* New York: William Morrow, 1994.

Beranbaum, Rose Levy. *The Pie and Pastry Bible.* New York: Scribner, 1998.

Bishop, Jack. *Vegetables Every Day: The Definitive Guide to Buying and Cooking Today's Fresh Produce.* New York: HarperCollins, 2001.

Bittman, Mark. *Food Matters: A Guide to Conscious Eating with More Than 75 Recipes.* New York: Simon & Schuster, 2009.

———. *How to Cook Everything: 2,000 Simple Recipes for Great Food.* Hoboken, N.J.: Wiley, 2008.

———. *How to Cook Everything Vegetarian: Simple Meatless Recipes for Great Food.* Hoboken, N.J.: Wiley, 2007.

Bubel, Mike and Nancy. *Root Cellaring: Natural Cold Storage of Fruits & Vegetables.* 2nd ed. Pownal, Vt.: Storey, 1995.

Carucci, Linda. *Cooking School Secrets for Real World Cooks.* San Francisco: Chronicle, 2005.

Chadwick, Janet. *The Busy Person's Guide to Preserving Food.* Rev. and exp. ed. Pownal, Vt.: Storey, 1995.

Costenbader, Carol W. *The Big Book of Preserving the Harvest: 150 Recipes for Freezing, Canning, Drying, and Pickling Fruits and Vegetables.* Rev. ed. North Adams, Mass.: Storey, 2002.

Dye Gussow, Joan. *This Organic Life: Confessions of a Suburban Homesteader.* White River Junction, Vt.: Chelsea Green, 2001.

Estabrook, Barry. *Tomatoland: How Modern Industrial Agriculture Destroyed Our Most Alluring Fruit.* Kansas City: Andrews McMeel, 2012.

FairShare CSA Coalition (as MACSAC). *From Asparagus to Zucchini: A Guide to Cooking Farm-Fresh Seasonal Produce.* Madison, Wis.: MACSAC, 2004.

Fallon, Sally, with Mary G. Enig. *Nourishing Traditions: The Cookbook That Challenges Politically Correct Nutrition and the Diet Dictators.* Deluxe ed. Washington, D.C.: NewTrends, 2005.

Gardeners and Farmers of Terre Vivante, with a foreword by Deborah Madison. *Preserving Food without Freezing or Canning: Traditional Techniques Using Salt, Oil, Sugar, Alcohol, Vinegar, Drying, Cold Storage, and Lactic Fermentation.* New ed. White River Junction, Vt.: Chelsea Green, 2007.

Gisslen, Wayne. *Professional Cooking.* 7th ed. Hoboken, N.J.: Wiley, 2010.

Greene, Janet, Ruth Hertzberg, and Beatrice Vaughan. *Putting Food By.* Updated ed. London: Michael Joseph, 2011.

Halweil, Brian. *Eat Here: Reclaiming Homegrown Pleasures in a Global Supermarket.* New York: W. W. Norton, 2004.

Herbst, Sharon Tyler, and Ron Herbst. *The Deluxe Food Lover's Companion.* Hauppauge, N.Y.: Barron's Educational Series, 2009.

Hewitt, Ben. *The Town That Food Saved: How One Community Found Vitality in Local Food.* Emmaus, Pa.: Rodale, dist. by Macmillan, 2011.

Hobson, Phyllis. *Garden Way's Guide to Food Drying.* Charlotte, Vt.: Garden Way, 1980.

Hupping, Carol. *Stocking Up III: The All-New Edition of America's Classic Preserving Guide.* 3rd ed. Emmaus, Pa.: Rodale, 1986.

Ivanko, John, and Lisa Kivirist. *Farmstead Chef.* Gabriola Island, B.C.: New Society, 2011.

Kafka, Barbara, with Christopher Styler. *Vegetable Love.* New York: Artisan, 2005.

Katz, Sandor Ellix. *The Art of Fermentation: An In-Depth Exploration of Essential Concepts and Processes from Around the World.* White River Junction, Vt.: Chelsea Green, 2012.

———. *Wild Fermentation: The Flavor, Nutrition, and Craft of Live-Culture Foods.* White River Junction, Vt.: Chelsea Green, 2003.

King Arthur Flour. *King Arthur Flour Whole Grain Baking: Delicious Recipes Using Nutritious Whole Grains.* Woodstock, Vt.: Countryman, 2006.

Kingry, Judi, and Lauren Devine, eds. *Complete Book of Home Preserving: 400 Delicious and Creative Recipes for Today.* Toronto: Robert Rose, 2006.

Kingsolver, Barbara. *Animal, Vegetable, Miracle: A Year of Food Life.* New York: HarperPerennial, 2008.

Krissoff, Liana. *Canning for a New Generation: Bold, Fresh Flavors for the Modern Pantry.* New York: Stewart, Tabori, & Chang, 2010.

Lair, Cynthia. *Feeding the Whole Family: Recipes for Babies, Young Children, and Their Parents.* 3rd ed. Seattle: Sasquatch, 2008.

Langton, Brenda, and Margaret Stuart. *The Cafe Brenda Cookbook: Seafood and Vegetarian Cuisine.* 25th anniversary ed. Minneapolis: University of Minnesota Press, 2004.

Lappé, Anna. *Diet for a Hot Planet: The Climate Crisis at the End of Your Fork and What You Can Do about It.* New York: Bloomsbury, 2010.

Lappé, Anna, and Bryant Terry. *Grub: Ideas for an Urban Organic Kitchen.* New York: Jeremy P. Tarcher/Putnam, 2006.

Lappé, Frances Moore. *Diet for a Small Planet.* 20th anniversary ed. New York: Ballantine, 2010.

Lappé, Frances Moore, and Anna Lappé. *Hope's Edge: The Next Diet for a Small Planet.* New York: Jeremy P. Tarcher/Putnam, 2002.

Lind, Mary Beth, and Cathleen Hockman-Wert. *Simply In Season.* Exp. ed. Scottdale, Pa.: Herald, 2009.

MacRae, Norma. *Canning and Preserving without Sugar.* 3rd ed. Old Saybrook, Conn.: Globe Pequot, 1993.

Madison, Deborah. *Local Flavors: Cooking and Eating from America's Farmers' Markets.* New York: Broadway, 2002.

———. *Seasonal Fruit Desserts: From Orchard, Farm, and Market.* New York: Broadway, 2010.

———. *Vegetarian Cooking for Everyone.* 10th anniversary ed., with a new introduction. New York: Broadway, 2007.

McGee, Harold. *On Food and Cooking: The Science and Lore of the Kitchen.* Completely rev. and updated ed. New York: Scribner, 2004.

McKibben, Bill. *Deep Economy: The Wealth of Communities and the Durable Future.* New York: St. Martin's Griffin, 2007.

Middleton, Susie. *Fast, Fresh & Green: More Than 90 Delicious Recipes for Veggie Lovers.* San Francisco: Chronicle, 2010.

Moosewood Collective. *Moosewood Restaurant Cooking for Health: More Than 200 New Vegetarian and Vegan Recipes for Delicious and Nutrient-Rich Dishes.* New York: Simon & Schuster, 2009.

Nabhan, Gary Paul. *Coming Home to Eat: The Pleasures and Politics of Local Foods.* Reissue. New York: Norton, 2009.

Parsons, Russ. *How to Pick a Peach: The Search for Flavor from Farm to Table.* Paperback ed. Boston: Houghton Mifflin, 2008.

———. *How to Read a French Fry: And Other Stories of Intriguing Kitchen Science.* Paperback ed. Boston: Houghton Mifflin, 2003.

Peterson, James. *Vegetables.* Rev. ed. Berkeley, Calif.: Ten Speed, 2012.

Pollan, Michael. *In Defense of Food: An Eater's Manifesto.* New York: Penguin, 2008.

———. *The Omnivore's Dilemma: A Natural History of Four Meals.* New York: Penguin, 2006.

Reinhart, Peter. *Peter Reinhart's Whole Grain Breads: New Techniques, Extraordinary Flavor.* Berkeley, Calif.: Ten Speed, 2007.

———. *Sacramental Magic in a Small-Town Café: Recipes and Stories from Brother Juniper's Café.* Reading, Mass.: Addison-Wesley, 1994.

Ruhlman, Michael. *Ratio: The Simple Codes behind the Craft of Everyday Cooking.* New York: Scribner, 2010.

Sass, Lorna. *Cooking Under Pressure.* 20th anniversary ed. New York: Morrow, 2009.

———. *Whole Grains Every Day, Every Way.* New York: Clarkson Potter, 2006.

Schlabach, Joetta Handrich, and Kristina Mast Burnett. *Extending the Table: A World Community Cookbook.* Scottdale, Pa.: Herald, 1991.

Schneider, Elizabeth. *Vegetables from Amaranth to Zucchini: The Essential Reference.* New York: Morrow, 2001.

Smith, Alisa, and J. B. Mackinnon. *Plenty: One Man, One Woman, and a Raucous Year of Eating Locally.* New York: Harmony, 2007.

Swanson, Heidi. *Super Natural Everyday: Well-Loved Recipes from My Natural Foods Kitchen.* Melbourne: Hardie Grant, 2011.

Thomas, Cathy. *Melissa's Great Book of Produce: Everything You Need to Know about Fresh Fruits and Vegetables.* Hoboken, N.J.: Wiley, 2006.

Vinton, Sherri Brooks. *Put 'em Up!: A Comprehensive Home Preserving Guide for the Creative Cook, from Drying and Freezing to Canning and Pickling.* North Adams, Mass.: Storey, 2010.

Virant, Paul, with Kate Leahy. *Preservation Kitchen: The Craft of Making and Cooking with Pickles, Preserves, and Aigre-Doux.* Berkeley, Calif.: Ten Speed, 2012.

Ziedrich, Linda, with a foreword by Chuck Williams. *The Joy of Pickling: 250 Flavor-Packed Recipes for Vegetables and More from Garden or Market.* Rev. ed. Boston, Mass.: Harvard Common, 2009.

INDEX

Page numbers in italics indicate photographs; page numbers followed by "t" indicate tables.

D

E

Q